John Walsh was born in Wimbledon to Irish parents in 1953, grew up in south London and was educated at Exeter College, Oxford, and University College, Dublin. In 1987, he became literary editor of the *Evening Standard*, and from 1988 to 1992 was literary editor and feature writer at the *Sunday Times*. In 1993, he joined the *Independent* as editor of the magazine, and spent the next twenty years as assistant editor in a variety of roles, writing features, reviewing restaurants and interviewing famous people – everyone from Václav Havel and Dame Ninette de Valois, to Vanessa Redgrave and Ozzy Osbourne. In 1996, he chaired the judging panel of the Forward Poetry Prize. From 1997 to 1999, he was editorial director of the Cheltenham Festival of Literature. From 1998 to 2015, he could be heard, alongside Sebastian Faulks and James Walton, on the popular Radio 4 book quiz show, The Write Stuff. Since 2007, he has been President of the Authors' Club.

He is the author of two memoirs, *The Falling Angels: An Irish Romance* (1999) and *Are You Talking To Me?: A Life in the Movies* (2003). His novel *Sunday* at the *Cross Bones* (2007) was shortlisted for both the Desmond Elliott Prize and the Bollinger Everyman Wodehouse Prize. He is married and has three grown-up children, Sophie, Max and Clementine, and lives in London and West Sussex.

Praise for *Circus of Dreams*

'Elegant and entertaining' *Critic*

'Very funny . . . I laughed long at the set-piece lunch with [Martin] Amis.'
Observer

'An entertainingly gossipy memoir of the period.' *Week*

'[An] elegant and elegiac memoir . . . the vigour of the book's attack and the
hilarity of its anecdotage . . . [shows he was] one of the great power-brokers
of literary London . . . He was (and is) a good thing and I salute him.'
D. J. Taylor, *Literary Review*

'Walsh makes London seem like the place to have been. The stage was
smaller; everything burned more brightly; more angels teemed on the head
of a pin . . . One of the best things about *Circus of Dreams* is Walsh's
memories not of the big beasts of literature, but of the smaller players – the
editors and agents and clubmen and hacks and P.R. people, the various
legends in their own lunchtimes.' *New York Times*

'This is by no means just a book of literary history, fascinating though much
of that is. Walsh also gives us plenty of terrific stories/gossip from those
far-off days when newspaper offices were full of typewriter noise and
cigarette smoke, and the choice of lunchtime drinks was definitely not
restricted to still or sparkling.' *Reader's Digest*

'[There's a] mixture of high and low, sacred and profane, running through
Walsh's account of literary London in the 1980s that makes it such a joy.'
Sunday Times

'Walsh's enthusiasm for the writing of the 1980s is infectious' *Irish Times*

'Through it all, Walsh was there. First as an eager wannabe, then as a
full-blooded insider. Any disappointment that his own efforts at a novel
didn't prove a ticket to the dream-circus was quickly mitigated once he
discovered his potential as a critic, commentator and general facilitator,
swishing through the forest as interviewer, literary judge, pundit, speaker,
partygoer *par excellence* . . . An immersive literary history . . . highly readable'
Financial Times

'Alternately fascinating and provocative' John Sutherland, *TLS*

CIRCUS OF DREAMS

ADVENTURES IN THE 1980s LITERARY WORLD

John Walsh

CONSTABLE

CONSTABLE

First published in Great Britain in 2022 by Constable
This paperback edition published in 2023 by Constable

1 3 5 7 9 10 8 6 4 2

Copyright © John Walsh, 2022

The moral right of the author has been asserted.

A CIP catalogue record for this book
is available from the British Library.

ISBN: 978-1-47213-347-2

Typeset in Caslon by SX Composing DTP, Rayleigh, Essex
Printed and bound in Great Britain by Clays Ltd, Elcograf, S.p.A.

Papers used by Constable are from well-managed forests
and other responsible sources.

Constable
An imprint of
Little, Brown Book Group
Carmelite House
50 Victoria Embankment
London EC4Y 0DZ

An Hachette UK Company

www.hachette.co.uk

www.littlebrown.co.uk

To Valerie Grove and Sarah Spankie – my friends and benefactors, confidantes and fellow carousers over 30+ years – this book is dedicated with love.

Contents

A Note on Memory

Any author who offers his reader personal remembrances of events from three decades ago risks being greeted with scepticism and accusations of invention. I'm happy to say that, in summoning up the past, I've been able to call on scores of newspaper articles, magazine interviews and diary items from the period, written by me and others, plus letters, cards and memos from authors and fellow journalists in those pre-email days, along with recent personal recollections from several people involved in publishing and journalism in the 1980s.

Many conversations fuel the story I tell in these pages, and some may wonder how I can replicate words that were spoken so long ago. The answer is that, at some points, I have recalled the gist of what was said and re-cast or embellished the exchanges for dramatic effect. My inspiration here has been the line taken by Pooh-Bah in *The Mikado*: 'Merely corroborative detail, intended to give artistic verisimilitude to an otherwise bald and unconvincing narrative.'

In other cases, I have simply sat with a pen and a sheet of A4 paper and summoned up the sentences that were uttered in this circumstance or that. I can't explain why I have a vast lumber of memories in my head. Why I should still be able to remember, as clear as daylight, the words with which the *Evening Standard*'s diary editor announced the lead item of his gossip column in the conference room one Wednesday morning in 1987, I have not the faintest idea. But I can. It's still there.

---·◆·---

Introduction

As so many things do, it started with a Bang.

For several days in 1971, the London *Evening Standard* ran quarter-page advertisements for something called the Bedford Square Book Bang. It was scheduled to run for two whole weeks, from 28 May to 11 June. It would, the organisers promised, cram the oval garden in the middle of the famous square with blowsy pavilions, where poets and novelists would recite or debate. There would be a massive tented bookshop selling ten thousand titles, a children's playground, a poets' corner, a cooking tent, a gardening display, several refreshment areas (alcohol served after 6 p.m.) and a candy-striped Big Top.

The air of skittish playfulness that hung over the event was compounded by the crazy variety of the participants. Alongside the serious novelists who would discuss 'The Future of the Novel' – Margaret Drabble, Stan Barstow, Alan Sillitoe, Penelope Mortimer – were the less highbrow authors of sex-and-showbiz bestsellers, Jacqueline Susann and Jackie Collins. For the modest entry fee of 50p, you might see such luminaries as Spike Milligan, Kingsley Amis, Stephen Spender, Barbara Cartland and Seamus Heaney among the crowd. Famous names from television were also featured. Percy Thrower would explain to the crowd 'How to Enjoy Your Garden', a young Mary Berry would present a cookery show, Dorian Williams – the BBC's equestrian commentator – would introduce 'The Ponies of Great Britain', Harry Corbett with Sooty and Sweep would entertain the book-lovers' children, who could win prizes dished out by Geoffrey Bayldon, the star of TV's *Catweazle*, while hilarious comic turns were promised from ancient vaudevillian Tommy Trinder, and from Johnny Speight, the writer of *Till Death Us Do Part*. And, continuing the circus-tent theme, Coco the Clown would open the proceedings with an exploding book.

During the first week, I took the Tube to Tottenham Court Road one evening, walked down through Bloomsbury, and saw a miraculous sight. Slap-bang in the heart of London, through a stand of plane trees, a constellation of fairy lights twinkled in the gloaming over a huddle of faces beside the main marquee. I remember how good it felt to walk into the garden, trying to spot writers. Was that bearded guy John Fowles, whose novel *The Collector* had chilled my blood? Could the posh, cream-skinned lady in the powder-blue coat be Antonia Fraser, whose *Mary Queen of Scots* I'd had to read for History A-level? In the Poetry Pavilion I watched as a bald man with a Scottish accent declaimed verses to a packed audience sitting on beer crates; as he read, he brandished his slim volume in one hand, slightly above the level of his face, as though perusing an exotic bird. I saw, from the books on the table, that he was called Iain Crichton Smith. I didn't know his name, but I remember admiring his bardic theatricality.

I spent only about ninety minutes at the Bang. I didn't talk to anyone. I bought a couple of bottles of Young's Special in the beer tent, but didn't have enough money to enter the songs-and-jokes cabaret. I bought one book – *Selected Poems of Louis MacNeice* – after flicking it open at a table and reading a poem called 'Les Sylphides'. But I glowed with pleasure at having hung out at an actual Literary Event, at having walked among the trees beside actual real-life novelists, playwrights, poets and critics, in the hallowed bit of London where, sixty years earlier, Virginia Woolf and her friends had taken tea and lolled in their deckchairs on warm June evenings like this one. Though they would, I fear, have regarded with horror any attempt to connect literature with a circus.

My fascination with meeting real-life writers went back to 1963, when I was ten. My sister Madelyn and I grew up in south London to Irish Catholic parents called Martin and Anne. Both were medical people. My mother was a former nursing sister, thrilling of bosom and stern of demeanour; my father a GP, Brylcreemed of bonce and genial of manner. Neither was an avid reader. When I went to Balham Public Library, Mum would ask me to bring home something by the American author Elizabeth Seifert, whose chosen creative path was signalled by the titles of her work: *The Doctor's Private Life*, *Doctor's Kingdom*, *Love Calls the Doctor*, *The Doctors Were Brothers*, *Two Doctors and a Girl*, *Katie's Young Doctor* . . .

Dad had a lot of respect for Victorian classics. He urged us to read *The Heroes* by Charles Kingsley, a re-telling of three Greek myths from a very Christianised perspective, although the bits about Jason and the Argonauts were fun. He told me I'd enjoy *The Coral Island* by R. M. Ballantyne, in which three English schoolboys are shipwrecked on an uninhabited Polynesian island and, through public-school resourcefulness and sturdy Victorian enterprise, manage to feed themselves, make clothes and fashion a shelter, while watching missionaries convert nearby islanders to Christianity.

It was, of course, the book that inspired William Golding to write *Lord of the Flies*, as a counterblast to its smug assumptions about human nature and the British spirit. I wasn't aware of the *Flies*, but I couldn't make much headway with the *Island*. The boys all sounded like pipe-smoking schoolteachers and their adventures lacked any actual excitement. I soon abandoned it for the familiar comforts of *Just William* and *Jennings and Darbishire*.

Madelyn, by contrast, was a passionate reader of historical fictions, especially those written by Jean Plaidy and Georgette

Heyer. She devoured the complete works of both, in their multitudinous entirety, several times. By the age of thirteen, there was no detail of the private life of Catherine de' Medici or the dance-card etiquette of Regency Bath with which my sister was unfamiliar.

One day she received in the post a novel about the burning of Rome called *City of the Golden House* by one Madeleine A. Polland. To her, and my, utter amazement it came with a personal note from the author. 'Lovely to be able to say hello to another Madeleine,' it read cheerily, explaining that Ms Polland came from Cork and had befriended a cousin of our mum's. This woman had explained that her family contained the world's most passionate eleven-year-old reader of historical fiction, so Madeleine was sending her newest book with compliments. My sister was delighted by such a grown-up gift. I was stunned by the revelation that an author wasn't, as I'd assumed, some anonymous alien in a far-off land, but could be someone human, chatty and unexpectedly keen to approach a reader. This made a deep impression on me.

There was a library of sorts at our home, a three-decker cabinet with glass panels that flipped up and slid back over the books. As I turned twelve, and buried myself in Sherlock Holmes and Agatha Christie, I thought it worth investigating to see what our parents had collected therein. It was, quite frankly, disappointing stuff. There were books of Irish folk tales (*The Turf Cutter's Donkey*, *The Grey Goose of Kilnevin*) and leather-bound copies of *Lord Jim* and *Oliver Twist* which looked like family heirlooms, but the main burden on the shelves was medical textbooks.

The Merck Index: An Encyclopaedia of Chemicals, Drugs and Biologicals was one appealing tome. Several works had titles like *Essentials of Nursing Practice*, and a really thick one was called *Manual of Midwifery*, which I remember leafing through for some time. I was confronted with pages and pages of what, in my days of making Airfix models of fighter planes, were called 'exploded views' (i.e. *really* detailed diagrams) of ladies' down-below arrangements: they included drawings of 'vulva vestibules' and a 'uterine prolapse', along with other phenomena to which I was a stranger. It was a relief to reach more understandable, if still alarming, territory: birthing procedures, illustrations of Caesarean incisions, pages of forceps, stirrups (*stirrups?*) and fearsome-looking theatre (*theatre?*) scissors. I was keen on all books but this, I felt, was a field of human knowledge I could do without exploring.

I entered the world of grown-up fiction when, on holiday in Italy, in the drawing-room bookshelf of the Hotel San Giorgio, I discovered a paperback of *Thunderball*. 'Now John,' said my mother sternly, 'I think you know the bits that I'd rather you didn't read.' (I sure did. I couldn't *wait* to not-read them.) I became a devotee of Ian Fleming and his famous creation, tut-tutting at any of the books (such as *From Russia with Love*, or *The Spy Who Loved Me*) that didn't stick to the Bond formula: 1) Outbreak of villainy in foreign city; 2) James Bond at home/in casino; 3) Briefing from M and cheeky inspection of lethal gadgetry with Q the Armourer; 4) Bond travels to exotic location; 5) Bond meets attractive lady in trouble . . .

After Bond, I thrashed around in the ocean of modern popular fiction. I tried thrillers by Alistair MacLean and Hammond Innes, but the narrators sounded like stolid military types who lacked warmth (and how thrilling could *Ice Station Zebra* be, about a British intelligence officer masquerading as a 'frostbite expert' on a submarine heading for a damaged meteorological shelter on an ice floe in the Arctic Sea?) I found Richard Gordon's *Doctor in the House* books funny, with their band of schoolboyish medical students and the stern, headmasterly Sir Lancelot Spratt, but they relied too enthusiastically on sniggery tit-jokes (Doctor, stethoscopically examining well-developed girl patient: 'Big breaths'. Girl: 'Yeth, and I'm only thickthteen . . .') for my fastidious taste.

The works of John Wyndham appealed because of their global-catastrophe plots in everyday settings. The first chapters of *The Day of the Triffids*, when the hero walks through London to find the whole world's population has gone blind except him, were troubling in a way I'd never come across before. But I never finished any of the books; things tended to become slow and moralistic in the second half of every one of them.

At fourteen, my favourite book was *King Rat* by James Clavell. In four hundred pages it evoked life in the Changi POW camp in 1945 Singapore, where a clean-cut English flight lieutenant called Marlowe falls under the spell of a US corporal, King, an enterprising but unscrupulous (and charmless) guy, who runs a black market in food, anti-malaria drugs and 'pygmy deer' – rats, offered as food delicacies. I'd hoped the book might serve up the kind of torture-porn that every schoolboy had read in *The Knights of Bushido*, but Clavell offered something other than flayed bodies. *King Rat* was more about the prisoners than the Japanese, about men in the last extremity of humiliation, starvation and filth who, in order to survive, must themselves become corrupted. It was a gritty, sometimes sickening descent into hell and I read it wide-eyed. I longed to have Mr Clavell come to my school, where I could introduce him to the boys, who'd be stunned like me by his brutal memories.

Around my fifteenth birthday, I had a wake-up call. I was doing well in English at school, but I'd become accustomed to reading rubbish at home. In the summer of 1967, on holiday in Ireland, I bought a paperback novelisation of an American TV spy drama – and ten pages in, I flung it to the ground and asked: What the *bloody hell* am I doing with this crap, when I could be reading something good? There and then I resolved to read the Western canon of literature, and to do so without delay.

On the actual birthday, I began this noble – if ambitious – project by making a list. I knew better than to start with *Beowulf* and move doggedly through the centuries. I resolved instead to mix classics from the Olden Days with more recent works, to intersperse the Defoe-Austen-Thackeray stuff I'd heard about, with the twentieth-century fiction featured in the new Penguin Modern Classics with their lovely grey-silver spines. The list read like this:

Gulliver's Travels
The Great Gatsby
Pride and Prejudice
What Ho, Jeeves!
Bleak House
Howards End
Crime and Punishment
Brighton Rock
Tom Jones
Lucky Jim

A certain specific worry nagged at me: what if I didn't enjoy the books that the world had admired for centuries? What if I didn't have the taste (or intelligence) to appreciate them? *Gulliver*, though, turned out to be a brilliant starting point. From the puzzlement of the Lilliputians about the contents of Gulliver's pockets (what are they describing? Oh of course, they're his *spectacle*s) to the grotesque close-up of the Brobdingnagian ladies' huge hairy moles, to the mad inventors on the flying island of Laputa, to the wild yahoos in the final story, sitting in the trees and raining shit down on Gulliver's head, it was a wild ride of a book. My main reaction wasn't to say, 'Goodness, what a fine piece of work!' but to cry, 'Why did it take me so long to discover *Literature*?' And to feel that Jonathan Swift, mad and wicked and shockingly funny, was sitting there in the room, smiling as he watched me read his words.

At the time of the Bang I was seventeen. I was shortly to sit my Oxford Entrance exam and, if all went well, to be interviewed at one of the colleges to see if I might study English Literature for three years. My callow desire to meet writers had never gone away, however. That summer, as I took a break from the Western canon, my favourite author was the Irish-American novelist J. P. Donleavy, whose book *The Beastly Beatitudes of Balthazar B* filled my heart with word-drunken bliss. It was raucously funny, swishily picaresque, swooningly romantic and shockingly tragic (Balthazar's love object, Fitzdare, falls off a horse and dies) and it hit my teenage-virgin sensibility amidships. My pooh-poohing English master, Joe Winter, tried to stifle my enthusiasm; he called Donleavy 'the poor man's James Joyce' and mocked as affectation the way he turned the last sentence of every chapter into a kind of haiku ('There was a man/ Who made a boat/To sail away/ And it sank.')

I told Joe I was planning to visit Donleavy at his home in Ireland, to explain how much I admired his writing, his characters and his prose style. I said I just knew he'd appreciate this heartfelt gesture by a sensitive reader, and that we'd soon become friends.

'I wouldn't do that if I were you,' said Joe gravely. 'I've seen photographs. He's a beardy, unsmiling and very grand American with delusions of being both a Celt and a squire. And he's got two enormous wolfhounds. Go and see him, and you'll end up as their lunch.'

The Bedford Square Book Bang was fifty years ago (I'm writing this in spring 2021) and – Big Top and *Catweazle* notwithstanding – it signalled a sea-change in the relationship between authors and readers, of the kind I craved with Donleavy. It wasn't the first-ever lit-fest – that title goes to the Cheltenham Literature Festival, which started life in 1949 – but it was the first time that authors came out from behind their desks and publicly mingled with their readers on the same level. It was the first sighting of a project that was to flourish mightily in the 1980s, as this book will show. Because, in those days, British publishing didn't believe in promoting authors or trying very hard to maximise sales. Publishing was an occupation for gentlemen who were fond of snuff and clubland lunches. Publication day might see a modest drinks gathering in the boardroom, but nothing more – no tacky razzmatazz, no throwing of parties with the press in attendance, no tours of bookshops or festivals. We were dealing with writers here, OK, not people from *showbiz*.

The brains behind the Book Bang, the man who persuaded British publishers and authors to take part in this jolly but undignified circus, was Martyn Goff. The son of an émigré Russian furrier now living in Hampstead, Goff was the author of several novels, many with gay themes, ran the Ibis bookshop in Banstead, Surrey before becoming a civil servant, and lived in Chelsea, next door to Peter Sellers. An engaging chap to meet, he sported kipper ties and the hairstyle of a Roman emperor, spoke in a raspy chuckle and was one of the British book world's key figures in the late twentieth century.

By 1971 he was director of the National Book League, a government-sponsored initiative to encourage more people to buy and read books. Goff was an enthusiast and world-class huckster, promising the *Evening Standard*, a week before the Bang, that 'People will be able to say to their friends, "I bought this Graham Greene book from Graham Greene himself and I paid him thirty shillings for it."' (Graham Greene didn't actually attend the event, but it was the thought that counted.) In his introduction to the programme, Goff explained why he believed that publishers and booksellers might need a marketing leg-up: 'Expansion of the number of hours and channels of television broadcasting,' he wrote, '[and] the arrival of video cassettes, microfilms and microfiches, to name but some of the competitors, will blot up hours and money that might otherwise have gone to books . . . Books must be shown to be *fun*.'

The Book Bang, then, wasn't a demonstration of the health of the book market but of its *fragility* under threat from other forms of entertainment. By coincidence, another warning was being sounded in another part of the literary wood. A book called *Jonathan Cape, Publisher*, a history of the noble publishing house by its outgoing chairman, Michael S. Howard, also appeared in 1971. In its conclusion, the new chairman, Tom Maschler, laid out his thoughts about the company's future. One part of his prognosis was startling:

'In the field of fiction,' he wrote, 'we are now very close to the point where, with the exception of thrillers, we are publishing no novels primarily for commercial reasons. Such books as *Portnoy's Complaint* and *The French Lieutenant's Woman* have become bestsellers almost despite their literary value. However, in literature, the bestselling author is relatively unpredictable.' It was a shocking admission – that British literary fiction didn't sell, and that Cape weren't going to bother with it any longer because British readers simply had no interest in books that were highbrow, experimental or challenging.

Ten years after this dismal pronouncement, how did things stand? Had the British novel succumbed to its predicted fate and expired? Had the British reader's flagging interest in fiction finally flatlined? To which the answers were emphatically No and No. The British novel was instead staging the beginnings of an astonishing recovery. By the end of 1981, newspapers were reporting massive sales, in millions of pounds and dollars, of four 'challenging' new novels by British authors, in the UK and USA. The work of a new generation of young novelists, boldly original in their style and intent, controversial, risk-taking, iconoclastic, blackly comic and bracingly rude, was starting to flood the market.

The brightest star in the new constellation was Martin Amis, a cool, unsmiling, perma-smoking, laser-brained literary star with a prose style 'as fast and efficient as a flick knife' and a chain-saw approach to reviewing new works by the old guard of the literary establishment. He was the flag-bearer of the new generation, and he watched with interest as the world began to flock to his door and treat him, not just as a maker-upper of stories, but as a political *savant*, a cultural soothsayer, a cosmic pundit. In the Introduction to his 2017 collection of essays, *The Rub of Time*, Amis wrote:

> *In 1972, I submitted my first novel: I typed it out on a second-hand Olivetti and sent it in . . . The print run was 1,000 (and the advance was £250). It was published, and reviewed, and that was*

that. There was no launch party and no book tour; there were no interviews, no profiles, no photo shoots, no signings, no readings, no panels, no on-stage conversations, no Woodstocks of the Mind in Hay-on-Wye . . . The same went for my second novel (1975) and my third (1978). By the time of my fourth novel (1981), nearly all the collateral activities [of promotion] *were in place, and writers, in effect, had been transferred from vanity press to* Vanity Fair.

Amis attributed the 1980s explosion of interest in literary fiction to the media, especially the newspapers: as they grew fatter and multi-sectioned, he said, they needed more content to fill the pages and – sated with features about 'ne'er-do-well royals, depressive comedians, jailed rock stars . . . and rapist boxers' – turned reluctantly to writing about Writers.

Amis was being disingenuous in claiming to be weary of being badgered, through the 1980s and beyond, by features editors and the convenors of literary festivals. The publication of each of his books became a media event, mainly because of his readiness to make pungently quotable remarks about consumerism, nuclear weapons, Communism, Nazism, Islam, world entropy, the cost of dental treatment, the state of England, the fate of the US. He became the novelist most sought out by newspapers for vivid copy – and he could be relied on to sign up. Like the nymphs of Arcadia, he was eagerly pursued but easily caught.

The 1980s renaissance was not caused by the media's need to fill pages. It was caused by the arrival of a flood of talented new writers, who were inspired to write fiction by several circumstances. The most potent was simply the challenge and example of their peer group, fronted by Amis, Ian McEwan, Julian Barnes, Rose Tremain, William Boyd, Salman Rushdie, Pat Barker and others who will appear in these pages: the baby-boomer generation, born between 1945 and 1955, who arrived at puberty or maturity in the wild sixties and felt empowered to do something more creative than join the professions or the financial world.

As the 1980s progressed, more new writers made their debuts and flourished. Many were naturalised foreigners – from India, Hong Kong, Australia and Japan, with names like Mistry, Mo, Carey and Ishiguro – and they used English in thrilling new ways. Many of their works were translated and published around the world. At the same time, a slew of innovations changed the way books were consumed: a revolution in bookselling, spearheaded by Tim Waterstone; the flourishing of new literary magazines after the temporary closure of *The Times* in 1978; a new visibility of book prizes that followed the televising of the Booker in 1981; and the success of promotional campaigns based on the personal appeal of authors as well as their way with words.

All these things transformed young British writers from cash-strapped anchorites into renowned public figures – 'gunslinger' prose stylists, much in demand. The shift in identity found a hitherto untapped audience of readers, who bought the books in great numbers. This led to competition between multinational publishing companies, fuelled by a new strain of sharky agents. The newspapers got involved. Rupert Murdoch put huge tranches of money into buying serialisation rights to the memoirs of famous public figures, into extensive books coverage in his newspapers, and into a soon-to-be-famous literary festival on the Welsh borders.

Margaret Thatcher was never likely to be a fan of *Dead Babies*, or *Oranges Are Not the Only Fruit* and certainly not of *The Satanic Verses* (where she appeared as 'Mrs Torture') but, on her watch, a lot of money was suddenly washing around the publishing industry. By 1985, every firm was looking for the next twenty-something wordsmith, the new precocious literary star, and would pay absurd sums to find one, and to tell the world of their signing. This encouraged writers to be more ambitious and productive, and inspired readers to spend more money in bookshops – not just to acquire their new work, but to buy into what today would be called their brand.

The opportunities for writers to meet potential readers in public
– for fans to see them on stage, hear their words up close, meet
them in bookshops and admire their appearance on TV chat shows
– grew like a rushing wave. Between the writers and readers sat the
publishers, desperate to monetise the new arrivals for an audience
no longer shy of innovation. This audience was already buying
Sony Walkmans, home computers, Body Shop cosmetics and
luxury holidays; now, for perhaps the first time in decades, novels
were trendy, authors were cool, bookshops were temples of
Mammon, and crazy sums of money were being exchanged in the
publishing marketplace.

This is a memoir of a long decade in the literary world, a heady
time to be alive, in love with books, trying to make it as a writer/
critic and feeling bowled over by the talent, the money and
the razzmatazz. It was a time of wild imagination, a period of
'strenuous dreaming', as Anne Enright (writing about *Ulysses*)
called the making of fiction. It was the time of *Midnight's Children*,
Granta and the *London Review of Books*, Adrian Mole, *The Hitchhiker's
Guide to the Galaxy*, Waterstone's, *Waterland*, The Best of British
Writers, the Merchant/Ivory productions of E. M. Forster, the Best
of Young British Novelists, *Flaubert's Parrot*, the launch of Fourth
Estate and Bloomsbury, Craig Raine and the Martian poets,
The Swimming-Pool Library, the New York copycat Brat Pack, *Lace*,
Pearls, Jeffrey Archer's libel case, Hay-on-Wye, the fatwa . . .

Amidst the book events, the launch parties, the hatchet reviews,
the gossip, the romances, the scandals, the rows, and the rises and
falls in reputation, I had a ringside seat as a book reviewer,
interviewer, prize judge, sometime media pundit, feature writer
and literary editor. Half a century after the Big Top went up in
Bedford Square, I want to present the UK book renaissance as
three things: a crucible of invention, a blizzard of commercialism
and a tumbling three-ring circus, whose jostling troupe of performers displayed to their astonished audiences the spectacular
fruits of their strenuous dreams.

CHAPTER 1

Amis and Company

My fascination with Martin Amis began long before the leading lights of the 1980s literary scene were christened 'the Amis Generation'. When I went to university, he seemed to be in the air I breathed.

In 1971, I'd gone to Oxford to be interviewed for a place at St John's College by John Carey (later to be the star of the *Sunday Times* Books pages) and at Exeter College by Jonathan Wordsworth. I chose to go to the latter, arrived in September 1972, and discovered that Amis had arrived to study at Exeter four years before me; he'd left in 1971. (By coincidence, he'd also been interviewed at St John's, where he'd impressed the hell out of Professor Carey.)

Even in my first term, Amis's name ('Kingsley's son, you know') already signified glamour and salience. Rumours flew about him. He had been, people said, almost wholly unfamiliar with the Western canon of literature until three years earlier, and had bluffed his way to success. On the contrary, others said, he was a scholar of Empsonian brilliance, who absorbed information all day in the Bodleian Library, leaving the building only to smoke roll-ups outside, looking like Jean-Paul Belmondo in *À Bout de Souffle*.

People spoke in wondering tones about his degree. He'd achieved the rare distinction of a Congratulatory First. This meant that when he was summoned to a *viva voce* in front of a panel of tutors (supposedly to be offered a chance to defend his exam papers in the hope of improving his results), the tutors applauded and drowned out his words: a quaintly academic way of congratulating a student for being, basically, too clever to need any more teaching from them.

People said Amis had been a swordsman of the boudoir – or, at least, of the squalid dung heap that constituted a college bedroom; they said he'd charmed his female 'scout' (the domestic servant who comes to clean college rooms each morning) into ignoring the presence in the bathroom of yet another exhausted Silvikrin siren from St Hilda's College or Lady Margaret Hall.

Amis's throwaway remarks were quoted as if they were Wildean shafts. When we first-year students were sent, one day, to a seminar room to undergo a kind of rehearsal for the Honour-Moderations exams, our young tutor – who'd been a contemporary of Amis's – told us how, when they'd sat a similar mock exam four years earlier, Martin had visited the bathroom halfway through and had reappeared, reporting to nobody in particular: 'I wouldn't go in there if I were you. There are *pencil-thick* pubic hairs in the bath . . .'

Towards the end of my first academic year, in June 1973, I attended the final Friday pre-lunch seminar class with Jonathan Wordsworth. In his studiedly casual get-up of brown jumper and rumpled blue corduroys, he was dishing out glasses of sherry to us and to the girls from St Hugh's College who shared our Practical Criticism class. With his usual genial attentiveness, Wordsworth would hold up two bottles in front of each student and ask, 'Would you care for the dry? Or the' – infinitesimal shudder – 'slightly *less* dry?' as if the latter would be the choice of a lunatic.

Jonathan was a firm believer in the old-fashioned lit-crit concept of the Close Reading – the first contact with a text, and the response it drew from you *right away, there and then*, before you'd worked out what other texts it reminded you of, or found out what academics had written about it. In the 1970s university world, where the critic's reaction was becoming increasingly intellectualised, where words like 'structuralism' and the names of Lacan and Derrida were being bandied about, Wordsworth clung to his belief that someone's pure emotional response trumped any academic reaction. Which is why Jonathan loved to have a roomful of people sitting around uttering their artless but (with any luck) truthful reports about what a new, previously unknown, poem did to their ears and brains and hearts.

As we filed out at the end, I noticed a new book on his desk that I hadn't seen before. You couldn't miss it because the cover design almost knocked your eye out – a black shiny dust-wrapper on which the title announced itself in a shouty diagonal of garish yellow and red: *The Rachel Papers*. The author's name featured in a red box: Martin Amis. I stood by the desk and turned the book over. The back cover showed the author's handsome face: longish hair, ironical eyes, sulky expression, cigarette held before his pouty (and apparently much-bitten) lips.

I flipped the book open to the title page, where a handwritten message ran: 'To Jonathan, my star tutor—with many thanks and much love.'

Gosh, I thought. So this is Amis's first novel, a copy of which he's sent to his tutor as if they were, you know, *mates*, a book in which he had *written down words*, probably with *his own fountain pen* in his own (amazingly small and neatly precise) handwriting.

And *hang on a minute*, I thought in growing excitement, this is the *actual room* in which Martin must have sat during tutorials and seminars with Jonathan, four years ago, making no doubt *brilliant* interventions, rather as I had done just half an hour earlier, shyly suggesting (to general derision) that the last two lines of T. S. Eliot's *La Figlia Che Piange* were a clear allusion to a section of *The Prelude* ... And perhaps – holy shit! – that dusty seminar chair in which I'd been sitting for two hours was *precisely the one* on which Mart (I'd begun to think of him as 'Mart') had actually parked his denim-clad bottom ...

This was my first experience of literary hero-worship, a frankly idiotic admiration not far removed from the devotion I'd once given to Popeye or William Tell, or Stirling Moss or John Edrich or Napoleon Solo in *The Man from U.N.C.L.E*. This was a kind of stunned respect for the sort of chap who had everyone talking about his student wonderfulness, who'd slept with several girls, who'd won a Congratulatory First, and who could write a book (at, what, *twenty-two?*) and get it published in dazzling livery, then dispatch it to his Oxford tutor with the insouciance of the guy in the TV ads who, clad in black polo-neck sweater and jeans, navigated motorbikes across perilous clifftops and leapt from a helicopter to deliver boxes of Milk Tray to his thunderstruck lady love.

It wasn't just Amis who occupied this shadow-life I felt around me. His friends showed up as well. His girlfriend Tina Brown, exactly my age, was already a star and, like Martin, she was the subject of hot gossip. The daughter of a film producer whose first wife was Maureen O'Hara (the fiery redhead romanced by a ludicrously Oirish John Wayne in *The Quiet Man*), and a mother who had been Laurence Olivier's press agent, she was dazzling, blonde, sharp-eyed and hectically successful: she was pointed out to me at St Anne's when I visited a girl from my sister's school, coincidentally another Christina. Ms Brown seemed to have become a journalist overnight: she'd snuck her way onto the pages of *Isis*, the more readable of Oxford's two student-edited magazines. She'd been invited to a *Private Eye* lunch by Auberon Waugh, an acid-sharp columnist on the magazine and an *Evening Standard* book reviewer, and had written about the experience in the *New Statesman*. In 1973 she won the Catherine Pakenham Award for Most Promising Female Journalist.*

---

* The Catherine Pakenham Award was founded and administered by the family of Lord Longford, in tribute to his daughter, a journalist on the *Sunday Telegraph* magazine, who died in 1970, aged twenty-three, in a car crash.

She'd sold an article to the *Tatler* entitled 'What It's Like to Be Up at Oxford' which most of the students I knew had read. Not only was it the work of someone who'd quickly become well-connected and in-demand; it was also thrillingly cheeky about the senior academics. Tina Brown had had the nerve to describe her English tutor, Dorothy Bednarovska, as 'a cross between Voltaire and Greta Garbo'. The fact that Madame Bednarovska would probably have wriggled with delight at being thus described didn't stop the student faculty from agreeing that Tina Brown had been, you know, *shockingly* rude and disrespectful to her exalted supervisor.

A close friend of Amis's at Exeter College was Craig Raine. In 1972, six years before he made his poetic debut with *The Onion, Memory*, he was assigned to guide the faltering steps of first-year English students. Annoyingly, I didn't have him as a tutor (I was assigned a lanky Australian called Rod, very much a runner-up prize) but I enjoyed meeting him around the college. He was very funny, scatological, crude and physically distinctive: profusely curly-haired, Marxianly bearded, granny-spectacled and swishy (he wore a black wool shoulder bag as he strode down Turl Street); and he liked a good argument.

One morning, Jonathan Wordsworth was conducting a seminar on Tennyson's 'Maud', the poet's favourite work, about a deeply unstable lover who goes mad after murdering the brother of Maud, the titular teenager whom he adores. I remember Craig sitting in a window seat, assessing the discussion in silence but with an occasional nod of encouragement to any student brave enough to argue with Wordsworth. After forty-five minutes – halfway through the seminar – Wordsworth asked: 'Craig? Any thoughts? Any points about the poem that we haven't raised?'

'There's one glaring omission,' said Craig. 'I can't understand how you can talk about "Maud" for the best part of an hour without a single mention of the vaginal imagery.'

Wordsworth's noble brow furrowed. 'I can't say it's something that *leaps out* when I read the poem,' he said. 'And I'm not sure whether, in a class like this, it's a fruitful area of—'

'It's absolutely central,' snapped Craig. 'The poem is full of allusions to holes and hymens and blood and lips. They have an important function. I'd be happy to run through the main ones for the class.'

'I don't *think* so,' said Jonathan Wordsworth firmly, like a teacher declining a cheeky fifth-former's offer to recite his own poetry.

Raine looked annoyed. It seemed odd that two tutors could have a battle of wills right in front of their students. Then Craig rose to his feet, crossed the room, yanked the door open and left. We could hear his feet clattering down the flagstones of Staircase 1.

Gosh, we thought: did he just *storm out*?

The seminar resumed, with much discussion of death in both 'Maud' and 'In Memoriam', the Tennyson poem that had immediately preceded it in his career. As the session was drawing to a close, we heard another noise on the stairs. This time the footsteps were clattering upwards.

The door opened. Craig Raine burst in, carrying a sheaf of A4 paper in his hand.

'Here you are,' he said dramatically to the room in general. 'I've done photostats for all of you. Every vaginal image in "Maud" from the very first line. Which is, let me remind you: "I hate the dreadful hollow behind the little wood" . . .'

I'd like to think we applauded his rather sexy bravado, but we probably also thought him a bit of a diva.

Sex and literature were the twin poles of Amis's writing career at its outset. I bought *The Rachel Papers* in the Long Vacation – I'd never bought a hardback novel before; my private library at home resembled a Charing Cross Road barrow of dog-eared paperbacks – and turned the pages as reverently as if I were leafing through the *Book of Kells*.

The first thing I noticed was the literary allusions: the names of (or titles by) D. H. Lawrence, Philip Larkin, E. M. Forster, Ernest Hemingway, Henry Fielding, Sigmund Freud, Oscar Wilde, Gerard Manley Hopkins, A. E. Housman and William Shakespeare are all dropped in the first thirty pages. By page 60, Dickens, Dylan Thomas, William Blake, Jane Austen, George Herbert and Franz Kafka have all been press-ganged into service in the twangy, torsional, first-personal narrative of Charles Highway.

Charles is compulsively literary. When he first meets the book's titular love object, Rachel, his opening gambit is to quote the first lines of Tennyson's 'Tithonus', which are, understandably, received with blank silence. And when Charles and Rachel finally have sex, we get a page-long passage of Charles trying to delay his orgasm by running disjointed shards of T. S. Eliot's early poetry through his head.

My first response to Amis's debut, however, was puzzlement. The opening sentence was: 'My name is Charles Highway, though you wouldn't think it to look at me. It's such a rangy, well-travelled, big-cocked name and, to look at, I am not one of these.' Well *that*'s not terribly good, I thought. Was 'Charles Highway' *really* a rangy, well-travelled, big-cocked name? (What, Charles as in Prince Charles, Charles Hawtrey and Charles de Gaulle? Highway as in Steve Heighway, the lugubrious Liverpool winger with the awful moustache?) Also debatable was the proposition which followed: that the age of twenty is 'the real turning point' in a man's life, 'the end of youth'. No it's not, I thought – the turning point is surely the age at which you buy a place to live, or acquire a kid.

The first few pages trundled some cumbersome plot machinery into view. This novel, Charles assures us, will take five hours for us to read, starting at 7 p.m., ending at midnight. In that time, he'll run through the events of the last three months, using all his 'sixth-form cleverness and fifth-form nastiness' to establish what kind of grown-up he will make. 'Anyway,' he lamely concludes, 'it ought to be good fun.'

The three months, we learn, were mostly spent by Charles having unfulfilling sex with one girl and planning to part another girl, Rachel, from her current boyfriend and her underwear, while studying for his Oxford Entrance Exam. That was pretty much the book's whole plot, with walk-on parts for his parents, sister and brother-in-law. The actual 'Rachel Papers' were the collection of writings which Charles consults in his sexual campaign, a series of self-penned behavioural stratagems, kept in folders with titles like '*Conquests and Techniques: A Synthesis*': they sounded to me like the 'Dodge Book' kept by ten-year-old Roger the Dodger in the *Beano*.

Rachel the Love Object proves surprisingly easy to win. The Hated Rival, an annoying American called DeForest, becomes, for no obvious reason, a weeping non-combatant. No obstacle of commitment or crisis of mortality threatens to derail Charles's acquisition of both The Girl and the Getting Into Oxford. At the end, Charles receives his comeuppance at the Oxford Entrance interview, when the Jonathan Wordsworth-ish English tutor points out that all the literary *aperçus* in his exam papers are a) pinched from famous critics and b) contradictory. But Charles ends the book unchanged, still committed to being a self-centred pillock.

The writing, however, was the important thing. Its prevailing mode was of blistering, take-no-prisoners, descriptive abuse, which started on page 13 with a description of Charles's mother ('The skin had shrunken over her skull, to accentuate her jaw and to provide commodious cellarage for the gloomy pools that were her eyes; her breasts had long forsaken their native home . . .') and seldom let up thereafter.

I read the novel over four days in a delirium of pleasure at its headlong malignity, its hilariously disgusted inspections of the surface of teenage life: pimples (the 'double-yolkers', the Big Boy that resembles 'a surgically implanted walnut'); venereal disease (Charles's friend Geoffrey's fantastical lies about the clap clinic, and its use of a urethra-invading miniature umbrella, are a nightmare

of horrific invention); bronchitis (the book is an extended paean to
'hawking'); problematic teeth ('For two years I went about the
place with a mouth like a Meccano set') – a theme that was to
become obsessive in Amis's books and, of course, his later life – and
the fear of being gay. Charles typically checks out his body's
response to the works of gay writers (Wilde, Gerard Manley
Hopkins, A. E. Housman, E. M. Forster) by taking a body-building
magazine to bed to see if turning the pages and scanning the
pictorial beefcake will give him an erection.

What most impressed me about the Amis debut, however, was
his writing about sex. No literary smut I'd encountered over years
of avid research could match Amis's descriptions of shagging and
its physical weaponry. He brought up the notorious American
erotophile Henry Miller and said that, since the publication of his
Tropic of Cancer and *Tropic of Capricorn* books in the 1930s, it has
become 'difficult' to describe female genitalia 'sensibly'. But it was
far from difficult for *him*: 'Rachel's was the most pleasing I had ever
come across. Not, for her, the wet Brillo-pad, nor the paper-bagful
of kedgeree, nor the greasy waistcoat pocket, the gashed vole's
stomach, the clump of veins, glands, tubes . . .'

For a moment, I felt I was back home aged twelve, leafing
through the *Manual of Midwifery*. It was writing that made you
think: Jesus – how can you write like this, knowing that parents,
friends and indeed girlfriends will read it? Doesn't it sound sweatily
disgusted by the female body, appalled by the physical homeland
of sex? Or is that Charles's attitude, rather than Martin's? (And,
come to that, Jonathan Wordsworth's distaste at Craig's delight in
poetic genitalia.) But that didn't matter to me. It was the fearlessness
that mattered, the boldness of attack, the inventiveness of the
comparisons (not always the accuracy, though – kedgeree? I mean,
what, *rice*? And *eggs*?).

He was also capable of a more subtle register of sexual description. When Charles is in bed with his girlfriend Gloria, post-coitally,
she is keen to repeat the process but he is not (Charles is oddly

unenthusiastic about sex – to him, 'It's not something you do, just something you get done.'). Charles turns to the wall and pretends to be asleep, while Gloria employs a repertoire of seductive manoeuvres to regain his interest. Her enthusiastic tuggings and tongue-scourings inspire in him a grudging respect. During their final fuck, while Charles feels only 'back pains, bronchitic gasping', he watches her coming to orgasm 'with clenched-teeth, bullwhip-shuddering yelps of dismay'. Every action she's performed has been full-blooded, volitional, generous; everything he's done has been grudging, detached, fake. And the long passage ends with three simple sentences and a significant final word:

'Gloria lay back, her race run. After a while she folded up and went to sleep. And I watched the ceiling, breathless with envy.'

I was amazed by how much Amis achieved in this passage. His determination to go miles beyond conventional ways of describing sex was fearlessly frank. But he'd also let Charles, a monster of egotism, be truthful about his emotional blankness. He showed the conflict in the head of a callow youth who wishes he could feel real emotion while lying beside someone overwhelmed by it.

I read the reviews of *Rachel* with fascination. What would the literary greybeards make of the egomaniacal bullshitter, Charles Highway? In the *Spectator*, Amis's exact contemporary Peter Ackroyd (another *enfant terrible*, he became the magazine's literary editor aged twenty-one) addressed the oldies directly: 'Well, you old fogies, you were right after all. Martin Amis has exposed the younger generation for the evil and wretched creatures you always supposed them to be,' before concluding that Amis had 'fashioned a substantial character out of the rag-ends of our frantic contemporaries.' In the *New Statesman*, Peter Prince gave Charles a ferocious drubbing. He called him 'the Early Bloomer, the Sixth Form Sneerer', a ghastly amalgam – 'that combination of middle-class privilege and A-level meritocracy who is such a delight for the dons and such a damn trial to everybody else until a few years pass and, mercifully, he either fizzles out or, more rarely, manages the breakthrough into joining the rest of the human race.' It was quite a demolition job.*

I began subscribing to the *New Statesman*, because Amis reviewed books there occasionally. In these caustic reports, he seemed to be on a one-man mission to trash the reputations of several dinosaurs of English fiction: especially Angus Wilson, Iris Murdoch, Anthony Burgess, C. P. Snow and Fay Weldon. His pitiless inspections of these old fogies combined the lordly omniscience of the career academic (he always showed his familiarity with the writer's complete works) and the shuddering fastidiousness of a modern style commissar.

Here's an example. Reviewing Angus Wilson's *As If By Magic* in 1973, he complains about the nastiness of Wilson's work and declares: 'One of the few things I would rather run a mile than do is have an Angus Wilson character over for the evening.' The 'nastiness' to which he refers is the gay milieu of Wilson's fictions, and his 'candour about the vulnerability of the homosexual to self-destructive guilt, rabid promiscuity, pleasureless bitching, vanity, greed and haemorrhoids'.

Amis introduces the protagonist, Hamo Langmuir, a sexually confused agronomist who is unable to achieve an erection with anyone over twenty. 'It is with some enthusiasm, then,' writes Amis, 'that he embarks on a working tour of the nubile East, and it is with increasingly little that we follow him on a long, diffuse, unfunny sexual picaresque.' I loved the use of the word 'we', as if Amis is speaking for a new generation of gerontophobic (and frankly homophobic) readers. The review proceeds to dismiss the book's plot, characters, twist and climax, and the 'scruffiness' of

---

* In his autobiography, *Experience*, Amis called Prince's 'the worst review that came my way' – though one could imagine Charles Highway raising an amused eyebrow at having caused Mr Prince such personal heartburn.

Wilson's prose, before concluding with a final putdown that mingles the tones of disappointed uncle and stern headmaster: 'Naturally one doesn't begrudge Wilson his Uproarious Jaunt, but one hopes that in future he will make better use of his travel diaries.' I remember thinking: Jesus – *how old* is this Amis guy now? Twenty-four? Or eighty-five?

Here's another one. In 1974, he reviewed Iris Murdoch's *The Sacred and Profane Love Machine*. He began by having some sport with the title, suggesting it was a highbrow version of Jacqueline Susann's *The Love Machine*; he briefly outlined the central *ménage à trois*, in which the improbably named Blaise Gavender juggles his home life (he has a serene, Buckinghamshire-based wife) with a sluttish, needy mistress in a Putney bedsit. With a typically Amisian sideswipe ('Whatever the prolixity of Miss Murdoch's scene-setting might lead one to believe, this can't go on for ever'), he concludes that the book lacks 'a linguistic centre of gravity', meaning that it rambles on too much. He concludes with what sounds, once again, like a school report:

'I suspect that Miss Murdoch's huge productivity is, paradoxically, a form of self-defence or self-effacement: three hundred pages a year disarms a lot of criticism. She can't, in the nature of things, revise much and probably she never re-reads; she just "gets on with the next one." Were she to slow down, she would be accepting a different kind of responsibility to her critics and to her own prodigious talents. She would, in short, begin to find out how good she is, that strange and fearful discovery.'

To put it another way: *'Hey, Will Shakespeare, could you just knock it off with all this production-line stuff? You probably don't re-read your plays – you're too busy – but if you took the odd year off, you might find that you're, you know, pretty talented. I certainly discovered I was!'*

In the same year, a new literary magazine was published with the help of some cash from the UK Arts Council. The *New Review* was a glossy, glamorous phoenix sprung from the ashes of *The Review*, a quarterly magazine of poetry and criticism founded in 1962 by

Ian Hamilton, who now edited the new incarnation. The cover promised plenty of marvellous things – new poems by Robert Lowell, a new story by Edna O'Brien – but I knew I'd find Martin Amis in there somewhere. Sure enough, he was lurking in the back pages like an assassin in a Venetian porch, reviewing, or rather crucifying, a new critical work by Denis Donoghue, the stratospherically distinguished Professor of English at University College Dublin and New York University. The book was *Thieves of Fire*, a re-jig of his 1971 T. S. Eliot Memorial Lectures on the theme of Prometheus in some major literary works, and was the perfect prey for Amis's stiletto-bladed takedowns of literary royalty.

He sounded a note of regret that Donoghue should interrupt his valuable work as a critic to wander into the theme-hunting groves of academe: 'As a result, this is a fidgety book, a venture into a critical mode not fully assimilated. It has neither the distinction of telling us something new about literature, nor the stimulative power of an intellectual exercise relentlessly seen through.' *Sorry Den*, the twenty-four-year-old reviewer says in his kindly, letting-him-down-gently way, *but your new book doesn't interest me either this way or that way. Frankly, I don't know why you bother.*

With indecent productivity, Amis's second novel, *Dead Babies*, came out in 1975, as I was sitting my finals. I read the reviews, and noticed that *Private Eye* had christened it *Dead Vomit* while its paperback publishers had insisted the title be changed to *Dark Secrets*, as if it contained chocolates. The cover was dazzling; another jazzy, neon-sign title, the author's name in a spidery sans-serif font against a jet-black background. The back cover displayed a more stylised version of the photograph from *The Rachel Papers* of the author, insolent and unsmiling, holding a cigarette before his rock-star gob. In the month after its publication, I saw two cool young geezers on the London streets, carrying the book ostentatiously like a prop, the way we used to tote a copy of *Sergeant Pepper* or *In the Court of the Crimson King* to let people know how cool and modish we were.

Dead Babies is set mostly in a single house, Appleseed Rectory, a cosy, English-cottage-y name, with a sextet of inhabitants. They were a vivid, if one-dimensional throng: elegant, suave, universally adored Quentin; leathery-aggressive macho thug Andy; porky, disgusting, self-loathing Keith; classy-but-mousy aristo Celia; neurotic, uncoordinated Diana; and the hopelessly alcoholic, teeth-obsessed posho Giles Coldstream. They were later joined by three visiting Americans, Marvell, Skip and Roxeanne.

The book proceeded on two levels. One was a pastiche of an Agatha Christie's *And Then There Were None* murder mystery in a cosy, village setting, where flat characters with generic names (upper-crust Coldstream, proletarian/spotty Keith Whitehead, foxy Roxeanne, rangy Yank Skip) gradually realise there's a malevolent, homicidal madman among them. The other was an undertow of nasty modern phenomena, new conditions of drug-induced fucked-up-ness. The conditions included 'cancelled sex' (where arousal and lust crumple to nothing for no apparent reason); 'lagging time' (a drug comedown 'with its numbness and dysjunction . . . its lost past and dead future'); 'street sadness' (the terror of being anywhere away from the snug confines of home); and 'false memory' (happy or serene remembrances of a past that never existed). These brain traumas are offered as if they're conditions of druggy confusion, like the elements of a bad trip; but in Amis's hands they're literary constructions that nod to the Beat poets: the *in transit* lostness of characters in *On the Road*, and the *Interzone* stories, all buggery and purgation, of William Burroughs from the days of *Junky* and *Naked Lunch*.

In *Dead Babies*, Amis revealed a new, hitherto unveiled strength in his writing: the wildly exaggerated character study, or origin history. His protracted thumbnail sketches of Quentin, Giles, Diana and the rest were wildly inventive – baroquely, Munchausenly extreme satires of behaviour.

Amis could take a random thought for a long walk down the page, elaborating it with perfectly chosen examples. On Quentin's versatility, for instance:

> *He can talk all day to a butcher about the longevity of imported meats, to an air hostess about safety regulations in the de Gaulle hangars, to an insurance salesman about post-dated transferable policies . . . Just so he can address a barrow-boy in rhyming slang, a tourist in yokel French, a Sunderlander in Geordie,* * *a Newmarket tout in genteel Cambridgeshire, a gypsy in Romany . . . He can swank into the Savoy in T-shirt and jeans, or sidle dinner-jacketed through the Glasgow slums.*

Behind what seems like the author's praise, of course, we're allowed to wonder if Quentin's marvellous adaptability masks some kind of confidence trickster . . .

The book also revealed a bravura skill at scenes of embarrassment and grotesquerie. One was the conversation that ensued when Keith Whitehead, the plump, dwarfish butt of his friends' contempt, steals away from a picnic to void his churning bowels under a tree and is followed by Skip, the tall, troubled southern boy, who squats down beside Keith and asks, chattily, if he would enjoy a threesome, a blow job, a fuck . . . Later, in an extended chronicle of nastiness, poor Keith, habitually used by Quentin and Andy as a guinea pig for sampling new drugs, is given an overdose. Fearful that he might die and cast a dampener over the weekend, his tormentors tie him to a tree and fill him with powerful laxatives and vomit-inducers that make him virtually explode with shit and puke. Then they clean him up by employing a Fire-Brigade-issue power-hose, whose cascade of water makes his eyes bleed.

---

* My friends from the north were appalled by Amis's carelessness here. Apparently, 'He could address a Sunderlander in Geordie' is like saying 'He could address a Scouser in Mancunian'. A Sunderlander is not a Tynesider (Geordie) but a Wearsider (a Maccam). The distinction is vitally important, apparently.

I was stunned by *Dead Babies*, astonished by how creepily the world of the Appleseeders insinuated itself inside me. The gleeful nastiness of Amis's imagination was something you could admire or condemn, depending on your taste. But the shiver it put inside your head was palpable, like a drug stealing through your bloodstream.

I couldn't help noticing, however, that every now and then his immaculate prose would slip into confusion or emptiness. The book's last line, for example, sees Keith walking up the drive to Appleseed Rectory, oblivious to the charnel house that it has become at the hands of 'Johnny', one of the inhabitants, now revealed as a murderer. At the rectory, we learn: 'Johnny was there. He leant forward eagerly by the window. As he watched Keith move up the drive, his green eyes flashed into the dawn like wild, dying suns.'

Well, I hated to nit-pick, but how can Johnny's green eyes, being green, resemble suns? How can eyes flashing into the sunrise resemble sunsets? And can sunsets be wild rather than elegiac? And why does this closing image make you think of the bad guys in *Captain Scarlet and the Mysterons*, the British TV puppet show, who signalled their malevolence by having their eyes flash with light when no one was looking?

Having logged these complaints, I realised that *they simply didn't matter*. I'd become, amidst a few thousand pretenders to the title (just *back off*, you lot) Amis's biggest fan. Nobody wrote prose like him. Nobody's writing was more eagerly awaited, and more voraciously devoured, than by me. I was in the throes of hero worship and I didn't care. I thought: we'll probably meet very soon. We'll get on *really well*. We'll talk for hours in west London pubs and wine bars. We'll probably end up, you know, *sharing digs* . . .

By the time I was starting my first job in publishing, in 1978, Amis's third novel had appeared. *Success* told the parallel first-person stories of two foster-brothers, Gregory Riding and Terry Service, who shared a flat in London. Gregory is another Quentin Villiers – tall, divinely handsome, irresistible to women – while Terry is short, squat, gingery and very ordinary ('I look like educated lower-class middle-management, the sort of person you walk past in the street every day and never glance at or notice or recognise again.') He's not exactly grotesque, like Keith Whitehead, but is nonetheless an exercise in self-loathing.

By now readers and critics had begun to notice Amis's obsession with the binary opposition of success and failure in his characters, and to wonder if they represented two sides of his character: the midget/god, the nobody/somebody, the sulky-taciturn brooder/ sparklingly hilarious wit. The real-life Amis, we'd learned, was the alumnus of a succession of crammer schools, who never read a literary work until his stepmother, Elizabeth Jane Howard, pressed a copy of *Pride and Prejudice* into his hands at seventeen, but who, in only four years, had picked up a fancy First at Oxford. The 'tiny ironist' (as Tina Brown called him) had, by twenty-eight, apparently slept with every available literary female in London (along with her sister, her mother and most of her girlfriends). Were his dual characters incarnations of his successful public persona and some night-time throb of inadequacy? I had no idea. His readers had no idea. But I'm sure lots of them *hoped* it might be so – hoped that Amis, no matter how handsome, cool and talented, might be terrified of being a fake, a charlatan, a loser with a small dick, as Terry wishes Gregory could be.

I enjoyed *Success*. I was perversely delighted to be back in *The Rachel Papers*' territory of male egomania, clicking my tongue with disapproval at every shocking detail of Gregory's lordly progress around town, his cold-hearted descriptions of orgiastic evenings at his friend Torka's, his hilariously extravagant clothes (an opera cloak? a silver-tipped cane?), his snobbery and revulsion about being desired ('It gets quite boring, being chased and squabbled over the entire time.') It read like the work of someone daring you to be revolted by the male ego.

What surprised me was that, for the first time, Amis identified some characters at work – existing in the world of labour, money and the socio-political universe, rather than a cut-off world of men and women engaged in mutual hostility while trying to get on with, or off with, each other.

We learn that Terry works in an office, something in telephone sales, but is hazy about the details (Amis himself worked in journalism in his twenties, as a sub at *The Times Literary Supplement*, and as literary editor at the *New Statesman*). There is talk of a takeover, of affiliating with a union, of rationalisation and staff cuts. Elsewhere you could find, for the first time in Amis-land, some warnings about a coming social, even universal, upheaval. There's a prescient nod to global warming ('The world is heating up. I've seen three oldsters drop down dead already this month . . .') and a warning for the upper classes ('The world is changing. You are not protected, your father is not rich any more, and what you do suddenly counts') and a rather Kingsley-ish high moral tone: 'You hardly dare open a paper these days: the news is all of cataclysm and collapse . . . everybody accepts the fact that they've got to get nastier to survive.' Had the gleeful depicter of teenage grot turned into a prophet of Thatcherism and union-baiting?

The book ends in an operatic shit-storm of mortality, as we learn how various women died and Terry and Gregory travel to the family home to view their father's body. We discover that their levels of success and failure have switched. Terry is last seen in the restaurant car of the train for London, triumphant, rich, socially popular and sexually confident – a modern *mensch*; nasty but in charge. Gregory watches the train go by; he has lost everything, he can't go back to his old life – and there's a strong suggestion that he will drown himself in the pond behind the old family home. It's a brutally downbeat ending to a fierce exploration of moral nullity – Amis's third success to be published before he hit thirty.

By 1978, another modern British writer, equally fascinated by sex and death, but operating on a tightrope between enthralling and creepy, had started to challenge Amis's grip on what the *New York Times* christened 'The New Unpleasantness'. This was Ian McEwan, born in Aldershot to a scary military father whose postings abroad – Singapore, Africa – kept the family on the move. Educated at a state-run boarding school in Suffolk, McEwan had begun writing at Sussex University and was one of the first signings at the University of East Anglia's MA in Creative Writing.

His first collection of stories, *First Love, Last Rites* was published by Cape in 1975 and made an immediate impact. 'The most devastating debut I've seen for a long time,' wrote Peter Lewis in the *Daily Mail*, 'devastating' being fastidious tabloid-speak for 'shocking' and 'degenerate' and 'sexually twisted'. Other reviewers, noting how flatly, and matter-of-factly his characters embark on sexual hanky-panky, sometimes with children, christened him 'Ian Macabre'.

The stories reeked of dark and cloacal themes. The first page of 'Homemade' explained that the story was not *just* about 'virginity, coitus, incest and self-abuse', before charting the steps of teenage obsession that led the narrator to rape his little sister Connie (aged ten, but she sounds about five) just in order to join the ranks of Chaps Who've Done It.

The second story, 'Solid Geometry', told us about the narrator's interest in his great-grandfather's diary. It's the journal of a Victorian autodidact, his passion for antique curiosities (among them the pickled penis of an army captain in a glass jar, which he bought at auction), his love of scientific experiment and his growing neglect of his wife. The diary mentions a Scottish mathematician called Hunter whose theorems include 'a plane without a surface' which, as he demonstrates to a startled Victorian audience, can make objects disappear. Back in the modern world, after his wife smashes his pickled-penis jar, the narrator takes revenge by making her vanish, still talking, into thin air. The coolly formal way in which McEwan handles the language of science gave this crackpot tale a weird verisimilitude. It felt like a new writer saying: Watch this – I can make you believe *anything*.

Other stories occupied a similar territory of the grim, the dark and the doomed: a fat nanny drowns on the last day of summer, after being rowed in a boat by a schoolboy on the cusp of puberty. On another summer day, the last person to see a nine-year-old girl who has drowned in a canal describes what happened: how he met her, took her to a toy shop, promised to show her butterflies, exposed himself and, when she fell over and banged her head, 'eased' her half-conscious form into the water. The title story, following the romantic summer of a teenage couple living by the sea, is obsessed with animal and human reproduction, with guts and slime and the dark embryo of creation. It features a slightly effortful metaphor of phallic eel-traps and a pregnant rat that explodes at the story's end.

First Love won the Somerset Maugham Award for 1976. McEwan's follow-up collection, *In Between the Sheets*, emerged in 1978 with seven new stories. The first, 'Pornography', followed a blankly amoral guy called O'Byrne who works in his brother's Soho porn-mag store and is having regular sex with two nurses. When he gets a dose of the clap, the girls take revenge by handcuffing him to his bed and bringing to his room a hospital steriliser, 'long-handled scissors, scalpels and other long bright tapering silver objects'. One of them says, 'We'll leave you a pretty little stump to remember us by.'

You couldn't help wondering how much more time and energy McEwan could spend in rubbing readers' faces in disgusting evidence of human (and animal) physicality, in sexual grossness and cruelty; but you had to admit he could show you fear in a handful of spunk, in butterflies, kitchens, bedrooms and bath time, in children's games. But was his intention merely to disgust readers, like an Aldershot Marquis de Sade? Or was he closer to the Fat Boy in *The Pickwick Papers* who says: 'I wants to make your flesh creep'?

When I met Ian McEwan, years later, he confessed to being hurt by his early reputation for perversity. 'People used to say, "Your stories are so horrible!",' he told me. 'I thought they were funny, but then I think Kafka is funny. Only a handful of people thought they were the work of a moralist, somebody rather squeamish, appalled but fascinated by grossness.' An interview by Ian Hamilton in the *New Review* in Autumn 1978 revealed some intriguing influences. McEwan said how much he'd admired John Fowles's *The Collector* when he began writing, and said the voice of Clegg, the titular obsessive – 'that kind of wheedling, self-pitying, lower-middle-class voice' – was the starting point for stories such as 'Confessions of a Cupboard Man'. Elsewhere, in discussing the story about a middle-aged man looking back on the time he raped his kid sister, McEwan says he was trying for 'a Henry-Miller-ish' tone of self-regard and self-aggrandisement. It was intriguing to find that he and Amis, the two *enfants terribles* of late-1970s English fiction, should both cite the long-discredited 'sex maverick' American author of *Tropic of Cancer* as a formative influence.

In the meantime, Amis's Oxford associates had not been idle. Tina Brown hit the journalistic empyrean like a sleek blonde rocket. Her one-act play, *Under the Bamboo Tree*, written while she was still at Oxford, won the *Sunday Times* National Student Drama of the Year award, and brought her to the attention of Pat Kavanagh, Martin Amis's agent, who introduced her to Harry Evans, the *Sunday Times* editor in 1973.[*] In his turn, Evans introduced her to Ian Jack, the paper's features editor, who gave her freelance assignments in the modish Look section.

Six years later, she hit the editorial jackpot. In the Introduction to *Life As a Party*, a collection of her magazine pieces published in 1983, she wrote: 'I took over the editorship of the *Tatler* in June 1979, the same month that Mrs Thatcher took over Number 10. The upper classes were in optimistic mood. "At last," the late Lady Hartwell commented at a Sunday lunch party, "we're going to live

---

[*] Harold Evans married Tina Brown in 1981, when she was twenty-seven, his junior by twenty-five years.

in a world where we can sack people again."' Brown's identification with the PM was cheeky but shrewd: just as the Iron Lady of Downing Street was going to shake up British politics for a decade, so the Tough Bunny at Hanover Square was to shake the British aristocracy from its ancient torpor and make it dance to her tunes.

Brown was a great introducer. She introduced Ian Jack to a then-unknown barrister called Julian Barnes, who had written an article about a bestiality case that had come to court. Jack turned it down.* Brown also introduced Jack to her friend Craig Raine, who had written a long piece about witnessing the birth of his new baby. 'It was immensely long,' says Jack, 'probably three thousand words. I told Harry, "We're going to have to cut it." "No no," he said, "don't cut it. Just throw away some ads." I'd never heard *that* instruction from an editor before.'

Over the previous year, Claire Tomalin, the literary editor of the *New Statesman*, had published several book reviews by Raine, with the encouragement of her deputy, Martin Amis. During a lunch with her, Raine had told Tomalin, 'Actually, I write poetry', hinting rather broadly that he'd like to see it in her pages. 'I watched her eyes turn to concrete,' he reported later – but his poems made it into the back half of the celebrated left-wing, politics-and-arts magazine.

The first time I encountered Raine's poetry, in his 1978 debut collection, *The Onion, Memory*, I was dazzled. The first poem was 'The Butcher', one of several about humble tradesmen who are re-created as heroes, by a simple twist of the visual kaleidoscope. Here is the butcher as swashbuckling romantic:

> *He duels with himself and woos his women customers*
> *offering thin coiled coral necklaces of mince,*
> *heart lamé-ed from the fridge, a leg of pork*
> *like a nasty bouquet . . .*

---

* 'I read it and thought no, it's trying to be funny about something which essentially isn't,' says Jack. 'It was tacky, not funny. Many years later, Julian Barnes came up to me and said, "I was always very grateful that you didn't publish that piece".'

It was brilliant. You had only to brandish a raw Sunday joint of meat to see how – with a flourish of the wrist and the brain – it turned into a bunch of flowers, a presentation of love or gallantry. And how often had I seen the local butcher stropping his longest carving knife against a metal poker like a one-man swordfight.

His second collection in 1979, *A Martian Sends a Postcode Home*, would give its title to a new kind of English poetry: Martianism, a style of poetic evocation, rich in similes, in which the physical world is seen through a new filter of noticing or understanding, which delights by its newness, its visual precision and shocking rightness. Its early exponents were just Raine and Christopher Reid (whose first books *Arcadia* and *Pea Soup* shared Raine's fondness for two-line stanzas) but its influence spread down the decade. Its originator became the most influential bard in the UK, by taking over the poetry list at Faber, some years after T. S. Eliot had the same job.

In October 1978, James Fenton, the poet and *New Statesman* assistant editor, announced the winner of the annual Prudence Farmer poetry award for the best work published in the magazine that year. It was a simple decision, said Fenton: Craig Raine was the obvious winner; the only problem was which of his poems to choose. Praising his book reviews and journalism, Fenton said:

'Mr Raine's penchant for the outrageous image can create some startlingly repulsive effects . . . I often wonder what it must be like to be Mrs Raine, whose lying-in was described by her husband in unloving detail. At one moment, readers of the *Sunday Times* were told, "her anus re-puckered like an Italian tomato". How does one face the neighbours after that?'

Well, quite. But Amis, Raine and McEwan were standard-bearers for a new frankness of physical, especially sexual, expression, of description, depiction, image and simile, and for a radical invitation for readers to see the world afresh, in prose and poetry that, in John Carey's fine phrase, was like 'a windscreen-wiper across the eyeballs'. Tina Brown, still only in her mid-twenties, would usher in a new form of style journalism: jokey, caustic, satirical, pitiless, but expecting no offence to be taken. In the years that followed, these four, the core of the Amis Generation, were to set the tone of the 1980s literary renaissance – a revolution in ways of seeing, and in our responses to the modern world.

CHAPTER 2

———— •◆• ————

Before the Storm

I knocked on the door of the London publishing world in 1978. I was twenty-four and looking for my second job. My first had been selling advertising space in a weekly Catholic magazine called the *Tablet*. The work was repetitive and frustrating, but I met some interesting people on the phone – such as Sister Concepta from the Holy Cross Convent in Mill Hill, whom I tried to interest in our special Vocations Issue. It wasn't a big success ('Now look, Mr Walsh. Didn't we take a *quarter-page* advertisement in the last Vocations Issue? And didn't it cost us 50 pounds? And did we get a single vocation as a result? We did not . . .')

On the whole, I felt I was wasting my two degrees in Literature from Oxford and Dublin. So when I saw, in the *Bookseller*, a job going in the publicity department of Victor Gollancz Ltd, I jumped at it.

I knew the name of Gollancz for three reasons: first, they (or rather he himself) had been George Orwell's publisher (*Down and Out in Paris and London*, *The Road to Wigan Pier*); second, they'd published one of my favourite novels, *Lucky Jim* by Kingsley Amis; and third, they'd been the purveyor of my Aunt Maud's obsessive choice of reading.

On family visits to her spinsterish, mouse-scented home beside the Thames at Putney, I used to gaze at the row of Daphne du Maurier romances and Dorothy L. Sayers crime mysteries on her mantelpiece, and marvel at how their garish yellow dust jackets drew the eye. Somebody (possibly Aunt Maud herself, in a rare departure from her tales of the flat-racing season) once told me that Mr Gollancz had asked a behavioural psychologist to name the most irresistibly eye-catching three-colour combination available, learned that it was the trifection of yellow, purple and black, and had a word with his book-jacket designer the very next day.

I liked the combination of Orwell (decent, clear-sighted, transparent), Amis (hilarious, subversive, omni-mocking) and Gollancz (manipulative, shrewd, sneaky), so I went along to their premises off the Strand for an interview.

Covent Garden had recently been renovated: the famous old fruit 'n' veg market, where Eliza Doolittle meets Professor Henry Higgins in *Pygmalion*, had recently been relocated to Nine Elms and replaced by bijou, arty little stalls that sprang up like bluebells in May. *Time Out* ran a special issue itemising the market's multifarious delights. It was all terribly modern and trendy. The same could not be said for Gollancz's office at 14 Henrietta Street. Even the street name belonged to another era, when daughters of well-born families were routinely christened Hermione or Millicent. The house looked stern and masculine, a rugged Victorian pile with a Scrooge & Marley doorknocker.

Victor Gollancz began to rent the place as his HQ on founding the company in 1928 (it was always considered a bad mistake not to have bought it outright). The half-century of its existence was marked by a biography by Sheila Hodges (*Gollancz: The Story of a Publishing House, 1928–1978*), several copies of which were piled on a table in the chilly reception area. A droopy woman of mature years, with a cameo brooch on her cardigan, announced herself as Margot, and asked me to wait, before returning to her conversation on an ancient telephone, the kind whose metallic dialling circle had little holes for the finger to tickle.

Things improved when I was interviewed by two women. One was Nellie Flexner, head of the publicity department, a quizzical

American in her late twenties, with jet-black hair and the whitest skin I'd ever seen. The other was Liz Calder, a brunette in her mid-thirties with Russian-model cheekbones, crimson lipstick, and a faint trace of Kiwi in her cool, sardonic voice.

They were an appealing double-act, their sharp wits a contrast to the schoolgirl informality of their names. Nellie and Liz were clearly as smart as Pythagoras and as unsusceptible to my boyish charm as Andrea Dworkin. Nellie had a habit of wrinkling her white brow at all my replies, while Liz let a disbelieving smile play around her carmined lips.

They asked about my life, and mocked my replies. When I explained that my MA thesis had explored the late prose of Samuel Beckett, they said, 'You'll need to lower your brow to read our crime and sci-fi.' When I announced my devotion to modern fiction, they said, 'If you're hoping to add to it, you can do it at home, not in the office.' When I urged my passionate interest in helping works of literature reach the best readers, they said, 'You'll probably spend more time helping children's books reach five-year-olds.'

After twenty minutes, they suggested I meet two other staff members. We ascended a flight of stairs, with a faded brown carpet and oak banisters that clearly dated back a half-century. In the kind of office you associate with the headmaster's study, I met the managing director, John Bush, a preoccupied-seeming, white-haired cove with a tic of fluttering eyelids and an abrupt manner.

He didn't have many questions. Mainly, he wanted to confirm that I lived in London and would be available for evening parties, promotional events '. . . and so forth.'

I said I'd love to.

'Married?' he barked.

'Er, no,' I said.

'Gay?' he barked.

'I beg your pardon?'

He glared at me through rimless specs.

'Are you en*ga*ged?' he repeated.

'Oh, er, no,' I said. A pause. 'Actually, I thought you said, "Are you gay?"'

'Did you now,' said Mr Bush neutrally. '*Did* you now.'

Nellie and Liz mentioned something about my academic background – how I was overqualified but keen.

He muttered some reply. He specialised in a kind of abrupt mutter.

'Better eat Nivea,' I heard, or thought I heard, him say.

Five minutes later, I was climbing another set of stairs, even dustier and narrower than the first, leading to ... what? The servants' quarters? An attic where some latter-day Mrs Rochester had been imprisoned since the 1870s? Or was it the Gollancz Holy of Holies?

It was the latter. The rickety door opened onto a cosy Edwardian parlour, Dickensianly crammed to bursting with books, magazines, newspapers, a three-bar electric fire, an elderly Xerox machine, files, boxes and, everywhere, toppling pagodas of manuscript pages. It was dominated by a huge desk on which an ancient black Remington typewriter held centre stage. Seated behind it was an extraordinary figure, someone out of Hans Christian Andersen.

Livia Gollancz's penetrating blue eyes, set in the face of an Eastern European peasant woman, regarded me sternly. A frizz of steely grey hair gave her enormous head a translucent halo. She sat bolt upright – not exactly hostile to my arrival so much as baffled as to why an unknown youth had been ushered into her presence. Cleopatra, I thought, would have worn that expression if a young Alexandrian pot-washer had been brought to her boudoir. Boadicea might have had that look, had some grubby teenage chariot-driver suddenly materialised in her chamber.

'This is John Walsh, Livia,' said Liz, offering a sweet nod of encouragement my way. 'He may be joining the publicity department, if all goes well.'

She rose and stood before me – an awesome sight. Victor Gollancz's daughter seemed at least six feet tall, commanding, unsmiling, majestic. Among the many images that flashed through my head was the Duchess in *Alice in Wonderland*, broad-faced, elaborate-hatted, blankly unsmiling. The alarm I felt beneath her gaze was mitigated by her clothes. She had chosen, on that April morning, to dress herself in a thin oatmeal sweater and a long, black, thick woollen skirt: her top half seemed to anticipate warm weather, her bottom half winter.

'Do you,' she boomed, icily polite, 'know anything about typography?'

I couldn't see what relevance typefaces could have to the workings of a publicity department, but felt it was better to keep the thought unspoken.

'I know about italics,' I said feebly, 'and upper and lower case. And somebody once explained to me what sans serif is, but I'm afraid, beyond that . . .'

'But this is *marvellous*,' she said, her great broad face breaking into a charming smile. 'If you know the difference between serif and sans serif, that puts you at a *huge* advantage in this industry.'

'Well I suppose—'

'Good day, Mr Walsh,' she said abruptly, and sat back down, her attention fully returned to the letter she'd been reading when I arrived.

To my delight, I got the job. I was now definitely 'in publishing'. This was the place that had published Martin Amis's dad, and would soon be looking after – I discovered in the catalogue – *Angela Carter*, whom I revered. It didn't mean that I was now going to rub shoulders in the pub with the entire A-Team of modern literature, but it was definitely a start.

I gradually discovered the *oddness* of the company. This was a world that predated computers: in the production office, the complicated schedule of dates for setting up the company's output of new books in proof, then final pages, then binding and jacketing, was all laid out on the wall in surprisingly home-made-looking cardboard sheets with capacious pockets. More surprising, in its antiquity, was the 'counting house', a dingy and fly-blown room where a telephone operator manned a switchboard. When Gollancz Ltd started life in 1928, it had been the room where the company accounts and cash were kept. It seemed that neither Victor nor his daughter had ever thought to have it stripped, plastered, repainted and ergonomically repurposed as something with, you know, photocopiers and electronic gadgets.

The publicity office was often chilly in the mornings, but I was kept warm by my frequent trips up and down stairs. Nobody had mentioned that part of my job was to be full-time flunkey and dogsbody to Livia Gollancz. Mid-morning, a red telephone behind my desk would shrill and her deep imperious voice on the line would say, 'Come!' I'd gallop up the stairs to her office where she'd hand me a sheet of paper to take to the printers in Fleet Street. I'd read her plain-as-a-pikestaff advertising copy, handwritten in the blackest ink (*The Ampersand Papers* by Michael Innes. Who stole the Byron and Shelley manuscripts from a locked room in a Cornish castle? An absorbing mystery from a leading British crime writer. Gollancz. £5.95) and surmounted by instructions to the typesetters, specifying type size and font.

She always chose the same fonts for every advertisement: they were called Gill and Grot, like characters from a Beckett play. The former was the invention of Eric Gill, the brilliant but deeply peculiar sculptor and printmaker whose biography by Fiona MacCarthy (to be published in 1989) revealed that he had sex with both his sisters, his two eldest daughters and the unfortunate family dog*. The latter typeface was a contraction of 'Grotesque', invented in Sheffield.

I don't believe Livia had the faintest clue about the sexual associations of the former or the dark provenance of the latter; I think she just liked using the plainest-sounding typefaces on the

---

* See page 321.

market. She was a very basic person and a no-frills publisher. She'd clung until recently to Victor's insistence that Gollancz books were so starkly distinctive, they needed no arty, or even coloured jackets; and, like him, she flatly refused to introduce paperbacks to the company's operations. And she certainly didn't believe in paying fancy advances, even to successful, in-demand novelists.

She never took authors out to lunch, and only grudgingly allowed launch parties for the stars of Gollancz's list. When I helped to arrange a launch party for Angela Carter's *The Bloody Chamber*, and booked the sunny terrace of a modest Italian restaurant in Fleet Street, I was upbraided as though I'd booked the entire Café Royal for the whole day and night.

In meetings, she was blunt to the point of rudeness. If someone talked for longer than she thought reasonable, Livia would reach into her capacious carrier bag, extract a fistful of spring onions (she grew vegetables in her back garden), tear the hairy tendrils off the tops and noisily munch the bulbs until the garrulous committee member lapsed into silence.

I gradually learned about her, um, salad days. When young, she'd been an accomplished player of the French horn. By twenty she was playing in the London Symphony Orchestra. At twenty-three, she saw a job for principal horn on offer at the Hallé Orchestra in Manchester. So she telephoned their headquarters, got through to the musical director, Sir John Barbirolli, and asked for the job at a salary of £2 a week.

Sir John said yes. People generally did with Livia. It saved time.

Of her other major talent, I soon became aware. On the second day, as I prepared to leave at 6 p.m., I heard a scary noise coming from upstairs, a faint but spine-tingling wail, like a lamentatious banshee that had just received some atrocious news.

I opened the office door, and found the racket wasn't coming from the first floor, but higher up. Apprehensively, I climbed the stair, turned at the corner, and realised the noise, with its graduated rise and curiously orgasmic top note – 'Ah – ahhh – *Ahh* –

Aaaarrrggghhh – Ahrrrr – Ah – Ahhh' – was Livia performing arpeggios in her study, with the door ajar.

I marvelled at her weirdness and witchiness – but also at her *chutzpah* in making sure the whole company knew she had a trained operatic voice and wasn't afraid to use it.

Liz Calder, it turned out, had been at Gollancz since 1971, initially as publicity director, then as an editor. I liked her company a lot. Every other day she'd come downstairs to snaffle a cigarette from me and stay to chat. She recalled her early days in the publicity department, where she'd been shown the ropes by her predecessor, Claire Walsh, the long-term companion of J. G. Ballard, the genius behind *The Drowned World*, *Empire of the Sun* and *Crash*.

One of Liz's first authors had been Lord George-Brown, the former Labour politician, deputy PM to Harold Wilson and, famously, a weapons-grade drunkard. His memoirs, entitled *In My Way*, had just been published in 1971. Liz took her unsteady author to the Manchester literary festival. 'We went up by train,' she said, 'and by 10.30 in the morning he wanted a drink. So we went to the bar and, finding it closed, he banged on the corrugated screen, shouting "Open Up!" They came eventually and he got his first G and T of the day – but not the last, I may say – at 10.45 a.m. By the time he made his speech, after lunch at the Free Trade Hall, he was extremely sloshed.'

In those unreconstructed days, when secretaries were mostly selected for their bosom-to-waist ratio and slenderness of legs, publicity girls were sometimes taken for professional hostesses. Liz remembered the time a journalist called Michael Bateman, who wrote the 'Atticus' column on the *Sunday Times*, phoned round the London publishing houses, and asked the publicity girls to meet for a group photograph. 'We went along,' said Liz, 'thoughtlessly, like lambs to the slaughter. The cameraman asked us to pose with our legs in the air, as if for a can-can line-up.' She kept the resulting photos, mainly because they show Carmen Callil, the Australian feminist powerhouse who later founded Virago Press, flashing a V-sign at the presumptuous snapper.

Liz explained how she came to sign up what would soon become her most high-profile author. 'In the early 1970s, I was spending time between Manchester and London. My partner then, Jason Spender, was at Manchester University, so I commuted up and down, and I needed a place to stay in London, three nights a week. One of my London colleagues said, "I know someone who has a house in Lower Belgrave Street, and they're looking for a lodger." So I went along.

'The person with the house was Clarissa Luard, and her husband was one Salman Rushdie. I got to know them very well. Salman was working as a copywriter for Ogilvy Benson & Mather, and every time I came in from work in the evening, he'd be holding forth to a group of mates from Trinity, Cambridge, telling them everything he knew about books. It was the first time I'd heard anyone mention Gabriel García Márquez. Salman was all over *One Hundred Years of Solitude*. And it transpired that, when I was out of London, he was using the room I slept in as a writing space. When I came back, I'd see the pages mounting up on the floor. The book turned out to be his first novel, *Grimus*, which I persuaded Victor Gollancz to publish in 1975. It wasn't my kind of book – it was rubbish in some ways, the story was all over the place – but I could see this guy had a facility with language which was dazzling.'

Rushdie wrote *Grimus* in response to a competition Gollancz was running – a SF/Fantasy competition, judged by Kingsley Amis, Arthur C. Clarke, and Brian Aldiss. Rushdie entered *Grimus* for it. Amis and Clarke rejected it, but Aldiss was impressed; he argued in its favour, but it failed to get the prize. Gollancz published it anyway, to an almost universal rubbishing by the critics. It received just one good review, from Isabel Quigly in the *Financial Times*. Despite this dispiriting response to his debut, Rushdie was determined to keep going. 'He brought me a story called *Madame Rama*,' said Liz, 'which I didn't exactly turn down, I just said, "I don't think this is *quite there*." And he went away and completely rewrote it.' The story became *Midnight's Children*, published three years later.

Liz consolidated her reputation as a talent-spotter by inventing a subgenre into which could be slotted ambitious works of fiction that were too edgy or perverse to fit anywhere else. She called it Gollancz Fantasy and Macabre, a home for prose that intertwined elements of modern myth, fairy tale, horror, Gothic, mutant romance, transsexual power and Celtic dreaming. There was no name in English publishing for this mongrel multi-genre; but soon it would be christened magical realism, a term that dated back to Latin-American writers of the mid-1950s, especially Jorge Luis Borges and Alejo Carpentier. Under the Fantasy and Macabre imprint she published four of her star writers – Angela Carter, D. M. Thomas and Salman Rushdie. The second and third were to meet in the public arena after Liz had left Gollancz to become editorial director at Jonathan Cape: Rushdie's *Midnight's Children* and Thomas's *The White Hotel* would go head-to-head for the Booker Prize in 1981.

I settled in at Gollancz, made friends with my new colleagues and heard their back stories. Nellie was the daughter of James Thomas Flexner, the author of a Pulitzer-winning, four-volume life of George Washington, and a life of the young Alexander Hamilton, whose political career was to become a world-beating Broadway musical in 2015. David Burnett, a commissioning editor, was a rumpled, curly-haired, cardigan-wearing, country-life enthusiast. He signed up books such as *Nature Detective* (about how you could learn to read animal tracks) and *A Sketchbook of Birds* by C. F. Tunnicliffe. A keen small publisher of limited editions, he didn't really belong in a serious London publishing house. I learned that Livia didn't approve of him: she thought him too quirky, too uncommercial, too keen on silly nature books – as opposed to books about mountaineering, her own outdoor passion and, you know, obvious million-sellers.

Though Gollancz was obviously an organisation stuck in the old days of the switchboard, the manual typewriter and the cardboard folder (Margot the receptionist and Livia the joint MD would have fitted nicely in an Ealing comedy), signs of modern style were visible elsewhere. The design department was a light and airy space where a perky young art director called Claudia Zeff (later to marry John Brown, who gave the world Johnny Fartpants, Sid the Sexist and the Fat Slags in the comic *Viz*) held court at a streamlined drawing board, her slender frame clad in a riot of primary colours; the 1970s had definitely made it as far as the first floor of Gollancz HQ.

Other members of staff stopped by to inspect the new boy. Joanna Goldsworthy, the children's editor, was elegant, forty-ish, expensively coiffed, serenely unflappable, and very un-child-friendly: you couldn't for a second imagine her reading a bedtime story to a three-year-old. She had the air of the posh eldest daughter of Gloucestershire gentry, whose best friends were still the girls she'd met at Cheltenham Ladies' College. Quite a contrast with the rights and permissions manager, Victoria Petrie-Hay, a tough, emphatic presence, who never smiled and seemed permanently affronted that she hadn't yet been given carte blanche to knock the company into shape.

I was driven a little mad by Emma, the energetic publicity secretary, who described with relish her adventures with her madcap schoolchums, Vick-*ee* and Nick-*ee* and Tish-*ee*, and sang numbers from *Grease*, which was then filling London cinemas. 'Tell me *mooooooore . . .*' she would sing, typically choosing the boring last line of 'Summer Nights', over the tuneful hook.

I was intrigued by the sales director, who seemed to work somewhere other than Henrietta Street, and appeared in the publicity department every few weeks. It seemed to me that sales and marketing were related, and should exist side by side. But what did I know? His name was Kenneth Kemp, and, like Livia and Margot, he seemed straight out of the 1950s. A tall, officer-class cove with a jovial manner, he was the dead spit of the detective inspector who rumbles Ray Milland's attempt to murder Grace Kelly in *Dial M for Murder*. Like the inspector, he had a bristly moustache which he liked to finger, mid-conversation.

He had an absolutely tin ear for advertising copy. He'd suggest terrible puns on book titles or authors' names. When, in November, we were brainstorming the words to accompany a big, colourful, double-page advertisement for a beautifully illustrated new edition of *Grimm's Fairy Tales* in the *Bookseller*, he banged his fist on the table: 'I've got it!' he cried. "Things are looking Grimm for Gollancz this Christmas!" What do you think?' I looked over at Nellie. Her eyes were closed; she was pinching the bridge of her nose with the air of one who cannot take much more.

My first steps in publicity ran into some snags. On my second day, Nellie brought me a children's book on which to perform miracles. It was called *My Brother Stephen Is Handicapped*, and was aimed at the family and friends of disadvantaged minors. 'Read this, John, and come and tell me what you think. I'll be with Joanna in the Children's department.'

I read it. It was *awful* – by turns sentimental, gloopy, whiny, carping and selfish, the words of a horrible sister who complains that her stricken brother won't play with her, on account of his spina bifida, and that she can't bring friends home because it's, like, *really embarrassing*, but then she realises she has to love him anyway because, you know . . .

Upstairs in the department, I said, 'Sorry, Nellie, I really don't like this. It's *terrible*. Not only does she—'

'What do you mean?' said Nellie, icily. 'I didn't ask for your opinion of the book.'

'But you said, "Read this and tell me what you think of it",' I said. 'Which I'm doing.'

'I meant,' said Nellie, 'tell me how you think we might publicise it. To bring it to the widest public. To steer it towards people who might want to read it.'

I must have looked crestfallen.

'This job isn't about you having *opinions* about the books, John,' she said. 'The decision to publish them has been taken. Our job is to get them to the public and nothing else.'

'Yes of course,' I said. 'By sending them out to be reviewed in the papers.'

'Yes, but no newspaper is going to review *My Brother Stephen Is Handicapped*, are they, when they've only got space for half a dozen novels and two biographies?'

'So what do we . . . ?'

'We phone up the organisations that might be interested – in this case, hospitals, schools, care homes, clinics, paediatric departments . . . You get the picture?'

I did. From that day on, I was determined to do everything to please her. I dug out Yellow Pages, found the numbers of medical institutions which might deal with handicapped children, and asked the people on the phone if they were interested in the book. To my delight, they all were. After three hours, I told Nellie, triumphantly, 'I've contacted all these people, and they've mostly said yes, so we have to send thirty-six books in the post.'

'That's great,' she said coolly. 'You mean they've said they'll buy them?'

'Not exactly,' I said. 'They said they were interested, so I said I'd send them a book.'

She pursed her lips.

'That isn't how it works,' she said with heavy patience. 'We can't just give away books to everyone you talk to, or we'll have none left to sell.'

'So what do we do?' I asked grumpily.

'We send *press releases*, saying, "Hi – here's some information about this book, perhaps you'd like to buy it, and buy one for every other hospital and children's home in the district while you're at it." And if they say "yes", we get the sales team onto it. You understand?'

Yes, I did. And thus, by missteps and clutchings at protocols that I was only starting to understand, did I get on in publishing.

* * *

A couple of months into the job, when I was still on probation, Nellie told me that the chairman, John Bush, wanted to see me. I went up the first floor with an apprehensive spider crawling in my stomach. Mr Bush was behind his desk. He surveyed me unenthusiastically through his Himmler spectacles.

'John, come in,' he said. 'Take a seat. I'll come straight to the point. How long have you been here?'

'Six weeks.'

'And are you enjoying your time here?'

'Very much indeed.'

'And you would like to stay on after your probation period is up?'

'Absolutely. Of course. Why?'

'It's rather delicate, actually,' he said, removing his glasses and wiping them with a handkerchief. 'It seems there's been a . . .'

He searched the perimeter of his desk for the word.

I couldn't stand the suspense.

'Complaint?'

'No. Not that. Ah . . . *remarks* have been made about you.'

'Oh God. What have I done?'

'It's not about what you've done. It's more – your attitude.'

'My attitude? You mean I've been obstreperous?'

'No.'

'Obstructive?'

'No.'

'Obnoxious?'

'No no no. It's perceived that you are too, ah, informal.'

'Informal? In what way?'

'David Burnett said that, after he came to brief you about the publicity campaign for *Nature Detective*, you squeezed his arm.'

'I did? I don't remember doing that.'

'And only yesterday, downstairs, you said to me, "Hi, John. How's it going, old bean?"'

'Are you sure,' I asked coldly. I wondered if he was confusing me with Bertie Wooster.

'Or "old fruit" or some such thing. And I hear you spend far too much time in the design department, chatting to Claudia and the girls, as if you're at a . . . a *cocktail party*.'

'I see.'

'The point is, Mr Walsh, this is a sleeves-rolled-up working environment. You are not here to socialise, but to get work done. There's plenty of time after work for informality.'

'I'm terribly sorry,' I said. 'I like being here so much, it just sort of . . . *spills over*.'

'Nobody wants you to leave,' said Mr Bush in a show of kindliness. 'But if you could rein it in a bit, we need have no further discussion of the matter.'

I slunk back downstairs and went to see Nellie, feeling like a dog whose nose has been plunged in its own shit.

'Sorry, John,' she said smiling, 'but you had to be told. You can't just stroll into my office and have a lovely chat with an author, as if you're staying at their house for the weekend.'

'Nellie,' I said firmly, 'if, henceforth, you *ever* see me do or say *anything*, to *anybody*, that's not strictly informative or inquisitorial on a need-to-know basis, I will shoot myself right in front of you.'

'Jesus, nobody wants *that*,' she said. 'Enthusiasm is fine. Just keep a lid on it, is all.'

I was ashamed. I was guilty of Excessive Informality in the office environment. So embarrassing. But again, I resolved to improve.

One day the phone in Nellie's office rang.

'Hello?' I said.

'Is Nellie there?' It was a sleepy-sounding, preoccupied voice, as though its owner were reading something, or trying to get a speck off her black sweater.

'I'm afraid she isn't. Can I help?'

A silence. 'Who are you?'

'I'm John. Nellie's deputy. Who's this?'

There was a significant pause, as the voice's owner considered the possibility that her publisher's new recruit might not know who she was, and could therefore be telephonically eviscerated.

'This is Angela Carter.'

'Oh my *God*,' I said, artlessly. 'How fantastic to meet you, Miss Carter.'

There was another silence.

'I've been a fan of your writing,' I burbled, 'for years.' It seems I had forgotten what I'd been told about over-familiarity.

'Not *that* many years,' she murmured, 'judging by your *voice* . . .'

I felt as if I was being patted on the head by a distant aunt for being a polite child, if not especially cute.

'No really,' I said. 'I've been a fan ever since I read the words, "The bar was a mock-up, a forgery, a fake, an ad-man's crazy dream of a Spanish patio, with crusty white walls . . ."' I subsided, pleased that I'd managed to recall the opening words of her first novel, *Shadow Dance*, which had been published in 1966, when I was thirteen, and which I'd read at university.

'Oh,' she said. 'And was that as far as you got?'

She was always like that, able to wrongfoot anyone in conversation, always able to disconcert, uttering her sharp little laugh at how easy it was to do so. I came to adore her. She had such presence – cat-like in rumpled cardigans, her hair a tangle of silver-grey, her voice a seductive but dangerous purr. Her dazzling prose stood out a mile from the polite, well-bred voices of the late-1970s English novel. The stories she told, the things that befell her characters, were far from cosy or comforting. They were harsh and terrible life lessons, played out against scary, eldritch landscapes peopled by masked execution-ers, scarred virgins and dominating androgynes. The flat, matter-of-fact cruelty of the Marquis de Sade lurked behind her rapturous use of language. It was like finding a clump of Venus Flytraps in the agreeable bluebell wood of contemporary English prose.

At twenty-four, I had definite views about whose writing was *really* good. There were only three contenders, A, B and C: Martin Amis, Anthony Burgess and Angela Carter. Having the last-named physically present before me in the publicity office on the day after the launch of *The Bloody Chamber*, and listening to her silkenly bitchy gossip about the guests who'd been at the party, and how her novelistic rival Emma Tennant had said, 'Darling, your publishers obviously love you, this is *so* much better than *my* last launch', was a delight to hear.

She could be scary, though, no question; she didn't let any slack or casual language get past her. One Saturday I went along to a lunchtime talk she was giving at the Institute of Contemporary Arts. It was about *The Bloody Chamber*, of course, and considered her interpretations of classic West European fairy-tale tropes of womankind: sacrificial virgins, passive wives, Cinderellas and fairy godmothers. The title story, with its decadent and wicked marquis, his love of depictions of dead or tortured women and his collection of sadistic porn, came in for discussion; in considering the passivity of some fairy-tale victims, the subject of rape came up. What was its real motivation?

'Nobody has ever explained to my satisfaction,' said Angela, 'why a man would want to rape a female stranger.' Her interviewer asked for contributions from the audience. One or two hands went up. 'Maybe it isn't about sex,' said a woman, 'but an urge to demonstrate male power.' A second woman opined that it was 'a throwback to the colonial thing, like slaveowners using slaves as sort of their property.' And then a man standing at the back by the door, a man in his twenties, blue jeans and a white T-shirt, without raising his hand, called out: 'Maybe they just do it for kicks.'

It was a shockingly simple observation, as if he was talking about hot-wiring a car and going for a burn down the A3. A small 'Mmmmpf!' of indignation rose from the audience.

'Whatever do you mean?' asked the moderator.

The young man seemed unbothered. 'You know,' he said, with a hint of a macho grin, 'just for the hell of it.'

Angela's voice burst out, explosively.

'*Wipe that smile off your face!*' she screamed at him.

The man's grin disappeared. He looked as if he would have liked to sit down. Angela's eyes blazed at him, as if she'd met the world's most shameless rapist in a Rapists' Holiday Retreat. We wondered what might come next, but while her words still quivered above the sudden silence, she didn't need to say any more.

'Ah fuck *this*,' said the young man. He turned, opened the Conference Room door and was gone.

Another favourite was John Irving, the American novelist, whose fourth book, *The World According to Garp*, had just been published in the US. I read it with amazement. It was full of solidly old-fashioned virtues – a narrative that took its time (bloody ages in fact), lovingly elaborate descriptions of umpteen complex characters, vivid dialogue, multiple viewpoints – which drew comparisons with Dickens from some critics. But it was also astoundingly perverse, raw and rude, full of casually shocking characters and horrifying events.

The hero T. S. Garp's mother is a prototypical feminist heroine who becomes pregnant when she impales herself on the turgid member of a brain-damaged and dying ball-turret gunner in a state of permanent priapism. She takes the airman's title ('Technical Sergeant Garp') for the child's initials and surname. Later she takes under her wing a group of women called the Ellen Jamesians, named after a young girl who was raped at eleven years by men who cut her tongue out so she couldn't testify against them – and the EJs cut their own tongues out in sympathy.

One of the book's three internal narratives, 'The World According to Bensenhaver', opens with a nasty scene in which a desperate backwoods hick invades the home of a young mother, slices the cheek of her baby son with his saw-bladed fisherman's knife and announces he's going to rape and kill her. Garp himself, a loving parent, strives to keep his family from harm; but towards the end of the novel, his wife Helen is giving her lover a blow job in a car parked in the family driveway, when Garp himself arrives with his children; in the ensuing crash, the lover's penis is bitten off, one child dies and the other loses an eye to the gear lever.

When we met, I found it hard to relate this youthful (he was thirty-six in 1978), good-looking, perma-smiling and wholly sympathetic man, to the imagination that had invented the pitiless fictional mayhem of the book. (The *New York Times Book Review* had been moved to ask, in honest bafflement, 'What traumas suffered by John Irving elicited *The World According to Garp*?')

I asked Liz Calder how it was that a novel of such explicit, gleeful horror could be accepted for publication by such an old-fashioned, old-school moralist as Livia Gollancz. And while we're at it, how did the shockingly obscene opening twenty pages of D. M. Thomas's *The White Hotel*, not to mention the clotted narrative contortions of Rushdie's *Grimus*, get past her quality control? Liz revealed that the company had a secret weapon. He was called Jon Evans, a 'publisher's reader' mature in years but rock-solid in judgement. He could say definitively whether a novel was Good or Bad Literature, and nobody questioned him. If a manuscript came before the Fiction Committee that seemed promising but problematic, Livia would say, 'Send it to Evans!' – and if Evans liked it, that would be the end of the matter. Livia sent him, Liz told me, up to nine typescripts a week . . .

In Irving's book, Garp as a child listens to stories told about the dangerous currents in a swimming hole, and mishears the word 'undertow' as 'undertoad'. For him, the Undertoad is a Stygian threat, an amphibian monster, lurking beneath the surface of his life. For publicity purposes, Irving had agreed to have a version of the Undertoad constructed in *papier mâché*. We showed the author our handiwork – a fat-bottomed, warty monstrosity with a foolish smile – and he laughed delightedly.

I thought it odd that a creature of nightmare had been turned into a comic item and asked if he was happy with it.

'Well,' said Irving kindly, 'I guess the book is a balance between laughter and darkness.'

I asked him if that had always been his intention. Or had the book started out as a comedy and become something darker?

'What I set out to do,' he said, 'was to invent the perfect family, the best family in the world, and have the most terrible things happen to them.'

I was impressed by his straight-talking. How many authors would tell you bluntly what the 'intention' of their work had been? And I was grateful to him when, about eighteen months later, I was at a supper party in Chelsea when the talk turned to books. A posh chap called Tony, yawningly passionless and superficial about everything he touched on, from politics and Third World debt to music and movies, suddenly surprised me by saying, 'Has anyone read this book called *Garp*? *The World According to Garp*, it's called, by an American chap. I just finished it. It's quite funny and very strange and really quite nasty at the same time. Anyone know it?'

There was a silence.

'Why do you bring it up?' someone asked.

'Well, *usually*,' said Tony, 'I have a fair idea of what's going on in a book I'm reading. I don't just mean the plot, obviously, I can understand *plot*, I read a lot of crime and that's *all* plot, isn't it? But this book – I enjoyed it but, by the end, and it's *jolly* long, I couldn't quite see what the chap had been driving at. You know? What had been the *point* of it all.' He sipped some wine. 'I wish there was a way you could, you know, *ring up* an author and ask him or her: "Well, what was *that* all about then?".'

'Well now,' I said. 'I may just be able to help you there . . .'

I enjoyed my time at Gollancz, not because I conceived a lifetime passion for publishing, but because of the energetic bustle always going on around me. Of course it was a terribly old-fashioned place, but the stirrings of magic realism and casual savagery in

Liz's books were about to become part of a revolution. I liked sitting in with Nellie as she planned contrasting strategies for the authors of *The Turin Shroud* and (one of the first-ever books on the computer revolution) *The Mighty Micro*. She was a very hard worker, forever on the phone to Liz Forgan at the *Guardian* or Sue MacGregor at *Woman's Hour*, trying to persuade them to run interviews with her authors. I loved hearing Liz talking about her encounters with new authors, such as D. M. Thomas, the Cornish visionary; at their initial meeting, he talked and talked, obsessively, about his first book, *The Flute Player*, for nearly an hour, 'until his lips became dryer and dryer and the corners of his mouth started to bleed . . .'

I liked the flap and excitement in the building when the new Diary editor of the *Evening Standard*, Adrian Woodhouse, called on Nellie and Liz to extract from them enough scandal from a forthcoming political memoir to make a diary item. The fact that Woodhouse was not an author, merely a twenty-seven-year-old, callow gossip-column hack seemed not to bother them. He was tall, curly-haired and worldly, with a commanding stride and the air of a chap who could make or break fortunes with a paragraph, like Burt Lancaster's venal columnist J. J. Hunsecker in *Sweet Smell of Success*. What, I wondered, might it be like to have his job? Would I enjoy it? (Only for a while, of course, while planning my assault on the London literary world . . .)

A different kind of *frisson* attended the arrival in the building of authors from a previous era, such as Naomi Mitchison, CBE, prolific novelist, poet, feminist, geneticist and birth control campaigner, whose autobiography, *You May Well Ask*, was full of mildly shocking revelations from the 1930s. By now aged eighty-one, she told Nellie, to my amazement, 'I very much regret that I never went to bed with Aldous [Huxley]. I know he *certainly* wanted to go with me.' As I watched her tiny but rotund form leaving through the front door, Margot the receptionist called me over. 'Did you *see* what Lady Mitchison had on the lapel of her overcoat? A big round badge which said: YOUR SAD STORY HAS TOUCHED MY HEART. SELDOM HAVE I HEARD A TALE SO DESERVING OF SYMPATHY. NOW FUCK OFF AND QUIT BOTHERING ME. Well I *mean*,' she concluded, 'it's just not what you expect from a peer of the realm!'

I stayed at Gollancz for a year, but I knew it wasn't going to be my career and, when I was offered a writing job on a magazine, I tendered my resignation. My colleagues made sorry-you're-leaving noises and, on my last day, suggested we all go for a farewell drink at the Cork & Bottle wine bar near Leicester Square.

As we gathered in Margot's office, Livia came through the front door, wearing (I think it was mid-September) a classic late-summer combination of long pastel frock and sturdy hiking boots. She had clearly been out for a late-afternoon constitutional around Covent Garden.

'What are you all doing here?' she asked suspiciously. 'Is this a meeting?'

'It's John's last day,' said Victoria. 'We're going for a drink to see him off the premises. Why don't you come?'

This was clearly not a serious invitation. Livia famously did not 'do' social events, not even launches of books she'd commissioned herself.

'I'm afraid I am not a great frequenter of pubs,' she said sniffily.

'We're not going to a pub,' said Nellie.

'It's a little early for a restaurant,' said Livia.

'We're going to a wine bar,' said Victoria. 'They're much more civilised than pubs.'

'Indeed?' said Livia, a famously teetotal vegetarian. 'I do not drink wine.' There was a pause. 'But maybe they will have an elderflower cordial.'

The jaws of every person in the vestibule collectively fell. Livia Gollancz going to an office piss-up? Unheard-of!

We set off through the market, a friendly crocodile in the late-summer sunlight. Livia took the lead, striding Amazonianly down Bedford Street. I thought it unwise to leave her walking by herself in case she berated some passer-by for smoking in the street, so I drew level. I tried to chat to her about things I'd learned in my time at the company, but it was like making small talk with Queen Victoria. 'I hope you enjoy journalism,' she said, putting the word in distasteful commas, 'but I feel you are leaving us too soon. You made yourself useful, and I think you might have learned more about publishing.'

'Such as?' I asked. But she had become distracted. I followed her gaze. On the corner of the Strand, a man of mature years, clearly down on his luck, was playing the fiddle.

Livia stiffened like an ageing pointer that had clocked a stag.

'I *must* give that man some money,' she said. 'He's playing *unaccompanied Bach*.'

And she was gone. She never became a fan of the new world of wine bars or the heady convivium of the corporate knees-up. She was, I realised, spectacularly far removed from the late twentieth century – a feeling reinforced for me a year later, when I attended the Publishers' Pantomime.

At the climax, an ancient chariot arrived on stage, and from it a powerful figure emerged in a spectacular silver toga and a silver helmet the size of a coal scuttle. Livia stood resplendent on stage, beaming like a visiting monarch, as the modest orchestra swelled and a familiar tune began. She lifted her silver trident in the air, pointed it over the heads of the audience and began to sing 'Rule Britannia'. It seemed to epitomise the whole style and voice of British publishing in 1979, just before everything changed.

CHAPTER 3

Directing My Steps

When I was interviewed by John Carey at St John's College in 1971, he asked at one point: 'Mr Walsh, have you any discernible ambition?' 'Yes indeed,' I said, 'I want to be a man of letters.' This elicited from the professor a charmingly incredulous laugh. Of course, John Gross's book *The Rise and Fall of the Man of Letters* had been published two years earlier; it reminded readers that Evelyn Waugh once referred to his father as a man of letters, 'a category, like the maiden aunt's, that is almost extinct'. No wonder Carey considered it an odd life goal to which a groovy young whippersnapper like me might aspire.

I explained that I didn't hope to become a whiskery recluse, writing nostalgic pieces about forgotten novelists ('Am I alone in my continuing regard for E. Phillips Oppenheim?') for *The Times Literary Supplement*. 'I want to make a living by writing articles and books about lots of things,' I said, my eyes almost certainly shining with the gleam of youthful idealism. 'I don't know yet what they might be – maybe a book about swimming in literature, or, I don't know, cricket or brandy or opera – and I hope to develop a fancy prose style to express my enthusiasm . . .' Or words to that effect. As Professor Carey listened, his lean, appraising features were set into a disbelieving mask, and his sharp eyes fixed on a point somewhere above my head; perhaps on the upper reaches of his library, whose volumes, he profoundly hoped, would never be joined by mine.

The path to becoming an actual *homme de lettres* wasn't a smooth glide in my mid-twenties. Getting a job in publishing had been a start, but after a year I realised I hadn't the patience to enjoy the gradual gestation of a book, the editing of the result or the planning of a publicity campaign to celebrate its birth. I wanted to write. I wanted to plant words in a certain order and watch them turn, magically, into an article or a book that would, ideally, make readers laugh or weep or sigh with contentment.

And I had to begin with journalism. That was how all the top writers started out. Martin Amis at the *TLS*. Julian Barnes at the *New Statesman*. Clive James at the *New Review*. Even if you didn't have the charmed life that led you straight into the literary mags, other kinds of journalism were available. The novelist Timothy Mo, for instance, had started out on *Boxing News* ...

While waiting to publish a Booker-snagging masterpiece, of course, the best thing would be to hit Fleet Street and make money writing features (or book reviews). But I knew that ambitious young arts graduates couldn't get within cab-hailing distance of the national press without 'doing time'. You either spent three lonely years in some Hardyesque village or gritty Yorkshire mining town, working for the local newspaper and reporting on stories of petty crime ('Yetminster Wheelbarrow Vandal Strikes Again') or pathetic reports on minor social events ('Pottle Memorial Service "A Touching Tribute" Says Widow'). The only alternative was to start out on a specialist journal or magazine – *Gravediggers' Gazette*, say, or *Cage and Aviary Birds* – in the hope that your contributions might come to the attention of a Fleet Street talent-spotter.

I left Gollancz, because I got lucky – or it seemed lucky at the time. I walked into a job on a business magazine called the *Director*. I arrived there by the time-honoured process of befriending a chap (a chap for whom my sister was working), who introduced me to another chap who, by coincidence, had gone to my school years before me, and was now editor of the magazine.

The two chaps invited me for a drink at the mag's headquarters, the Institute of Directors in Pall Mall. Tightly clad in my first-ever suit, a stylish, three-piece, heather-coloured number from a Chelsea backstreet, I sat in the institute's fabulously plush bar, clutching a rum and Coke served by Clive, the inscrutable barman. Surrounded by club members, presumably chairmen and boardroom executives, I felt like H.G. Wells's hero Arthur Kipps might have felt had he strayed into the bar of the House of Lords.

The editor's name was George Bull. Born in 1929, he was fifty when we met, but seemed older – his hair a crinkled silver, the collar of his grey suit dandruffy, his demeanour donnish, his conversation droll but pedantic and his personal manner always conciliatory, as if he felt it would be bad manners to argue or confront anyone.

The two men reminisced about the school we'd attended in Wimbledon, although they'd been there in the mid-1940s and I in the late 1960s. Anxious to impress, I tried to relay uproarious tales of my fellow scholars' cheekiness in the refectory or pubescent hanky-panky in the bogs, but it was tough going.

Things lightened when we were joined by George's colleagues on the magazine, Richard and Carol, who were younger, sassier, and less obviously the denizens of clubland. Thirtyish Richard Barber, the associate editor, was camp, sleek and witty, and wrote freelance pieces for glossy magazines aimed at sixteen-year-old girls; when not writing for the *Director* about marketing and technology, he was 'Pandora' the agony aunt, dishing out advice on snogging and periods to the readers of *Fruity Teen* or whatever it was called. Carol Kennedy, forty-something, was immensely tall and fantastically old-fashioned: she wore spectacles that recalled the typing pools in 1960s TV comedy shows, and wore her hair in a bouffant meringue last seen on the head of Dusty Springfield.

Both were chatty and charming with the newcomer, laughed at George's courtly manner (he'd say, 'Shall we have the other half?' rather than, 'Shall we have another drink?' – a clubland construction, just as annoying as the barman's way of saying, 'Similar, sir?' rather than 'Same again?') and discussed Mrs Thatcher's recent elevation to Number 10 with tremendous verve and fluency. Carol turned out to be professionally clued-up about current affairs. She wrote a weekly 'Letter from London' for a Canadian news mag called *Macleans*. I was dead impressed: it was the equivalent of being the London correspondent for *Time* or *Newsweek*.

I looked at these two people, so amusing and sophisticated, so cool and confident, so versatile in writing for different markets, so airily at home in the Pall Mall club with their benign and venerable boss. Gosh, I thought, I would *love* to be like them, working in this Versailles-like temple of Mammon, freelancing for teen glossies and news-breaking international journals of record. Could it be possible?

George Bull and I met on many occasions during my time at Gollancz. He'd ring me up and say, 'Come for a drink next week, if you're not too busy. I want to find out what's happening in the Young Mind.' Tragically, the only things in the young mind were a greedy desire to make lots of money, an ungovernable passion for a fat singer called Meat Loaf, and a faint suspicion that I shouldn't be spending evenings out in my heather-pink suit with a smooth-talking, middle-aged man. But George and I rubbed along surprisingly well, given that his job was to monitor key events in the City, the Treasury and the British boardroom, whereas I just knew some stuff about books.

He seemed to have amazing contacts – not just the business titans whom the *Director* magazine profiled, but everyone in posh Catholic circles, London clubland and Fleet Street. He moved around a tight circuit of religio-politico-literary pals at the Garrick, the Savile and the Travellers Clubs; at The Cardinal near Westminster Cathedral, where the nation's top Catholics gathered for power dinners and lectures on eschatology); and in the pubs around Gray's Inn Road, home of *The Times* newspaper and its cognate titles.

I discovered that he'd been a literary Infant Phenomenon among translators. While still at Oxford, he'd begun translating Renaissance Italian classics. Five of them, published in the 1960s and 1970s, were still in print with Penguin Classics. When it came to twentieth-century books, George was very well-read, but disapproved of much that was new. 'Have you read this chap Ian McEwan?' he would ask. 'Writes well but with a very cold eye. Very nasty stories. And absolutely no moral perspective at all.' I felt this was a bit rich coming from someone who'd brought a new edition of Machiavelli's shocking volume of advice about how to be a successful tyrant – *The Prince* – into the world, but decided to keep it to myself.

A favourite memory of George, some years after we first met, was of an evening in the Garrick Club; he was telling me about his recent trip to New York and his fondness for the Gramercy Park Hotel, when he heard a stentorian American voice at the bar. Garrick rules allow any club member wearing the club tie to talk to any other one without waiting to be introduced, so George piled in.

'That's a splendidly American voice,' he said. 'Do you come from New York?'

The man turned around. He was at least six feet four, and his face was instantly recognisable; it had appeared, on screens forty feet high, in three global blockbusters in the 1950s.

George showed no sign of knowing who he was. 'I've just come back from New York, you see.'

'I'm originally from California,' said the Incredibly Famous Film Star. 'But I have had occasion to visit Noo York on many occasions. Often in the Broadway area.'

George failed to pick up this stonking clue.

'I was staying at the Gramercy Park Hotel. Do you know it? It's very reasonably priced.'

'When in Manhattan I tend to stay at the Pierre,' said the IFFS smoothly. George seemed not to notice that this translated as: 'I don't stay in mid-town flophouses. I stay at the most expensive hotel in the city, overlooking Central Park.'

'And are you over here on holiday?'

'No sir,' said the man. 'I'm here to work.'*

'May I ask,' asked George, cluelessly, 'where your work is?'

'Oh, quite near here,' said the man. 'In the Strand. As a matter of fact, I'm working this evening and I must be running along.'

'You mustn't let us keep you,' said George, clearly not disposed to wonder how such a striking man could be working at seven o'clock in the evening. 'Lovely to meet you. My name is George Bull.'

'Nice to meet you, George.'

'Do you know my young friend, John Walsh?'

The man nodded in my direction, noting from the aghast look on my face that I, at least, knew who he was.

'And you, John,' he said.

'Lovely to meet you,' I said, 'Mr Heston.'

Another evening at the Garrick, I met someone whom I would meet a lot thereafter. He was a tall, loose-limbed, blue-eyed chap, with an easy manner, a friendly conversational style and a shock of golden curls like those on the head of the boy in Millais's *A Child's World*, better known as *Bubbles*. This was my first sighting of Sebastian Faulks. He wasn't a Garrick member (too young by at least twenty-five years) but was the guest of a friend of George Bull's called David Hughes. Introductions were swift and hearty as the two old friends welcomed their blushing Ganymedes to each other.

---

* The IFFS was in town to direct his critically acclaimed LA production of *The Caine Mutiny Court Martial* starring himself as Captain Queeg.

George and David knew each other from schooldays in Wimbledon – George at the Sacred Heart (Catholic), David at King's College (Protestant) – and undergraduate life at Oxford: George at Brasenose, David at Christ Church. They were an interesting contrast: George was a polite, fastidious, episcopal presence, who small-talked in a soothing, agreeable murmur. David was a more raffish and eager figure, with a receding hairline and merry eyes, alive to the possible laughter in whichever twist the conversation took. When meeting an old friend he'd say 'My *dear fellow*...' clutching the chap's elbows in a fond parody of clubman bluffness; he laughed easily, revealing shockingly nicotine-stained teeth.

I can't remember precisely how Sebastian and I bonded in the company of these two fifty-year-old, alpha-male show-offs, but it was the first time I'd heard of the New Fiction Society, to which both he and David were connected. The society had been cooked up by the Arts Council to persuade more people to buy new hardback novels. It was, effectively, a government-subsidised plug for modern literature, a notion unthinkable today. Through the National Book League, run by the ubiquitous Martyn Goff, the society published a monthly magazine, *New Fiction*, which carried articles and recommendations by reliable literati about new publications that members might enjoy, and could buy at bargain prices.

Sebastian was a member when he wrote to David, its editor, offering a feature about the life of the modern reviewer; it was published and they became close friends. When Hughes left to write his own novels, he suggested that Sebastian apply for the job, which meant being inspected by the Board of Directors. For such a modest concern as the New Fiction Society, they were an impressive bunch: Liz Calder (my ex-colleague at Gollancz), Ion Trewin (literary editor of *The Times*), Deborah Rogers (agent of, among others, Amis and McEwan) and Michael O'Mara, a Philadelphia-born publisher, whose bestselling work would be *Diana: Her True Story* in 1992.

It took the distinguished company an age to choose Sebastian as the magazine's new editor in 1978, but once in, he was (at twenty-five) a hot new figure on the London literary scene. Because *New Fiction* shared a typesetter with the *New Review*, then in its final year of existence, Sebastian found himself, once a month, in Greek Street drinking pints at the Pillars of Hercules pub with Ian Hamilton, who had published the early work of Amis, McEwan, Julian Barnes, James Fenton and Clive James. How I envied him.

The year 1979 was significant, not just for the quality of the books being published, but for being the year *The Times Literary Supplement* disappeared. The *TLS* was required weekly reading for any would-be young Amis-clone like my friends and me: so serious, ambitious and perverse in the titles it chose (Sanskrit cookery? Medieval Albanian politics?), so nuanced and fastidious (and seldom praising) in its treatment of fiction. Its disappearance from the literary scene was, therefore, a disaster. It came with the temporary closure of *Times* newspapers after a long battle between the proprietor, Lord Thomson of Fleet, and the print unions of Fleet Street. On 30 November 1978, the papers shut down for a year, leaving a vacuum that had to be filled. And in that year, four new book-related journals arrived.

Quarto, a monthly journal, was founded in 1978 by Craig Raine and John Ryle the writer, anthropologist and great-nephew of the philosopher Gilbert (*The Concept of Mind*) Ryle. It was later edited by Richard Boston, journalist, literary editor of *New Society*, biographer of Osbert Lancaster, *bon vivant* and real-ale fanatic. It was a laid-back, serious, determinedly non-glossy production which promised high seriousness.

The *Literary Review*, founded Dr Anne Smith, head of Edinburgh University's English department, kicked off in October 1979 with an appreciation of Antonia White by Hermione Lee, a Paris Diary by someone I'd never heard of, and an evaluation by A. S. Byatt of the just-announced Booker Prize shortlist (*Confederates* by Thomas Keneally, *A Bend in the River* by V. S. Naipaul, *Joseph* by Julian Rathbone, *Praxis* by Fay Weldon and *Offshore*, the eventual winner, by Penelope Fitzgerald).

In June 1979, Professor Frank Kermode, the nation's most eminent literary academic, wrote a piece in the *Observer*, 'on behalf of all the new books that don't get reviewed' and calling for a new magazine to fill the *TLS*-shaped gap. Up stepped the *New York Review of Books*, offering to fund, launch and publish a transatlantic version of itself and carry it – the *London Review of Books* – tucked away in its pages. The relationship between the literary journals of the Big Apple and the Big Smoke would, said Karl Miller, the *LRB*'s first editor, be 'marsupial'.

Seven months later, the main paper had had enough of its joey. 'Good writers are thin on the ground,' wrote the deputy editor Mary-Kay Wilmers, 'and we didn't like their using ours any more than they liked our using theirs.' So in May 1980, the *LRB* quit the parental pouch and went out into the world alone.

Also in the spring, another literary magazine with an Anglo-American provenance appeared in British bookshops. It was a glossy paperback that glowed with confidence. Its name was *Granta*, a re-launch (or perhaps exhumation would be a better word) of a student magazine originally founded in 1889. It was edited by Bill Buford and Pete de Bolla, both American academics at Cambridge, and it would make waves in the book world all through the 1980s and beyond.

Issue number 1 was called 'New American Writing' and the contents featured essays and fiction extracts from stateside authors both well-known (Joyce Carol Oates, Donald Barthelme) and obscure. An unsigned introduction, presumably by Bill and Pete, issued a sorrowful, then crushing, then downright rude bulletin about the state of British fiction.

Its first words bizarrely echoed the famous opening sentence of *Pride and Prejudice*: 'It is increasingly a discomforting commonplace that today's British novel is neither remarkable nor remarkably interesting. Current fiction does not startle, does not surprise, is not the source of controversy or contention ... And so the complaint: British fiction of the fifties, sixties and even most of the seventies variously appears as a monotonously protracted, realistically rendered monologue. It lacks excitement, wants drive, provides comforts not challenges.'

My initial response, like that of most British readers of *Granta 1*, was to think: 'Of all the bloody *cheek*.' The editors were so obviously trying to pick a fight with the British literary establishment in order to get their mag noticed, it was laughable. But the rude Americans hadn't finished. 'Current British fiction,' they sneered, 'seems to be characterised by a succession of efforts, the accomplishments of which are insistently [I assumed they meant 'persistently'], critically, and aesthetically negligible.'

Was this dismissal of British fiction really a 'commonplace'? Was everyone talking about us behind our backs? Were readers across the English-speaking world meeting in bars in Sydney Harbour or Fifth Avenue and making finger-down-the-throat gestures about the work of, say, Iris Murdoch?

The introduction claimed that 'a few apologists' (unnamed) had tried to stick up for British fiction, and insist it wasn't mediocre. They were, apparently, OK with David Storey and Alan Sillitoe (both northern and about as 'experimental' as Heinz tomato soup), B. S. Johnson, Roald Dahl, John Berger, Malcolm Bradbury, John Fowles, J. G. Ballard and Ian McEwan. And that was it.

Had they never heard of Angela Carter, by 1979 the author of seven novels and two collections of stories, turbocharged with magic realism and magnificent witchy prose? Had none of them read Anthony Burgess, the most prodigiously gifted master of language, whose books could feature parallel narratives, musical versions of *Ulysses* or pastiches of Italian Renaissance poets? How had they failed to spot Martin Amis – already, with three novels, making the English language fizz and coruscate? How could they be unacquainted with the extremely *un*-mediocre Michael Frayn or Beryl Bainbridge or Fay Weldon, who had seven fine novels to her credit, including *Little Sisters*, *Female Friends* and the Booker-shortlisted *Praxis*?

The wretched Buford also brought up a recent essay in the *Bookseller* by Robert McCrum, the new commissioning editor at Faber. 'Writing Without Risk' made three damning complaints about modern British fiction. First, that it was lifeless, 'happier adding to the myths, writing about the world we have lost.' Second, that 'British writing seems immune to the philosophical and intellectual fevers of the time, inoculated against innovation by its native pragmatism.' And third, that writers and publishers 'take too much for granted and are incapable of the determination and artistic integrity of those from politically repressed nations.'

The second complaint had some justification to it – many British novelists seemed unenthusiastic about borrowing foreign modes of expression, European forms of experimentation (such as Alain Robbe-Grillet's *nouveau roman*) or South American innovations with language or narrative such as magic realism. But it seemed a bit harsh to blame British publishers for lacking the risk-taking and bravery of their counterparts in countries that were 'politically repressed'. Maybe British preoccupations *were* simply a) to make a profit and b) to publish stuff that appealed to a reasonably well-defined, if heterogeneous, readership. That seemed to me a pretty sensible modus operandi. Maybe they had grown stale in being thus preoccupied – but they could hardly be blamed for failing to disseminate *samizdat* literature, divisive or inflammatory tracts, dangerously unpopular screeds of blasphemous material or depictions of wantonly cruel or sexually bizarre human behaviour that might get them banned or put in prison for their transgressions. It just wouldn't be British.

I found myself bridling with indignation at these attacks on the home-grown product. The Americans, I concluded, were only being rude about our novelists because they felt irritated by the lack of interest we showed in their nation's overwrought sagas about priapic Jewish academics in New Jersey or disgruntled car dealers in Wisconsin. And Mr McCrum at Faber was simply behaving like a callow new broom, determined to replace the lumber, the antimacassars and dusty old carpets of T. S. Eliot's old firm with cool pine Conran furniture, gleaming chrome and ambient sound systems. From now on, I decided, I would read all the new literary journals and see for myself how things were faring in the English-lit jungle.

When George offered me the job of associate editor of the *Director*, I jumped at it. There was a good salary, colleagues whom I knew to be good company, an easy journey from my home in Clapham to Trafalgar Square, a handsome workplace, a bustling environment flanked by Soho and the Strand. The only thing wrong, the substantial fly in the otherwise agreeable ointment, was that I knew absolutely fuck-all about business.

I made elementary moves to familiarise myself. I bought *Teach Yourself Commerce*, and frowningly absorbed the chapters about 'Starting Your Own Business'. I'd barely got beyond the section on Articles of Association and the page on Limited Liability when I realised that nothing was sinking in. Flicking the pages, glancing at later chapters on 'Zero-Based Budgeting' and 'Discounted Cash Flow' gave me attacks of cardiac flutter and acid reflux. I studied the lives of leading businessmen – John Harvey-Jones at ICI, Richard Branson at Virgin, Hector Laing at United Biscuits – and sullenly digested the crucial events in the companies' histories ('United Biscuits was prepared to admit defeat when appropriate; in 1977, the company withdrew from the packaged cakes market . . .'). With a sinking heart, I swotted up on present and previous governors of the Bank of England, trying to guess what combination of mathematical skill and personal ruthlessness might qualify them to run the operation. I began to wonder if I had made a grotesque blunder.

My lack of any basic grasp of commerce prompted a dinging memory. What was it? Oh yes, Dickens. I remembered from university days how interested I'd been to discover that he never had a clue about business people or what they did all day. Rather than ascribe the success or failure of businessmen to such things as investment, risk management, profit margins and customer service, he simply described them as being fantastically *tidy*, reducing huge piles of invoices, orders, receipts, dockets, letters and legal documents to manageable proportions.

Where had I read this? Then I remembered – at Oxford, during the weeks in which John Carey had given the lecture series, *The Violent Effigy: A Study in Dickens's Imagination*. I recalled how brilliant it had been and I rushed off to buy a copy, to refresh my memory. In the chapter 'Dickens and Order', Carey has fun with the recurring scenarios (in *Little Dorrit*, *Martin Chuzzlewit* and *Our Mutual Friend*) where a Dickens character demonstrates his *heroism* by writing neatly, tidying up and turning chaos into order.

'The vagueness in all these episodes is remarkable,' writes Carey. 'The reader gains no inkling of how the accounts of a firm are actually kept, or of what the merits of different accounting methods might be. Nor does he acquire any confidence in Dickens's understanding of these matters. The neatness is self-justifying, unrelated to any real occurrences in the world of finance, and does not extend beyond elementary gestures like dotting i's and tying papers in a bundle. It is what one would expect in a novel written for a child.'

It was gratifying to think I shared a quality – *any* quality – with Dickens, but I began my career in business journalism with a heavy heart. Over the next four years I got through by confining myself to writing only about non-technical subjects, such as advertising campaigns, film moguls, charities, sponsorship, publishing (which meant I got to interview the famous literary agent Ed Victor, who told me: 'I'm very lucky to be an American in English publishing. Most of my English publishing friends consider it a good day's work if they get to their desks before lunch') and management. There was never any danger of my being required to write about stock options, or sent to interview the chancellor of the exchequer.

I rather enjoyed the theory of management, though, and read several works on the subject, marvelling at how fatuously simple-minded they were. They explained to nervous, brand-new managers how everything can be made to work in perfect systems and structures, powered by departmental teams of ruthlessly efficient men in Cutler & Gross spectacles and women in Armani pencil skirts, who never put a foot wrong. Their power-meetings, power-presentations, power-walks, power-naps and other collective or solitary endeavours invariably resulted in an 'arrowhead' of unstoppable force that got whatever-it-was done in record time, leading to praise from their department boss, who (after reading *The One-Minute Manager*) devoted much hand-clasping and eye contact to his underlings, to make them feel his approbation.

One day I was sent to meet the nation's top piss-taker of management theory, Professor C. Northcote Parkinson. He was the naval historian who, in 1958, wrote an article for *The Economist* that gave the world 'Parkinson's Law'. The law stated that 'Work expands so as to fill the time available for its completion', an aphorism that found its way into the *Oxford Dictionary of Quotations*.*

He had a new collection of essays out in Penguin, and I set off, with my new cassette-tape recorder, to conduct my first interview. This, I told myself, is going to be good. No, like a successful piece of management, it's going to be *perfect*.

I'd read all his clever essays with relish. One mapped the ways in which people navigate the room during a cocktail party; another revealed that the increase in naval personnel at the Admiralty was in direct proportion to the dwindling number of actual ships. I boned up on his life story, I even checked out the history of Malaya in the 1950s, when he was Raffles Professor of History in Kuala

---

* Along with 'Expenditure rises to meet income'; and 'Men enter local politics solely as a result of being unhappily married'; and 'Delay is the deadliest form of denial'.

Lumpur. I left nothing to chance. I practised the tape machine, bought extra batteries, rewrote my questions. I set off in good time to see him in a hotel lobby. What could go wrong?

Parkinson, seventy that year, was large, rubicund, fantastically bald with alarmingly piercing blue eyes. He surveyed my twenty-six-year-old features without enthusiasm, as if he'd been sent a pimply naval rating to grill him about his life's work. But the interview went OK. In fact, until disaster struck, it was going extremely well. Parkinson talked fluently. He was pleased I'd read the whole book. He coolly extemporised bullets of wisdom as he discussed how Mrs Thatcher's degree in Chemistry could help her build a strong Cabinet.

I looked at this super-intelligent, battle-scarred, indomitable man talking with evident pleasure about the folly of human planning, and I thought, 'This is going really well.' I watched the little red unblinking eye on the tape machine and the tape serenely circling round its little spool, and I thought, 'This is my first interview and it's going to be *really good*.'

I smiled. I may even have uttered a tiny, interior giggle of satisfaction. '*Heh!*'

Parkinson stopped talking. I looked up. His blue eyes were glaring directly into mine.

'Have I said something humorous?' he asked, in a voice that would freeze mercury, 'or were you just thinking about something else?'

Fuck fuck *faaaaarck*. I'd made the worst blunder you could make as an interviewer. I'd lost concentration and *tuned out*, as if I'd been listening to the radio instead of trying to extract information. I'd just insulted a septuagenarian genius. Now he'd cancel the interview and storm out, and I'd be completely screwed.

'I'm *so sorry*, Professor,' I said, my voice wobbling with supplication. 'But you see – this is my first-ever interview. I was *really* nervous about it. But you've been so fluent, and your answers are so interesting, I just thought, *This is going really well*, and the thought sort of . . . came out.'

'Humph,' he said. 'Seemed a bit odd, that's all. Let's move on.'

I didn't take my eyes off him thereafter. I adopted an expression of deranged alertness, and concentrated on making each question appear to spring organically from his last answer. At the end we shook hands. Amazingly, when the piece was published, he sent me a thank-you note at the magazine, inviting me, rather bizarrely, to accompany him to his daughter's birthday party in Canterbury.

After this gruelling experience, I wrote a *Memo to Self: Things Not to Do While Interviewing Someone*:

1) Laugh or smile at something not occasioned by interviewee.
2) Talk to self.
3) Sing under one's breath.
4) Yawn voluptuously.
5) Fall asleep.
6) Examine fingernails.
7) Go to check out interviewee's CD collection.
8) Scrape at blemish on shirt front.
9) Rearrange publications on interviewee's coffee table.
10) Start to cry.

So I spent my late twenties meeting people – businessmen – whose lives and works I cared nothing for, writing about things in which I had zero interest. It wasn't a dull existence, though. For one thing, I travelled a lot. I flew to Sri Lanka for a week to hang out with a charismatic businessman called Upali Wijewardene, who showed me around his confectionery factories and racing stables, while two bare-footed teenage boys hurried along behind him, one bearing his wallet, the other his fags and lighter. Though he was as camp as Christmas, Upali had married the niece of Sirimavo Bandaranaike, Sri Lanka's three-term prime minister. He flew me in his helicopter to his summer retreat in the balmy uplands of Nuwara Eliya, and then to Malaysia to explain how he was attempting to corner the market in coca plants there. Such airily ruthless expansionism might perhaps be the reason why his private Learjet mysteriously disappeared over the Straits of Malacca in 1983 and was never found.

Over the four years I spent lashed to the mast of the *Director*, while I pretended not to notice I'd taken a catastrophic misstep in my career, small hints and nudges and shadowy manifestations from Providence kept trying to tell me what I should be doing. For one thing, I wrote a book, for a publisher called Sphere. But it wasn't a first novel, nor an outpouring of limpid verse. It was a handbook of management, gleaned from all the interchangeable business tomes I'd digested; it was written to be thrust into the hands of any spotty youth who found himself at sea in a management role shortly after leaving school. It featured a hundred and fifty Q&As of blinding predictability about every aspect of managing a project, for which I was paid £5,000. Of this, £500 went to my old schoolfriend, Paul, now, at twenty-seven, a thrusting finance director, who helped me write the difficult stuff about How to Read a Balance Sheet or What Is a Profit-and-Loss Account, subjects about which I remained shrouded in ignorance.

For another thing, my girlfriends in these years arrived in my life like hints about where my career should go. One was Elizabeth, the serene daughter of a Hampshire bank manager. She worked for a firm called Rainbird, which packaged books on wine and travel for other publishing houses to produce and sell. Another *inamorata*, Belinda, a Bohemian vamp in gypsy skirts, sold advertising space in the *Bookseller*, and brought home gossip from the party circuit about my old employers, Gollancz. (Yikes! Liz Calder has left to become editorial director of Jonathan Cape!)

Belinda's boss was a ramrod-backed ex-public schoolgirl called Joanna Hastings-Trew, who was later to marry Nigel Newton, the co-founder of Bloomsbury Publishing. Their daughter, Alice, was later responsible for getting *Harry Potter and the Philosopher's Stone* published, after she was given the first chapter to read, aged eight, and, on finishing it, demanded to see the second. It was Belinda who pointed out that the *Bookseller*'s distinguished editor, David Whitaker, lived around the corner from my parents' house.

Sebastian Faulks and I had become friends and we used to visit pubs together, talking about fiction. He told me he'd tried writing his first novel in 1974, just after leaving Cambridge, and said he was grateful to Martin Amis for writing *The Rachel Papers*. It was so funny, the turns of phrase so sensational, that it had killed the young-man-coming-of-age novel stone-dead, and blocked off that avenue for ever. 'You can't try and be funnier than that,' he sadly observed. 'You're just wasting your time.'

Even at home I couldn't escape aspiring writers. One evening I came home to my Putney flat to find my co-habitant, Heather – a journalist then working on *Vogue* – entertaining a new beau on the sofa. 'This is Philip,' she said, 'Philip Kerr.' I said hi, got myself a drink and scrutinised the new arrival. He was swarthy, brown-eyed, well-dressed, rather too emphatically cool to be friendly, and he worked in advertising – but only (of course) until he made enough cash to become a full-time writer.

We circled each other warily, and talked about books and writers we admired. They seldom overlapped. He loved Graham Greene, whose Catholic novels I found overwrought with metaphysics, their plots hinging on elements of sin, damnation, and the likelihood of the characters' imminent plunge into Hell. I banged on about Burgess, whose style Philip found too baroque and word-drunk for the stories he himself was trying to tell. We both, however, admired Amis Junior and talked about his work like co-religionists. We probably both hoped we were Quentin Villiers in *Dead Babies*, while nursing a ghastly suspicion that we were actually Little Keith.

Philip shone at plotting. He was full of notions of where a genre story might go, if the writer were bold enough. Agatha Christie might have contrived a murder mystery in which the entire cast of suspects did it, or the narrator did it; only Philip would suggest a murder mystery in which the reader of the book did it. And would explain exactly how it could be contrived.

We talked about Ian Fleming's James Bond plots and wondered: where do you go after *Goldfinger*, with its heist on Fort Knox, that would render the entire gold reserves of the USA radioactive and worthless? Could there be a robbery on a bigger scale? Oh please, he said – it was obvious. 'In the future, the most valuable resource for the human race won't be gold, it'll be uncontaminated blood. So I'm going to write a thriller about a blood bank orbiting the Earth in 2030 or so, and a gang of robbers in a module coming after it.' Years later, when he was a Hollywood player, he pitched this idea to a roomful of executives at United Artists and was paid $3,000 for it. Yeah, I know: $3,000. For a single sheet of A4. What a shame he hadn't gone over the page.

A couple of years after we met, he asked me if I knew any agents. After writing four or five school-of-Martin novels that had got nowhere, he was, he said, trying his hand at a thriller set in Berlin, and it was going well. Also, he'd been turning over the possibility of editing a book on the best falsehoods ever written and published, in political, historical or literary circles. '*The Penguin Book of Lies*,' he said, 'has a nice ring to it.' I had to agree. He had such confidence, it wouldn't have surprised me if he'd had the manuscripts of both books in the briefcase he carried every morning to Saatchi & Saatchi. But yes, I'd met a few agents by then. The sharpest seemed to be Caradoc King at the A. P. Watt agency, who had represented Graham Swift at the time of *Waterland* and, after it failed to win the Booker Prize, asked publishers to bid for a two-book deal for Graham's next two books. The bidding had peaked at £130,000 . . .

I rang Caradoc, told him about Philip and suggested they meet for a chat about publishers. I told Phil to expect nothing, should Mr King get in touch; maybe a telephone conversation and some murmured exhortation of 'Keep at it, laddie . . .' Nothing of the sort. They had lunch, Caradoc loved everything about Phil and his big ideas. He signed him up on the spot and remained his agent until Phil died in 2018. Oh, and a month after their lunch, Caradoc rang and offered *me* lunch to thank me for putting him and his new best friend in touch. The new friend who would go on to make a rumoured £30 million from his Bernie Gunther thrillers and children's books.

Wherever I looked, there were would-be authors and publishing people. Through George Bull, I met Sue Bradbury, deputy boss of the Folio Society, which brought out beautifully produced editions of literary classics, with Japanese endpapers and silken bookmarks, and newly commissioned illustrations by trendy artists (Paula Rego on *Peter Pan*, Tom Phillips on *Waiting for Godot*), and flogged them to rich bibliophiles as collectors' items.

Sue was an avid reader, a passionate Hispanophile, and a biker. She would arrive at the Institute of Directors astride a Kawasaki 9000 (I was always hazy about bike makes, models and CCs), extract her slender limbs from her battered leathers (insulated with copies of the *Guardian*) in a bathroom, and reappear, appropriately clad, in the *Director* office to shoot the breeze with Carol, George and me about literature. She put George's book about the Vatican into Folio covers, and commissioned me to write an introduction to Thomas Hardy's *Wessex Tales*. She was six years my senior and was spoken for with some lucky businessman. It didn't stop me nursing a massive crush on her.

George's books, Carol's books, Sue's Folio books, Elizabeth's Rainbird, Belinda's *Bookseller*, Sebastian's advice, Philip's ambitions – were the Fates trying to tell me something? Were they hinting I should stop arsing about in management and get back into the literary world?

And as well as meeting several almost-writers – aspiring novelists, tyro poets, thriller-plotters, genre-fans, people who spent evenings and weekends pounding typewriters and failing to find girlfriends or boyfriends – I befriended some writers who'd already made it.

Through my friend Jon Canter, a genial and awesomely witty Cambridge law graduate who was president of the Footlights in 1974, I met a droll gang of Fenland wits and sketch-writers, of whom the drollest (and by some way the largest) was Douglas Adams. I'd meet him at the flat he and Jon shared in Kingsdown Road, near Islington in north London, and found myself caught up in the tsunami of elegantly crackpot scientific inventiveness that became *The Hitchhiker's Guide to the Galaxy*.

I loved Douglas's way with fantastical names and throwaway remarks: I yelped with delight on reading that the coolest man in the universe, Zaphod Beeblebrox, had been described by Eccentrica Gallumbits, the triple-breasted whore of Eroticon Six, as 'the best bang since the Big One'. I loved Marvin the paranoid android, he of the Eeyore-like gloom and downer pronouncements ('I didn't ask to be made. No one consulted me or considered my feelings in the matter'), and I was impressed to learn that one of Marvin's keynote lines – 'Life? Don't talk to me about life . . .' – was supplied by Jon Canter.

Douglas had strong opinions about many things. One was music. He thought nothing of inviting people to dinner and, as they tucked into the lasagne, lecturing them about the sadly underrated musical brilliance of Ringo Starr. The more the guests mocked his championing of the skin-walloping Scouser, the more Douglas would turn up the volume and sit, smiling, as their complaints were lost in the racket.

I'd listened to *Hitchhiker* on Radio 4 in the spring of 1978, with a feeling of tuning in to something stunningly modern, insanely clever and strangely empathetic. Then Pan Books persuaded Douglas, an idle and reluctant writer, to extrude a full-sized novel out of the radio show. It was published in October 1979 and hurtled to the top of the bestseller chart.[*]

_____

[*] See Chapter 11.

I remember standing in my local bookshop, gazing at the cover and thinking: Douglas is the first person of my generation – the first person I actually *know* – to become a real writer and now, overnight, a famous one. I felt it was right and proper that such things could happen to us, born in the early 1950s, schooled in the *totally cosmic* wonder years of the sixties, and now (surely) about to form a new British generation of genius . . .

Through Jon I also met a beautiful Geordie called Sue, whom I mention only because she was the first person I knew who owned a Sony Walkman, that compact emblem of 1980s grooviness; also she drove a Citroën Mahari, a kind of automative plastic tray with some canvas material precariously stretched across its spindly aluminium struts. It was more suitable for driving on Malibu Beach than Marylebone High Street, and therefore also achingly on-trend. I adored her beyond idolatry and wrote poems to her loveliness. One began: *The way your freckles dot your nose/Like truffles in a fish terrine* . . . and sustained the '-ose/-een' rhyme-scheme for a whole page until running out of steam with: *The way your pink and fragrant toes/Hold nothing nasty in between* . . . unconsciously revealing me to be a real-life avatar of Adrian Mole, aged 13¾, whose *Secret Diary* would soon be published (in 1982) and would sell two million copies in three years.

David Hughes, back in charge at *New Fiction* magazine, asked me if I'd like to interview Martin Amis about his new novel, *Other People: A Mystery Story*. Obviously I jumped at the chance – but I had some trouble with the book. I'd devoured Amis's previous three novels, felt the weight and complexity of their characters, believed in their interactions, been shocked by their fates. But I didn't know where I was with Mary Lamb, the dazed, indistinct figure at the centre of *Other People*.

At the start, Mary wakes up from some kind of oblivion. 'Her first feeling, as she smelled the air, was one of intense and helpless gratitude. I'm all right, she thought with a gasp. Time – it's starting again.' She hears someone say, 'Are you all right now?' So, is she coming round from an operation? Coming to after an attack? Returning to life from death? She's lost her memory – and also any understanding of the physical world, even of her own body. She doesn't understand basic sights: clouds, shops, children, cars. And we're given her foggy interpretations of these familiar things, poetically defamiliarised, like the subjects of Craig Raine's 'Martian' poems.*

As we follow Mary's progress, she falls in with a cast of lowlifes, alcoholic women and pub lechers – and we wonder what connects her to the book's narrating voice. It's that of a policeman called Prince, who wants to tell Mary about the life of a murdered girl called Amy Lamb, who might or might not be Mary herself. At the end of the novel, we read 'Her first feeling, as she smelled the air, was one of intense and helpless gratitude . . .' and we're back at the start, only this time the voice saying, 'Are you all right now?' is her mother's . . . So has she died *twice*? And is the policeman her Handsome-Prince saviour? Or her murderer? I had no idea, and struggled to care. For the first time in ten years, Martin Amis had written something that I didn't understand and frankly didn't care for. And I was just about to meet him.

Amis's flat was in Kensington Gardens Square, the kind of blue-chip address you associate with diplomatic palaces and chaps with uniforms standing in wooden booths, dissuading motorists from entering the street. But the actual square was a let-down: a cramped, nondescript rectangle off Westbourne Grove, arrayed around a dagger-thin triangle of greensward. The staircase echoed dully as I

---

* We know from his published letters that Martin's father, Kingsley Amis, disliked Raine's poetry, and the influence it had on *Other People*. He wrote to Robert Conquest in March 1981: 'Young Martin's new novel is out. Tough going I find. You see there's this girl with amnesia shit you know what I mean, so she's forgotten what a lavatory is, and she thinks the cisterns and pipes are statuary, but then how does she know what statuary is? It's like a novel by Craig Raine, well not quite as fearful as that would be I suppose . . .'

rushed up them to meet the young maestro at last. The bell rang, the door creaked open, and Martin Amis stood before me. He was short, handsome and preoccupied, as if interrupted in the midst of an unusually fine piece of lexical pyrotechnics.

'Come in,' he said in that voice I'd heard a few times on TV, flat and precise and slightly disgusted. 'Would you like some tea or something?' The 'or something' clearly didn't mean that a margarita or a Flaming Zombie was available. It meant, 'Or how about *nothing*? Is *nothing* good for you?' I asked for water. He proffered it without enthusiasm. 'Can we keep this quite short?' he asked.

'I'll be out of here in twenty-eight minutes,' I said. It was a line used with interviewers (or so I'd read in *Melody Maker*) by the bedraggled Goth-rock star Alice Cooper.

Amis smiled: 'That's very exact.'

'I know how busy you must be,' I replied, looking around the sparsely furnished flat, with its desk, nondescript sofa, schoolroom table and prop guitar. It was not obviously the domestic set-up of London's most successful young novelist. Were someone to add an ironing board, it could have been the set for a 1980s production of *Look Back in Anger*.

Things got off to a sticky start.

'*Other People*,' I began, keen to impress, 'reminded me of *The Third Policeman* by Flann O'Brien, which also involves a circular plot after the main character goes into a police station and the cop behind the counter asks, "Is it about a bicycle?" At the end, the last line is a policeman asking, "Is it about a bicycle?" And we discover that the guy is in hell after murdering someone and is condemned to go round and round, doing the same things for eternity. There seems to be an obvious connection.'

Amis looked down at the cigarette he was rolling, held it to his lips, licked the edge and sealed it.

'Go on,' he said neutrally.

'And of course,' I went on, 'there's that line, "Hell is other people" in the Sartre play, *Huis Clos*, although of course the Greek concept of Hell is actually to be locked inside your own mind for eternity, picking over the terrible things you've done.'

'Sorry,' said Amis, 'but what's your question?'

'To be honest,' I said, dropping my cunning strategy of presenting a theory about his work and inviting him to agree with it, 'I didn't understand the ending of *Other People*. So my question is, "What the hell happens to Mary at the end?"'

'All I can say,' said Martin Amis, 'is go back and read it again.'

'I'm sorry,' I said, 'I don't really have time to.'

Instantly I regretted it. It was rude. Here was the writer I'd longed to meet since my student days, and I'd dismissed the idea of reading his new book twice. But then (a grumbling countervoice muttered in my head), how many times did one have to read a novel before you understood it? It's not like it's a bloody *symphony*.

Not a great start, then – and it made supplementary questions about *Other People* a bit redundant. But things improved. I asked how he'd managed to go straight from university into writing fiction, without an intervening period of going crazy with girls and drugs.

'I made a deal with my tutor,' said Amis, 'that I could spend a year trying to write a novel and if I managed to, well and good. And if not, I'd return to Exeter College and do a postgraduate degree.'

'What would you have studied?'

'Probably Shakespeare. I don't think any other writer's worth spending such a lot of time on, do you?'

We talked about lots of things unconnected to his new publication: how long one can spend being an *enfant terrible* (he was coming up to his thirty-second birthday), the differing grades of nastiness at work in *Dead Babies* – in Andy, Quentin, Marvell and Skip ('I'm fully conscious of the moral weight of all my characters,' he said defensively), and about his books' preoccupation with the twinning of Dazzling Success and Grubby Failure. I even dragged in his fondness for science fiction, just so I could point out that an early sentence in *Other People* was clearly pinched from the last line of *The Nine Billion Names of God* by Arthur C. Clarke.

After twenty-seven minutes, I was exhausted by my efforts to a) impress Amis and b) become his best friend. That fact that I'd be going home with a very sub-optimal interview didn't bother me. Then, right at the end, something unforeseen happened. As I put my tape recorder away, Amis, perhaps relieved the ordeal was over, chattily asked:

'So, do you travel much for journalism?'

'Yes I do. Actually, I'm flying to the States in July.'

'Which part?'

'I'm off to Chicago for a week to see a friend and write a travel piece.'

'*Chicago?*' At the name, his face lit up. An artless smile animated his face. 'You *lucky* thing.'

'Do you know it well?' I said. 'Have you been there a lot?'

He shook his head. 'No, never. But Saul Bellow lives there.'

'OK,' I said, wondering how my trip to the city could be enlivened, or my stay there rendered more fortunate, by the existence, somewhere in the mid-town region, of a sixty-something Canadian Nobel laureate.

'Are you planning to go there?' I asked. 'You know, pay him a visit?'

'Yeah,' he said, vaguely but dreamily. 'Maybe next year.'*

And there before me, as I looked at the living writer whom I admired above all others, I saw a fanboy, having a little hero-worship moment of his own.

The *Director* featured a small section on directorial hobbies, relaxation pursuits, holidays, cars and the like, plus a page of book reviews, commissioned by George and Carol. One day, a Jiffy bag disgorged a book called *Hacks and Dunces: Pope, Swift and Grub*

---

* And so he did, in December 1982, to interview Bellow for the *Observer*, an encounter rapturously evoked in *Inside Story*.

Street by an American author called Pat Rogers. 'This is your kind of thing, isn't it?' Carol asked me. 'Swift and Pope, and satire and gossip?'

'I'd love to read it,' I said, 'if you don't fancy it yourself.'

'No, I mean, maybe you should review it,' said Carol. 'Seven hundred words by Friday week. What d'you think?'

I spent that lunchtime blissfully locked in the streets of seventeenth- and eighteenth-century London, amid the periwigs and beauty spots, the gin palaces and coffee-houses, the new phenomena of gentlemen's clubs, newspapers and magazines, of political fights and pamphleteering, of the tiny, vituperative Pope and the scatological, divine Swift, and the way the noble profession of journalism was rated as on a par with prostitution. 'This is terrific,' I told Carol, 'but we can't review it, obviously.'

'Why ever not?'

'Because there's nothing about business or entrepreneurship anywhere,' I said. 'There's nothing on trade – well, apart from the South Sea company of course, but that's all over in, like, ten pages.'

'For heaven's sake,' she said, 'not everything we write about has to be one hundred per cent focused on business. What a crashing bore *that* would be. The back of the mag is about anything that might amuse or interest company directors – and, you'll be amazed to hear, that includes history. Even literature, provided it's not your awful friend Beckett . . .'

So I read Professor Rogers's splendid book, reviewed it at twice the length I'd been given and almost wept to find my words mercilessly blue-pencilled – but there it was on a glossy page, with a heading someone had spent a whole minute thinking up ('Grubbing for Gold'), and hurrah, my name at the end. I left the new issue of the magazine open on my desk at my review, to dazzle anyone who came near. 'Not bad,' said George, 'but you'll need to watch the boyish enthusiasm. Restraint and cautious approval should be your watchwords.'

He and Carol wrote actual books that ordinary, non-business people could read with pleasure. George's book *Venice: The Most Triumphant City* hit the bookshops in 1982, with a slightly condescending puff from Jan Morris on the cover. Carol Kennedy was a whizz on the English aristocracy and their living quarters: she published *Harewood: The Life and Times of an English Country House* in 1982, and a comprehensive study of posh London in *Mayfair: A Social History* four years later.

I liked Carol a lot. She was a throwback to an earlier time, not just in her choice of hairstyle, but in her interests and adventures. She liked being photographed standing with a foot perched on the fender of one of the vintage cars she adored. I could picture her alongside the hearty girl hikers played by Margaret Lockwood and Googie Withers in Hitchcock's *The Lady Vanishes*. She came from legal and theatrical stock: one great-grandfather had been chief magistrate of Dublin, another owned theatres in Portsmouth and Southsea. One of her cousins was the lynx-eyed actress Kate O'Mara, who starred in every TV action series of the late 1960s – *The Saint, Z Cars, The Avengers* – and, in the 1970 Hammer classic *The Vampire Lovers*, where she appeared in a sweat-inducing lesbian love scene with Ingrid Pitt that (she told me) required several takes because the Polish-German vampire's fangs kept falling into the O'Mara cleavage.

I went to dinner several times at Carol's flat, and it was there that I met Giles Gordon, a charismatic book-world star. By then pushing forty, he'd worked at Secker, Hutchinson and Penguin before becoming editorial director at Gollancz aged twenty-seven, a decade before I arrived there. As Carol served up Elizabeth David casseroles, Giles told stories of his brushes with literary immortals: how he'd sat behind Cyril Connolly at the memorial service for Cecil Day-Lewis; how he'd met Sonia Brownell, the second wife of George Orwell and Connolly's deputy at *Horizon* during the war, and found her a 'literary groupie' and 'an actressy fake'; how he'd taken tea with Ivy Compton-Burnett, interviewed the playwright

Joe Orton about his experience of prison after being nicked for defacing library books, and recalled drinking whisky out of tooth mugs with Iris Murdoch in a hotel room in Buxton, Derbyshire.

I brought up Martin Amis's name, expecting a ringing endorsement of his brilliance, energy and zingy style. This was a mistake. Giles dismissed him as a jumped-up *arriviste* on the literary scene, a trendy and vicious little shit, desperate to prove he wasn't a clone of his much more talented dad. It was only years later, when I read Giles's memoirs,* that I realised the reason for this toxic dislike. In 1975, Giles had co-edited an anthology of essays entitled *Beyond the Words: Eleven Writers in Search of a New Fiction*, featuring such avant-garde talents as B. S. Johnson, Ann Quin, Gabriel Josipovici and Robert Nye. By coincidence, in the same week, Giles's second collection of short stories, *Farewell, Fond Dreams* was also released. Hearing there was a review of both in the *New Statesman*, Giles had rushed to the newsagent's – only to find that, over a page and a column, Amis had taken a hatchet, a chainsaw and an entrenching tool to every word in both books. He had administered brief, insulting slaps to the faces of all the 'New Fiction' contributors, one by one, and thought Giles's own stories were rubbish: 'Mr Gordon's prose,' he wrote, 'is put together without skill, sensitivity or affection, and does nothing at all to animate his drab musings on static scenes and fabricated paradoxes. Perhaps it's meant to be as dull and discourteous as it is . . . Another possibility, of course, is that Mr Gordon can't write very well.'

Pretty much everything about Giles Gordon struck me as admirable. His airy familiarity with the publishing world, his cool name-dropping ('Do you know I once got Antonia Fraser to write a ghost story, her first piece of prose?'), his combative spirit, his breezy reports of the literary giants he'd interviewed, his gossipy inside track on love affairs and the corrupt jungle of book prizes – I

* Giles Gordon, *Aren't We Due a Royalty Statement?: A Stern Account of Literary, Publishing and Theatrical Folk* (Chatto & Windus, 1993)

lapped it up. How marvellous, I thought, to be, like him, a kind of giant squid of the book world, his long, searching tentacles poking about everywhere. But then again (I sighed), his main job was being an agent, a skilled negotiator about money, backing hunches, gambling on outcomes, knowing stuff about licences and sales to foreign 'territories' – it was all part of that busy, besuited commercial world in which I'd totally failed to immerse myself.

Then came the day somebody had an idea about handwriting.

A small article in the *Financial Times* had noted that some important banks – Morgan Stanley, Goldman Sachs, Citigroup – had started asking prospective employees to apply for jobs, not in typescript but in handwriting. Why? Because they were experimenting with *graphoanalysis* – the science of determining someone's character traits from the way they sloped their capital Ts or gave their surname a loopy flourish.

The article explained how no standard curriculum vitae could convey vital pieces of information about employees the way that handwriting could. Applicant X might persuade the Personnel department that he was a whizz at glad-handing potential clients; but it took a study of his curly Ys and bloated Bs to rumble the fact that he was a raging drunkard.

I was given the brief: find the City's top graphoanalyst, and send them samples of the handwriting of a dozen captains of industry, without (obviously) saying who they are, and ask for his or her comments.

It wasn't hard to find samples. The magazine's files were full of signed letters and handwritten cards from company bosses complaining about this or that article. I chose the 11 best examples, named their owners only by letter, from A to K, put the sheets in an envelope – and, at the last minute, for a laugh, I included a sample paragraph of my own writing.

You can guess what happened. The script inspector gave her judgements in crisp, no-nonsense bullet points, identifying lots of 'iron will', 'firm ambition', even 'a degree of ruthlessness' in over half the sample. Elsewhere, more benign boardroom virtues were given a nod: 'clear instructions' and 'unafraid to compromise' were both cited. It would all make for a perfectly readable article.

And then there was me. 'Sample L,' the analyst wrote, 'is a puzzle. While there is some evidence of strength of character and fluency of thought in this handwriting, no qualities of leadership are discernible, nor rigorous problem-solving, nor imaginative flair, nor, to be frank, any powerful ambition. I'd be surprised to discover that Sample L held any corporate position higher than that of middle manager, and one of an unusually disputatious character.'

Jesus. This was a blow. I went to see Carol. She laughed heartily.

'He's got you to a T, darling,' she said. 'But you mustn't be upset. You weren't really put on this earth to be a company director, were you?'

'But Carol,' I said, 'do you think I have no ambition?'

She considered this for a while. 'I think you have a *sort of* ambition, which is to become the youngest-ever Nobel Prize-winner for Literature. But since you haven't written anything apart from some journalistic pieces about sponsoring hot-air balloons, it's not an ambition that's stoking a fire in your guts, is it?'

I was crushed. I asked her what I ought to do.

'What you will do is this, John,' she said, as if she'd been saving it up. 'You'll go out this lunchtime and take a long walk around St James's Park, during which you'll think about the job you want to have by the time you're a certain age. I don't mean a *job market* or an *industry*. I mean a job that's currently held by *that* person, sitting in *that* chair, whom you will supplant when you're *that* age. OK?'

It was the best career advice I'd ever heard. So I went. The trees in St James's Park were like bosky sentinels. In the blue-and-white candy-striped bandstand, whiskery musicians in crimson uniforms played bits of Gilbert & Sullivan. I fed the last of my sandwich to a suspicious duck. Everything shouted of a new beginning. I thought of all the things I'd most enjoyed over the last couple of years – the people, the conversations, the excitements, George's friends. And I suddenly knew what I wanted.

Back in the office, I waited for Carol to get off the phone.

'How was the park?' she said eventually.

'Beautiful.'

'And did you—'

'Yes I did. So listen. You heard it here first. By the time I'm thirty-five, I'm going to be literary editor of *The Times*.'

'You see?' she said. 'Now *that's* an ambition. It means you must leave here, go freelance, meet new people, and write lots of reviews and literary articles – but anyone can see that's what you should've been doing for ages. You've now got seven years of working your way through Grub Street. I'll watch your progress with interest.'

CHAPTER 4

———— ◆ ————

Among the Bookmen

A few weeks after Carol's excellent advice, Fate decided to speed things up. On 8 June 1982, the post brought an invitation to a launch party that very evening for a book called *Recipes from a Château in Champagne*. Carol said it was far too short notice for her; would I like to go? Cookery and French castle management weren't things in which I had either expertise or passionate interest; but the book was co-authored by Sheila Bush, the wife of my old employer John Bush at Gollancz. I had happy memories of her, and thought I'd enjoy an hour of gastro-chatter and pricey alcoholic bubbles in her warm, engaging company.

The venue turned out to be Alexander Macmillan's grand house in Chelsea Square. I was impressed by the sweeping staircase, the *hauteur* of the flunkies and the trays of Dom Pérignon, but I knew no one. I moved through the bearded publisher's drawing room, feeling as at home as a horse in a swimming pool, while polished chatter rose and subsided around me. I tried to catch the author's eye but Mrs Bush was ringed by admirers, apparently avid for guidance about the correct preparation of *blanquettes de veau* at a château banquet.

Beside the table where copies of the book lay in piles like castle battlements, I fell into conversation with an American chap of my age. Cosmo Landesman was handsome, voluble and charming, and had a punchy verbal delivery, like someone pretending to be a 1930s Chicago gangster. 'Whaddya mean?' he'd ask, or (directed at a waitress who glided by without topping up his glass), 'Who da hell does she think *she* is?'

He punctuated his remarks with a repertoire of gestures and expressions, widening his eyes in shock, crinkling his brow with disapproval. He even did that thing James Cagney did in movies: he jerked his index finger towards his interlocutor to make a point ('I dunno about *choo* . . .'), then jerked his thumb towards himself to emphasise an opinion ('. . . but *I* think he's an asshole').

After we'd discussed Ry Cooder's recent triumph at the Hammersmith Odeon, as though looking for inspiration Cosmo suddenly cried, 'Hey! You wanna meet someone?' and walked me through the room to the drinks table. A short and slender young woman stood there, her eyes fixed on me, as if she'd silently summoned me to an audience; as if Cosmo had been some form of emissary.

'This is John,' said Cosmo, dialling down his tough-guy *shtick* to a low simmer. 'John, this is Carolyn Hart.'

Our eyes met. Hers were bushbaby-huge and River-Styx-dark, and they regarded me without warmth but with a kind of detached interest.

'Hi there,' I said. 'So, er, will this book come in handy next time you're in your castle in Champagne?'

'I haven't got one,' she said coolly. 'Though my cousin has a fortress in Puglia.'

'I wish *I* could brag about the old family seat,' I said, feeling outclassed, 'but it's just a ruined abbey in Galway.'

We drank some more fizz, and talked about travel and holidays, while Cosmo, having established that we'd connected, slunk away to startle some more English partygoers with his act. Carolyn turned out to be deputy editor of *Books and Bookmen*, a glossy but old-fashioned journal I'd seen in WH Smith's, along the shelf from *Dance and Dancers*, *Plays and Players*, *Art and Artists* – and, had I looked further, probably *Balloons and Balloonists* and *Tortures and Torturers* too.

By the time waiters started gathering empty glasses and Sheila Bush could be heard trillingly bidding farewell to her hundred best friends, Carolyn and I were still talking. She looked around, as though for a mislaid spouse, and was joined by Cosmo and two women. One was Sally Emerson, editor of *Books and Bookmen*, young and cheerful (I expected elderly and grave for such a venerable publication), with a feather-cut mane of jet-black hair and an endearing way of speaking into your face, as though she was trying to kiss you while conveying information. The other was Patricia Miller, a poodle-haired American dame with hard, suspicious blue eyes and a curious tic of shaking her head while making a point.

They stood on either side of Carolyn, as though protectively, and inspected her new friend. 'There's another book launch going on at a nightclub near here,' Carolyn said to me. 'You can come along if you like.' Sally and Patricia exchanged glances. I half-expected one of them to turn a thumb down, like Nero in the Colosseum. Cosmo intervened. 'You should come,' he said. 'It's the McEnroe party. Big night for the Yanks. C'mon!'

And suddenly, we were a little gang, as we rounded Chelsea Square, gained Fulham Road, filed down a long garden plot with globes and, beneath an awning, entered a club called Barbarella's. There I encountered, for my first time, a bank of paparazzi snappers brandishing giant cameras like a jostling and impatient firing squad.

This was a quite different affair from the sedate *politesse* of Lord Macmillan's château-nosh crowd. This was a cheap-white-wine-and-lots-of-it gathering, full of noise, flashing lights and excitement. The publishers of *The John McEnroe Story* had invited the sports staff of the national press, who were milling stolidly around in their burly sports jackets, drinking beer and asking the catering staff when the tennis brat – who'd won the Wimbledon singles championship the year before – might arrive. But they'd also

clearly asked a random crew of non-sporty Chelsea rich kids
(presumably the club's regular clientele) who lolled at the tables
beside the dance floor. As time went on, and the publishing chaps
assured the guests that the tennis star would arrive at any moment,
I drank a lot of Pinot grigio and talked to my new pals.

Cosmo's background was wild. His dad, Jay, from St Louis
Missouri, had published several of the Beat Poets in the 1940s, in
a magazine called *Neurotica*, and opened a nightclub where Woody
Allen and Lenny Bruce used to hang out. His mother was Fran
Landesman, a singer from New York, who wrote the song 'Spring
Can Really Hang You Up the Most' which I knew from the Ella
Fitzgerald songbook. Suddenly Cosmo's finger-clicking routine
seemed understandable. He wasn't playing at being a gangster; he
was being a finger-clicking 1950s hepcat. And I discovered he was
a sparkling and cynical wit.

Carolyn and I seemed to have hit it off pretty well – enough for
me to casually mention that I might be able to find a small hole in
my busy freelance schedule to review the odd thing for her
magazine. She'd agreed, without showing wild excitement at the
prospect: 'Maybe I'll send you something,' she'd said (probably
followed, sotto voce, by '. . . and maybe I won't.') By the time we
left the party and went for a nightcap in a nearby pub, I was elated.
I'd found a new professional home – not with a salaried job, true,
but I was suddenly linked – *associated with*, *in orbit around* – a
literary magazine, just as surely as was John Updike attached for
years to the *New Yorker*. I was on my way.

A few days later, the first Jiffy bag arrived from *Books and
Bookmen*. Hooray, I thought. This will be a major new novel by V. S.
Naipaul. Or perhaps John Fowles. It wasn't. The bag contained a
collection of humorous journalism by Miles Kington, the *Punch*
humorist and *Times* columnist. Was Carolyn serious? Should I
complain? But it soon dawned on me that I was being tried out,
like a new plumber, and they weren't wasting anything important
on the new bug.

I got over myself and got on with it. Kington's work was predictably brilliant – I loved the list of 'Badly Timed Publications' which included *So You Want to Be a Dirigible Pilot* (1937) – and said so as amusingly I could. After a few days, a note arrived, making no comment on my debut, but asking if I'd like to try a biography of Frank O'Connor, the Irish short story maestro. I rang the *B and B* office and asked: 'Are you holding the book right now? Can I come over and exchange it for a large bunch of roses?'

'No you can't,' she replied. 'But you can buy me supper at Manzi's if you'd care to.'

So now I was a *regular* reviewer – and I became part of the *Books and Bookmen* weekly party gang.

Every Thursday, and some Tuesdays too, Sally and Carolyn would hold court at Winston's Wine Bar in Museum Street, the magazine's HQ. We'd drink wine and gossip and the same people would join us: Sally's husband, Peter Stothard, a Trinity Oxford classicist, charming, benign, and keen to downplay his sharp political intelligence – he was then deputy editor of *The Times*, later to become editor and, later still, to edit the *TLS*; Patricia, the blue-eyed, curly-topped Kansas dame with the sharp appraising eye; Terence Blacker, late of Wellington and Cambridge, a publisher turned author; and Tim Satchell, a suave, chortling gossip columnist. Something of a clone of his one-time boss Nigel Dempster, Tim always wore yellow socks and parlayed valuable chitchat from his drinking cronies at Annabel's and Tramp, the Strangers' Bar at the House of Commons, and the less reputable bar of Soho's notorious Colony Room, into sophisticated paragraphs for the *Mail* and the *Telegraph*; he kept the bookish anecdotes for our magazine.

One June, he came to our wine-bar gathering, and to the launch parties that followed, straight from the train, still in his Ascot regalia (navy tailcoat, grey trousers, dove-grey waistcoat, tie, tie-pin) from earlier that day. I clocked the little metal tags that hung from his waistcoat, telling the world he was an honoured guest at the royal racetrack rather than a gossip hack. I thought him a slightly ludicrous show-off. But he grew on me.

Three years had passed since the launch of the new magazines in 1979, and the literary landscape had changed in some crucial ways. One was the belatedly explosive effect of the Booker Prize. By 1980, the prize had been around for a decade and, despite being the UK's answer to France's classy Prix Goncourt, had become colourless and lacklustre, enlivened only by some outbreaks of controversy at the prize-giving dinners.

Things changed in 1980, when, on a shortlist of seven books, two literary heavyweights, both men, each the author of a rock-solid twentieth-century classic English novel, were in the ring: Anthony Burgess, the crazily prolific, omnilingual, breezily polyglot author of *A Clockwork Orange*, was shortlisted for *Earthly Powers*, while William Golding, the grave, patriarchally bearded, ex-RN former schoolteacher and author of *Lord of the Flies*, was his main rival with *Rites of Passage*.

The promise of an elderly (Golding was sixty-nine, Burgess sixty-three) punch-up between modern versions of Dickens and Thackeray caught the public's attention. It was sharpened by three things: a terrific *Sunday Times* caricature by the political cartoonist Richard Willson, of the two men with tiny bodies and monumental heads like the presidential bonces on Mount Rushmore; by Burgess's snarky summation of *Rites of Passage* ('A bad book . . . all too easily put down'); and by the prospect of their meeting each other for the first time at the prize-giving dinner in Stationers' Hall. Newspapers speculated, chauvinistically, about which author would prevail; look at these two brilliant Englishmen (read the subtext), two home-grown world-beaters showing the world that British culture is best.

In the event, the contenders didn't meet, and the dinner was anticlimactic, because Burgess failed to show up. According to

Martyn Goff, of the Booker Prize Foundation, he spent the evening sulking in his room at the Savoy Hotel after being told he hadn't won. Burgess himself denied the sulking; he said he was jet-lagged and hadn't brought a dinner jacket.

A year later, in 1981, the Booker was back in the news for a different reason: it was, for the first time, to be televised as a stand-alone show. In 1976 the proceedings had been shown live as a segment in BBC's *Tonight* programme, at the prompting of a young arts correspondent called Melvyn Bragg. Bragg's boss on *Tonight* was Brian Wenham who, in 1981, came to an agreement with the prize organisers to broadcast the dinner and prize-giving on BBC2, annually. The show would offer viewers live footage of the milling crowds of publishers, authors, journalists and Booker management, a panel discussion between three literary pontificators – then cut to Stationers' Hall for live broadcast of the chair of judges announcing the winner.

There was excitement in the air. Everyone remembered the clash-of-the-Titans drama of the previous year. The shortlist featured two young-ish writers (Salman Rushdie, thirty-four, and Ian McEwan, thirty-three) squaring up to three veteran literary dames: Doris Lessing, sixty-two, Muriel Spark, sixty-three, and Molly Keane, seventy-seven, along with the forty-ish Ann Schlee and D. M. Thomas. This Youth-versus-Age dynamic hadn't been seen before. And, most important, people were curious to see how serious-minded literary figures (especially the glamorous ones, especially Nigella Lawson) scrubbed up for the TV cameras.

The judges were heavyweights: Brian Aldiss, the SF writer who had helped Rushdie's first novel *Grimus* win a prize in 1975; Joan Bakewell, the arts broadcaster; Hermione Lee, the biographer of Virginia Woolf, and with Malcolm Bradbury, professor of English and American literature at the University of East Anglia, in the chair. But when Rushdie accepted the prize and stood, modestly smiling, looking young and awkwardly student-like with his owlish spectacles, his hooded, Garfield-the-cat eyes and slightly askew bow-tie, he managed to eclipse them all.

Because he was a major part of a second crucial change in the literary landscape. The English novel, so recently considered moribund, backward-looking and stale, had experienced a startling new wave of excitement, ambition, novelty and achievement. Hardly had *Granta*'s sneery denunciations hit the bookshops, when a new generation of talent had emerged to join Amis and McEwan. Writers such as Timothy Mo, a twenty-eight-year-old, British-Hong-Kong Oxford graduate, whose day job was fight reporter on *Boxing News*, and whose debut novel, *The Monkey King*, was a dazzling serio-comic family saga set in postwar Hong Kong. Or Julian Barnes, whose *Metroland* took the temperature of middle-class Englishness; we see its hero, Christopher, as a schoolboy would-be sophisticate and mocker of the bourgeoisie, who learns to love his backyard and to embrace happiness rather than see it as a despicable enemy of progress. Or Kazuo Ishiguro, whose *A Pale View of Hills*, a brilliantly original ghost story set in England and post-war Nagasaki, tells the story of two women who meet in the wasteland their city has become. The narrative proceeds with haunted formality like a Kabuki drama, where everything is indistinct and contingent, especially the lives of children. Or Rose Tremain, whose *Letter to Sister Benedicta* is a heartbreakingly jaunty depiction of a woman reflecting on her childhood in India and her husband's paralysis. Or William Boyd, whose *A Good Man in Africa* relates the gloriously funny adventures of Morgan Leafy, a minor apparatchik at the British Deputy High Commission in the west African state of Kinjanja. Fat, lazy, horny, and in constant danger of being fired, Morgan becomes mired in corruption with a local politician, is tasked with the removal of a dead body without outraging voodoo protocol and, while recovering from gonorrhoea, yearns for his boss's daughter Priscilla. *Lucky Jim* meets *Black Mischief*, with a bracing undercurrent of moral enquiry. Or D. M. Thomas, whose *The White Hotel* begins with a poem of eye-popping sexuality and violence, proceeds through Freudian case history, and ends with the massacre at Babi Yar in a delirious amalgam of *Eros* and *Thanatos*.

Or, of course, Rushdie, with his prize-winning novel, *Midnight's Children*, the most remarkable literary phenomenon of the early 1980s. Its qualities and uniqueness may take some explaining. It stood out from all the other books I read in 1980 and 1981 in being borderline impenetrable. The first dozen pages gave us – no, *flung* at us – a handful of characters who weren't so much described as *muttered about* in a rambling, disjointed, elliptical fashion.

There was Saleem Sinai, the book's narrator, born on the stroke of midnight, 15 August 1947, the exact second that India won its independence from the British Raj; Saleem's life, we learn, is going to be intertwined with the new life of India. Then we read about his grandfather Aadam Aziz, a doctor just back from Germany in 1915, who bangs his nose while trying to pray: the blow produces blood, which becomes rubies, and sweat which turns into diamonds. Then we flounder amidst allusions to Kashmir, Srinagar and Heidelberg, hearing the voices of friends, of prayers, of his mother, of the lake boatman Tai. We learn also about the presence of big noses in the Aziz family. As I wondered what to make of the author's style, he supplied an answer: he described Tai the boatman's chatter as 'fantastic, grandiloquent and ceaseless, and as often as not addressed only to himself.'

That wasn't quite fair, though. The grandiloquent chatter was also addressed to readers with a specific interest in eighteenth-century English and twentieth-century Euro-Latin-American literature. As Dr Aziz went visiting patients, some familiar notes could be heard bonging away beneath the text. There were several allusions to Laurence Sterne's multi-volume novel *Tristram Shandy*, published between 1759 and 1766. On the first page of *Midnight's Children*, in the middle of all the stuff about chiming midnight clocks, I read 'A few seconds later, my father broke his big toe' – itself a chime with page one of *Shandy*, when Tristram's mother, with disastrous timing, asks her husband while they're making love, 'Pray, my dear, have you not forgot to wind up the clock?', disturbing the balance of 'humours and dispositions' that would otherwise have formed a perfect child. Things became more explicit by page 44, when Padma ticks off Saleem for his long-windedness and says, 'At this rate, you'll be two hundred years old before you manage to tell about your birth'. This is exactly Tristram's problem – the myriad digressions in his narrative mean that he won't write about his own birth until Volume Three.

Other notes derived from the more modern musical register of magical realism. From early in *Midnight's Children*, people and things change their essence, get born or die in unnatural ways. Just as Dr Aziz's blood and sweat become rubies and diamonds, a vision of his mother becomes a lizard and sticks its tongue out at him. When the boatman Tai gives up washing, his bodily fumes make flowers die and birds flee from window ledges. Time itself is stretched and foreshortened. When Dr Aziz is called in to examine a rich landowner's stricken daughter, he finds a bedchamber in which three muscular handmaidens hold up a large bed-sheet in which a hole has been cut, through which his patient gradually obtrudes bits of her body that are supposedly afflicted with ailments. Dr Aziz is gradually allowed to put his healing hands only on his patient's extremities; later he gets to touch a breast, then a buttock. And we learn it's taken him only *three years* to be allowed such access.

I found a distinct whiff of *The Benny Hill Show* about this coyly leering disclosure of flesh – but a more obviously literary predecessor was Gabriel García Márquez. In his *One Hundred Years of Solitude*, torrential rainstorms go on for years, cows crop green baize from billiard tables in dilapidated mansions, and trickles of blood from a murder victim climb the stairs looking for the victim's mother. Rushdie explores the comic potential offered by the elasticity of time and emotion. So we learn about an 'epidemic of optimism' breaking out in India in 1942. A row in the Aziz household leads to Naseem (known as the 'Reverend Mother') refusing to feed her husband for years; it becomes 'a war of starvation'. The Reverend Mother is a termagant who starts to dream her daughter's dreams (an *Arabian Nights* equivalent of the phrase 'woman's intuition'), and yells at her husband for one hour, nineteen minutes.

A more striking innovation of Rushdie's book was the appearance, in the narrative, of real historical figures from India's path to independence. Brigadier General Reginald Dyer – the infamous Butcher of Amritsar, who in 1919 ordered his fifty troops to fire on a gathering of unarmed Indian civilians, killing at least four hundred and precipitating the end of the Raj – has a walk-on part, as do Gandhi, Sir Stafford Cripps and Lord Wavell.

Gradually, I made out the enormous scale of Rushdie's ambitions. I'd read the *Arabian Nights* as a kid and knew that, alongside stories about genies and beggars, they could involve real people such as Harun al-Rashid. I dimly knew that the *Mahabharata* was about a family and the battle between members for control of something-or-other (a jewel? A round table? A palace?). When I saw that the narrative of *Midnight's Children* hurtled around parents and children, aristos and lowlifes – boatmen, spittoon-hawkers, chutney-makers – with walk-on parts for real people, I had an inkling of what the author was up to. He was trying to construct a whole new literary language for India.

I wondered if Rushdie had become wearied by the obsessive treatment of India on successive Booker shortlists since 1971. V. S. Naipaul won it that year for *In a Free State*; as did J. G. Farrell for *The Siege of Krishnapur* in 1973; ditto Ruth Prawer Jhabvala for *Heat and Dust* in 1975, ditto Paul Scott for *Staying On* in 1977. Naipaul was on the shortlist again in 1979 with *A Bend in the River* (set in Africa but narrated by an Indian Muslim called Salim), and Anita Desai was shortlisted for *Clear Light of Day* in 1980, the year before Rushdie lifted the trophy himself.

The narrating voices in these books were, almost without exception, polite British-literary. They sounded like this: 'The first sign of trouble at Krishnapur came with a mysterious distribution of chapatis, made of coarse flour and about the size and thickness of a biscuit'. The voices never came close to authentic Indian, whether in Brahmin or demotic registers. Even V. S. Naipaul's first-person voice, supposedly that of a deracinated Indian merchant, sounds like an irritable Englishman far from Surrey: 'It wasn't only the sand-drifts and the mud and the narrow, winding, broken roads up in the mountains. There was all that business at the frontier posts ... I had to talk myself and my Peugeot past the men with guns – just to drive through bush and more bush.'

Disdaining the Booker-English idiom, Rushdie plunged into a wondrous Babel of effects, vocal and stylistic: there was babu-speak and boatman-speak ('nakkoo', 'babaji', 'tahkt', 'funtoosh', 'nibu-pani'), and family-servant-speak ('It's going to be a real ten-rupee baby; yes, sir! A whopper of a ten-chip pomfret, wait and see!') and stylish upper-crust English food-related metaphors: 'Family history, of course, has its proper dietary laws. One is supposed to swallow and digest only the permitted parts of it, the halal portions of the past, drained of their redness, their blood. Unfortunately, this makes the stories less juicy ...' Or 'the feasibility of the chutnification of history; the grand hope of the pickling of time!'

By halfway through, I was dazzled, impressed, bewildered and frankly exhausted. It was brilliant – and it was just too much to process. All the dreams and mythologies, the births and deaths, the arguments and magic transformations, the tumbling, endlessly distracted logorrhoeic cascade of words and subjects, the jumping-bumping, hyperadrenalinated, huggery-muggery, jiggery-pokery tsunami of special effects. It was all very impressive but just a touch *frantic*.

I thought Rushdie was trying too hard to convey *hilarity*, Keystone Kops slapstick, the speeded-up fun of the fairground, while simultaneously dealing with weighty matters of Indian history and identity. James Joyce had a word for this quality: 'jocoserious', the business of being both earnest and strenuously farcical at the same time.

Evidently the judges hadn't allowed such objections to sway their admiration. Everyone agreed that British fiction had suddenly taken a giant leap forward, taking a million playful liberties with the language, virtually inventing a new Anglo-Indian idiolect while throwing cheery nods to the European past in a way not seen since *Ulysses*.

The transatlantic reading public pricked up its ears. A few months later, in the *Sunday Times*, Hunter Davies reported excitedly on a new boom: 'Two years ago, the average publisher in Britain was a deeply pessimistic figure. His sales were slipping, his costs soaring and his catalogues being cut back. The bestseller lists were dominated by a dispiriting combination of royal-family books, "TV tie-in" books, guidebooks . . . In the fiction market, pulp carried everything before it.

'Since then, something strange has happened. Four novels, all winners or finalists in the annual Booker Prize, have sold in such staggering quantities that they have begun to change the whole attitude of British publishers to their trade. The serious novel is back.'

The books in question were, of course, *Earthly Powers, Rites of Passage, Midnight's Children* and *The White Hotel*. 'None is an easy read, they are intellectually demanding,' Davies warned his readers, 'A lot of innocent buyers will have found them thoroughly daunting. But they have sold and sold. By the end of this month [February 1982] there will be half a million copies of these four books, in hardback and paperback, either sold or on sale in Britain. In the US, the figure is closer to two million. Between them the four have sold foreign rights in forty foreign countries. On book sales around the world, the total turnover should in the end be worth around £8 million.'

This was a startling development. Not only was the serious British novel having a rebirth; it was, amazingly, a commercial success. And the Booker Prize and its shortlists had woken up the British reading public to the spectacular richness of the fiction worlds abroad, especially India, Canada, Africa and Australia, and some names that would come to dominate the English-language novel: along with Rushdie would come Atwood, Carey, Desai, Coetzee, Okri and Ondaatje.

Luckily for British readers, a third development in the book world now made it possible to access new books in numbers unheard of in the days of WH Smith and John Menzies. The new phenomenon was called Tim Waterstone. He had been born in Glasgow in 1939 and grew up in East Sussex. He went to Tonbridge School with Frederick (*Jackal*) Forsyth and studied English at St Catherine's College, Cambridge, attending lectures by the quarrelsome, belligerent F. R. Leavis and the sainted C. S. Lewis. In his student years, Waterstone spent hours browsing in Heffers, the 'anchor bookseller' of Cambridge, the city's equivalent of Blackwell's in Oxford. One term-time afternoon, he experienced an epiphany, 'a stunning moment of sudden, unexpected, joyful clarity.' As a friend walked past, 'I told him that, one day, I was going to do this, like Heffers but better than Heffers, the best in the land, and all over the land.'

He left Cambridge with a third-class degree, but never relinquished his bookseller ambition. He became a successful businessman, first with Allied Breweries at the tender age of twenty-six, before moving to WH Smith at thirty-five. He found the UK's largest bookshop chain 'highly nepotistic' and 'excruciatingly feudal'. For years he nursed in his bones a detailed business model of how a new kind of bookshop chain might work; and got his chance when he was fired by the WH Smith chairman, Simon Hornby in 1981.

Waterstone had identified a niche in the bookselling market. He had noted how WH Smith, despite its 35 per cent market share, were keener on flogging bestsellers than literary fiction and were pulling back from selling books *in general*, in favour of videos, music, toys, cards and stationery. Much space was given up to best-sellers and 'gift' books.

Waterstone recalls in his memoirs that, although the capital could boast some old-fashioned shops that operated like gentle-men's clubs (John Sandoe in Chelsea, Heywood Hill in Curzon

Street), 'we all found it inexplicable that a city as great and as culturally diverse as London had within it ... no stockholding literary bookshops at all, and certainly not one – Foyles, Hatchards, Dillons, not one of them – that was open at the weekend after lunchtime on Saturdays, let alone on weekday evenings.'

He wanted to produce a chain that sold only real books, literary fiction, poetry from small houses, biographies, art tomes, film books, science books – and fill the shops, floor to ceiling, with titles that people longed to buy; he wanted to cram the shelves with vast amounts of stock, and to staff the shops with people who knew their subject and could enthuse with the punters about what was on the shelves. And he wanted to have his shops stay open until 10 p.m., every day and at weekends.

With bank and family loans amounting to £125,000, he found a site for the first branch in the Old Brompton Road, Kensington and bought a lease. In July 1982, he put a now-famous advertisement in the Recruitment section of the *Evening Standard*:

> *Required: Experienced Booksellers for a new bookshop – Waterstone's in Old Brompton Road. Opening in September. The first of many. Our object is to have the best literary bookshops in the land, staffed by the best, happiest, literary booksellers.*

There was an unusual, hippie-ish ring to the word 'happiest' in the advert, but it worked. In no time, four of the six available jobs were snapped up by staffers from Hatchards in Piccadilly. It wasn't a coincidence. The main reason for their enthusiasm was that they hadn't had a pay rise for two years.

The first bookshop bearing the chairman's name and the company's W logo opened its doors at 9 a.m. on 30 September 1982. The seven staff, including Tim, watched with interest as the first customer walked in, headed for the Reference section, bought a copy of the Koran and took it to the till to pay. Waterstone's was in business. In the next ten years, it would revolutionise British bookselling.

* * *

Books and Bookmen differed from *Granta*, *Quarto*, the *Literary Review* and the *LRB* in three ways: a) in being a venerable old warhorse of a books magazine, dating back to 1955, when it was launched by Philip Dosse as part of his stable of art publications, Hansom Books; b) in never, but *never*, expressing any opinion whatsoever about the imminent death of the English novel, and c) in soliciting book reviews, not just from academics and literary hacks, but from luminaries in the worlds of politics, the army and the aristocracy.

Books and Bookmen was home to the Old Guard of British literary-political culture, the *ancien régime* of the Men (and Women) of Letters that had supposedly died out in the war. Every month, its cover carried the names of elderly literati and people who'd spent their working careers in ermine: Virginia Woolf's nephew, Quentin Bell, Harold Acton, Lord Quinton, Lord Hailsham and Lord Soper. Alongside elderly historians and biographers such as Lady Longford and A. L. Rowse, you'd find Roger Lancelyn Green (the children's author who had been one of the discussion group, the 'Inklings', in the late 1930s, along with Tolkien and C. S. Lewis), Hugh Montgomery-Massingberd, former editor of *Burke's Peerage* – and Sir Iain Moncreiffe of That Ilk, self-confessed snob, absolute whizz at matters of heraldry, and reviewer of such esoteric works as *Equestrian Splendour: The Royal Office of Master of the Horse* by M. M. Reese.

I wasn't surprised to learn that Christina Foyle, venerable owner of the dustily chaotic Foyles bookshop in Charing Cross Road, was so fond of the magazine that she used to send copies through the post to her best customers (cheekily renaming it 'Foylibra') and would leave a copy on every chair around the table at Grosvenor House, where she presided over her monthly Literary Lunches.

The mistress of our revels at Winston's Wine Bar, Sally Emerson, was precisely my age (twenty-eight) and was a living bridge between two literary generations. She'd first worked for *Books and Bookmen* aged seventeen in 1971, just before she went up to Oxford to study English (at St Anne's, the same college as her friend Tina

Brown). It had been an amazing stroke of luck: her parents lived in Vincent Square, around the corner from the Hansom Books HQ, and Sally's mother had a university friend who reviewed for the magazines. She'd heard that Philip Dosse was looking for an editorial dogsbody, for the generous stipend of £12 a week. Sally applied, and got the job.

What she found there was straight out of the 1950s. As a boss, Dosse was both tyrannical ('Everyone was terrified of him. Lots of mood swings and people being sacked one day, then reinstated the next') and secretive ('No one ever knew what anyone was being paid') and gay. It soon dawned on the new arrival that the magazine was a gay ghetto. 'That's one reason why it was so successful. They could get really good people, who might find it hard to work in a straight milieu, for very reasonable prices.' The presence of a fire station just down the road, staffed by brawny firefighters, was a source of daily excitement.

The people she met in 1971, when she attended bookish events, were from a different era: the days of Bloomsbury, Modernism, the Bright Young Things. She interviewed Olivia Manning, author of the *Balkans Trilogy*, whose first novel was published in 1937; and William Gerhardie, the Anglo-Russian author of *Futility* and *The Polyglots*, whose work in the 1920s was praised by Evelyn Waugh and H. G. Wells.

'I went to see Gerhardie in Hallam Mansions off Oxford Street,' Sally told me. 'He was a very strange person. He was wearing a completely plastic suit, possibly with several other clothes underneath.' She once met Jorge Luis Borges, the great Argentinian surrealist and magical realist, after he gave a talk in Victoria, aged seventy-two. She visited Waugh's friend and Oxford contemporary Harold Acton, the seraphic, immaculately well-mannered super-aesthete, at his family home, La Pietra, in Tuscany, and found him 'a man of enormous charm and intelligence', though he displayed utter helplessness when trying to entertain Sally's baby daughter, Anna.

After Oxford, where she edited *Isis*, Sally returned to Dosse's
embrace in 1976, working on *Plays and Players* under Michael
Coveney and writing her first novel *Second Sight*. Two years later,
she was moved to *Books and Bookmen*, where she resumed relations
with the *B and B* reviewers and, to her pleasure, in meeting giant
figures – good, bad and ugly – from the past.

Sally once shared with me the entry from her diary of 27
September 1978, after a lunch to which she was taken by
Philip Dosse:

> *Yesterday I had lunch with Oswald and Diana Mosley at the
> penthouse flat they borrowed from Mark Longman. The Duchess of
> Devonshire, Diana's sister, was there, as was her son and his wife,
> a very beautiful girl. Oswald M. has long, ape-like arms and a
> large head, with enormous ears sticking out. He shuffles. Diana's
> eyes are immense, an incredible blue, her bone structure quite
> beautiful and her voice ultra-upper class – rather like Virginia
> Woolf's, I imagine.*
>
> *They talked about the Sitwells and 'Evelyn' as though they were
> still alive, and remarked that Sacheverell Sitwell's son was oafish.
> 'When he goes to people's houses,' said the Duchess, 'he spends half
> an hour before each picture. I suppose it's rather sweet that he
> should be impressed.' Diana still had a cook and butler who, she
> says, 'behave with civility'. Oswald propounds 'the importance of
> each according to their gifts . . .'*
>
> *As we sit down to lunch, builders stomp up and down the roof,
> which seems to amuse Lady Mosley no end. We had perfectly cooked
> anchovy eggs, chicken in sauce, cheese and crunchy cinnamon apples
> from the Temple de la Gloire, her beautiful château in Paris.*
>
> *After the meal, Oswald looks blue in the face; he's a sinister-
> looking man. Diana is strange, ethereal, with her soft, cajoling
> voice – so concerned about her friends. Harold Acton, whom she
> writes to regularly, said that looking into her eyes is 'like looking
> into an enormous blue dome, with the same sense of emptiness.'*

> *Philip [Dosse] who went with me, chattered in the car about the Mosleys' time in Holloway prison: 'apparently, quite soon they were moved into a little house in the prison grounds, where they grew vegetables.' 'Of course!' I thought with a shiver, they would have been.*

Reading this encounter, one is conscious of the chasm of sensibility and social understanding that separates the Mitford generation and that of the early 1980s, a chasm that the creative works of young British writers – the Amis generation – were about to exploit.

One of that generation was Sally herself. Her first novel *Second Sight*, published in 1980, was an immersive dive into the psychology of a fifteen-year-old London girl, Jennifer, who's trying to come to terms with the death of her best friend, Rebecca, killed in a road accident. Also troubling her is the cheerful amorality of her mother. In the opening pages, Jennifer goes to her mama's restaurant after hours and, in the basement, discovers her *in flagrante delicto* with her lover, Saul. The sight of her mother Sarah 'spreadeagled, a sacrificial victim, over one of the drinks tables [and] the mat of pubic hair, the nipples, the red distorted face' do nothing to improve Jennifer's emotional equilibrium, but things soon become more complicated. Saul, an LA-based crime writer, visits Jennifer's father at Sarah's behest, to persuade him to write about some of the murder cases being tried at the Old Bailey that year – one of which involved a victim who resembles Rebecca, her dead friend.

Showing a flair for physical description, especially of bodies and rooms, Sally also introduced an effect I hadn't come across before: Jennifer's vivid relationship with Percy Shelley, the poet, who, far from being dead for 158 years, is enlisted as a friend and guide (and walker at parties) to the virginal adolescent; so is Aphra Behn, the Restoration playwright and subject of Jennifer's father's recent biography. Just as Martin Amis crammed his debut novel with literary allusions amidst the carnival of adolescent sex, Sally Emerson went one better by bringing two dead writers back to life, to help her main character's journey through adolescence.

It seemed amazing that someone like Sally could have had lunch with the Mosleys only three or four years previously, and was now lunching with the *jeunesse dorée* of modern young writers such as Amis and Barnes. I mentioned, in a callow, braggartish way, that I'd recently had dinner with some people that included Douglas Adams, and she'd nodded sweetly. Perhaps she didn't want to steal my thunder by mentioning that she'd been having a raging affair with Douglas for some months, after meeting him at a literary event.

The talk, at the pre-party, catch-up sessions in Winston's Wine Bar, was all publishing gossip. Everything seemed to be about sex and money. Pat Miller, who wrote gossip for *Publishing News*, seemed to have an amazing inside track about who was currently shagging whom. Her information seemed to come largely from editors and agents with whom Pat had herself enjoyed sexual congress in the past. She came across as a tireless, and shameless *horizontale*, with a slightly shocking determination to dish the dirt, and a fabulously throaty laugh. There was much talk of Alan This and Patrick That, of how one had propositioned a foreign rights buyer, or the other had invited a married-but-bored agent to join him on a trip to Paris. Of shocking behaviour at the annual Frankfurt Book Fair, and of panty raids and bathroom jiggery-pokery at the Grandhotel Hessischer Hof, many stories were repeated.

Stories of money and deals and sky-high advances on forth-coming books were meat and drink to Terence Blacker, with Pat supplying extra details. Amid our little gang of magazine regulars, Terence was the only one with authentic publishing experience. His CV spoke of an eclectic life. After Cambridge, he'd worked as a jockey, but given it up and moved to Paris to work in a bookshop. Back in London he'd found a job as a foreign sales rep at Hutchinson, and travelled around Europe for two years. Then, in a move that resembled the junior footman in Downton Abbey being invited to join the gentry in the dining room, he was made an editor at Hutchinson's paperback imprint, Arrow. 'It was regarded as a very

odd, irregular and risky appointment,' he told me, 'as if they'd
hired a chimpanzee.'

   He and Pat, Sally and Carolyn talked about the main shakers in
the publishing world and, from a starting position of blank
ignorance, I gradually familiarised myself with the leading players
in late 1982. They were, alphabetically:

Liz Calder
Age (in 1982): 44
Appearance: American model turned TV news anchor
Defining quality: Serenity under pressure

Though as English as treason, Calder spent much of her youth on
the other side of the world. Born in 1938 to a former coal-miner
and lay-preacher father, and a piano-teaching mother, she and her
siblings lived over their parents' grocery shop in Edgware, north
London, until they emigrated to New Zealand in 1949. After
graduating, Liz married a Rolls-Royce engineer whose work sent
their growing family to England, Canada, America and Brazil,
where Liz worked as a fashion model and journalist. Back in
London, newly divorced, she worked writing reports on new
fiction for MGM, before joining Victor Gollancz (see Chapter 2) as
publicity director, then head of editorial. She discovered Salman
Rushdie, John Irving, D. M. Thomas, Julian Barnes and, after Tom
Maschler persuaded her to move to Jonathan Cape, signed up
Anita Brookner, Margaret Atwood, Isabel Allende and Lisa St
Aubin de Teran. 'I wasn't trying to build a feminist list, but I was
definitely on the lookout in a determined way for women writers,'
she said in interview. 'I published a lot of overtly and inherently
feminist fiction reflecting on people's lives.' Universally liked in a
combative industry, she co-founded Women in Publishing in 1979,
and the Groucho Club in Soho (see Chapter 7). Calder was
credited with having perfect pitch when it came to judging the
quality of a newcomer – her taste was uncompromised by her not

going through the Oxbridge system and sharing the taste of other
British publishing editors. She always looked, she said, for books
that offered the 'opening of another world – whether of the
imagination or another place – that's exhilarating to enter.'

Carmen Callil
Age (in 1982): 44
Appearance: Menacing nanny
Defining quality: Being difficult

The tough, tempestuous but game-changing Callil brought a
wild colonial spirit to London publishing when she set up Virago
Press in 1972. But she showed her independence from the start.
In 1964, newly arrived in London, she put an advertisement in
The Times, reading 'Australian, BA, wants job in book publishing'
(note: it did not say 'seeks'). Inside a year she was working at
Hutchinson's, as publicity boss of Panther paperbacks, and later
at Andre Deutsch. Then she took a career break and worked for
the flower-children/Underground magazine, *Ink*. There she met
the journalists Marsha Rowe and Rosie Boycott and formed a
kind of feminist alliance. Her new friends set up *Spare Rib*
magazine; Carmen founded Spare Rib Books, which became
Virago, dedicated 'to publish books which celebrated women
and women's lives and which would, by doing so, spread the
message of women's liberation to the whole population.' Starting
out by reprinting classic proto-feminist novels (*Frost in May* by
Antonia White was an early success), Virago began to publish
new work, guided by four other women: Ursula Owen, Harriet
Spicer, Lennie Goodings and Alexandra Pringle. There were
reports of heated discussions among the quintet, of Carmen's
strength of character and occasional intransigence, of emotional
outpourings and young secretaries fleeing in tears to the lavatory,
but Virago flourished.

In 1982, Carmen was named as managing director of Chatto & Windus, part of a new three-way conglomerate with Cape and Bodley Head. She stayed on as chair of Virago, prompting some commentators to suggest that her commitment to feminism might be eclipsed by her commitment to the bottom line. Few people said this to her face.

Richard Cohen
Age: (in 1982) 35
Appearance: Charismatic maths teacher
Defining Quality: Geniality

In a world where most publishers' only connection with sport is a game of squash, Richard Cohen stood out a mile. The Brummie beanpole was introduced to fencing at Downside School, was British Sabre Champion five times and represented the UK at four Olympic Games. He's still the only publisher in history to appear in a Bond film – *Die Another Day*, where he impressed Madonna and Rosamund Pike with his cool swordsmanship.

His career in the web of words started on *Frontier*, an Anglican-based current-affairs magazine which brought him to the attention of Lady Collins, with whom he discussed religious books. Summoned to her husband's publishing company, Cohen found himself, at twenty-six, responsible for editing the work of many established authors with 'difficult' reputations. Among them was Alistair Maclean, who disliked being told that his plot featured too many 'luscious blondes', or that four of his characters were called Jackson, Johnson, Jackman and Johnstone. As fiction editor at Hodder & Stoughton, Cohen edited John le Carré and James Clavell, took on Morris West and Thomas Kenneally, who won the Booker for *Schindler's Ark*. In 1985, Cohen left Hodder to become publishing director at Hutchinson, in the middle of a massive industry shake-up that involved a score of imprints, enormous investments from the City of London, and the sharky manoeuvres of the American Random House group. Cohen survived it all and oversaw the careers of Fay Weldon, Anthony Burgess, James Herriot, Kingsley Amis and later Sebastian Faulks. He is, however, most famous as the man who helped Jeffrey Archer write his massive-selling early thrillers, possibly the most successful (though perhaps not most highbrow) author-editor partnership since Edward Garnett and D.H. Lawrence.

André Deutsch

Age (in 1982): 65
Appearance: Mitteleuropean leprechaun
Defining quality: Parsimony

Short, prickly, mercurial and penny-pinching, but ferocious in promoting good writing, Deutsch was one of a group of European Jewish refugees – along with Tom Maschler, George Weidenfeld and Tom Rosenthal – who put down postwar roots in England and flourished in London publishing. Born in Budapest and educated in Vienna, like Maschler he fled the Austrian capital at the Anschluss and made it to England. When the war began, he was interned as an enemy alien on the Isle of Man – but there he met a European publisher who impressed him enough to want to follow his choice of career.

He started Andre Deutsch Ltd in 1951. His first success was the minor comic masterpiece of national stereotyping, *How to Be an Alien* by George Mikes, with illustrations by Nicholas Bentley. Less amusing were the memoirs of Franz von Papen, Hitler's top diplomat. Deutsch managed to sell the serial rights to an English Sunday paper for £30,000, and it became a bestseller, but protesting voices were raised about the propriety of selling books by people who had only recently been mortal enemies.

Deutsch changed tack and contacted his Jewish-immigrant friends in the New York publishing world. He had a coup with Norman Mailer's gritty first novel, *The Naked and the Dead*, set during the Korean War. Its most notable feature was the presence on every soldier's lips, of the word 'fug'. When the actress Hermione Gingold met the author at a party, she said, 'Oh yeah – you're the young man who can't spell "fuck".'

Deutsch also presided over the careers of John Updike, Laurie Lee, V. S. Naipaul, Peter (*Jaws*) Benchley and the economist J. K. Galbraith. He was the most beadily focused of publishers; at parties he would target a writer for an hour, insisting that he or she write a book for him. But he was also famously mean: he saved bits of string, reused old brown paper, measured out the sugar in his employees' tea and put 20-watt lightbulbs in the company loo to discourage reading therein. He was, however, awesomely well connected: when he commissioned the sports writer Frank Keating to write about the England First XI cricket tour of the West Indies in 1980, he offered him 'expenses' in the form of letters he'd sent to some Caribbean people asking for their help. He showed Keating the names: among them were three of Deutsch's former Black Movement student authors: Eric Williams, Forbes Burnham and Michael Manley. They were now prime ministers of Trinidad and Tobago, Guyana and Jamaica respectively.

Pat Kavanagh
Age (in 1982): 42
Appearance: Regal dominatrix
Defining quality: Inscrutable silence

Raised in South Africa, the top literary agent had an early brush with literature when she came to England in 1964: she landed a part (uncredited) in the classic 1972 recording of Dylan Thomas's radio play *Under Milk Wood*. She was unpaid but still (she said) 'got to snog Richard Burton'. She had an early break after she answered a newspaper ad, and found herself being mentored by an early doyen of the agenting world, Augustus Dudley Peters.

Under his tutelage she found herself negotiating serial rights for Arthur Koestler, Rebecca West and Tom Wolfe. She was the first agent of the literary stars of the early 1980s, Martin Amis, Tina Brown, and Julian Barnes, whom she met in 1978 and married a year later.

As an agent, she was admired and respected, but was a tough negotiator (Koestler called her 'my little shark'), feared because of her way with few words. She would name a figure that a publisher had to pay to secure her client's next book. Then she would greet with silence all her interlocutor's shocked attempts to haggle or bluster. Later, at Peters, Fraser and Dunlop, she looked after the fortunes of bestselling authors who included John Mortimer, Ruth Rendell, Sally Beauman, Robert Harris, Joanna Trollope and Posy Simmons; but she attracted more highbrow figures to her side. 'If I must travel to London to lunch with an agent,' William Trevor once told me, 'I'd rather it was Pat sitting across the table from me than anyone else.'

Robert McCrum
Age (in 1982): 29
Appearance: Head prefect
Defining quality: Bounce

Tall, boyishly enthusiastic, nervously charming, and suspicious of all received wisdom about writers or their reputations, McCrum had perhaps the easiest *entrée* into the book world since John Murray IV, in 1892, took over the job of being Queen Victoria's publisher from his father John Murray III. Robert's father, Michael McCrum, was headmaster of both Eton and Tonbridge schools, and vice chancellor of Cambridge University. Robert went to Sherborne and Cambridge, before winning a scholarship to Penn University, Philadelphia. Back in London, he was reading *The Times* in his parents' garden in Eton, when he spotted, among the classifieds, a job going for a publicity assistant at Chatto & Windus.

He applied, and was interviewed by the legendarily dragon-like Norah Smallwood. Also at the interview was her deputy, Christopher Maclehose, who happened to be a relative: his father was McCrum's great-uncle.* McCrum got the job. When the vacancy for a commissioning editor at Faber came up, McCrum didn't see it. He was in New York on a 'placement' with the grand firm of Farrar, Straus and Giroux. The vacancy was pointed out to him by Ann Faber, daughter of the company's founder. By coincidence, the current Faber chairman was heading for New York to see Roger Straus. They met, took to each other like duck to *l'orange*, and one of the great double-acts of 1980s publishing was born.

When McCrum moved into Faber's office in Queen Street, Bloomsbury, he was appalled. To his eyes, it was chauvinistic, patriarchal, managerial, clubby, and dominated by committees. Though Matthew Evans was, at thirty-five, a youthful boss, McCrum was the only staffer in his twenties. Even the secretaries were spinsters, with names like Mavis. Staff communicated in formal terms: memos went to 'Mr Evans' from 'Mr McCrum'. Spontaneity was not encouraged.

The top man was Charles Monteith, a God-like figure who had plucked William Golding's *Lord of the Flies* (as it became) from the slush pile. McCrum found Monteith ('as grand as they come: a Bentley to my Ford Fiesta') extremely lazy. In commissioning books, he relied on the judgement of others – many firms had their own troupe of dedicated readers. McCrum decided that, henceforth, he'd do all the reading himself. He contacted literary agents and told them there was now an open door at Faber for new young writers.

---

* Christopher Maclehose was later to become a considerable publisher in his own right at Harvill Press, where he introduced UK readers to the work of Raymond Carver and Richard Ford and (as 'the champion of translated fiction') *The Girl With . . .* novel sequence by Stieg Larsson, among other prize-winning authors. Tall, of Scottish descent and ineffably grand, he had a curious habit, on meeting people, of offering his left hand to be shaken rather than his right. If anyone enquired what was wrong with the right, he'd say, 'Got it trapped in a taxi door', or a similar tall story.

He had two early successes. When he revived the 'Faber Intro-ductions' story anthologies and asked agents for contributions, through the post came three short stories by Kazuo Ishiguro (he'd been encouraged to send them by Malcolm Bradbury, his tutor at East Anglia); after they were published, McCrum was sent the first half of *A Pale View of Hills*, Ishiguro's first novel. The Faber board were shocked by the suggestion that they should buy a half-writ-ten novel, but McCrum persuaded them; he signed up Ishiguro for £1,250. When two collections of stories by the Australian Peter Carey failed to find an English publisher, McCrum brought out a selection culled from both, repackaged it as *The Fat Man in History*, and launched the UK career of the double-Booker winner.

Tom Maschler
Age (in 1982): 49
Appearance: Mediterranean pirate
Defining quality: Bustle

Seafaring images were never very far from descriptions of Maschler. He was 'swashbuckling' and 'buccaneering', swarthy, bold, dashing, charismatic and attractively risk-taking, the Douglas Fairbanks Junior of the book trade. In the 1960s and 1970s, he'd turned Jonathan Cape into the most successful and high-profile publishing house in the country. He signed up *Catch-22* for an advance of £250 after Fred Warburg (of Secker & Warburg) turned it down for being 'so American that nobody in England could possibly understand it'. He seduced Philip Roth away from his English publisher, Andre Deutsch, and published *Portnoy's Complaint*. Through the doors of the company's Georgian mansion at 30 Bedford Square crowded Joseph Heller, Doris Lessing, Philip Roth, Edna O'Brien, John Fowles, Len Deighton, Tom Wolfe, Gabriel García Márquez, Kurt Vonnegut and Thomas Pynchon. In the 1980s, the game-changing new cabal of young British novelists gravitated to his office as though drawn by magnetic waves.

He was unlucky enough to be born into a Jewish family living in Berlin in 1933, the year Hitler came to power. Tom's father, Kurt, was a publisher himself, his star author being Erich Kästner, author of *Emil and the Detectives*. In 1938, when Tom was five, after Kristallnacht covered the streets with smashed glass from Jewish shops, the family relocated to Vienna – unlucky again because the Nazis soon arrived in the city. Tom and his mother planned to flee to America, but their connections were faulty and they came to England instead – and stayed there. Tom's four grandparents stayed in Germany. Three were gassed in concentration camps.

In his early twenties, Tom lived in Rome, making money by teaching English while trying to break into film-making at Cinecittà, but although he met Vittorio De Sica and Federico Fellini, his heroes in the neo-realist cinema, he didn't get further. Reluctantly, he went into the one profession he'd always ruled out: becoming a publisher like his dad. He started at Andre Deutsch, and was paid £25 for three months' work. But there he met Len Deighton, who was employed to design catalogue covers, and went on to publish him at Cape, and discovered Colin Wilson, the precocious author of *The Outsider*, whom he sent to Gollancz to be published and cause a sensation.

Stories abounded of his ability to spot sales potential where others couldn't, and of his marketing of books in unusual ways. He persuaded John Lennon to turn his handwritten verses and line drawings into a book, though Lennon himself considered them no better than 'light-hearted scribbles'. (*In His Own Write* and *A Spaniard in the Works* sold four hundred thousand copies in the UK and the same in the USA.) At a party in Primrose Hill he met the curator of mammals at London Zoo, and listened to him talk about what humans might learn from other mammals. When he used the phrase 'the naked ape', Tom recognised a brilliant title for a book with a potentially worldwide sale, and badgered Desmond Morris for three years until he wrote it. The worldwide success of *The Naked Ape* (1967) made Morris a tax exile; it brought him a grand villa in Malta, a Rolls-Royce – and a fan letter from Niko Tinbergen, the Nobel laureate, congratulating him on 'making ethology a subject of concern to the general public'.

'I'm not a particularly scholarly person,' Tom would say. 'My instincts in publishing are very much a gut reaction. The only thing I can claim is that I have a very broad range, broader than most.' Broad enough to encompass the post-war US novel, the rise of South American magical realism, and the English fiction renaissance of the early 1980s.

Liz Calder later told me of Tom's mad energy. 'He'd be there in his grand room, sitting behind his desk, on which there was always a bowl of white sugar, and his leg would be agitating like crazy and he'd lick a finger and dab it in the sugar every so often, and lick it. He'd have a constant sugar rush – like a train driver gradually feeding the furnace with coal – and a hole would gradually appear in the carpet.' Tom assured Liz that he never had affairs with his female (or male) staff and never slept with his women writers. But he often told people (including me) that he'd had a love affair with Doris Lessing (which she denied).

Sonny Mehta
Age (in 1982): 40
Appearance: Bollywood film mogul
Defining quality: Invisibility

The black-clad, chain-smoking, whisky-sipping genius behind Picador Books was born in Delhi to a diplomat, whose travels took him to world capitals from Nepal to New York. Mehta Junior won a scholarship to Cambridge to read History and English and in 1966 co-founded Paladin with a university pal. Four years later he hit the jackpot when lunching with Germaine Greer. She told him her agent was nagging her to write a book about sexism – and he found her so admirably fluent on the subject that he marched her back to his office to sign a contract for *The Female Eunuch*. When he launched Picador in 1972, its aim was to publish top-quality British fiction in paperback – something more readily associated with 'commercial' and 'genre' novels. The leading lights of the 1980s literary renaissance – Ian McEwan, Salman Rushdie, Angela Carter, Julian Barnes – happily signed up to appear in the Picador branding: striking glossy colour covers, white spines (if rather poor-quality paper inside), housed in spinning metal carousels in bookshops. Mehta relied on his own taste, rather than the recommendations of others, to guide him. He signed up *The Hitchhiker's Guide to the Galaxy* and sold millions of copies. When Douglas Adams revealed that he had failed to write a word of the fourth book in the series, *So Long and Thanks for All the Fish*, Mehta booked Adams and himself into two rooms in a hotel and refused to let him move, except to receive room service, until the book was finished. His authors loved him. Journalists seldom got a chance to meet him, but admired his enthusiasm for books. 'Reading . . . is still the most joyful aspect of my day,' he once said. 'I want to be remembered, not as an editor or publisher, but as a reader.'

Tom Rosenthal
Age (in 1982): 47
Appearance: Dandified patriarch
Defining quality: Stubbornness

Beetling-browed, bushy-bearded, bow-tied, cigar-smoking and flamboyantly egocentric, Rosenthal stood out from his publishing confreres like Moses at a sales conference. Only Tom Maschler could match his combination of alpha-male authority and intellectual rigour. He grew up in Manchester, then Cambridge, where his father was a fellow of Pembroke College. An early fascination with twentieth century painting led him first into art-book publishing at Thames & Hudson; then the ailing firm of Secker & Warburg sought his advice about whom they might approach to take charge. Typically Rosenthal suggested himself, and said he'd join as long as he could be chairman and managing director. His brazen *chutzpah* proved justified. On his watch, Secker & Warburg published top-dollar talents from around the globe: Gunter Grass, Umberto Eco, Italo Calvino, Carlos Fuentes and Saul Bellow along with Malcolm Bradbury, David Lodge, George V. Higgins, Melvyn Bragg and Tom Sharpe.

Rosenthal liked to publish highbrow books by serious writers, but had a shrewd commercial eye. When offered the dense and demanding prose works of Nicholas Mosley, he agreed to publish it as long as the author wrote a life of his fascist father, Oswald, a sure-fire seller. He published the stylish fictional farces of Tom Sharpe (including *Wilt* and *Porterhouse Blue*) but also established a poetry list, which lost money but brought James Fenton, John Fuller and Peter Reading to public attention. When Secker was bought by a conglomerate in 1983, Rosenthal resigned and hooked up with Andre Deutsch (q.v.) whose star authors, John Updike, Norman Mailer, Jean Rhys and Gore Vidal were among his charges.

His enthusiasm for painters (especially Jack B. Yeats, Sidney Nolan, Ivon Hitchens, Paula Rego and John Piper) saw him becoming art critic of the *Listener* and the *New Statesman*. Shortly before he died, he gifted his whole art library to Pembroke College, his Cambridge alma mater. He also achieved immortality in a popular magazine. The bearded publisher Lord Snipcock in *Private Eye*'s 'Pile 'Em High' strip cartoon is unmistakeably Tom Rosenthal.

Christopher Sinclair-Stevenson

Age (in 1982): 43
Appearance: Chivalrous beanpole
Defining quality: Sincerity

Freakishly tall, bespectacled, and possessed of an ironclad charm, Christopher SS was the most gentlemanly of publishers and the most quixotically generous with his advances. He joined Hamish

Hamilton in 1961, took over from the founder Jamie Hamilton in 1974, and published some of the key writers of the late seventies and early eighties, most especially Paul Theroux, William Boyd, Peter Ackroyd, Philip Norman and Jane Gardam. Later in the 1980s he presided over the surge of interest in literary biography after bringing out Richard Ellman's life of Oscar Wilde and seeing it sell seventy-five thousand copies in hardback. He sent me a card in 1989 saying: 'I gather someone has told you I'm paying Peter Ackroyd a million for the Dickens. It ain't true. I wish we had that sort of money. So, no doubt, does Peter!' By that time his fantastic spending on advances had caused a rift with Hamish Hamilton and he resigned to start his own company, Sinclair-Stevenson. The first fruit of his one-man firm was the 1,095-page Dickens biography by Peter Ackroyd, published in 1990. It sold extremely well.

Ed Victor
Age (in 1982): 43
Appearance: Old Testament squash player
Defining quality: Ubiquity

The Bronx-born son of Russian Jewish immigrant shopkeepers, Victor made his way to Cambridge on a Marshall scholarship and moved to London. He started at Weidenfeld & Nicolson working on coffee-table books but, after buttonholing Lord Weidenfeld in the lavatory, switched to fiction, overseeing the publication of Saul Bellow and Vladimir Nabokov. In a striking career shift that mirrored Carmen Callil's, he co-founded the underground magazine *Ink* with the men behind the now-defunct *Oz*. In the mid-1970s he became a literary agent, a fixture on the party circuit and a swinger of enormous advances for his clients, who included Carl Bernstein, Harry Evans, Eric Clapton, Keith Richards, Mel Brooks, Nigella Lawson, Edna O'Brien and Roman Polanski. He was most famous, however, for bamboozling a clutch of publishers into bidding at auction for a book that wasn't worth beans.

The Four Hundred by Stephen Sheppard was a Victorian crime caper in which four American crooks attempt to swindle the Bank of England out of £400,000, in order to crash the posh Florida social set known as 'the 400'. The swindle depended on the quartet of master criminals setting up a fake-but-plausible company producing notes of exchange signed by the Baron de Rothschild.

The book sounded to some like a turkey, but Victor, without actually lying, let it be known that he'd sold the film rights to Hollywood. The fact that he'd probably achieved this by convincing Hollywood he'd got a huge book deal with a major publisher wasn't mentioned. But Victor knew the British publishing world had an inferiority complex and, if TV or film showed interest in a book, its value would skyrocket. Suddenly everyone was talking about *The Four Hundred* and its unknown first-time author. 'Everyone was so desperate to be a player,' Terence Blacker told me. 'Nobody wanted to hear a rival say, "Oh dear, weren't you in on the bidding?" My friends at Hutchinson and Arrow and I all read it, and we all thought it was a load of bollocks. By now, though, the bidding was up to £48,000, and Penguin were involved. We had to tell Ed Victor we weren't bidding, and endure his contempt: "Well that's just *great*," he said. "I've gone out of my way to include you in this auction and you've wasted my time – well, just *forget it* the next time something else good comes along . . ."'

As it turned out, Penguin bought it, and it sold well – but there was no Hollywood movie and everyone lost money on it, except for the author ('he's probably still living off the proceeds today') and, of course, Ed Victor.

It was the first time UK publishers were stampeded into offering umpteen thousands for a pig in a poke. And the first sighting of a major eighties theme: the stratospheric transformation of the meek, helpful figure of the agent into a 200-pound shark.

Lord Weidenfeld
Age (in 1982): 63
Appearance: Off-duty pope
Defining quality: Networking

Arthur George Weidenfeld was born in Vienna, the son of a university-lecturer-turned-banker, and was studying to be a diplomat when the Nazis invaded. Through a friend who knew the British consul in Salzburg, he escaped to England in 1938, and arrived with 16s 6d (82p) in his pocket. Eleven years later, in 1949, he started Weidenfeld & Nicolson with Nigel Nicolson (son of Harold Nicolson and Vita Sackville-West), helped by a contract with Marks & Spencer for the mass-supply of cheap books. His first signing was *The Future of Coal* (not the world's most gotta-read title) by the then-unknown Harold Wilson. They printed two thousand copies and sold three hundred, but it was the start of a lasting friendship that culminated in Wilson's much-denigrated resignation Honours List, in which Sir George graduated to the Lords. He was married four times (his second wife was Barbara Skelton, who left Cyril Connolly to be with him, although she was also carnally entwined with King Farouk of Egypt) and was a bit of a braggart. 'I am,' he used to tell friends, 'the Nijinsky of cunnilingus.'

Weidenfeld specialised in commissioning big biographies of megawatt celebrities and heavyweight politicians – his big books in 1983 were a life of Princess Margaret, Laurence Olivier's autobiography, and the memoirs of Zbigniew Brzezinski, President Carter's National Security Advisor – though he wasn't above such opportunistic titles as *War in the Falklands* by the reportage team from the *Sunday Express*.

Andrew Wylie

Age (in 1982): 35
Appearance: Alien being from Close Encounters of the Third Kind
Defining quality: Sinister intent

The founder of the Wylie Agency, which would become the most influential (and most feared) collection of authors' representatives in the Anglo-American publishing world, Andrew Wylie comes from a family of Boston aristocrats. After Harvard, he plunged into Manhattan decadence, hanging out with Andy Warhol, writing atrocious erotic poetry and driving a cab, before starting an agency in 1980.

He was an innovator in two regards. First, he wanted to deal with the finest writers rather than the most popular: 'I'm not interested in mass culture,' he told Robert McCrum. 'When I started out I saw nine out of ten [agents] heading for the door marked Money, Commerce, Trash. So I chose the door marked Quality, Interest, Significance.' Second, he wanted to have the agent deal directly with writers rather than make arrangements with their publishers. Wylie began to approach writers directly, saying he could get them book advances that were double what their current publisher paid. His willingness to 'poach' writers from their creative home at Weidenfeld or Hamish Hamilton (something that just wasn't done in the books world) led to his acquiring the nickname 'The Jackal'; he scared publishers to death. His strategy was to acquire the best and secure 15 per cent of their backlists. He could be found approaching authors at parties, securing their attention by quoting whole paragraphs of their prose verbatim, and pitching an offer they couldn't refuse. His biggest coup was to sign up Salman Rushdie, to steal him away from his long-term agent Deborah Rogers, and secure him an advance of $800,000 for *The Satanic Verses* in 1988. A later coup saw him persuade Martin Amis to leave his agent of twenty-two years, Pat Kavanagh (wife of Amis's close friend Julian Barnes) for an advance of £500,000 for *The Information*. By the millennium, he was the man you had to deal with if you wanted to publish the works of Philip Roth, V. S. Naipaul, Saul Bellow, Vladimir Nabokov, John Updike, Jorge Luis Borges, Evelyn Waugh, Yukio Mishima or Giuseppe di Lampedusa.

After I'd reviewed a few titles for *Books and Bookmen*, without actual protests from its editor, I asked if I could have a go at interviewing writers. To my delight, Sally and Carolyn agreed. My big discovery of 1983 was *Waterland*, one of the great novels of the 1980s. I was bowled over by it and longed to meet the author.

Set in the modern-day Fen country, it's a boundingly rich tale of empire-building, land reclamation, brewers and sluice minders, whiskery Victorian patriarchs, insane and visionary relicts – an amazing cast of professional burghers and local eccentrics that constitute a sort-of history of England over the last three hundred years. And the whole spilling chronicle issues from the mind of one man – Thomas Crick, a middle-aged schoolmaster who faces the sack because of the crackpot quality of the history lessons with which he regales a class of sullen, nuclear-age children.

Crick is supposed to be teaching kids about the French Revolution, but instead he throws a ton of Fenland history at them, with digressions on all manner of things (some of the fifty-two chapters are two- and three-page lecturettes) including 'About the Fens', 'About the Lock-Keeper', 'About the Question Why' and 'About Nothing'. His project, if that's the word, is to search through his own and his family's past, looking for something to explain his present-day catastrophe – his wife has gone mad and abducted a baby from a supermarket. So he looks for clues in the history of England, and the weirdness of his family.

There's Thomas, who had drained 12,000 acres of the Leem River by the time of Trafalgar; his wife Sarah, who loses her marbles and becomes a spooky presence at an upstairs window; then Ernest, who, at the turn of the twentieth century, spoke out about the coming of war, was refused a seat in Parliament, and invented an ale of such mystic potency that the whole town went crazy on Coronation Day and the brewery burnt down; also of Ernest's wife Helen, who gives birth to her own father's child, who is the schoolmaster's doomed brother.

I interviewed Swift in the County Arms (est. 1852), a substantial three-bar Youngs pub on Wandsworth Common, patronised by burly, shirt-sleeved warders from the nearby Wandsworth Gaol. Swift was a modest, unassuming, drolly amusing man of thirty-four, a drinker of Youngs beer, a smoker of French cigarettes, a public schoolboy (Dulwich College, which he clearly loathed) and a Cambridge graduate. I was surprised to find that he had no personal connection to the Fens. He turned out to be a Londoner – born in Forest Hill, grew up in Croydon – who first clapped eyes on the soggy realm through a window. 'I saw all that flat, wet, depressing, utterly unpromising landscape through a train window one day, with a field and a lock – and imagined a body floating in it . . .'

Swift wrote a PhD thesis on 'Dickens and the City', later abandoned in favour of writing fiction. His choice of subject was no surprise, since *Waterland* has a Dickensian richness in its evocations of place and childhood. The lock-keeper's cottage beside a river seemed to come from the same imaginative universe as the blacksmith's forge in *Great Expectations*. And the bravura passages about the effects of Coronation Ale on the town of Gildsey combined orotundity and carousing in a way Mr Pickwick would have approved:

> *It was no ordinary ale that they drank by the Ouse . . . For when the men of Gildsey jostled into the Pike and Eel and The Jolly Bargemen . . . they discovered that this patriotic liquor hurled them with astonishing rapidity through the normally gradual and containable stages of intoxication: pleasure, satisfaction, well-being, elation, light-headedness, hot-headedness, befuddlement, distraction, delirium, irascibility, pugnaciousness, imbalance, incapacity – all in the gamut of a single bottle.*

One other writer's name kept occurring to me as I read Swift's third novel. The first-person narrative, with its constant self-questioning, its ellipses, its way of letting secrets leak out between the protestations of the narrating voice – it seemed to echo the voice, endlessly self-contradicting, of Samuel Beckett in his 1950s trilogy, *Molloy*, *Malone Dies* and *The Unnamable*. Had Swift learned anything from Beckett?

'Everything in *Waterland* comes from nothingness,' he said, 'from that landscape of water and darkness, in which people tell themselves stories to keep it at bay. Yes, Beckett influences me strongly – I wrote a number of stories in his manner, which thankfully were never published. He's a wonderful experimenter with words, he writes with a voice that you know you can trust, and there's a persistent humour in his writing, even in the middle of an utter pessimism.'

By the time we emerged, blinking, into the darkness on Wandsworth Common, Swift and I had become comprehensively sloshed and euphoric, like John Wayne and Lee Marvin singing 'The Moon Shines Tonight on Pretty Red Wing' in *The Comancheros*. I had explained several times, with decreasing intelligibility, that he was definitely going to win the Booker Prize that year. I told him I'd already put £20 on at Ladbrokes, it was a racing certainty, and we would celebrate together at the Guildhall. Which is why it was a crushing disappointment when *Waterland* lost out to the South African J. M. Coetzee, whose novel, *Life and Times of Michael K*, won the big prize. The book was about a lowly Cape Town gardener, disfigured by a hare lip, who takes his tragic mother, burdened by grotesquely swollen legs and arms, on a long, recuperative journey to the place of her childhood. Despite its Kafka-esque title, Coetzee's book also took its cue from Beckett's *Trilogy*, but without a trace of the wild, anarchic humour of the original – or of *Waterland*.

A month later saw me standing in a telephone booth on the main concourse of Paddington Station, trying to describe myself to William Trevor.

'I'm quite, er, tall,' I explained, 'Six-one or so, devastatingly handsome, brown hair prematurely grey at the front, and I'm wearing a long blue trench coat. Would it help if I were carrying a copy of *Books and*—'

'I don't think it will be *very* hard to pick you out,' said Trevor in a voice that was dry, ironic and surprisingly un-Irish. Admittedly he'd been living in England long enough to have shaved off most traces of his native Cork, but I hadn't bargained for the formal, high-table delivery.

The train ride to Exeter took two hours, in which I re-read the ending of *Fools of Fortune*, his bewitching new novel. I'd read lots of his stories, mostly set in Ireland, and loved his way of evoking small-town boredom, the oddly formal conversation of people with trapped lives and cancelled futures. But I hadn't been wildly gripped by his early novels set in Dublin and London; the narrative tone of voice never seemed to settle for being dignified English (on the lines of, say, Evelyn Waugh) or cod-formal Irish (like, say, Flann O'Brien).

Now here was *Fools of Fortune*, Trevor's first full-scale excursion into the imaginative territory of his past. It was also his contribution to the Anglo-Irish 'Big House' novel, in which the grand homes of the Anglo-Irish Ascendency are celebrated as places of civility (if you're Anglo) or condemned as symbols of tawdry colonial grandeur (if you're Irish).

The novel tells about the childhood and tragic life of Willie Quinton, who is born into an Anglo-Irish family living in an old mansion, Kilneagh, in Cork, but grows up hearing tales of Irish history from a Republican perspective. After the body of a local informer is found at the house, Kilneagh is torched and most of the family murdered by the Black and Tans. Years go by. Things settle down. Willie falls in love with an Irish cousin, Marianne. Then one night, Willie's adored mother, who has lapsed into alcoholism, slashes her wrists. Willie takes a savage revenge and disappears – and the reader, along with Marianne, has to piece together what happened, and wait for his return. It's an intensely moving story, told with all Trevor's peerlessly textured descriptive skill.

At Exeter Station, a dozen people alighted. William Trevor was leaning against his car, the living embodiment of an Irish farmer, complete with tweed trousers, wrinkled brow, and a battered wool hat randomly plonked on his mostly bald head. He was taller than I expected, and seemed older than his fifty-four years. As he drove, he admitted to being a landowner of sorts – 30 acres of fields across which he strode every day with his beloved red setter, Rory – and talked about small-town life, English and Irish style.

'If you take away the VG supermarket and the Lloyds Bank,' he said, 'many of the little villages on the edge of Dartmoor are indistinguishable from Irish ones.' He found it amazing that England and Ireland, two countries so close, could be so different. 'Though of course they influence each other in many ways, particularly since the rise of television. You can walk through Athlone and see kids with Manchester United scarves round their necks, and the women will get addicted to *Coronation Street* – but the influence is mostly by default, like parents becoming influenced by the habits or interests of their children.'

They mostly differed, he said, in their sense of the past. 'Here in England, the past is dealt with very well, all neatly arranged and tucked away under a glass case, just to be looked at. History in England is found in the gardens, and castles and parks and monuments. It's all very pleasant and charming. It implies contentment. In Ireland you just don't find that kind of ease, simply because there hasn't been enough time for it to grow. The Rising, the civil war and the arrival of independence took place more or less within living memory. Ireland, in consequence, is still living *through* her history, without having had time to settle down.'

It was oddly pleasing to find that the Trevors, like Willie Quinton, lived beside a ruined mill. But their home on the road north out of Exeter wasn't a grand estate, it was a two-hundred-year-old farmhouse, a paradigm of snugness. Ancient beams lined

The way they were: the cream of British 'publicity girls' in 1975. Liz Calder with extended arms top left, Carmen Callil seated extreme right (flashing V-sign at the photographer). *(Author's collection)*

The author, Oxford 1975, channelling the bumptious Charles Highway from *The Rachel Papers*. *(Author's collection)*

Sebastian Faulks: a Millais in the Garrick Club. *(© Norman McBeath/National Portrait Gallery, London)*

Martin Amis, at home in west London, early 1980s.
(Homer Sykes/Alamy Stock Photo)

Ian McEwan. 'I was a moralist, somebody rather squeamish, appalled but fascinated by grossness.' *(Martin Goddard/Shutterstock)*

Martian chronicler: an ebullient Craig Raine, poetry editor at Faber throughout the 1980s. *(Shutterstock)*

Livia Gollancz. 'Her penetrating blue eyes, set in the face of an Eastern European peasant woman, regarded me sternly.' *(akg-images/Purkiss Archive)*

Angela Carter in a characteristically disputatious mode. *(Fairfax Media Archive/ Getty Images)*

Liz Calder, fiction *maestra* at Gollancz, Cape and Bloomsbury. *(David Montgomery/Getty Images)*

The Best of British Writers, 1982. See Chapter 5. *(Photograph by Snowdon/Trunk Archive)*

The Best of Young British Novelists, 1983. See Chapter 5. *(Photograph by Snowdon/Trunk Archive)*

Tom Maschler: 'The Douglas Fairbanks Jnr of the publishing trade', and Doris Lessing, Nobel laureate, with whom he enjoyed a long relationship. *(Author's collection)*

Duelling ciggies: Sonny Mehta, master of the upmarket bestseller at Picador Books. *(Dafydd Jones)*

New broom at the old factory: Robert McCrum takes over at TS Eliot's publishers, Faber & Faber. *(Fairfax Media Archives/Getty Images)*

Feminist pathfinder tries on new outfit: Carmen Callil in January 1983, now Managing Director of Chatto as well as Chair of Virago. *(Fairfax media/Getty images)*

Queen of Books and Bookmen: Sally Emerson.
(Author's collection)

Shock tactics: one of
Adam Mars-Jones's edgy
stories imagined HM the
Queen with rabies.
(Jason Alden/Shutterstock)

Beryl Bainbridge
and Anna Haycraft:
best friends, love
rivals and creatively
symbiotic authors.
*(© Guardian News &
Media Ltd 2022)*

(left) Power couple: super-agent Pat Kavanagh and her husband, the novelist Julian Barnes.

(Photograph by Jillian Edelstein, Camera Press London)

(below) Close Quarters: William Golding, Nobel Prize laureate, at the Gala banquet in Stockholm City Hall with Princess Christina of Sweden, 1983.

(Roger Tillberg/Alamy Stock Photo)

he said, he wasn't, and didn't, though he would allow the description of 'a dealer in the absurd'. 'I suppose no writer can resist being so described,' he said, 'I'm far more *that* than a tragedian, which is altogether too heavy a mantle to bear. But nobody writes books very seriously any more, as far as I can see – they don't have the gravitas, the length, the vision. Dickens, I suppose, managed to combine the comic, the tragic and the absurd – and that's what I, in a very minor way, am trying to do myself.'

I asked him why, like Hardy, he never seemed to give his characters a break – why their choices doomed them to misery, why their actions invariably led to trouble or misery.

'But John,' he said with sudden heat, 'I see this happening *all* the *time*. It's not my *vision* of *humanity*, it's my *observation* of *people*. I constantly see people walking into *terrible* relationships or courses of action with their *eyes wide open*.'

At lunch (delicious roast lamb, roast potatoes and parsnips from the garden), they asked about my Irish parents, and their decision to return to the old country after thirty-three years in London. And they expressed amazement at my current employment.

'Surely, though,' said Mrs Trevor, 'you're not going to *stay* on that trade magazine, are you?'

'Oh *God* no,' I told them. 'I intend to be literary editor of *The Times* before I'm thirty-five.'

They looked at each other.

'Mm-hmm,' said Trevor, noncommittally.

'That's the spirit,' said Jane, 'I'm sure you will.' Had she not been across the table from me, I'm sure she'd have patted my hand.

On the train home, I thought how I envied William Trevor. Not just his talent and the heartbreaking restraint of his storytelling, but the times he'd lived in and lived through: the aftermath of the Rising, the split of allegiances that tore families apart in the civil war, the reheating of the Troubles after 1969, the fuzzy identity of being a Protestant Irishman, dwelling in England but better able to express the ache and yearning of Irish country life than anyone in Ireland. Where, I asked the train window, is my subject? Where do I find the material that can be turned into spectacular fiction?

I was also keen to meet Adam Mars-Jones, the author of *Lantern Lecture*, a damned odd, *sui generis* collection of stories that weren't stories: they were three explorations of the British establishment – its aristocracy, its legal system and its royal family – that followed no rules, and played fast and loose with concepts such as 'truth' and 'fiction'.

The main story, called 'Hoosh-Mi: A Farrago of Scurrilous Untruths', concerned a national tragedy. We read of how an American hoary bat flies across the Atlantic and lands in the bracken of Aberdeenshire. Before expiring from exhaustion, it comes to the attention of Evesham Pontius Meggezone the Third, a pedigree corgi, which it bites on the nose. Later the dog is cuddled by its owner and, in drawing its tongue across her face, passes on an infection. And that is how HM Queen Elizabeth II of Great Britain falls ill with rabies and dies.

It's a mad premise for a story, and Mars-Jones tells it with relish and touches of farce. The Queen Mother arrives to break the grim news to Prince Edward just as he's listening to his new cassette of BBC sound effects: *Volume 13 Death and Horror*. 'The Queen Mother entered without knocking, heavy with news, just as Number 10 Red Hot Poker Into Eye, 7', was giving way to the eighteen seconds of Number 14 Nails Hammered Into Flesh . . .' And it keeps the reader amused with bizarre, apparently true-life stories from the Queen's reign. Gradually the reader wonders: are these stories true? Has Mars-Jones made up some of them? And does it actually matter?

We met at the Inns of Court where he lived with his parents (his mother is a barrister) in an attic suite at the top of a spiral staircase. He made us Darjeeling tea, and talked at a torrential rate. I asked why was he so keen on writing about real-life, factual, observed-by-many events such as a trial or a royal visit. 'I enjoy fiction when it's stiff with facts,' he said. 'When I start writing, I immediately begin to import the virtues of documentary rather than fantasy. But you have to decide how far to go with the various versions of truth available – and from those impure sources, you start paying attention to timing and tone of voice and things from the sphere of fiction, eventually to produce something a bit different that doesn't depend on the apparent truth of any of them.'

Mars-Jones airily dismissed my objection that his work is short on psychological truth. Why didn't he give an inner voice to the Queen? 'I think it's impertinent to assume you can get into someone's mind,' he said. Instead he dealt in 'different registers of impersonality ... It's the writer's job to suggest a space within which feelings exist.'

The interview was published in *Books and Bookmen* – and when we next met, at a Faber party, I said I hoped I hadn't misrepresented him.

'What you wrote about the book was fine,' he said, 'though I wasn't wild about the way you described me.'

'Really? What did I say about you'

'You called me "Tall, crop-haired, prognathous and gangling."'

I looked at him. He was wearing a striking pair of trousers with a vertical red stripe, like Tissot's cavalry officer.

'Well you *are* tall,' I pointed out. 'And your hair *was* very short. And you have a pronounced jawline which is why I used the word "prognathous". As for the gangling ...'

'It's not a recital of attributes,' he said, 'that's going to get much response in the small ads of *Gay Times*, now is it?'

I was shocked. I'd met several gay men at university, who made no secret of their sexuality. But this was the first time I'd met anyone in public life who blithely admitted – no, who *broadcast* the fact, and didn't care who knew it.

There was another revelation for me around the launch of Mars-Jones's career: the invented controversy. Robert McCrum told me about it. He and Mars-Jones had been at Cambridge together (though they hadn't been friends). When the manuscript of *Lantern Lecture* arrived in July 1980, McCrum knew he'd have a hard time getting something so odd past the Faber board. So he went to his chairman, Matthew Evans, and said, 'Matthew, these pieces are fantastic, but it's highly unlikely Faber will want to publish them because of the one about the Queen dying of rabies.' Evans loved the idea of an in-house kerfuffle between the old guard and the avant garde. He approached Charles Monteith, the company's *éminence gris*, and told him the problem. Monteith urged caution, and asked a solicitor to read the story. 'I can visualise,' the lawyer wrote, 'that if Faber were to publish this book, it would be considered by many an outrage, would harm Faber's high reputation and even possibly lead to one or two authors wishing to change their imprint.'

McCrum refused to give in. He was the new broom in the company, and he knew he was right. When Monteith suggested they seek the advice of a good 'literary' lawyer – John Mortimer – he readily agreed. So Evans, Monteith, Mars-Jones and McCrum trooped off to Mortimer's chambers in Gray's Inn, round the corner from Mars-Jones's flat. They filed in, gravely handed over the seventy-page manuscript, and sat outside the barrister's office, waiting for the jurisprudential thumb to point up or down.

Eventually, the door to Mortimer's private sanctum was yanked open. He looked at them, one by one, as if they were completely mad.

'I cannot see what on earth all the fuss is about,' he said. 'This is absolutely marvellous work.' And that was that. No crash. No drama. But it could now be leaked to the press that a Faber book about the Queen, written by the son of a High Court judge, had had to be inspected for *lèse-majesté* by one of the leading lawyers in the land . . . Honestly, when it came to manipulating the truth, publishers could teach the newspaper world a thing or two.

CHAPTER 5

————— ◆ —————

The Best of British

There were two photographs that the whole literary world – publishers, authors, agents, TV executives, and the Great British reading public from Aberystwyth to Zennor – gazed at in 1982 and 1983. The photographs were first seen in the *Sunday Times* magazine, but were reproduced at least a million times and appeared in the windows of every bookshop and on the walls of every library in the UK. They were our – the nation's buyers and readers of books – chance to inspect the creative superstars who were giving the literate world its new stories.

Look at the first photograph and what do you see? Upstairs in a pub in the Gray's Inn Road, London, on a freezing cold January in 1982, ten distinguished faces are peering at a camera wielded by the Queen's brother-in-law. Only two are smiling into the lens. The others are radiating, if not exactly hostility, a kind of grudging acquiescence, as if they're undergoing some dull civic duty. Nobody would guess that these ten glum, middle-aged-to-elderly people are involved in a major promotional exercise. For they're here to celebrate their hot status as the Best British Writers in the United Kingdom.

Reading from left to right, Rosemary Sutcliff, sixty-two, best known for her children's books, especially the *Eagle of the Ninth* series about family life in Roman Britain, smiles like an indulgent aunt under a voluminous shawl. Leon Garfield, sixty-one, also a writer of historical adventure tales for children, looks heroically suave in a tuxedo and bow-tie. Beside him is Malcolm Bradbury, in this company a mere stripling of forty-nine, best known for writing *The History Man*, about a venal and hypocritical academic called Howard Kirk (made into a TV show the previous year), but also for teaching at the University of East Anglia, and launching the MA in Creative Writing that kick-started the careers of Kazuo Ishiguro, Ian McEwan and Rose Tremain.

Beside him, Rosamond Lehmann is a sternly thrilling presence in a cloak with elaborate frogging around the throat; now eighty-one, her literary friendships date back to the Bloomsbury Group and bang up to the present day with the new feminist publishing house, Virago – her 1930s novels *Invitation to the Waltz* and *The Weather in the Streets* have recently been revived as Virago Modern Classics.

In the middle of the group, looking uncharacteristically stern, is Sir John Betjeman, seventy-five, the British Poet Laureate and National Teddy Bear. Sitting beside him, smiling and rubicund, is Sir V. S. (Victor) Pritchett, at eighty-two the oldest of the group, the doyen of British short-story writers, a Companion of Honour and President of PEN International. Looming in the background is Sir Laurens van der Post, seventy-six, South Africa-born novelist, Jungian mystic, author of *The Lost World of the Kalahari*, intimate of Mrs Thatcher, guru to Prince Charles, godfather to Prince William – and apparently compulsive fantasist, liar and seducer of young girls, according to a disobliging biography, *Teller of Many Tales: The Lives of Laurens van der Post*, that would be published in 2002.

Perched on a blanket-covered box, his hands nursing a cup of whisky (with wise anticipation, he's brought a bottle in his briefcase; there it is on the floor beside him) is Laurie Lee, sixty-six, poet, spinner of the most beautiful prose in England, and author of the immortal rustic memoir, *Cider with Rosie*. Standing slightly back from the others, a spookily umbral presence, is Anthony Burgess, sixty-four, polymath, polyglot, linguist, composer, author of *A Clockwork Orange*, *Earthly Powers*, the *Enderby* trilogy and thirty other novels. Last of the group, wearing a fur coat against the January chill and pleased to be sharing Laurie Lee's Scotch, is Beryl Bainbridge, forty-nine, a Liverpudlian actress turned novelist, whose slender, macabre tales of desperate working-class women on Merseyside and in north London have won critical acclaim and respectable sales from the mid-1960s to the early 1980s.

It's a fabulous line-up – but these ten don't, unfortunately, constitute *all* the writers who have been awarded that impressive title, Best of British Writers. Only, in fact, half of them. Twenty writers were originally chosen for the honour but, sadly, ten couldn't make it. Ian Jack, the journalist who covered the photo shoot in the *Sunday Times*, was merciless about the excuses that were put forward by the non-attendees:

'V. S. Naipaul, William Golding and Graham Greene did not like the idea of being photographed like a school cricket team. Margaret Drabble's parents were ill. Iris Murdoch's husband fell in the snow and hurt himself. John le Carré was travelling abroad. Lawrence Durrell couldn't be bothered. Ted Hughes and John Fowles got snowbound in their rural homes. Rebecca West was unwell.'

The reluctance of the veteran literary superstars to co-operate with this exercise – despite the excitement of being photographed by Lord Snowdon, five years divorced from Princess Margaret and generally agreed to be the nation's second-best snapper after David Bailey – was easy to explain. There was just no precedent for it. Distinguished authors did not, as a rule, get together (and certainly not, good heavens, in a *pub*) for a promotional exercise. They did not, as a rule, present themselves for collective photographs – or for *any* professional photographs, except the occasional sober portrait that would adorn the inside-back jacket of a new book, paid for from the publicity budget of Cape or Chatto or Faber or Hutchinson.

Sometimes, of course, they might meet their writing peers socially – at the Society of Authors or the Royal Society of Literature, perhaps, when a palpitating new member was being inducted – but they seldom, if ever, met the reading public. The concept of the Author Signing Session or the 'An Evening With' event in a bookshop were phenomena of the future. Literary festivals had been around since 1949, inviting well-known authors to be interviewed in front of admiring readers, but they seldom managed to snare the super-distinguished writers – the Goldings, the Lehmanns, the Van der Posts. The proliferation of festivals that followed the success of Hay-on-Wye in 1989 was almost a decade in the future.*

Ian Jack wrote about how strange it was to see the Magnificent Ten gazing into the Snowdon camera lens. 'It was odd to see them together; it looked like a piece of cultural nationalism that belonged to the Second World War: 'Writers against Hitler'. Odd, in fact, to see them at all; we were still in the time when writers were private figures, their public lives confined mainly to what was printed on the page. What they looked like, how they sounded, where they lived, what they believed: these things – always excepting the case of Betjeman – were mysterious to most people outside the world of London publishing houses.'

The mastermind behind the 1982 photo shoot was a thirty-seven-year-old promotional genius called Desmond Clarke. He was a military man by training (Sandhurst and the Royal Artillery) before entering the publishing world. In 1979 he'd led something called the Lost Book Sales Research Study, the first industry-wide project to investigate what might be done by publishers to make their books fly off bookshop shelves. It was influential in the development of book retailing, and was supported by the Booksellers Association. Out of it came the Book Marketing Council, with Clarke in charge as director of promotions.

---

* The earliest literary festival was the Cheltenham Literature Festival, founded by George Wilkinson, manager of Cheltenham Spa, and John Moore, a Tewkesbury-based author of over forty books on rural and conservationist themes. Among the guests at the debut festival was Cecil Day-Lewis, later to be professor of Poetry at Oxford and Poet Laureate, reading some of his verses, and the actor Ralph Richardson, who arrived by motorbike and set a festival precedent: the organisers inviting a non-literary celebrity, to guarantee Bums on Seats.

His aim in helming the 'Best of British' was simple: 'To increase the buying market for books of literary quality'. Behind the word 'quality' lay a shrewd understanding that he wouldn't just be selling the idea of reading in general; he knew readers wanted to be steered towards The Best, the *aristos* of modern literature. And the best way of promoting The Best was by presenting a list – something that could be argued and fought over – and making it a news story.

The first people to whom he sold the idea, in summer 1981, before he approached any publishers, were WH Smith and Penguin paperbacks. The former sold around fifty million books a year, 20 per cent of all book sales in the UK; the latter had a virtual monopoly on quality paperback fiction; they published about one hundred and fifty titles from seventeen of the twenty authors who were finally selected.

Clarke pitched his plan bluntly. Would Penguin be able to supply the enormous volume of paperbacks for which there would be a sudden demand? And would Smith's agree to back the promotion in all their high street and railway station stores? The answer was unsurprisingly positive. So he went to the publishers and told them: 'We are going to succeed in stimulating consumer interest by an effective PR campaign while ensuring that demand can be satisfied immediately in bookshops. We must have the active support of each of you in getting PR coverage for your authors . . . We should sell, by our collective efforts, about one million paperbacks and between fifteen and thirty thousand hardback books. Please remember this is a backlist promotion and author identity is critical to selling across the range of an author's titles.'

Then Clarke convened a judging panel; it comprised two literary bigwigs (our old friend Martyn Goff of the National Book League, and Frank Delaney, the presenter of Radio 4's *Bookshelf*) plus three representatives of the bookselling trade. He asked them to make their choice, from one hundred authors put forward by their anxious publishers, of who should qualify for the big league.

The rules were simple: publishers could nominate novelists, of course, but should suggest children's authors, poets, and the odd travel writer as well.

In autumn 1981, gossip columns in *The Times* and the *Sunday Times* ran little stories suggesting that certain British authors were furious because their names hadn't been put forward by their publishers for this important list. Where did the diary stories originate? From Desmond Clarke himself, of course. According to Ian Jack, Clarke later confessed that, by that stage, only a single author had been put forward by a publisher: Margaret Drabble. But once the diary item appeared, the floodgates opened. Publishers were suddenly demanding that their authors should be considered; that it would be an outrage – no, a national *insult* – if they were left off this vitally important index of recognition.

From the hundred-odd names submitted to the panel, the list was narrowed down to twenty. And if anyone thought the judging criteria were a bit odd, what did they make of the eventual choice of writers? Where, for example, was Kingsley Amis, still productive at sixty and soon to win the Booker Prize with *The Old Devils*, four years later? How, if they chose John Betjeman and Ted Hughes, could they overlook Philip Larkin? If they'd decided to honour Iris Murdoch and Margaret Drabble, shouldn't there have been a place for Doris (*The Golden Notebook*) Lessing? If Malcolm Bradbury, master of the campus novel, was selected for the team, why not his friend and fellow campus novelist David Lodge? And where, pray, was Angela Carter? Was she just too wild and fanged and contrary to be proper company for Rosemary, Laurie and Victor?

But there at last was the Best of British list, a *fait accompli*, and there, in January 1982, were ten of the twenty ageing literati posing for a double-page spread in the *Sunday Times* colour magazine, for which, coincidentally, Lord Snowdon had been the artistic advisor twenty years before.

Desmond Clarke's plan was brilliant, because not only did it bring the idea of 'the Best' to an audience who might be glad to hear of its existence (Clarke reckoned that only 2 per cent of the UK population had even heard of, let alone read, the majority of the twenty); but it involved a *lot* of titles. An impressive 2.5 million people had read *Lord of the Flies*; now, maybe, finding Golding's name in the list, they might try *The Spire* or *Rites of Passage*. John le Carré's *The Spy Who Came in from the Cold* had, by 1982, already entranced 1.4 million people; perhaps they might fancy blowing some cash on *Tinker, Tailor* or *Smiley's People*. Fans of modern poetry had already bought one hundred and fifteen thousand copies of Ted Hughes's *Selected Poems*; might not another hundred thousand fans of literature, who didn't usually buy poetry, take a chance on Betjeman and Hughes after learning that they were the 'best' English poets in the land?

The shifting of units, however, wasn't the main effect of the promotion. What made it a cultural milestone was its demystifying of The Writer, turning him or her from a hermit-like recluse into a full-blooded figure, wise and sociable and available for public pronouncements, political opinions, even lifestyle tips. The BoBW and its successors made writers visible and then fashionable, on radio and TV, in the newspapers. In the next decade, they'd begin to appear on stage, at bookshop readings and literary festival debates. They began to be *brands*: marketed for their personae as much as for the quality of their new books. Their youth or good looks or performance levels started to matter, to be important. A new trendification of authors had come centre-stage. You could date its arrival from the mid-to-late-1970s advertising campaign for Sanderson, purveyors of expensive living-room wallpaper and boudoir fabrics for one hundred and fifty years. The campaign featured Diana Rigg on a William Morris print sofa with Japanese silk wallcoverings, Britt Ekland titivating a modern dining room with monochrome-and-silver decor, Peter Hall relaxing at the piano surrounded by cheese plants, Petula Clark on the 'settee' of her Swiss chalet, and the chef Robert Carrier on a four-poster bed with Biba-esque fabric. Now came a bespectacled Kingsley Amis and his then wife Elizabeth Jane Howard perusing a manuscript in a living room that resembled a stage set with prodigiously swagged peach curtains. 'Very Kingsley Amis, very Sanderson' murmured the caption. That was the kind of company – actresses, singers, famous beauties, theatre directors and, er, chefs – with which top writers were now bracketed.

Desmond Clarke was brilliant at promotional wheezes. When he became sales and marketing director at Faber & Faber in the 1980s, he persuaded a clutch of distinguished poets to read from their work at Waterloo Station – an unheard-of public performance (imagine T. S. Eliot or W. H. Auden debasing themselves in that way). His other clever stroke was arranging to send Faber's most famous bards, Seamus Heaney and Craig Raine, on a poetry tour *by helicopter*. The proposal was covered by newspapers for months before Heaney decided he couldn't face it. So the tour never happened, the helicopter wasn't rented, Faber saved a lot of money – and Raine and Heaney got acres of coverage for doing nothing. The headlines of the coverage ('Here come the Whirlybards'? 'Stand by for the Rotating Rhymers'?) have, sadly, not survived. Clarke was also a favourite with Faber writers: P. D. James based a minor character in her book *Devices and Desires* on him, while Wendy Cope's adoring 'The Desmond Clarke Poem' appeared in a limited edition.

Clarke's Best of British promo had worked. The Book Marketing Council reported that 276,406 extra books were sold as a result of the campaign. Less welcome had been the news that, when a team of pollsters around the UK asked the general public how many of the writers they'd heard of, the news was disappointing. Twenty per cent of people polled (one in five) hadn't heard of *any* of the Best of British – and among those who had, some thought John le Carré was a TV chef (or was that Robert le Carrier?) and Anthony Burgess was one of the Cambridge spy ring.

But could the BMC have a second go? Whom could they promote this time? Best Poets? Not really a money-spinner. Best Children's Books? Of limited interest to the childless. Best Travel Books? Stroll on . . .

Desmond Clarke told me that he was lying at home in his bath when the solution came to him – a genuinely Archimedean 'Eureka!' moment. The solution was – Youth! Young Novelists! Twenty more writers to promote in every bookshop in the land! Admittedly, many of their names would be even more unfamiliar to the book-buying public than the first lot, and few would have the name-recognition of Betjeman or Drabble, but would that matter? Readers would love to be steered once again, this time towards promising, fresh-faced new talent in British fiction.

As he towelled his portly frame, Clarke refined his selection. Twenty Young Writers? 'The Best of Young British Novelists'. Young meaning 'in their twenties'? Too callow. In their thirties? How about 'The Best Under Forty'? Yes! How about 'Twenty Under Forty: the Best of Young British Novelists'? Yes again!

For a second time, he took the idea to the publishing world and the 351 branches of WH Smith and asked what they thought. Predictably, they welcomed it with enfolding arms. But this time, the promotion was bolstered by something new.

That something was *Granta* magazine, last seen performing the final obsequies over the stricken and moribund English novel in issues 1 and 3. In the *Granta* office, editor Bill Buford read the *Sunday Times* write-up by Andrew Stephen in February 1983, gazed at the Snowdon multi-portrait and thought: a lot of these names seem familiar. Gradually he realised that, of the twenty, he had extracts of the work of fifteen or sixteen in his Pending file; extracts from their new novels or works-in-progress had been sent by their publishers in the hope that they might find a home in the new magazine.

Buford sat up with a jolt and thought: we could make this the Best of Young British Novelists Special Issue. It would cost the magazine nothing, since the extracts had been offered for publication, *gratis*.

And it would precede the bookshop rollout of BOYBN titles, provided they moved like greased lightning.

He didn't, however, have the production wherewithal to get several copies of his new magazine into all 351 WH Smith outlets. Could he get into bed with some partner, perhaps a mature and enterprising veteran publisher who would take on the gigantic burden for a suitable fee?

Soon he and Clarke arranged a meeting with the head of Penguin, who undertook to handle the mass publication and distribution of three thousand copies of *Granta* 7, and get them into bookshops everywhere. In the event, two thousand booksellers, including hundreds at WH Smith and Menzies agreed to display books by the featured twenty novelists prominently on their shelves and in their windows; the books were also stocked by a thousand public libraries. Clarke arranged to give publishers and booksellers advance warning about who the featured writers would be, so that they could make sure they had enough stock.

The *Sunday Times* jumped at the chance of doing another of their trademark group portraits. Lord Snowdon was persuaded to come back and take the picture.

It's an extraordinary photograph. Eighteen of the Young Twenty are regarding the camera with expressions of studied neutrality and occasional hostility. Ian McEwan, wearing a curious combination of ochre corduroy trousers, grey wool jacket and stripey school tie, is looking away from Snowdon's lens as he listens to Martin Amis beside him, who, holding the morning paper, looks slight and schoolboyish in a white shirt. In front of them are three of the six women in the line-up: Maggie Gee, in pearls, earrings and flesh-coloured jacket, seems to have come, hot-foot and irritable, straight from a *Harper's* fashion shoot; Rose Tremain appears as a pissed-off, frizzy-haired Bohemian in a bright red smock and shapeless russet cardie (even her string of pearls seems to be flashing a V-sign at the camera); Lisa St Aubin de Teran is unreadably cool in her pageboy fringe and black leather knee-boots.

The centre of the group is a five-star cluster of masculinity: Christopher Priest is, basically, a TV cop in this photograph, with his tough-bastard physiognomy, leather blouson and open-necked shirt; before him are Philip Norman, resembling a kindly art teacher, from his brown velvet jacket to his white socks and the hands that cradle his beige slacks at the knee, and Graham Swift, whose bespectacled face is a study in I-don't-want-to-be-here, while his wool scarf is a promise that he won't be sticking around for long.

Behind Priest stand two men who, in markedly different ways, resemble his minders, his hired muscle. Julian Barnes eyes the camera as if about to invite its manipulator to come outside and say that; he looks polite, but the thumbs hooked into his belt-loops tell a different story; beside him, Adam Mars-Jones is slight and thin-shouldered, but the combination of rolled-up sleeves, folded arms and thin braces over collarless dun shirt all yell 'skinhead!' (You can't see his Doc Martens but you just know they're there.)

Nobody looks very happy to be among the Chosen Few. Shiva Naipaul, on the extreme left, formally clad in jacket, white shirt, spotty tie and red V-necked jumper, glares at the camera like a schoolmaster about to demand that a quaking fifth-former explain his behaviour. Kazuo Ishiguro sports a cowboy moustache to go with his home-on-the-range gingham shirt, sheriff's waistcoat and Timberlands under rolled-up denims. Buchi Emecheta, in a red-and-black plaid frock modelled on Marlon Brando's bomber jacket in *On the Waterfront*, looks as if she's had a row with A. N. Wilson, who is half turned away from her; his face in profile is that of a medieval saint painted by Carlo Crivelli.

Behind him, looking as if he's just received disappointing news, is a handsome-but-troubled William Boyd in a brown suede jacket. Ursula Bentley is a highly strung presence, her hands clutching each other for comfort, her neck soothed by a high-collared grey jacket, while Pat Barker, by contrast, is a confident northern martinet with a direct gaze and the look that says she's not to be mucked about. Last in the group, hovering at the back in a lilac shirt and grey waistcoat, is Clive Sinclair, his right shoulder hunched, his bearded face and balding head suggesting a trickster-craftsman from folklore, perhaps the cobbler in a Grimm's Fairy Tale.

There were two notable no-shows. One was Alan Judd, thirty-six, the author of one novel, *A Breed of Heroes*, about a British army officer in the thick of the Troubles in Belfast. Judd's name was a *nom de plume* – his former career in the army and the diplomatic service meant he couldn't use his real name, which was Alan Petty. The other was Salman Rushdie. Failing to have the winner of the 1981 Booker Prize in this gathering was a bit *Hamlet*-without-the-Prince, but there was presumably a good reason, other than just Rushdie's famous superiority complex.

The job of selecting Twenty Bright Young Novel-Writing Things fell to a curious quartet, chosen once again by Desmond Clarke. They were: Martyn Goff, back again in the judging room; Beryl Bainbridge the novelist, who'd been one of the Best of British the previous year; Michael Holroyd, the nation's most eminent biographer, and Alison Rimmer, the fiction buyer at Heffers bookshop in Cambridge. Their task was to choose the twenty under-forty novelists who, in their view, best 'illustrate the quality and promise of contemporary fiction'. And to reassure potential readers that they wouldn't be steered towards a pack of nobodies, the promotional material said, 'Without a doubt, there will not be a single unknown writer' in the line-up of fortunate fictioneers.

Really? Some doubts were soon voiced. Who was Maggie Gee? (She'd published one novel, from the obscure Harvester Press, in 1981.) Wasn't Philip Norman a *Sunday Times* journalist and author of a group biography of The Beatles? Clive Sinclair's story collection *Hearts of Gold* won the Somerset Maugham Award in 1981 – was he a novelist too? Ditto, Adam Mars-Jones, known only for stories. Shiva Naipaul, the brother of the more famous V. S., had written only journalism in the last ten years. Who was Buchi Emecheta? And Ursula Bentley? And wasn't Christopher Priest an SF writer – did he qualify?

As Desmond Clarke had noted a year earlier, lists bring easy publicity, because they can be argued over in just this way. And some splenetic reactions followed. The choice of judges was abused. 'Admirable as Michael Holroyd is as a biographer, I have not noticed his name as a fiction reviewer, nor that of Beryl Bainbridge, although she is known as a minor novelist,' Geoffrey Elborn sniffily observed in *Books and Bookmen*. 'And I don't think that Alison Rimmer's position as fiction manager of a bookshop makes her any better suited to be a judge of fiction than a grocer to comment on cans of soup.' Mee-*ow*. Other voices complained about the judges' failure to identify more than six women writers as against fourteen men (where was Shena Mackay, the sixties-dreamboat author of *Music Upstairs*, now thirty-nine? And where, for goodness' sake, was Sally Emerson?)

The *Sunday Times* article which accompanied the group photo-graph, written by Andrew Stephen, sounded less like a celebration of youthful talent, and more like a lament for their feeble earnings. Only a tiny minority, wrote Stephen, currently made enough money to live on. 'Christopher Priest made only £1,500 last year and has had to sell his house,' he sadly pointed out. 'Another signs on for the dole. Philip Norman made just £350 for his first novel. Graham Swift wrote a much-praised first novel, but relies on [the] earnings of his girlfriend. Maggie Gee received £500 when *The Times* printed extracts from her novel, which is more than she made elsewhere from it. Buchi Emecheta is finding it pays to publish herself; Clive Sinclair has to work in advertising . . .' When it came to lucrative ways of making a living, Stephen made novel-writing sound barely a step up from taking in washing.

He went on to explain that, despite buoyant reviews and 'a well-advertised launch', Adam Mars-Jones's *Lantern Lecture* sold only 1,319 copies in nine months. After taking into consideration

Faber's costs of paper, printing, cover design and promotion, Mars-Jones netted a princely £791.54. Stephen admits the author made some cash from the paperback and American rights but, he reported, 'he still needs to supplement these earnings by reviewing fiction for the *Sunday Times* and other journalism.' Well, *really*. As George III observed, on being told that some of his aristocratic subjects washed and reused their dining-room napkins, 'I didn't know such poverty existed.'

Andrew Stephen was, of course, right to sound a warning that there wasn't a multitude of readers in the UK who were avid to spend money trying out unknown literary talent. Which is why he praised Desmond Clarke for fighting an uphill battle ('the whole unlikely operation, pushing unknown names in a difficult genre to a mass market, has needed discipline and stamina') and running a campaign with military precision over seventeen months. For this was a new world of bookselling: a promotional assault, based not just on talent but on furiously targeted marketing. As he concluded: 'If OMO can be pushed into British homes, why not our best young novelists?'

The promotion worked. A quarter of a million additional copies of the featured books by The Young British were sold. *Granta 7* reprinted six times in the next ten years and brought out its own Best of Young British Novelists updates in 1993, 2003 and 2013. Many people are under the impression that the whole 'Best of' idea originated with *Granta*, rather than the marketing genius of Desmond Clarke. The 1983 promotion made literary fiction cool, visible and aspirational as a career choice, in a way it had never been before.

But were these newly promoted authors any good? I knew the quality of Amis and McEwan, of Barnes and Mars-Jones, Ishiguro and Rushdie and Swift, but the others? I couldn't buy the works of thirteen novelists – who was I, Paul Getty? – but I could borrow some from Putney Library, near my new home in Lower Richmond Road. I set to work with three novels by writers I hadn't heard of before.

Union Street by Pat Barker began disastrously. Two sisters, Kelly and Linda Brown, wake up in their shared bed somewhere north of Tyne and Wear. Three pages in, we're knee-deep in northern working-class misery and grot: everyone says 'Eee!' and 'nowt' and 'mucky sod' and 'jammy bugger'. There's a bearded stranger in their ma's bedroom, a hole in the bedroom window, another hole in the downstairs floorboards, and a pair of bloodied sanitary towels in the girls' chest of drawers. Many things make eleven-year-old Kelly dread puberty: 'She looked at the hair in Linda's armpits, at the breasts that shook and wobbled when she ran, and no, she didn't want to get like that. And she certainly didn't want to drip foul-smelling, brown blood out of her fanny every month. 'Next time I find one, I'll rub your bloody mucky face in it.'

Charming. Downstairs, the girls meet their ma's new conquest – bearded, feckless Arthur, a replacement for her last *inamorato*, Wilf. Ma and Kelly discuss how much food they might get on credit at the grocer's. Linda enters in her bra and knickers, diverting Arthur by adjusting one breast inside its stretchy mooring. It was all a cascade of clichés, evoking not so much proletarian life in Durham so much as a Monty Python parody of it.

Then, abruptly, the book went up a dozen notches. Bunking off school, Kelly goes for a walk in a vista of horse-chestnut trees, remembering her father and how he could make the tattooed snake on his arm wriggle by tensing a muscle. She is not to know that she has strayed into Ian McEwan Land. She finds the green carapace of a conker in the grass and becomes aware of a man nearby; in his polished shoes he is 'menacingly elegant' against the shabby detritus of leaves and grass.

A conker, seen in its green housing, becomes the locus of some heavy symbolism. 'It's not ready yet,' says Kelly. 'Sometimes they are,' says the creepy man. 'You can't always tell from the outside.' Whereupon, 'She watched his long fingers with their curved nails probe the green skin, searching for the place where it would most easily open up and admit them.' And soon, he'd got it open. 'Through the gash in the green skin, she could see the white seed.'

Whew! This was decidedly good writing, charged with sexy menace, even if its imagery derived a little too obviously from D. H. Lawrence and Ian McEwan, undermined by touches of *Cold Comfort Farm*. When the stranger asks Kelly to go with him to feed the ducks, she feels his strange magnetism ('His eyes created her. And so she had to go with him. She could not help herself. She had to go') and heads for the lake. He gives her a bag of sliced bread, which she tears into pieces, inching along the branch of an overhanging tree and scattering the bread to the birds in the lake. With the bread gone, the geese come hissing and swaying after her, 'yellow beaks jabbing at her hands and thighs. She pushed them away, sickened by the wet plumage over bone.'

Already a hapless plaything of erotic literature, Kelly has, unknowingly, entered a tableau of Leda and the Swan. She is no longer an eleven-year-old about to be raped, she is a Spartan queen about to cohabit with the supreme god of Greek mythology. Pat Barker could pile on the earthy stuff by the shovelful, but there was clearly a strong personal talent behind all the allusions.

Hearts of Gold by Clive Sinclair was a revelation, a magnificent, fizzing display of literary styles pressed into narratives of heartless cruelty, amorality and sin. The title story was a Raymond Chandler pastiche, set in LA and Las Vegas, seen through a kind of Jewish filter: a gumshoe called Smolinsky is hired by a female pimp called Virginia Lyle to deliver a letter to her daughter Laura, a dancer at Mikel Ratskin's joint on the Strip at Vegas.

The Bogart-lite delivery and the laconic narrative were pin-sharp Chandleresque ('I got my money and spent the rest of the day beside the cool blue pool, watching couples move silently from their autos to their motel rooms as if their thoughts were too dirty for the open air'), while the story of hookers, corrupt business practice, fatal gunshots and casual incest were a nod to *Chinatown* (1974). But was it anything more than clever pastiche?

The first story in the collection, 'Uncle Vlad', offered a voluptuously written hymn to Mitteleuropean decadence, about a family descended from Vlad the Impaler: just as he used to toss Turkish captives in the air and catch them on the point of a spear, so his descendant, the narrator's uncle, likes to mount butterflies by driving a needle through their bodies. Preparations for dinner in the family's Great Hall involve trapping a score of thrushes and biting their heads off, catching silver trout in the moonlight, wringing the necks and pressing the breasts of mallard ducks. The climax is a dessert of *crêpes aux papillons* or flambéed butterflies.

After this display of strenuous decadence, Sinclair's story turns into a visual work of art: 'I lit many candles and covered the table with the chequered cloth and spread out upon it the remains of the picnic: there were a few cheeses, a little pâté, some fruit, and most of a bottle of wine, so that I was able to compose a creditable still life.' When he finally bites the girl's innocent neck, sucks her blood and whispers, 'Now you really are one of the family', it's almost an anti-climax to the steady, dreadful, scene-setting brilliance of Sinclair's prose. He was clearly a mad combination of Edgar Allan Poe, Vladimir Nabokov and *The Decadence Cookbook*.

A key moment in *Second-Class Citizen* by Buchi Emecheta saw a young Nigerian wife Adah and her feckless husband Francis trying to find a flat in Kentish Town in early 1960s London. On the phone to the new landlady, Adah disguises her voice to conceal her African delivery. She and Francis visit the flat at night the better to disguise their black faces (she considers painting them white). Their destination, sadly, resembles a bombsite or burial ground. The landlady greets them from an upstairs window – but at ground level, she explains that the rooms have, just a minute before, gone to someone else. The wife is stunned:

'Adah had never faced rejection in this manner. Not like this, directly. Rejection by this shrunken piece of humanity, with a shaky body and moppy hair, loose, dirty and unkempt, who tried to tell them that they were unsuitable for a half-derelict and probably condemned house with creaky stairs. Just because they were blacks?'

It's a terrific moment, and it's also the moment you've been waiting for since noting the book's title: this'll be the story of wretched black immigrants abused and ground down by the racist-bastard English. But it hasn't been that simple. In the eighty pages preceding this confrontation, Emecheta has introduced us to several other levels of class distinction, tribal warfare, social discrimination and sexual waywardness, both in Africa and the UK.

The book starts in Nigeria, where it's natural in Igbo families for boys to be educated and for girls merely to learn to write their names, count numbers and become skilled at sewing. We hear about the condescension felt by young Igbos for their Yoruba neighbours whom they consider inferior. When Adah gets herself an education, and swings a good job at the American Consulate Library in Lagos, she dreams of visiting England and making her family's fortune. But in London, her securing a good job with a white company, and refusing to send her children to be fostered, as was the Nigerian way, means that she's thrown out of the family home. The joy of her vividly written (and irreducibly auto-biographical) novel is its constant discovery of new ways in which human beings, whose lives superficially harmonise, spend so much energy preying on each other.

So: three successful novels out of three. I couldn't wait to get stuck into the rest of the list. But later, a question occurred to me: was there ever such a skillful, if anonymous, manipulator of the British reading public as Desmond Clarke of the Royal Regiment of Artillery (retd.)?

CHAPTER 6

—— •◆• ——

The Carmelite of Camden Town

In the spring of 1983, I finally parted company with the *Director* and hit the primrose path of freelance work. My goodbye present was a ream of personal stationery, in a fabulous rust-and-cream livery, on which I would write to scores of prospective employers around the world and send invoices for the umpteen thousands of pounds and dollars that I'd soon be earning. My pals at the magazine promised to steer lucrative commissions my way. My now-regular work for *Books and Bookmen* had been joined by just-about-lucrative features for *Time Out*, *Executive Travel*, *Publishing News* and a few others. Even my first employer, the *Tablet*, asked me to review new fiction, on the tacit understanding that it wouldn't be the kind with pages of extreme violence, blasphemy or anal sex in it. I had become a hack, pure and simple. In his 1939 book *Enemies of Promise*, Cyril Connolly warned the would-be writer to beware freelance journalism, because it would fritter away the time, talent and concentration that should go into creating a literary masterpiece. Connolly invented the hapless figure of Walter Savage Shelleyblake, as the typical innocent, unsuspecting young fritterer, put to work by the evil, serpent-in-paradise figure of the literary editor, Mr Viper. I'd now become Walter, but I didn't mind.

I wasn't going to make my fortune this way, but I was content. Carolyn Hart and I had been An Item for months, our group of friends in south London included lots of young things in publishing and journalism, and the life we led was pleasingly full of books and imaginative minds. The 1980s books renaissance was getting into its full swing, and we were happy.

A year before my departure from business journalism, I'd become captivated by the work of a writer called Alice Thomas Ellis. Her second novel, *The Birds of the Air,* featured a heroine unlike any other I'd met in fiction. Mary Marsh was a woman aghast with sorrow for the death of her only child, a son; her grief took the form of a pitch-dark, caustic wit. She had no intention of counting her blessings or looking forward to raising more children. She burned 'in a blazing exaltation of grief'. Sentence by sentence, she inspected and icily rejected the visible world and embraced the black carnival of sensations in her head.

The book was set at Christmas, when Mary's mother, sister and brother-in-law were arriving to share festive good cheer. Mary greeted the prospect with utter resignation. She saw the Yuletide bacchanalia as sharing a truth with Newton's Second Law of Thermodynamics, which 'suggests that all construction, movement, devoir merely hasten that time when the world and all its works will be utterly undone, a whirling mass of dust in an infinite desolation.'

As a kind of bonus, Mary's mother, Mrs Marsh, had a biting wit of a different register, more worldly and seen-it-all, caustic but forgiving of the follies of others. When she looks at her son-in-law, Sebastian, an English professor, she is reminded 'of hard roads under a film of rain ... of slugs and Nazis and the minister she sometimes met in the terminal ward of the cancer hospital when she was arranging the flowers ...'

I asked Sally Emerson if she'd come across the author. Sally knew the name from reviews of her debut, *The Sin Eater* ('A first novel of startling wit and malice ... Shamelessly clever and never vague,' Christopher Wordsworth, evidently a scourge of imprecision, had written in the *Guardian*). She also knew that the author's real name was Anna Haycraft, and that she was married to Colin

Haycraft, the publisher. 'Funny you should bring her up,' she said. 'Her new novel's out soon. It's called *The 27th Kingdom*. Why don't you go and interview her?'

Camden Town in 1982 was a north London enclave of honking trendiness. Both sides of the Tube station opened onto streets of polychromatic front doors, strenuously crazy murals, and shops and cafés apparently designed by people recently returned from a Marrakesh souk. Yet only ten minutes away, Gloucester Crescent was a millpond of English serenity. Surely nobody would ever consider speeding down its wide curving roadway, or climbing on its trees, whose branches seemed to wave at you with frail, exquisite gentleness, like the Queen Mother.

The Haycraft residence, at number 22, was reached down a long, overgrown garden shaded by magnolias, their creamy blossoms like thick communion wafers. At the house, I stood before a gigantic front door, feeling like Pip calling on Miss Havisham, and rang the bell, without success. Minutes of indecision crept by. It took some time to notice, down some steps, a partially open basement door. What should I do? It seemed rude to just push my way in.

'Hello?' I cried, falteringly.

'Come in, for *God*'s sake,' came a man's voice, not entirely friendly in tone. I pushed the door. Inside was a cavernous kitchen with a huge wooden table on one side and a black Aga cooker on the other. The walls had been painted several decades ago, in a shade of teal or turquoise, through which patches of undercoat could be seen. The shelves were full of earthenware bowls – very Camden peasant-chic – and on the tiled work-surface stood a two-foot-high statue of Jesus Christ, his extended arms encased in wizard sleeves, his sacred heart displayed like a giant strawberry.

Two people regarded me coldly. The man, Colin Haycraft, was sitting back in a deep cushiony armchair, holding a book in his right hand. I saw a corduroy jacket, identical to the one worn by my old geography teacher, a pair of spectacles above which spiky black eyebrows stuck out at angles, a jaunty blue bow-tie and a cigarette that burned in his left hand. He looked very absorbed, and rather cross to have been disturbed by a nervous stranger hovering outside his door. Colin was the boss of Duckworth, the famous publishing house, whose founder Gerald Duckworth is a pariah of literary history for having interfered sexually with both his half-sisters, Virginia and Vanessa Stephen, long before they became Virginia Woolf and Vanessa Bell.

The woman stood beside the black range. My first impression of Anna Haycraft was of a beautiful, pissed-off nun. She was clad in a long, black, button-fronted frock that fluted out around her ankles, as though she'd just come from a rather louche memorial service. Her brown eyes held no warmth and her mouth was set in a dispirited droop. There was something of a sneer about her face, a superior flare of nostril. Like her husband, she was smoking, holding her fag at cheek-height, her right elbow cradled by her left hand. Her whole attitude was defensive. It said: '*On the whole I'd rather you went away.*'

'What an amusing jacket,' she said, looking at a candy-striped number I'd bought in Chelsea three years earlier, and ill-advisedly still wore, long after its trendiness had evaporated. 'Would you like some tea?'

It was as though a light had been switched on in this dark, unwelcoming room. The key to Anna Haycraft was her voice, an exquisite cooing of perfect politeness and motherly welcome. It made most of her pronouncements seem graceful and kindly, even when she was radiating disapproval.

The magazine interview began. I told her how much I'd loved *Birds of the Air*, and asked about the passive figure of Mary.

'Surely,' I said, 'nobody in a state of such terminal sadness could possibly be as articulate as she is, could they?'

'You found her an unconvincing character?' Anna asked, a hint of steel in her voice.

'Er, no,' I stumbled, 'I think her voice sort of *transcends* realism, and . . .'

She looked away, into the room. 'I once knew a woman who died of grief,' she said dreamily. 'They said it was cancer but – of course – cancer is an emblem of sorrow.'

It quickly became clear that Anna had not the slightest interest in questions about her writing process or her narrative point of view. When I remarked on her aptitude for getting inside the minds of all her Yuletide *dramatis personae*, she said, 'Well actually, the narrator is the cat . . .'

Things changed, however, when I said Mrs Marsh reminded me of my mother, especially her rude remarks about men. (Of visitors to the family home who arrived without a gift, Mum used to say, 'That fella – he'd leave you with one arm as long as the other.' Of overly puffed-up officials, 'If conceit was consumption, he'd be dead long ago.') Anna was suddenly all ears. She wanted to hear all about my mother, her Irishness, her red hair, her directness with coarse market traders, her semi-erotic adoration of Catholic priests.

Anna's favourite subject was, it turned out, the Catholic Church in England and its many shortcomings. I later learned that she'd been a postulant nun for a year in her early twenties, but had slipped a disc and was considered by the sisters to be unsuited for life in the public community. With a shift from the sublime to the earthy that was very characteristic, she'd left the convent and gone to work at a tearoom near the British Museum, where she met Colin, who popped in daily for a buttered bun. They married in 1956, when she was only twenty-four.

It was hard to imagine what she looked like behind the counter at that age, offering her regular customers a virginal smile. She looked – not old, but timelessly stuck in a dark, umbral melancholy, from which she uttered sentences oddly perched between elegance and slang.

'I have written to Basil Hume many times since he became archbishop,' she said as she poured tea, 'to explain that, since the abandonment of the Latin Mass, I can barely bring myself to attend even the Sunday service; and, while there, I find myself alongside only six or seven co-religionists, all similarly dismayed by that iniquitous betrayal. Yet not a word of thanks do I get. Not a dicky bird.' The last four words were a riot of glottal stops: 'No'a'di'e'bird.'

From the depths of the armchair came a rapid quacking. It's the only way to describe it. 'Quoke, quack, quick, quock . . .'

I wondered if her husband, dismayed by his wife's disparagement of the country's top Catholic, had gone mad.

'I'm sorry,' I said. 'I didn't catch what you . . .'

'*Desine de quoquam quicquam bene velle mereri*,' Colin intoned, as if making some perfectly obvious point in English, '*aut aliquem fieri posse putare pium.*'

'Which means?' I asked.

'Give up wanting to deserve any thanks from anyone, or thinking that anybody can be grateful,' he said with a chuckle. 'Catullus, you know.'

I'd met a few classical scholars at university, but I'd never before met one who could quote a relevant thought in a perfect Latin couplet. I found out later that he composed occasional squibs in the supposedly dead language. A year after we met, he recited a couplet he'd just finished. It concerned the Women's Peace Camp at Greenham Common, where protests were being held against the presence of Cruise missiles at an RAF air base. A woman friend of the Haycrafts had paid a visit, to show solidarity with the group, but had been shocked to see an American airman pull down his jeans and expose his bottom. 'It's a rather clever play on words,' said Colin, 'because *anus* is Latin for *old woman* as well as meaning a circle, which is where the English word "anus" comes from. So . . .' (here he read out the two Latin lines, in which '*anum*' and '*anus*' followed each other) 'the ending translates as "I do not like this arsehole, said the old bag". Rather good, don't you think?'

Colin was odd in other ways. He liked making provocative statements that weren't just idiotic on the lips of a clever person; you couldn't believe a publisher could say them. When Anna brought up a famous writer whose recent work had been poorly received, Colin said, 'He's hopeless. But then, only women can write novels, you know; women and queers.'

When the interview was published in *Books and Bookmen*, I had a letter from Anna, telling me off for describing her as 'a perfectly bell-shaped woman'. I think I'd meant 'bluebell-shaped', since that had been the contour of her frock, but somehow it had become mangled. On the first sheet of the letter she drew a picture of a vast, wide-skirted Liberty Bell, and wrote, '*This*, John, is what a bell looks like. *No woman* is going to thank you for the comparison.' But she liked the rest of the write-up, and my praise for her book, and invited me to dinner.

When I arrived, Colin gave me a glass of wine and ticked me off for describing him in the article as 'a raffish and chortling classicist'. 'I'm not a *classicist*, for God's sake,' he said, 'I'm just an *educated man*.' The other guests at the kitchen supper brought to mind the card-table scene in *Sunset Boulevard* that featured *monstres sacrés* from the film world including Buster Keaton and Erich von Stroheim. There was Patrice Chaplin, with her huge alpaca eyes, the daughter-in-law of Charlie Chaplin, and the one-time friend of Sartre and De Beauvoir, Dalí and Cocteau; Anna's best friend, Beryl Bainbridge, with her helmet of black hair, her schoolgirlish white blouse and stripy tie; Terence Kilmartin, the handsome and wolfish literary editor of the *Observer*, and most recent translator of *À la Recherche du Temps Perdu*, plus a couple of Colin's donnish pals.

The dinner was memorable for three things. First, I noticed that Anna, having dished up a richly aromatic casserole, didn't actually eat anything. She served herself a doll's-house plateful and occasionally poked it with her fork. She drank white wine with gusto, and lit a Silk Cut as soon as the company had finished eating.

Second, she had a kind of seizure during pudding. Her face became contorted as if she couldn't breathe, her brow furrowed, her eyes full of agony. Beryl took her hand and tried to calm her by cooing sympathetically. Colin chuckled, 'Come on, darling, the stew isn't that bad . . .' The other guests looked on neutrally. I got the impression they'd seen this before.

'Is your heart palpitating?' asked Patrice in a detached way, as one might ask if it had stopped raining.

'No, it's all right,' gasped Anna, raising an eloquent hand. 'I know what it is. It's . . . *unshed tears*.'

I'd heard about the tragedy in her life, which was echoed by the trauma of Mary Marsh in *The Birds of the Air*. Two years earlier, the Haycrafts's beloved son Joshua had fallen through a plate-glass roof at Euston Station while trainspotting, and had spent ten months in a coma before dying. He was nineteen. His devastated mother had been able to keep going only by writing her grief onto the pages of her books. Hence the biting melancholy of *The Sin Eater* and *The Birds of the Air*. The 'unshed tears' bit was a touch drama-queen, a bit *mater Misericordiae*, but it wasn't an affectation. She was genuinely heartbroken. I thought it perfectly possible she might feel a sisterhood with the Virgin Mary of Michelangelo's *Pietà*.

The third thing was the courtly flirting between Beryl Bainbridge and Terence Kilmartin. The distinguished, Irish-born Kilmartin had a stern, craggy authority that promised little in the way of romantic skittishness; but when Beryl talked to him, he softened visibly. She brought up the hackneyed line about French (in which of course he was fluent) being a more musical and sexy language than English and he nodded. Then she looked straight into his face, and said:

'Terence, how do you say, in French, "I love the sun, the moon and the stars . . ."?'

'*J'aime le soleil, la lune et les étoiles*,' said Terence in his soft, Anglo-Irish lilt.

'But most of all,' Beryl continued, 'it's you that I love.'

'*Mais surtout, c'est toi que j'aime*,' Terence gamely concluded.

Her big brown eyes blinked.

'Oh, *Terence* . . .' she said, a little breathless.

In the months that followed, I found myself happily, if a little dazedly, welcomed into Anna's north London court. I had been 'taken up' by the sad-eyed sorceress, regularly summoned to her side for teatime chats, or to be her walker at publishing parties. I got used to her dark, womb-like kitchen, with her children (four boys and a staggeringly beautiful daughter called Sarah) wandering in and out at random, and Beryl constantly dropping by for cigarettes and wine.

Our growing friendship didn't mean that she abandoned her reserve with me or began to confide about her life. ('Colin used to say he'd as soon sell his wife on a street corner as discuss her with other people,' she said. 'And I feel much the same about him.') But Anna showed me a different side of her personality – a gossipy fascination for other people's bad behaviour, for oddity, for curious choices of marital partner or personal presentation. Once at a party she gazed with fascination at a six-foot, Oxford-graduate, former First XV rugby-playing Blue, now a transsexual author of books on popular culture, in a PVC bustier and a purple fright wig. 'You know who people are, John,' she said. 'Who is that man over there with the tits?'

Tales of adultery, instead of shocking her Catholic soul, elicited worldly remarks along the lines of 'Men are like fires – if they're not tended, they tend to go out' (was she quoting Zsa Zsa Gabor?) She looked with fond indulgence on the atrocious behaviour of Jeffrey Bernard (who once vomited on the Queen Mother's feet at Ascot) because he had 'such a wonderful sense of humour'. Later in the 1980s they had side-by-side columns in the *Spectator*. She was 'Home Life' to his 'Low Life'.

Devoutly religious (she often told people that she'd probably go back to being a nun some day), she had a brisk way with mysticism, with angels and apparitions; she didn't believe in their existence, but was entranced by people who did.

'The Welsh are always seeing fairies,' she told me once, 'but not your usual ones with wings and so forth. There's lots of different sorts. Some of their fairies are little tiny people with little tiny horses, richly clad. Some of them are like dwarves, terribly ugly. They've such a range of fairies, you never meet two of the same.'

Was that, I asked, the folklore stuff she'd heard when growing up in Wales? 'It's not just folklore,' she said. 'Until very recently they believed implicitly in fairies. Only thirty years ago, one old farmer still put out milk for them. You'd get "corpse candles" – when someone was going to die, you'd see the light flickering at the doorposts – and you'd see phantom funerals go by, just above the hedgerow. Someone would die a week later and be taken for burial along the same route.'

Had she actually seen one herself? 'No no *no*,' she said sadly. 'I never see anything.'

I learned about the modus operandi of Duckworth the publishing firm. That it was run on very old-fashioned lines, as befitted its company address: The Old Piano Factory, Gloucester Crescent, London NW1. That Anna, as fiction editor, encouraged burgeoning talent without caring too much about its commercial viability; some of her authors told me they were offered a two-book deal on the strength of a rough outline of the plots. Nor would dismaying sales figures dissuade her from asking her charges how their next book was getting on.

Colin, by contrast, was shrewd about money to the point of meanness. He published works on Latin and Greek classics – but these were mostly projects whose only alternative outlet would have been the university presses of Oxford and Cambridge. Since their authors would expect no advance or recompense from the presses, and were overjoyed to find a commercial publisher in London prepared to print their book inside a year, Colin could keep their advances and revenues low. Amazingly, he did the same with his fiction writers – even with his bestsellers. It was common knowledge that Beryl Bainbridge never received an advance of more than £2,000, no matter how high her profile, nor how wide her fame. Michael Holroyd once told me he'd seen one of Beryl's contracts. 'It stipulated that the more books she sold, the smaller, not larger, her percentage of sales. It was the most perverse contract I've ever seen.' But Colin was seldom indulgent about his authors. 'A publisher is a specialised form of bank or building society,' he once wrote, 'catering for customers who cannot cope with life and are therefore forced to write about it.'

I later learned the chequered, not to say patchworked, nature of the relationship between the Gloucester Crescent bohemians: that Colin and his biggest-selling author Beryl had embarked on an affair early in the 1980s; that Anna, notionally Beryl's best friend, knew all about it; and that both women had had an affair with the same man, Austin Davis, in the 1950s. Anna, despite her Catholic rigour, had become pregnant by him and endured an abortion, which she'd always regretted; and it was just possible that Beryl's affair with Colin was her dark recompense for Anna's having stolen her man, back in 1952.

Anna brought me with her to a party given by Lady Caroline Blackwood in her second-floor apartment in Redcliffe Square, Chelsea, where I gazed for whole minutes at the portrait of our hostess on the wall. It was *Girl in Bed* by Lucian Freud, her former husband, and it emphasised her enormous tigerish eyes and stroppy-teenager expression. (It must have been a copy – the original was in her New York home at Sag Harbour.)

In the large, richly furnished living room, a throng of beautiful faces, celebrities and grotesques milled about: one or two Guinnesses (Caroline's mother Maureen was there, an heiress to the brewery fortune, once described by Cecil Beaton as 'the biggest bitch in London'), George Melly, the jazz singer turned *Observer* film critic, Marianne Faithfull, the sixties rock *chanteuse*, Nigel Dempster the gossip columnist. Caroline's two daughters from her second marriage, Evgenia and Ivana Citkowitz, were real beauties at twenty and seventeen, with their plump cheeks and lips, their mother's feline eyes, and their air of well-bred contempt for the stammering men to whom they were introduced.

When Anna led me over meet to Lady Caroline, I had to pinch myself to stop blurting out, '*Oh my god you were married to Robert Lowell – what was that like?*' In fact I knew approximately what it had been like because Ian Hamilton's biography of the manic-depressive American poet had recently come out from Faber. It contained a vivid account of Caroline's early meetings with Lowell in 1966, when she was regularly placed next to him at dinner. This was during one of Lowell's manic periods, when he couldn't hold a conversation about anything except poetry. Caroline had described their 'ghastly silences'. Once, to break an especially heavy one, she'd said she admired the soup. To which Lowell had replied, 'I think it's perfectly disgusting', before lapsing into taciturnity. But after he invited her to a Faber party four years later, he'd moved in with her – into the very flat where we were now standing.

We found a problematic common ground in a chapter of her first book, *For All That I Found There* (the title comes from the lovely Percy French song, 'The Mountains of Mourne'); in it she dealt with the ghastly subject of burnt flesh. It seemed that her daughter Ivana had been seriously scalded by a boiling kettle at the age of six, and Caroline's description of a hospital burns ward was the result. I felt able to commiserate, having had, in my student years, a holiday job as hospital porter in Roehampton, where I did everything in my power to avoid going near G Ward, with its smell of roasted pork and its appalling groans. Caroline listened politely but her Snow Queen eyes revealed that we weren't talking at the same level of gravitas: she'd been writing about the trauma of a child with incinerated flesh, whereas I'd been chatting about my callow disinclination to go anywhere near such a child.

I loved the parties Colin and Anna Haycraft threw at the company HQ. In the same way that, in her kitchen, she'd hover by the Aga, smoking and listening to the conversations around her, throwing in the odd silkenly caustic observation, at Duckworth parties Anna would park herself in one place – an armchair by the French window – and wait for the social world to come to her.

I used to park myself alongside, in the hope of being introduced to writers and thinkers as they came to pay court.

The first I attended brought a series of shocks, as a succession of famous names filed into the garden. I knew Jonathan Miller from television, but couldn't place the stern, thin-faced cove he was talking to. Was it Bertrand Russell? No, it was another philosopher, A. J. Ayer, whose book on Hume had been reviewed a month before. The *Beyond the Fringe* polymath and the author of *Language, Truth and Logic* were standing beside me in a worldly corner of Philosophy Heaven. Kingsley Amis was unmistakeable with his Garrick Club tie and his look of dyspeptic grumpiness; he was, I learned from Colin, "a terrific asset" at parties because of his readiness to talk to, or preferably confront, absolutely anyone, including twenty-something strangers who came under his heading of 'little shits'. Once he turned to me, as I hovered on the edge of a conversation he was having with the playwright Ronnie Harwood and asked me, out of the blue: 'What about you? *You* believe that torture's a good thing, don't you? I mean, *you*'d torture someone if you knew they'd planted a bomb somewhere. Wouldn't you?'

As I opened and closed my mouth like a koi carp, Harwood came to my rescue. 'I'd say that one's enthusiasm for torture, as with oral sex,' he said sleekly, 'rather depends on whether one is giving or receiving.'

I remember Amis being unimpressed by the drinks available and asking for a malt whisky. I wasn't surprised because Colin Haycraft's champagne cocktails were vicious bastards. A look in the kitchen would confirm that they contained neither French brandy nor actual champagne. They were a mix of Fundador Spanish cognac and Pomagne. The first time I tried one, I went deaf in one ear for half an hour.

Anna's gang of lady writers – Beryl, Patrice and Caroline – were all in the garden. I gave them a wide berth, because I'd published an article in *Books and Bookmen* about how they formed a literary clique that, in public, sometimes resembled a Women's Institute meeting. Lady Caroline had rung me up after it came out, roundly abusing me for being so bloody cheeky, before asking me for the telephone number of some Irish friends of mine in County Wexford whom she was hoping to write about: especially a mad aunt who had established a transatlantic cult devoted to Isis, and had turned the basement of the family's Big House into a shrine to the Egyptian goddess. It was an odd experience, being asked a favour by someone who was simultaneously ticking you off.

In the magazine piece, I'd explained that these slender, sharp-eyed, intense and Bohemian women wrote books that closely matched that description: slender novels of about one hundred and fifty pages, set in both modern London and some coastal extremity (Cornwall, Wales, Ireland), starring a woman whose domestic or marital traumas prefigure unpleasant physical outcomes, including murder. They didn't deal in black humour so much as the bizarre, the driven, the obsessive, the Gothic, the Grand Guignol. What I'd failed to emphasise was that there was nothing marginal about their work. They were very much in the 1970s fiction mainstream. Caroline Blackwood's *Great Granny Webster* had been shortlisted for the Booker Prize in 1977, as had Beryl's *The Dressmaker* and *The Bottle Factory Outing* in successive years, 1973 and 1974, while Anna's third novel, *The 27th Kingdom*, had been shortlisted in 1982.*

A distinctive figure in the garden was Angela Carter, whom I'd met four years earlier at Gollancz. Angela was friends with all the Haycraft gang, and clearly liked their parties. To my delight she remembered me, and we talked, in a small knot of her admirers, about the articles she'd been writing for *New Society*. Beryl Bainbridge

---

* The ubiquity of slender fictions by female authors had led the press to note that the Booker Prize shortlist invariably featured every year something called 'the Thin Woman's Novel'. Bainbridge, Blackwood and Haycraft were joined in this skinny sorority by Penelope Fitzgerald and Anita Brookner, when they won the Booker Prize with the very thin *Offshore* (1979) and *Hotel du Lac* (1984) respectively.

came over to join us, just as the conversation turned to Simon Raven, the rackety but fabulously prolific, Deal-based author of the *Alms for Oblivion* novel sequence. Beryl listened for a few minutes and asked:

'Sorry, who is this Simon Raven?'

Angela turned to me with an eyebrow raised. Who would go first in defining this notorious rake, this modern-day Earl of Rochester?

'After you,' I said.

'You're the journalist,' said Angela. 'Go ahead.'

'OK then,' I said. 'Simon Raven is, um, a badly-behaved, broken-veined, ex-Charterhouse public school novelist, whose works tend to deal with cricket, buggery and vampires.'

There was a silence, as the others looked at Angela. She'd closed her eyes, as if she was thinking hard.

'Yes, that's all true,' she said, her eyes still shut, 'but it's not the most interesting thing about him, is it?'

'What's that?' asked Beryl nervously.

Angela tilted her face to the blue sky. 'Only that he is reputed to have . . .'

Our faces must have been a picture as we waited.

'. . . eaten . . .'

Angela's closed eyes fluttered.

'. . . human . . .'

Bloody hell, I thought. Is she having a turn?

'. . . *ffflllessssshhhh*.' Angela put a lot into the last word, as if savouring the exquisite tastiness of what it signified. If she was winding up the company just for larks, she was doing it very convincingly.*

The garden was filling up nicely by 2.30 p.m. Colin and Anna, for all their apparent oddness – her melancholy, his peremptory abruptness – seemed to know a lot of impressive literary types.

---

* Raven may have encouraged the suggestion that he had cannibalistic tendencies because of the true story about the baby. Once when he was travelling in foreign parts, his wife Susan, then nursing their son Adam, sent him a panicky telegram. It read: 'WIFE AND BABY STARVING. SEND MONEY.' He telegraphed back: 'NO MONEY. EAT BABY.'

Michael Frayn, the playwright and novelist, was there with Claire Tomalin, literary editor of the *New Statesman*. Sebastian Faulks, now working at the *Daily Telegraph*, stood with Marcel Berlins, the legal whizz and *Times* crime fiction reviewer, discussing *The Archers*, and the exact location (Dorset? West Midlands?) of the fictional Ambridge. Derwent May, literary editor of the *Listener*, was in earnest conversation with Michael Holroyd, biographer of Lytton Strachey and ubiquitous books-committee *apparatchik*.

A frequent visitor was Oliver Sacks, the great neurologist and anthropologist, who made a starry career out of writing about the vivid inner lives of people in persistent vegetative states or victims of neurological confusion. His most famous book was *The Man Who Mistook his Wife for a Hat*. He was an imposing presence, bald-headed, bushy-bearded, granny-spectacled and charmingly hesitant in speech. People offered each other random bits of information about him: 'Did you know he comes from Cricklewood?' 'Did you know he's first cousin of Jonathan Lynn, who co-wrote *Yes Minister*?' 'Did you know that he's a biker, that he was once in a Hell's Angels chapter, and was a big Grateful Dead fan?' Only the first two of these turned out to be true (I checked), but Sacks's oddness and peripatetic, transatlantic career encouraged speculation.

I can't recall whether the Sacks incident I witnessed was at a Duckworth garden party or at the Piano Factory, but the details are straightforward. He brought with him a sufferer from Tourette's Syndrome, called (I think) James – a skinny, sweet-faced youth of eighteen or nineteen, with a beguiling air of innocence and lots of brown wavy hair under a baseball cap. Sacks introduced him, explaining that he'd brought him on this trip to England to help him feel 'normalised' in society, and to monitor his reactions to the everyday world.

James looked at our enquiring faces with abrupt shifts of gaze, like a robbery victim inspecting a line-up of suspects. When someone asked, 'How are you enjoying London?' he replied, 'I love London. It's my favourite city after New York.' When another said,

'I hope Dr Sacks is showing you some interesting sights,' he said 'Dr Sacks is showing me a lot of cool places. I've been to Bucking-*ham* Palace.' His replies sounded a little pat. But I'm ashamed to admit I wasn't waiting for words of wisdom to fall from his lips; like the others I was waiting for him to utter some terrible curses, or a fusillade of effing and blinding, to bark or snarl or ululate.

He didn't do any of these. Then Beryl stepped towards him. Driven by a motherly impulse, or perhaps her natural sympathy for the downtrodden, she said: 'You *poor boy*. To be taken around London and shown off, as if you were – an exhibit! A prize *pig* somebody won at a fair! You poor—'

Her sympathetic words prompted James into action. He said nothing, but his right hand shot out uncontrollably, and clamped itself over Beryl's left breast. It wasn't, I'm sure, a sexual assault, more a clutching at a kindly, sympathetic female by a boy whose pubertal affections had been skewed by illness.

Somebody near Dr Sacks must have gasped at the sight, because the great man wheeled round. 'James!' he shouted across. 'That's very rude! Stop it *at once*!'

James looked at Sacks. We looked at James. His hand remained attached to Beryl's white-cotton-shirted breast. What on earth would she do?

She laid her hand softly over the boy's, and smilingly disengaged it.

She looked at Sacks. 'Leave him *alone*!' she said. 'He seems a *perfectly nice young man* to me.'

I left the party about 5 p.m., rang the *Director* and explained I'd been taken unexpectedly drunk, then went home awash with Fundador 'n' fizz, and hit the sack for several hours. Now *that*, I thought, was a party. And *that* was a glimpse of *la vie haute Bohème*, bang in the heart of 1980s London. And that was a publishing house to fall in love with, because of, rather than in spite of, its ramshackle air. Above all, there was Anna, whom I felt proud to know because she not only appreciated good writing, she was a fabulous modern practitioner. The big world of readers would catch up with her one day, I thought – I was just glad to know she existed, with her melancholy poise and her perfect sentences. She had let me into the magic garden, where literary dinosaurs crashed about and wide-eyed young pretenders could have their first glimpse of greatness – and wonder how to join it.

There were lots more positive vibes in the air than ever before. I'd become part of a venerable literary journal, with whose deputy editor I was in love. I was mates with a top agent – Giles Gordon – and had been 'taken up' by the fiction editor of a famous publishing house (Anna). And I had friends toiling in the groves of actual creativity. Sebastian and I could still be found in pubs across the metropolis, talking about the books we'd write. I remember an evening in The Clarence, an ancient boozer in Whitehall where, as we were serenaded by a red-faced lute-player singing 'It's All For Me Grog' in a tight-fitting harlequin costume, Sebastian said, 'I mean, for God's sake, John – if someone as rubbish as Norman Carpet [or the name of any annoyingly precocious recent debut scribe] can publish a novel, surely *we* can?' and we clinked glasses and vowed to take the fiction world by storm *very soon*.

Everything was in place. The stars were aligned. The entrails of a million chickens were giving a haruspicatory thumbs-up. All that was missing was The Great Book.

I'm sure you've read Michael Frayn's first novel *The Tin Men* (winner of the Somerset Maugham Award in 1965). It's a witty depiction of a computer laboratory where one of the scientists, Hugh Rowe, is obsessed with writing a novel. He has no idea about plot, characters, style or treatment, but is keen to get it done.

As *The Tin Men* progresses, we're given samples of his ever-changing plot and prose style. One minute, *R* is 'the story of a whisky priest, tortured by the consciousness of having committed every sin, from blasphemy to murder'; next minute, '*R* is the story of four men – a refugee dictator, an advertising copywriter, an alcoholic war-hero and a class-conscious trade unionist – who find themselves marooned on a tiny island in the steaming heat of the Torres Strait . . .'

Later, having got nowhere with *A Knot of Worms* (a torrid tangle of sexual relationships in the style of Iris Murdoch), he embarks on *Take a Bloke Like Me*, in which four modern chaps lay siege to the virginity of Annie Crumpet, in a dire pastiche of Kingsley Amis ('A moment later she could feel a dirty great hand fumbling with the moorings of the good ship brassiere . . .'). The opening of *No Particle Forgot* offers a scene under the Mediterranean sun *à la* Lawrence Durrell, where a description of the hero starts in confusion ('Rick Roe was tall. But his shoulders were broad, so that the first impression you got of him was that he was a man of average build standing some way off . . .') and becomes bogged down by over-precision. ('The fingers grew from strong well-formed hands, with russet hair on the back of them, and the hands were attached to the muscular arms by broad, sinewy wrists. There were four fingers and a thumb on each hand . . .')

Finally, in *Hear Me Punnin' to Ya*, an excruciating attempt at beat-poet prose, some way after Kerouac, the narrator is a jazz pianist ('I loped across to the piano and flipped the lid. My eighty-eight little friends smiled up at me. Black and white together – no segregation at this lunch counter . . .'). But Rowe can't sustain the groovy rigmarole and comes to a poignant finale. 'He looked down at his twenty-six little friends on the keyboard . . . "All right" [he says to the typewriter keys] "it's twenty-six to one and I surrender unconditionally. I swear I'll never lay another finger on any of you again."'

Frayn's virtuoso pastiches deliver a dismaying picture of the modern writer floundering in a sea of plots and voices, unable to find one that's personal, idiolectal, true. And this was precisely my problem. I must have started, and abandoned, seven or eight books in my twenties, none of which came to anything. They were a mixed bunch. Among them were:

1. *The Island of Nowhere*, a satire on modern sightseeing, in which Antonio, a minor official at the Italian Department of Tourism, is tasked with finding a new holiday destination, now that every island from Capri to Torcello is packed to saturation with holiday-makers; he chooses for a makeover the atrocious hell-hole of Serbellini, with its dormant volcano, its population of scorpions and visiting flocks of deadly locusts ... (*Sadly the story collapsed under the complexity of the set-up and the cast of thousands ...*)

2. *The Drug Museum*, starring thirty-something alcoholic Annabel, recently split from her husband, who is taken by her best girlfriend on a recuperative holiday to New Orleans. Annabel is intrigued by the Old Pharmacy, where a curator shows her some ancient voodoo potions. When she falls for a local musician but is rejected, she breaks into the museum and drinks a potion called 'Come to Me', with phantasmagorical consequences ... (*This would have been a thing of fireworks and wonder if written by Angela Carter. It wasn't.*)

3. *Cooking the Wolf*, set in 1910–11, brought together two stars of the Edwardian world: Angela Brazil, author of schoolgirl-hockey-sticks stories and Auguste Escoffier, the celebrity *chef de cuisine* at the Ritz-Carlton hotel. They're linked by a young doctor, an early fan of Freud, who gets entangled with a group of Latvian anarchists called The Wolf, who are planning to bomb the House of Commons ... (*This attempt to write a British version of* Ragtime *simply became overwhelmed by multi-story-osity.*)

So I didn't write a novel in my twenties. I still wanted, though, to join the great literary circus. But what should I write? At university, I'd been inspired by Cyril Connolly, whose 1938 book *Enemies of Promise* asked, simply: 'How is one to write a book that will last for ten years?' His answer suggested it was down to the kind of prose style you adopted. Connolly recommended would-be writers to borrow elements of both the 'Mandarin' style (grand, sonorous, old-fashioned and ruminative, the language of Dr Johnson, Carlyle and Ruskin, Virginia Woolf and Lytton Strachey) and the 'vernacular' style (plain, direct, journalistic, close to spoken

English, the prose of Hemingway, Orwell and Christopher Isherwood.) But who, in the 1970s, could get away with writing like Dr Johnson? And did one have to adopt Orwell's view that 'Good prose is like a windowpane' when it clearly could be a great deal more?

In the summer of 1975, after graduation, I'd read a *New Statesman* review of *The Metropolitan Critic* by Clive James, and was intrigued by the book's advocacy of a similarly 'mixed style', of highbrow thought and lowbrow (or amusingly slangy) expression. James's hero was evidently the great American literary critic Edmund Wilson, whose genius, James said, was to combine the smart language of the city street and the discourse of the university campus. James himself, though, sounded nothing like Edmund Wilson. When writing about authors, such as Ford Madox Ford, he sounded like this:

'Even at his youngest and trimmest, Ford looked like an earless Bugs Bunny on stilts, and by his own admission he was more interested in chat than sex. Nevertheless the Grade A crumpet came at him like kamikazes, crashing through his upper decks in gaudy cataracts of fire. Violet Hunt took him away from his first wife, Elsie ... A woman who had somehow managed to hit the sack with Somerset Maugham was a sexual force of primal urgency.'

Whaat? 'Bugs Bunny on stilts'? 'The Grade A crumpet'? '... hit the sack ...'? This wasn't the language of modern metropolitan-critical intelligence. It was the hard-boiled, side-of-the-mouth wisecracking *patois* of American gumshoe writers like Raymond Chandler and Dashiell Hammett. It was also, coincidentally, the same voice that appeared weekly in Clive James's *Observer* TV reviews – and nobody could write like this except Mr James.

Then I heard from an old college friend that *The Metropolitan Critic* had been the subject of an essay in the *New Review*, by none other than John Carey. It turned out to be a glorious takedown of James's noisy desire to show off his erudition, his vast range of allusions and grasp of concepts. For Carey, James's book was simply an Olympian display of name-dropping:

'Immortal names drop from him like dandruff, so that . . . the airily planted erudition can take on the tone of a Sixth Form Prize Essay . . . for instance, "Croce wrote to Vossler pointing out that Heidegger was Germany's Gentile, an acute remark."' Carey sleekly remarked that one shouldn't really mock a show-off: 'To scoff at Mr James for knowing a lot could be the reaction only of ignorance and envy. His versatility merits respect.'

Carey then takes a rubber truncheon to James's critical language. James evaluates intellectual affairs, says Carey, 'as if they were sporting events. Star literary critics are like "the Continental circuit of Formula 1 drivers"; a Keith Douglas poem is "like skiing on one ski"; in Seamus Heaney, "a punchy line travels about two inches" . . . The traditional image of the thinker and writer as lonely, contemplative, unspectacular, dissolves and in its place comes a composite Jamesian super-sportsman, goggled, helmeted, swinging punches from a surfboard.'

I read these words and felt exhilarated. So *that* was how a critic wrote a memorable review: you quote a lot of the author's sillier observations, then throw them together into one fabulous, killing image. It was indeed an amalgam of things – not the Mandarin and the vernacular styles, not the language of city street and university campus, but the combination of expressing polite interest in the writer's obsessions, and simultaneously taking the piss. From then on, I resolved to try my best to write like Carey, guided by my reading of everything he wrote in the future. Who knows (I thought)? Perhaps, one day, I might meet him again.

CHAPTER 7

————— •·• —————

The Big Time 1984–6

For British literary journalists, 1984 was a godsend, simply because of its Orwellian connection. It meant that every newspaper and magazine would want to run a piece headed something like: 'How Close Are We, in 1984, to Orwell's Nightmare Vision of Britain in *Nineteen Eighty-Four*?' The answer was, quite frankly, 'Not very close at all', but that didn't stop people like me teasing out all manner of correspondences for *Books and Bookmen* or *Time Out*.

Like these:

1. *In Orwell's book, the UK has become 'Airstrip One', a tiny province of a totalitarian state called Oceania, which also includes North America. But what was real-life England in 1984 but a version of Airstrip One, when we were being used by the USA to house their cruise missiles, targeting the USSR from Greenham Common?*

2. *Remember 'the Two-Minute Hate', when the citizens of Oceania were encouraged to yell and curse at their TV screens every night, when the image of Emmanuel Goldstein (head of 'The Brotherhood' and Enemy of the Party) was shown at 11 p.m.? The obvious modern equivalent was the face of Arthur Scargill (head of a variant of the Brotherhood called the Miners' Union) appearing on the TV News every night in real-life 1984.*

3. *Remember the fanatical Junior Anti-Sex League in Orwell's
    book, which deemed that any sexual act not designed for the
    procreation of children was a 'sexcrime'? In real-life 1980s,
    Mary Whitehouse and her Senior Anti-Sex League were
    campaigning to effectively ban the portrayal of sex on TV.
    In 1982, she'd called for the resignation of Jeremy Isaacs, chief
    executive of the new Channel 4, for allowing a sex scene to be
    shown on Brookside.*

See how easy it was? But when we weren't busy updating Orwell,
we were marvelling at the epic argosies of quality new fiction from
British writers. We watched them arrive every week, and rubbed
our eyes at the levels of imaginative achievement on display: *Money*
by Martin Amis, *Stanley and the Women* by Kingsley Amis, *Empire of
the Sun* by J. G. Ballard, *Blow Your House Down* by Pat Barker,
Flaubert's Parrot by Julian Barnes, *Stars and Bars* by William Boyd,
Hotel du Lac by Anita Brookner – and we were still only in the Bs.
We could also read *The Paper Men* by William Golding, *The Pork
Butcher* by David Hughes, *Small World* by David Lodge, *The
Glamour* by Christopher Priest and *1982 Janine*, a story of erotic
and suicidal longing told partly in a blizzard of typographical
explosions, by Alasdair Gray, the unclassifiable writer-artist whose
1981 debut, *Lanark*, ushered in a new cultural identity for Scottish
writing. And *The Wasp Factory*, the viscerally powerful debut novel
by another rambunctious Scot called Iain Banks.

   We said to each other, well *that* was a red-letter year for British
fiction, one that probably won't be repeated for a century. Amazingly
the following year, 1985, keenly rivalled it. Jostling for readers'
attention were *Hawksmoor* by Peter Ackroyd, *The Kingdom of the
Wicked* by Anthony Burgess, *A Maggot* by John Fowles, *Light Years* by
Maggie Gee, *The Good Terrorist* by Doris Lessing, *The Tenth Man*
by Graham Greene, *Black Robe* by Brian Moore, *The Good Apprentice*
by Iris Murdoch, *Blood Libels* by Clive Sinclair, and *Star Turn* by
Nigel Williams. Astonishingly accomplished new women writers

set out their stalls: among them Jeanette Winterson with *Oranges Are Not the Only Fruit*, and Hilary Mantel with *Every Day Is Mother's Day*. Iain Banks followed *The Wasp Factory* with *Walking on Glass*.

If 1986 brought a smaller fleet of individual talents (the key debut that year was *Continent*, an exercise in cross-cultural imagineering by Jim Crace), some significant new work appeared by established writers, as if they were on a celestial production line: *Staring at the Sun* by Julian Barnes, *An Artist of the Floating World* by Kazuo Ishiguro, *An Insular Possession* by Timothy Mo, *Love Unknown* by A. N. Wilson, *Vacant Possession* by Hilary Mantel, and the third outing from Iain Banks, *The Bridge*. When, before the 1980s, did serious writers turn out a book a year, as if they were Agatha Christie or Georgette Heyer?

One memorable debut in 1984 was *The Final Passage*, about a Caribbean family's gruelling experience of emigrating to London in 1958. Its author was the St Kitts-born Caryl Phillips, who would go on to publish twelve novels, six plays and four story collections, win a dozen awards, including the Commonwealth Prize and the James Tait Black Memorial Prize, and become Professor of English at Yale in 2006. The publication, and reception, of Phillips's work pulls into focus the journey that had been made since about 1970 to bring diversity to the British book world, long before the word became a shibboleth of the British press, media, advertising and sport.

British publishers welcomed the arrival of talented black and Asian writers such as the Guyanese Roy Heath, whose novel *The Murderer* won the *Guardian* fiction prize in 1979; and Ben Okri, who moved to England from Nigeria in 1978, published his first novel, *Flowers and Shadows* in 1980, and became the youngest-ever winner of the Booker Prize in 1991 with *The Famished Road*; and Buchi Emecheta, whom we met in the 1983 Best of Young British Novelists promotion, and whose published works pre-dated those of Heath and Okri by years. Her two novels, *In the Ditch* and *Second-Class Citizen*, strong, moving, quasi-autobiographical accounts of immigrant life on a London housing estate, were published in 1972 and 1974, and conjoined in 1983 under the title *Adah's Story*. In many ways a pioneer of black UK writing, Emecheta owed her success to a key figure in the advancement of black writers, the redoubtable Margaret Busby.

Born in Ghana in 1944, it was while studying at Bedford College, London, that Busby met a fellow student called Clive Allison and with him formed the publishing company Allison & Busby in 1967. In doing so she became (at twenty-three) the UK's youngest publisher and its first black female book publisher, and became a rousing voice for greater representation of ethnic voices in this country. In 1984 she wrote an article for the *New Statesman*, which asked: 'Is it enough to respond to a demand for books reflecting the presence of "ethnic minorities" while perpetuating a system which does not actively encourage their involvement at all levels? The reality is that the appearance and circulation of books, supposedly produced with these communities in mind, is usually dependent on what the dominant white (male) community, which controls schools, libraries, bookshops and publishing houses, will permit.'

During the 1980s she was co-founder of GAP (Greater Access to Publishing) which ran campaigns to increase the presence of black writers in the UK – especially black women. Later, in 1992, she published the ground-breaking *Daughters of Africa: an International Anthology of Words and Writings by Women of African Descent, from the Ancient Egyptians to the Present*. Zadie Smith later called her 'a cheerleader, instigator, organiser, defender and celebrator of black arts for the past 50 years, shouting about us from the rooftops, even back when few people cared to listen.'

Elsewhere, writers of Indian and Pakistani heritage, most notably Salman Rushdie, Vikram Seth and Hanif Kureishi, all gave the literary world seismic shocks by respectively a) inventing a new multi-language in which to express Indian life and history; b) publishing a novel about San Francisco written in 590 stanzas in the style of Pushkin's *Eugene Onegin*, followed by a novel 1,349 pages long which was shortlisted for the Booker; and c) having a film screenplay, about a gay, Pakistani-British boy growing up in south London in the 1980s, published by Faber with the kind of brouhaha attending on a major novel, and following it with *The Buddha of Suburbia*, which won the 1990 Whitbread First Novel award.

Five years before it won, in 1985 the Booker was won by Keri Hulme, a woman of mixed Maori/Orkney/Yorkshire/Faroe descent. The book, *The Bone People*, was the first New Zealand novel to win the prize, and came with a five-page glossary of Maori words and phrases.

It became a rather idiotic truism to say that all UK authors in the 1980s were writing the same novel. There was such heterogeneity in British fiction in this decade, such contrasts of voice, style, language and psychology. But three themes and preoccupations were shared.

One was the use of twentieth-century historical events and people in fiction. In 1980, *Earthly Powers* by Anthony Burgess had featured Chicago under Prohibition, voodoo in Malaya, Buchenwald and assorted massacres, while the central character, Kenneth Toomey, periodically ran into famous literary figures – among them James Joyce, Ernest Hemingway, Rudyard Kipling, T. S. Eliot, E. M. Forster and P. G. Wodehouse. Such encounters became a key trope of the decade.

The White Hotel by D. M. Thomas ended with the massacre of thirty thousand Kiev Jews at Babi Yar in 1941. The main character of *Midnight's Children*, Saleem, is imprisoned during the real-life state of emergency imposed by the prime minister, Indira Gandhi, which curbed civil liberties and suspended elections. In 1984, J. G. Ballard moved on from the SF natural-disaster theme of his early novels (*The Drought*, *The Drowned World*, *The Wind From Nowhere*) to recreate, in *Empire of the Sun*, the natural disaster of his boyhood, the Japanese occupation of Shanghai (where he lived with his parents) after Pearl Harbor. *The Pork Butcher* by David Hughes offered a fictional evocation of the Nazi massacre of the French village of Oradour-sur-Glane in 1944. A popular success in British bookshops in 1984 was the English translation of Milan Kundera's *The Unbearable Lightness of Being*, whose story of a skirt-chasing Czech surgeon unfolds against the Prague Spring and its suppression by Warsaw Pact countries in 1968.

Other novelists had their characters experience historical events and meet literary-historical figures. *The New Confessions* by William Boyd saw his hero, John James Todd, fighting in the First World War, surviving the Wall Street Crash, living in Berlin during the rise of the Nazis, becoming a war correspondent, witnessing the invasion of France and appearing before the House Un-American Activities Committee. Following a similar trajectory, the narrator of Nigel Williams's third novel, *Star Turn*, was taught by D. H. Lawrence, joined the First World War beside General Haig, ran into Virginia Woolf during the General Strike, bumped into Proust, lay on Sigmund Freud's psychiatric couch and was molested by Ramsay MacDonald *en travesti*. In the same spirit, David Hughes's *But for Bunter* charts the real-life avatar of Billy Bunter, the famous fictional fat boy, as he precipitates, through his behaviour, many of the twentieth century's disasters (the sinking of the *Titanic*, the General Strike, the Suez crisis) and provides the germ of some big literary landmarks, including *The Waste Land* and *Lady Chatterley's Lover*.

A second popular theme was homosexuality. One reason, of course, was the gradual revelation across the decade of the existence of the Aids epidemic: the term was used for the first time in 1982 and investigated by the World Health Organisation late in 1983. By the end of 1984, 7,699 cases had been reported in the US and 762 in Europe.

In publishing circles the founding in 1979 of the Gay Men's Press was a pioneering move, offering explicit fictions about contemporary gay life that hadn't been rendered 'suitable' for mainstream readers, such as the bestselling coming-out novel, *The Milkman's on His Way* by David Rees. Perhaps helped by the GMP's success and the transatlantic popularity of Edmund White's *A Boy's Own Story* (1982) and Armistead Maupin's San Francisco-based sextet of novels, *Tales of the City* (1978–89), a miasma of transgressive behaviour could be felt rising from the groves of fiction, like steam above a Louisiana bayou.

In *Earthly Powers*, Anthony Burgess's protagonist, Kenneth Toomey is gay (clearly modelled on Somerset Maugham); the book starts with a flamboyantly gay opening sentence: 'It was the evening of my eightieth birthday and I was in bed with my catamite when Ali came in to announce that the bishop had come to tea.' Toomey's sexual partners in the novel are mostly crude, venal and unloving (his only successful erotic relationship is with his sister), but his sexuality seemed more emblematic of his role as a sinner than that of a lover. During the book we're treated to Toomey's own comically pretentious prose in extracts from his book, *A Way Back to Eden*: 'And the boy took his lover like a beast, thrusting his empurpled royal greatness into the antrum, without tenderness, with no cooings of love, rather with grunts and howls, his unpared nails drawing blood from breast and belly.'

Seekers after homoerotic jiggery-pokery could have combed the novels of William Golding for years and found nothing until *Rites of Passage* came out, so to speak, in 1980. The first novel of the 'Sea Trilogy' sails along for 280 pages of eighteenth-century diary entries and Regency chat (Golding had been reading lots of Jane Austen before starting it), shot through with seafarer's *patois*. But its central concern is for what becomes of Robert Colley, a socially awkward clergyman, easily bullied by the commander, Captain Anderson. Trouble begins when Colley ventures into the fo'c'sle to pray with the lower orders; he emerges later, drunk, half-clothed and strangely pleased with himself – but when he reaches his cabin, it's the end of him. He turns his face to the wall, ignores words of encouragement, and expires. We discover he had developed a gay crush on a young sailor, Billy Rogers; below decks, he got drunk, caroused with the crew and ended up performing *fellatio* on the handsome *matelot*. The book's penultimate paragraph reads: 'In the not too ample volume of man's knowledge of Man, let this sentence be inserted. Men can die of shame.'

'Shame' was not a word many would come to associate with Peter Ackroyd – the most publicly 'out' gay man in 1980s literary London, who could regularly be found at parties comprehensively refreshed and demanding that some attractive young man in the room should be led away, stripped, lubricated and brought to his tent. His 1982 debut novel, *The Great Fire of London*, however, was rather tentative and un-explicit in its delineation of gay sex. But that it existed at all was pretty shocking. The main plot involved a successful TV director's attempt to make a film of Dickens's *Little Dorrit* in modern-day London. The gay strand was secondary: two men, a Canadian professor of English at Cambridge called Rowan Phillips and a handsome, asexual Cockney plank called Tim strike up a friendship, in which the latter offers to guide the former around London. After their first encounter came the first description of a gay bar I'd ever read: 'The pub was now filling up quickly; solitary men came in and sailed up to the bar like tugs looking for a berth. Once a drink was safely in their hand they would wander across the floor, smiling at someone here, pressing accidentally against someone there, generally ending up, aloof, in a convenient area of shadow or half-light . . .' After some inconclusive encounters, Rowan invites Tim to his flat and gives him oral sex, which leaves him in tears. Their relationship teeters back and forth unconsummated, while the movie in which they're both involved is burnt to the ground. But the very sighting of such scenes in a novel published by mainstream Hamish Hamilton and Penguin marked a new frankness.

Sexual confusion turned up in *The Natural Order*, the first novel by Ursula Bentley, in which three south London schoolgirls form a romantic bond, *à la* the Brontës, and find themselves teaching at the same boys' grammar school in Manchester. Caroline ('Carlo') and tall, impetuous Damaris share a tiny house, and, for convenience, a bed. When Damaris develops a hopeless passion for a cute sixth-former, she kisses Carlo on the mouth by way of substitution. 'Damaris,' reports Carlo, 'had become an alien creature, to be watched in fear.' Alarm at the threat of lesbianism is joined by the characters' curious conviction that sexual orientation may be irrelevant in choosing who you might have sex with – as in this exchange:

> '*Do you think she'll sleep with him?*' *I said.*
> '*Terry?*'
> '*Yes. To music probably.*'
> '*I wouldn't think so. He's homosexual, isn't he?*'
> '*Yes but that doesn't mean his balls have dropped off. It's usually a matter of choice rather than incapacity, I think.*'

When twenty-six-year-old Jeanette Winterson published *Oranges Are Not the Only Fruit* in 1985, it was a revelation – a coming-of-age lesbian novel that was neither coy nor physically explicit but showed the workings of a young brain filled with Christian missionary zeal. It's also filled with confusion about her mother, whom the main character Jeanette loves and hates, about the absurdities of her northern neighbours, and her own sexuality. The book is wonderfully assured, with digressive bursts of myth-making, fairy tales and literary speculation (her mother brought her up to believe that, in *Jane Eyre*, Jane marries the missionary St John Rivers rather than Mr Rochester). It also showed the fictional-Jeanette puzzled by her own sexual desires ('Quite suddenly I turned and kissed her. We made love and I hated it and hated it, but would not stop'), and welcomes falling in love as a relief from confusion ('She was my most uncomplicated love affair and I loved her because of it'). It was gratifyingly abrasive and very funny about missionary life, and won the Whitbread First Novel award and became a big hit on GCSE and A-level reading lists.

When Alan Hollinghurst's *The Swimming-Pool Library* appeared in 1988, it came with several shudders of expectation. *The first mainstream gay novel that goes all the way!* – that was the gist, the rumour, the *on dit*. Any unsophisticated heteros who remained unsure about the mechanics of gay sex would have their curiosity slaked at last. Some (straight) literati reported their responses; one shyly confessed to getting an erection while reading the famous passage involving an Arab youth and a can of Mazola Corn Oil.

The book begins with a subterranean epiphany, in which the main character, William Beckwith, rides a train with two Tube maintenance workers, one black, one white, and wonders how it feels to be working underground through the night. The language wasn't erotic, but phrases such as 'long-handled ratchet spanners' and the black workman's 'air of massive, scarcely conscious competence' gave the texture of the everyday a surging, erectile presence. Whenever actual gay sex appeared to be in the offing, however, Hollinghurst body-swerved the action. When William goes home to his flat, where he's installed a teenage lover, the action discreetly cuts to the next day. In a park, William spots an Arab boy he fancies and enters a public lavatory hoping the boy will follow – but instead of having sexual contact with him, he saves the life of a peer of the realm who is having a cardiac arrest. At the Corinthian Club, William describes the swimming arrangements, and the etiquette of flashing a hard-on in the changing-room shower – but still no actual smut.

I realised Hollinghurst was doing something subtle and rather beautiful: alerting the straight reader to a new world of visual textures, complex feelings and nuanced conversations, normalising gay life and perceptions as being just as worthy of attention as the Corinthian Club's stately architecture. We got to the hot sex eventually, and that was pretty shocking in a never-read-*that*-before way; but also shocking were the sexual encounters inscribed in the 1920s and 1940s diaries that were kept by the gay octogenarian whose life Will saved. Hollinghurst was offering, among other things, a history of twentieth-century gay life, before it became legal; before the modern threat, not from Aids (which isn't mentioned anywhere in the book) but from 'queer-bashing' and *agent-provocateur* cops hanging out in gay cottages.

The third major theme was religion, or, more precisely, the clash between religious transcendence and worldly corruption. Dominating the landscape was Umberto Eco's *The Name of the Rose*, published in the UK in 1983. Though essentially a murder mystery, it was an unlikely bestseller: five hundred pages long, written by a world-renowned Italian professor of Semiotics, Aesthetics, History and Philosophy, it was set in northern Italy in 1327 and is studded with long disquisitions on metaphysics, blasphemy, necromancy and Aristotelian comedy. Despite these drawbacks, it sold over fifty million copies worldwide.

The plot is cloister-Gothic whodunit. Our hero, William of Baskerville, a Franciscan friar, arrives at a Benedictine monastery to take part in a theological dispute between Pope John XXII and the Franciscan brotherhood. While it's getting under way, several monks are murdered: an illustrator of illuminated manuscripts, an Aristotle scholar, a herbalist and the librarian's assistant are found dead, some with black stains on their tongues and fingers. William, possibly inspired by the big hint in his honorary title, turns to sleuthing and deduction to find the killer. The book features an ingenious murder weapon, one that suits the library-haunting author to a T – a lost copy of Aristotle's *Poetics*, whose pages have been poisoned, and will prove fatal to anyone making the mistake of licking their fingers to turn them. Many readers congratulated Professor Eco for suggesting a way to dispose of people who indulge in such a revolting habit.

I met Eco at a dinner for literary editors just off Knightsbridge. He was a big, rumbustious, black-bearded, contemptuous, Rabelaisian, garlicky, cigar-chomping, voluptuously greedy man, with black-framed spectacles and snuff stains on his waistcoat, and he regarded the British literary journalists around the table with undisguised loathing. The Secker publicity director kicked off dinner by telling us we wouldn't be able to chat to the prof during or after dinner but, if we were lucky, he might agree to answer some questions. I like to start a ball rolling, so I tried a simple one.

'Professor, I believe you're a passionate book collector and when you're in London you always visit antiquarian bookshops. Can you tell us which shops you go to, and which writers' works you hope to find there?'

He took a languorous pull on his Montecristo.

'In London are the best rare book shops, yes. I always visit Maggs, Quaritch, the obvious ones. As for whose works I weesh to find, I would say anytheeng by Roberto Fludd.'

He looked around the table for signs of appreciation among the guests. Everyone wore their best I'm-absolutely-fascinated expression.

'E was British polymath. E knew about everytheeng. E was physician, e speculate about the circulation of the blodd before Weelyam Harvey, e knew all about magic, the creation of the earth. E believe in cosmic harmony.'

He paused. I thought I ought to acknowledge his answer with some pleasantry.

'How fascinating,' I said. 'And isn't it extraordinary, Professor, that Robert Fludd, an Englishman, should be such an object of fascination to you – and yet is completely unknown to the English.'

Eco removed the cigar from his mouth, inspected the glowing tip and said to it: 'E is onnnly unknown . . .'

Then he looked straight at me. The grizzly-bear eyes regarded me with hatred.

'. . . to *you!!!*'

It came out as 'to *yowwww!*' He put a lot into it. And you know what? All my friends around the table, all my buddies, co-evals, fellow-toilers in the literary vineyard, made the same noise – a clucking of disapproval: '*What?* Oh *really*, John. Speak for your*self*. *We* all know *everything* about Robert Fludd, the celebrated astrologer, mathematician, cosmologist, Qabalist and Rosicrucian apologist . . .'

Dammit. If only I had read *Fludd* by Hilary Mantel. But cruelly, that didn't come out until a few years later.

Errant pilgrims could be found in *Flying to Nowhere* (1983), a slim (eighty-nine pages) fiction by the poet John Fuller. Vane, the emissary of a bishop, comes to a bleak island trying to find why no pilgrims visit the holy well any longer. Seemingly unimpressed by his visit, the abbot, meanwhile, is embroiled in his task of finding the physical root of the human soul.

In 1985, *Black Robe*, by the Canadian-Northern-Irish writer Brian Moore, set in the Nowhereland of seventeenth-century North America, showed us a Jesuit missionary, Father Laforgue, clad in the titular garment of religious conversion, travelling to the wild and dangerous territory of the Huron Indians to bring them the good news about Christianity. Though the priest calls the Hurons 'savages', Moore shows the collision of cultures as a tragedy for both sides; but especially for Laforgue who, as well as losing his faith, is subjected to torture at the hands of the Iroquoi, which is almost as harrowing as the scenes of gobsmacking violence wreaked by a gang of murderous white scalp-hunters on Amerindians and Mexicans in Cormac McCarthy's *Blood Meridian*, published in the same year.

Religious matters informed the final novel by John Fowles. It was called *A Maggot*, one of the least appealing titles in novel history. Set in 1736, it offered readers the sight of five people on horseback riding through the murky Devon countryside. Strange, unsettling things happen. A dead man is found with violets stuffed in his mouth, a maidservant turns out to be a London prostitute, an aristocrat disappears and a lawyer arrives to take legal depositions from everyone, like an eighteenth-century Hercule Poirot. The testament of one witness, Rebecca, takes over the narrative, with her reports of seeing visions of paradise and a female Holy Trinity. And Fowles reveals that the book is intended to be little more than a sermon about Ann Lee, the founder of the United Society of Believers in Christ's Second Appearing – which is remembered today only by its stripped-back 'Shaker' architecture, furniture and tableware.

I was sitting on a train from Paddington to Lyme Regis in the summer of *A Maggot*'s publication, on the way to interview John Fowles at his home, Belmont House. I was halfway through the book, taking copious notes, looking forward to the conclusion of what was evidently a murder mystery and preparing my questions – when suddenly the plot abruptly shifted direction. An intriguing investigation into a disappearance was abandoned without warning, and the narrative now concentrated on the dull visionary who founded a religious movement. What the hell? The author's unforeseeable swerve of direction was almost perversely obscure – and I was due to meet the author for an in-depth chat about his new masterpiece in, let's see, fifty-seven minutes . . . Luckily, when I arrived, he was keener to talk about his terrible current writer's block, and his dark suspicions about which people at the *TLS*, the *London Review of Books*, the *Listener* and the *Observer*, had it in for him. He didn't mention anyone on *Books and Bookmen*, and gave me a courteous *namaste* when we parted company.

So that was the 1980s novel: fascinated by twentieth-century massacres and writers, homosexual urges and religion – and, of course, monkeying around with the English language in ways that hadn't been seen before. Wherever you looked, there was newness, innovation, hybridity, and a perverse and gleeful delight in breaking ancient rules and moth-eaten conventions.

In October 1984, *Harper's & Queen* ran a collective interview with four writers, presenting them as a kind of super-clique. The article (by the possibly pseudonymous Garth Blaine) was headlined 'Mutual Admiration Society' and the clientele around the table in the Café Pelican in St Martin's Lane would have been familiar to anyone *au fait* with British fiction and poetry. They were Martin Amis and Julian Barnes, the Butch and Sundance of the new novelistic prairie, and Craig Raine and Blake Morrison, the Wyatt Earp and Doc Holliday of the poetry corral. By coincidence they all had books out that year: Amis's *Money*, Barnes's *Flaubert's Parrot*, Craig Raine's third poetry collection, *Rich*, and Morrison's debut volume, *Dark Glasses*. Two years before, he'd been co-editor (with Andrew Motion) of *The Penguin Book of Contemporary Verse*.

Their conversation, as recorded by the magazine, sounded a bit stilted. The quartet discussed exclusively literary matters, as though that (rather than money and sex) was what writers talk about over lunch. But there were some good moments. How, they asked, does one deal with the prospect of getting a bad review? Simple, said Barnes, just pre-empt it by writing yourself *the worst possible review* it could get, and the actual review won't seem that bad. They shared a story about the hectic omnicompetence of Anthony Burgess: 'An *Observer* secretary got her books muddled up and sent him a music book intended for [a musicologist reviewer], but before they could correct the error and send him the *right* book, his review of the *wrong* one had arrived. Then they sent him the *right* one, and he reviewed that as well.'

What the piece didn't mention was that the Café Pelican lunchers were veterans of a literary friendship-group that dated back over a decade.

It had been formed as a sort of in-joke by Clive James and his friend Terry Kilmartin, of the *Observer*. The joke was that F. R. Leavis, the ferocious Eng Lit don at Downing College, Cambridge, used to salt his discourse with references to 'the modish London literary world', to their sick-making mutual preening and creative orthodoxy. One Friday, after delivering his TV review at the *Observer*, James was lunching with Kilmartin in Mother Bunch's Wine Bar, under the arches at Blackfriars. When the conversation turned to Leavis's latest attack on the reviled trendsetters and taste-makers, James (he later explained) 'hit on the idea of making Leavis's mad fantasies of a London conspiracy come true by actually starting one up. Couldn't we whistle in a few recruits and make the Friday lunch look like a plot to control the collective mind of the capital?' Kilmartin 'thought the idea silly enough to work' and they decided to call the lunching cabal The Modish London Literary World.

The first lunch at Mother B's was on Friday 7 December 1973 and, around the table with Clive and Terry sat Martin Amis, Kingsley Amis, Tina Brown (then still at Oxford), Russell Davies, John Gross (editor of the *TLS*), the agent Pat Kavanagh, the poet Peter Porter and the *Evening Standard*'s Valerie Jenkins (before she became Valerie Grove). The Friday lunches moved house to other establishments (notably the Bursa, a Turkish-Cypriot kebab joint in Theobald's Road), but brought together a spectacular line-up of writerly and critical talents – among them Craig Raine, Piers Paul Read, Ian McEwan and several Oxbridge friends, many of them newly housed at the *New Statesman*, under its benign editor Anthony Howard.

Amis's best friend Christopher Hitchens and the poet James Fenton (later to become professor of Poetry at Oxford) wrote for the political pages at the front, while Amis and Barnes, who had met through the *Statesman*'s literary editor Claire Tomalin, ran the back half, with its book reviews, arts coverage and competitions.

Word of the glamorous literary lunches spread to readers of the *Statesman* in the 1980s, causing ripples of envy and outraged *amour-propre* among the brilliant-but-uninvited. My friend Gordon told me he was ashamed of his longing to be invited; he'd even considered making the journey to Great Turnstile, the *Statesman*'s editorial home in Holborn, just to watch the trendy scribes walking through the front door.

I knew how he felt, without sharing his urge to visit the magazine and hang with the staff. I felt pleased that there should exist in London an analogue of New York's 1920s 'Algonquin Set' (Robert Benchley, Dorothy Parker, Harold Ross, Alexander Woollcott, George S. Kaufman), who met regularly to satirise colleagues, trash reputations and improvise dazzling shards of wit. OK, the Algonquin gang met at a ritzy hotel noted for its Manhattan cocktails, not a reeking Clerkenwell shambles noted for its throat-scouring house red, but still. Given the quality of the prose and poetry for which the Friday lunchers were responsible, future generations might even regard them as a latter-day Bloomsbury Group, but without the deckchairs, reading parties, or cat's-cradle of polysexual affairs. Whatever their status, it felt good that The Literary Lads and Ladesses Who Lunch had got together in a kind of parody of a power clique – and, ten years later, in the mid-1980s, were an actual power clique and a pungent cultural force.

Very much *not* part of the charmed circle was Howard Jacobson, with whom I became friends after interviewing him about his second novel, *Peeping Tom*. 'I got so sick of hearing about Martin and Ian and the beautiful people,' he told me. 'I'd hear people saying, about me, "Is he quite up to them yet?" And I'd think: I'm with Lawrence and Conrad here, I'm not with Martin and Ian. I grew to like them all, but they knew each other and if you turned up in town as a new writer, you felt excluded. You weren't part of the gang. You know, Clive James and Ian Hamilton drinking at the Pillars of Hercules. Julian playing tennis with Martin. John Carey reviewing Clive James in the *New Review* . . . When I arrived with my first novel, I was forty-one and already too old to be part of it.'

When he fired his agents after they'd failed to secure him a decent advance for his fifth book, *In The Land of Oz*, Howard was taken on by Pat Kavanagh, very much *in* the charmed circle. 'My second wife Rosalin and I would go round to dinner with Pat and Julian, and it was always just us. One time I saw something on the table that suggested there had been a dinner with someone else recently. Pat said, "Oh yes – we had Marina Warner over, but we *couldn't trust you with her*." It was like I was this wild man who'd say terrible things. Pat was lovely, but in some odd way they were frightened of me.'

He wasn't a fan of Salman Rushdie. '*Midnight's Children* felt very second-hand to me. And I thought *The Satanic Verses* was preposterous. I thought Rushdie yearned to be amusing and he wasn't. And what kind of human being are you when you can't conceal the fact that you think you should win *everything*?'

His early days in the literary world were busy and restless. A Jewish Mancunian academic, he was taught at Cambridge by F. R. Leavis, whom he idolised. After a spell working at Sydney University (where 'everybody had affairs, the women staff with the men and both with the students'), he found himself teaching at Wolverhampton Polytechnic. He was in the boondocks, career- and creativity-wise.

'I was always going to be a novelist,' he told me. 'I never wanted to be anything else. But by 1978, I'd written fuck-all fiction. I'd co-written a book called *Shakespeare's Magnanimity*, but the world hadn't changed. Beautiful women weren't throwing themselves at me. I was trying to be Tolstoy, Dostoyevsky, D. H. Lawrence and, most of all, Henry James. But I'd write three sentences, and could see they were no good. Here I was, living on my own, at the end of my first marriage, eating curries non-stop in Wolverhampton. I was approaching forty. I had charts on my wall, showing how old George Eliot was when she published *Adam Bede* and *Middlemarch*. I was panicking about running out of time. So I started writing a novel about the absurdity of Wolverhampton Poly.'

His breakthrough was the decision to make his hero Jewish. 'I wrote the words, "Being Jewish, Sefton Goldberg . . ." and I thought "That's it! I'll say that again and again like comedians do." I was the only Jew interested in English Literature – all the others were doctors, lawyers, economists or ecologists.'

Jacobson's entry into the Parnassus of novelists had a matter-of-fact quality that bordered on the surreal. He finished his first novel, called it *Coming From Behind*, and took it to Chatto & Windus because they had published his Shakespeare book. The publishing director Jeremy Lewis took him to lunch and asked if he had an agent.

Learning that he hadn't, Lewis took him back to the office and said, 'Go upstairs one flight and you'll find a man called Mark Hamilton. He's an agent.' Jacobson left the manuscript with Hamilton and was told to come back in a fortnight. He returned, went up the creaky stairs and was told by Hamilton: 'I quite like this book because there's a party in it. You keep waiting for people to go to the party. I think it's quite funny.' Howard then learned, in the same understated British way, that his new agent had sold the book to the chaps downstairs for a thousand pounds. 'Until then, all I knew about publishing was from reading Henry James's trouble with it, and Conrad's and Lawrence's troubles. They never had any money. And now these people were paying me a fucking thousand pounds!'

Things became rather less rosy after his publishing company acquired a new boss. This was Carmen Callil, the Australian whirlwind who invented Virago, and, in 1982, took over Chatto. 'It was just before *Coming From Behind* came out,' he said. 'I'm afraid I got on with Carmen about as badly as it's humanly possible for a person to do. We hated each other from the start. Jeremy Lewis had edited my first novel, but Carmen decided to *re*-edit it. She put a blue pencil through any word that denoted a part of a woman's body – breast, thigh, flank, elbow – as if to say, "Who are *you* to possess a woman's body?"'

Because of the strong likelihood that the academic population of Wolverhampton might see themselves in the book, Jacobson resigned from the faculty and relocated to Boscastle, Cornwall, where Rosalin ran a tearoom and restaurant. But he was not safe from his publisher. 'Carmen rang and said, "I really don't know how we're going to sell this book. You need to have an affair with somebody famous. Come to London and have an affair!"' Howard declined to take her advice on that, but did come to the party she threw in London for new Chatto authors. 'Carmen was going up to the guests, one by one, saying "I love your book" and praising each in turn. She came up to me and said, "Well, I don't know *how* I'm going to sell you. If you ran down Bond Street stark naked, I don't think I could sell *you*."'

As it turned out, unclad public scampering wasn't required to make the book a success. After the rights were sold to a new imprint called Black Swan, the paperback of *Coming From Behind* was given a spanking new cover (featuring a caricature of the author by Charles Griffin, the *Daily Mirror* cartoonist) and widely advertised. It shifted one hundred and fifty thousand copies.

A follow-up novel, the hilarious *Peeping Tom*, in which a Jewish Londoner tries out the rustic idyll in the depths of Cornwall and discovers he may be the reincarnation of Thomas Hardy, came out in 1985 and sold one hundred thousand copies. Hardly had Jacobson decided to revisit his Australian heyday in Sydney for a new fiction called *Redback*, when he got an excited phone call.

'It was my agent, Mark Hamilton. He just said, "You haven't got a book on the go, have you? How soon can you have it ready? Because there's a LOT of money sloshing around . . ." It was the Booker effect. Every publisher was keen to put money into the kind of literary novel that might win the Booker. Advances were going through the roof.' Howard bestirred himself to finish *Redback* in double-quick time and, as his agent had predicted, there was a feeding frenzy.

'*Redback* was auctioned. I'd got £1,000 for my first book, £5,000 for *Peeping Tom*. Now there was an auction and Bantam Press won it with a bid for £50,000. The chairman, Mark Barty-King, came round to the house in person to seal the deal. Of course we were bitterly disappointed because we didn't win any prizes. *Redback* sold fourteen thousand copies – and we thought that was a *flop*. That was the excitement of the time."

---

* It hasn't been easy to find the exact sums publishers were prepared to pay for their star signings, but a few were widely known. After *Waterland*, Graham Swift received £130,000 from Viking Penguin for his next two novels, Fay Weldon got a staggering £450,000 from Collins for her next three fictions, and Michael Holroyd trousered a whopping £650,000 from his old friend Carmen at Chatto for his projected three-volume biography of George Bernard Shaw. The daddy of all advances, however, was the sum that Andrew ('The Jackal') Wylie secured for Salman Rushdie and *The Satanic Verses*: he sold British and American rights to Peter Mayer at Viking Penguin in the US for $850,000 (£525,000), an unheard-of sum for a serious literary novel.

For readers of the modern novel, it was bliss in that dawn to be alive. To live in London and be in a position to socialise with writers, reviewers and publishers, was very heaven. The main reason for such a state of bliss was the founding, mid-decade, of the Groucho Club. It was such a wild success almost from the start, so full of media tarts and TV faces and down-at-heel artists and wary-seeming rock stars putting their heads round the brasserie entrance after midnight, it was such a cool and trendy 1980s *thing*, some members wouldn't have believed it got started by a gang of publishers.

The idea initially came from Liz Calder and her partner, Louis Baum, editor of the *Bookseller*, who had been on holiday in Amsterdam frequenting the 'brown cafés' where you could drink at any time without worrying about licensing laws. Back in London, they were in a bar in Kentish Town one night, with a jazz singer performing in a corner. 'If she can sing in a pub,' Baum said to Liz, 'then so can I.' 'You'll have to start a club,' said Liz, and the idea was born.

Publishers are natural convivialists. They seek out places where one can follow serious business with gossipy chat. But the only place they could take a writer after work was a pub or a wine bar. Once Liz and Louis began talking about a club, things accelerated.

In Carmen Callil's garden, along with the super-agent Michael Sissons, they discussed what kind of club they had in mind: somewhere they could meet, work and socialise at any time of day; somewhere that resembled a bar, a café, a restaurant, an office *and* a living room, and would (crucially – this was a frankly startling innovation) welcome women who arrived on their own, without assuming they were prostitutes.

The next step was to invite a squad of publishers to a meeting and pitch the idea. Twelve of them, including Tom Maschler from Cape, Andre Deutsch from his titular imprint, and the literary agent Ed Victor, were wildly enthusiastic and pledged start-up money. Next they approached Anthony Mackintosh, a veteran starter-upper: he was the guy behind Dingwalls Dance Hall in

Camden Lock and the Zanzibar members' bar in Covent Garden. The crucial status of Zanzibar was that it was a members-only club and therefore had an all-day and until 1 a.m. drinking licence. Mackintosh and his friend, the architect Tchaik Chassay, thought about the big townhouse at 45 Dean Street. For years it had been Gennaro's restaurant, where European royalty regularly dined along with Dame Nellie Melba and Enrico Caruso. But since Signor Gennaro died, it had fallen into disrepute.

The cost of acquiring it was £450,000 freehold, with a further half million needing to be spent on doing it up. The banks seemed inexplicably reluctant to cough up £1 million in seed cash to found a new Soho drinking hole, so the rugby team of fifteen founders tried an early example of crowd-funding. They shared their address books and sent a cheery prospectus, about the club and the need for multi-financing, to all their rich friends, contacts and associates. A total of four hundred publishers, artists, theatre aficionados and media luminaries together raised the wind to buy the club, renovate it, refresh the cellar and employ lots of young and groovy staff to run the bar, the restaurant and front of house.

The Groucho Club opened its doors on 5 May 1985, and by the time its first birthday rolled around, it was swinging along. I joined in 1986 and, like many others, soon wondered how I'd ever been without it. It was the perfect place to meet literary friends (and how embarrassingly soon we were looking down our noses at the advertising chaps in the bar, saying 'God, who let *them* in? This place has gone *right* downhill'), to enjoy a brisk, modest dinner in the brasserie, or to drop in after a launch party. For the committed fan of mid-1980s book-launch parties, once the waiters in Kettners or L'Escargot began carrying around sad little trays of empty glasses, there was only one place to go with other party revellers in search of a debrief and a nightcap.

By the time I joined, stories and rumours about the club were legion. Princess Diana came for lunch there with her friend Wayne Sleep, after their famous 'Uptown Girl' *pas de deux* onstage in 1985.

David Gower, recently named England cricket captain, dropped in one evening, alongside his pal Gary Lineker, the England football team's star striker. Writers, artists and rock stars, themselves no strangers to success, gazed at the pair like schoolboys. The artist and dandy Sebastian Horsley, a Soho neighbour, was said to have been thrown out of the club for urinating, while standing at the bar, into the jacket pocket of a critic who had annoyed him.

I witnessed some exciting encounters. Once I was part of a group, with Melvyn Bragg and two others, who'd made it to the club after a launch party at the Ritz. We were sitting at a table in the bar, flooring the club Merlot, when a man came up, knelt reverentially beside Melvyn and spoke urgently into his ear, while gesturing towards the brasserie.

Melvyn took a deep breath and ostentatiously unbuttoned his tie.

'I don't think so,' he said. 'We've been to a party, I'm relaxing with some friends. I don't feel like saying hello to anyone right now.'

The guy redoubled his efforts. 'Please, Melvyn. It would mean *so much* to them. It'd be a personal favour. I'd be really grateful. Just come and say hi, that's all. Just for a minute. Will you do that for me?'

'Look,' said Melvyn, 'if they're so keen to say hi, bring them in *here*. Like I said, I'm relaxing with friends, and I'm not moving. Tell 'em I said, Come on over.'

But the man wouldn't give up. No *way* were his sacred charges going to be forced to come, cap in hand, to Melvyn-in-the-bar. The mountain had to visit Muhammad. Eventually Melvyn, with a smile that suggested he really didn't want his post-party equilibrium disturbed by this pushy git any longer, said yes.

I watched them walk past the piano and disappear into the brasserie. With whom was Melvyn being granted an audience he hadn't sought? I had to find out. I was a journalist, for heaven's sake. I strolled over, beyond the piano, and looked. It took a minute to spot Melvyn at the furthest-off, I'm-incognito table in the brasserie. He was standing with one hand on the chair occupied by Bono, while the rest of U2 smiled and laughed as if they'd been friends with Mr Bragg for years. It was interesting to witness a hierarchical battle between the world-beating rock band and the TV arts titan. U2 could be forgiven for thinking themselves pretty important: a year before, *Rolling Stone* had described them as 'the band that matters the most, maybe the only band that matters.' But then, meeting Melvyn could mean a one-hour profile on *The South Bank Show*, which would matter a great deal.

A generational shudder could be felt at the news, in May 1984, that Sir John Betjeman, the Poet Laureate, had died, and that his successor would be Ted Hughes. The whimsical Edwardian antiquary, passionate defender of Victorian architecture and national teddy bear was gone, yielding the stage to the craggy myth-maker from Mytholmroyd in the West Riding of Yorkshire, whose passions were salmon fishing, conjuring goddesses and being haunted by the suicides of ex-lovers.

The poetry scene of which Hughes was now chief executive appeared to be in rude good health in these years, with the publishing of Seamus Heaney's *Station Island*, Craig Raine's *The Electrification of the Soviet Union* (a libretto based on a Boris Pasternak story, and partly conducted in limericks), Peter Reading's anarchic *Ukulele Music*, Andrew Motion's *Dangerous Play*, Carol Ann Duffy's first collection *Standing Female Nude* and – a revelation – *Making Cocoa for Kingsley Amis*, the debut of Wendy Cope, a forty-year-old primary school teacher from Erith, Kent. Her poems could be simple, witty and wise about men and romantic relationships; they could also be wickedly subversive of the modern poetry world. Through her creation Jason Strugnell, a Tulse Hill poet with fine insights but not quite enough skill, she parodied T. S. Eliot, Geoffrey Hill, Seamus Heaney, Ted Hughes and Philip Larkin, and became an unexpected bestseller. I imagined her Faber editor,

Craig Raine, reading her parody of his own Martian style in 'The Lavatory Attendant' ('In overalls of sacerdotal white/He guards a row of fonts/With lids like eye-patches. Snapped shut/ They are castanets. All day he hears/Short-lived Niagaras, the clank/And gurgle of canescent cisterns') and thinking, 'Christ – that's *really good*.'

My favourite poet, Kit Wright, had two collections out, *Bump-Starting the Hearse* (1983) and *Short Afternoons* (1989). I loved his commitment to 'what vamped me/In my youth:/Tune, argument,/ Colour, truth'. I loved both his sense of humour and his ability to combine Martian-style visuals with Rumi-style transcendence, as in his poem, 'The Burden of the Mystery', in which his discovery that 'the dead outnumber the living by thirty to one' calls up some fabulous images, including, 'thirty slow shadow dancers/Round a lit candle' and 'the radiating hub of a many-spoked wheel.'

Martin Amis did something new with *Money*. Rather than repeat his narrative strategy of matching a squalid, low-rent character against a snootily over-achieving character (like Quentin versus Keith in *Dead Babies*, or Terry versus Gregory in *Success*), Amis now put a low-rent guy centre-stage and gave him a first-person voice with which to harangue the reader. His monologue, however, wasn't vulgar; it was super-cynical, hyper-alert to details of the modern world, endlessly questioning and terribly funny. It belonged to John Self, a successful British (though half-American) media wrangler, maker of scuzzy TV commercials and avid consumer of junk culture, from airplane food to overpriced hand-jobs in massage parlours. When the book starts, he's in New York to direct a film (called *Good Money*, though he wants to change it to *Bad Money*) starring some Hollywood grotesques: there's the Kirk Douglas-like ageing hard-nut Lorne Guyland (say it aloud and it becomes 'Long Island'), Caduta Massi, the troubled matriarch (whose name, meaning 'Falling Rocks', is seen on road signs all over Italy), Butch Beausoleil, a luscious Californian leading lady, and the high-principled, church-going Spunk Davis.

The characters don't matter a jot, however, compared to the novel's language. It was twangy, propulsive, interrogatory, stroppy, slightly hysterical. Even when John Self wonders about things, he wonders right in your face ('Martina's present was called *Animal Farm* and was by George Orwell. Have you read it? Is it my kind of thing?') I loved the way his concern about his teeth grew until it encompassed the whole of Manhattan ('I was starting to worry about my Upper East Side . . .'). I loved his new-minted US brand names: the souped-up Fiasco motor, the American Way burger, the Tuckleberry Pie. I loved his hero's passion for one thing above all other modern blessings – money. When making love to his girlfriend, Selina, they talk about money ('I love that dirty talk') and he exults in the knowledge that she does all the inventive, athletic, skilfully depraved things she does in bed 'not for passion, not for comfort, far less for love . . . she does all this for *money. I love her corruption.*'

Around the mid-1980s, British readers had become accustomed to finding young British writers mining seams of degradation – sex, drugs, porn, mutilation, casual murder – in a heartless but stylish manner. Now we couldn't help but notice that, across the Atlantic, a parallel universe of young talent was breaking out. As the postwar giants – Updike, Heller, Roth, Mailer, Bellow, Styron, DeLillo – got older, a new gang of literary gunslingers was out to shock the establishment, taking their cue from the British model.

In 1984, *Bright Lights, Big City* by Jay McInerney, took us on a cool, amusingly jaded whizz around Manhattan, from the nightclubs on the Upper East Side to the Palm Court at the Plaza, to the offices of the unnamed weekly magazine (clearly the *New Yorker*) where our hero works at the Department of Factual Verification, and spends his evening getting wasted on Bolivian marching powder, i.e. cocaine. The book's slender plot – his life is in free-fall after his mother dies and his wife leaves him – was enlivened by McInerney's confiding, second-person-singular address. The book opens: 'You are not the sort of guy who would be at a place like this at this time of the morning . . . You are at a nightclub talking to a girl with a shaved head.' His observations were sometimes hilariously caustic, and would get him into deep trouble in the current publishing climate. Like this moment in a subway car, when he sits opposite a Hasidic Jew from Brooklyn and considers his appearance: 'This man has a God and a History and a Community. He has a perfect economy of belief, in which pain and loss are explained in terms of a transcendental balance sheet, in which everything works out in the end, and death is not really death. Wearing black wool all summer must seem like a small price to pay. He believes he is one of God's chosen, whereas you feel like an integer in a random series of numbers. Still, what a fucking haircut.'

Bret Easton Ellis was twenty-one when he published *Less Than Zero*. Set in 1985, it follows an eighteen-year-old student called Clay as he returns home to LA for the Christmas holidays and proceeds to wade through endless days and nights of drugs, under-age sex, snuff movies, prostitution and rape. Its main theme was moral blankness. Ellis liked to show his characters preoccupied with their pursuit of nasty fun (joking while their friend Muriel shoots heroin, visiting a drug dealer who keeps a twelve-year-old girl as a sex slave), while failing to notice the atrocities happening under their noses. It was a trope that would be repeated a dozen times in the work of the New York 'Brat Pack' from *A Cannibal in Manhattan* to *American Psycho*.

Slaves of New York by Tama Janowitz came out in 1986. The stories in her debut collection, clever sketches of the lives of Greenwich Village artists, sounded as if its author had learned from Amis and McEwan how to create a striking instant effect. This is the opening paragraph of the first story, 'Modern Saint #271':

'After I became a prostitute, I had to deal with penises of every imaginable shape and size. Some large, others quite shrivelled and pendulous of testicle. Some blue-veined and reeking of Stilton, some miserly. Some crabbed, enchanted, dusted with pearls like the great minarets of the Taj Mahal, jesting penises, ringed as the tail of a raccoon, fervent, crested, impossible to live with, marigold-scented. More and more I became grateful I didn't have to own one of these appendages.'

McInerney, Ellis and Janowitz conquered the Manhattan literary scene with amazing speed, and the social scene shortly afterwards. The men (both in their early twenties) blithely adopted the lifestyle of their fictional characters and were regularly reported to be getting down at fashionable nightclubs. McInerney later noted on his website that he'd snorted coke with Hunter S. Thompson in the New York Library; Janowitz hung out at Studio 54, partied with Andy Warhol, and became a regular guest on late-night talk shows.

They were clever, spiky newcomers to the book scene, with a talent to shock and a lifestyle to match. But in the long view, they didn't really hold a candle to their US/Canadian seniors: Margaret Atwood with *The Handmaid's Tale*, Cormac McCarthy with *Blood Meridian* (both 1985) and Tom Wolfe, whose all-conquering *Bonfire of the Vanities* (1988) was the key US novel of this rumbustious decade. The first of its twenty-seven instalments ran in *Rolling Stone* in 1984. It was frankly amazing that Dickens's nineteenth-century publishing strategy should be resurrected by the coolest rock-generation magazine of the twentieth century.

'Would you like to meet Jilly Cooper?' *Books and Bookmen* asked me one day in 1984. 'She has a new book out called *The Common Years*, about her neighbours in south London.' Well yes, indeed I would. This was before she'd embarked on her massively successful shagging-in-the-shires blockbusters (*Riders, Rivals, Polo*), but I'd enjoyed Ms Cooper's newspaper columns on Soho (she thought nothing of descending into the seedy *milieux* of lunchtime strip clubs and confronting the clientele), and her witty dissection of the British class system in *Class*. I'd also admired her presence on television: the tumbling blonde locks, the merry eyes and the slightly *distraite* delivery. She *chortled*, that fine portmanteau word coined by Lewis Carroll, meaning to chuckle and snort together. I thought she'd be very good fun. Also, we had something in common, literally. I had moved into a flat in the Lower Richmond Road, near Putney Common, at about the time she was moving out of the district. In fact, my road featured on the pencil-drawn map of her dog-walking route that formed the endpapers of *The Common Years*.

So I took the train down to The Chantry, the lovely house in Gloucestershire she shared with her husband, the publisher and military historian, Leo Cooper. The great lady sat in her favourite upright armchair while her two dogs, Fortnum and Mason, took up positions on either side of her, like attendant lords. She was wearing tight black jeans and a ribbed cappuccino sweater down which her hair tumbled and jostled when she turned her head. She laughed a lot, revealing an enchanting gap between her front teeth. I knew instinctively that Chaucer's much-married Wife of Bath, the sexiest gap-toothed fictional character in Literature, must have been like Jilly.

We talked about the Common that we had in common, and she explained the origin stories behind certain landmarks: 'Alimony Villas' ('because at one time there were so many divorced women and their children living there') and 'Dogger Bank', 'Lurkers' Paradise' and, regrettably, 'Flashers' Point', 'Muggers' Tunnel' and the 'Eternal Triangle' ('a three-sided parking space, so-called because so many lovers – usually adulterers who could meet only during the day – park their cars there during lunch hour'.) Jilly dilated on the amusing/irritating characters she met on her daily dog-walks. Some were frustrated writers, among them a tramp called Old Dick, who seemed to live in the park ranger's hut. One day he presented Jilly with a bunch of roses and promised her a lovely surprise the following day. True to his word, next day he scuttled out and handed her a brown-paper package that wrapped his autobiography, written in longhand in a scrapbook, hand-ruled in pencil. A note called her 'the Goddess of the Common' and expressed his confidence that she could get it published. When, three days later, she broke the news that it might not be snapped up by Weidenfeld & Nicolson, the old man reacted 'as though I'd just turned down *Hamlet* or *The Iliad*', so she promised to try it on her publishing friends. Days of embarrassment followed, as Old Dick kept popping up on the Common to enquire about developments in London, while Jilly invented more outlandish white lies and squirmed with shame.

Elsewhere in the book she encounters famous faces – Roy Plomley of *Desert Island Discs*, David Dimbleby of *Question Time*, and the actor Anthony Andrews, then appearing on the BBC adaptation of *Brideshead Revisited*; inevitably, he and Jilly are made co-judges of the Fancy Dress component of the Putney Show. It was both charming and counter-intuitive to find a south-London suburb evoked as if it were a Sussex village.

Jilly proved to be a terrific flirt – her breathy contralto voice was made for sotto-voce confidences – and an eighteen-carat gossip. I stayed far longer than my allotted hour, revelling in her stories. Leo entered the room thrice to see if I'd gone yet. The first time, he gave me a hard look. The second time, he gazed meaningfully at his watch. The third, he actually tossed an actual British Rail timetable on the chair beside me.

'Sorry,' I muttered, 'I really must go and get my train.'

But Jilly always had time for more.

'What are you up to this evening?' she said, as I put my tape recorders away.

'I'm going to the cinema to see *The Company of Wolves*,' I said. 'How about you?'

'We're going to dinner with Godfrey Smith,' she said. 'Do you know Godfrey?'

'I've met him once or twice.' It was true. My old boss George had introduced me to the portly ex-editor of the *Sunday Times* magazine (and connoisseur of all things English) at his club.

'What do you think of him?'

'He's sort of . . . Falstaff in a Garrick tie,' I said, 'but very genial and charming. A real English gent.'

'He's not quite as innocent as people think,' said Jilly. 'I sat beside him at a dinner party a couple of years ago and, after the first course, he turned to me and said, "So Jilly. Would you be interested to know what I was doing at five o'clock this morning?" I said, "Actually, I'd *really* rather not, Godfrey, but I can see you're dying to tell me." He said, "As a matter of fact, I was being sucked orf by the former winner of the Booker Prize." I didn't hear the word "former" so I thought, "My God, that's – *William Golding*?" But of course it wasn't. It was Bernice Rubens.'

I rode home on the train comprehensively dazzled by Ms Cooper, and struggling to get the image conjured up by her final story out of my brain.

Exciting book-related initiatives were breaking out all over in these middle years. The *Independent* newspaper was launched on 7 October 1986 by three journalists from the *Daily Telegraph*, Andreas Whittam Smith, Matthew Symonds and Stephen Glover. The literary editor, Sebastian Faulks, arranged that, as well as weekly books pages, the editorial page should carry a book review every day. I dropped by to see him and encountered the joint charm offensive of his PA (and the future Mrs Faulks) Veronica Youlten and his deputy, Robert Winder, a cricket-obsessed wit who, I was pleased to note, had undergone the same wayward career trajectory as myself: he'd worked for years on the bible of investment finance, *Euromoney* magazine, before realising that his destiny lay in literary journalism.

Two new publishing companies were born, in the teeth of a massive shake-up of the industry. Since the end of the 1970s, many British companies had found themselves in financial trouble. In 1980, Cape made a profit of £800,000. Soon after, they were trading at a loss of £200,000. They linked up with two other houses, Chatto and Bodley Head, and tried to merge with a major paperback house, but to no avail. The trouble was that UK publishing was stuck in an elderly business model. Once they could rely on guaranteed sales of new books to the nation's libraries, which were now suffering local-council cutbacks. The cost of producing hardbacks had quintupled from the mid-1970s. And many old-fashioned houses refused to bring out their big sellers in paperback imprints of their own, relying instead on flogging the rights to Pan or Penguin. Sales of hardbacks were now a drop in the ocean compared to the units shifted in soft covers. So the early 1980s saw many companies either banding together in new conglomerates with streamlined operations (such as Cape, Chatto and Bodley Head), or found themselves bought up by rich paperback houses (as when Penguin acquired Hamish Hamilton, Michael Joseph and Sphere). Others began, like Faber & Faber, to set up their own paperback imprints.

It was absolutely the wrong time to start a small or medium-sized publishing company. Only a madman (or madwoman) would have thought it a good idea . . .

Victoria Barnsley is a short, dynamic, no-nonsense woman with lustrous dark hair, a voice of aristocratic plumminess and an air of omnicompetence you'd be wise not to confront. Her first job, at twenty-seven, was working for a small south London publisher; when it went bust, she decided to start her own firm, publishing books on politics by journalists – hence the name, 4th Estate. She raised £80,000 from four backers, used the money to buy the titles she'd commissioned at her old company (by then with the receivers) and rented an office in fashionable Notting Hill.

Barnsley soon realised that books of current affairs by newspaper hacks had a problem. Few of them would have much relevance, or sales, after a year or so. So she decided to specialise in fiction. In a few weeks she'd got lucky and plucked a winner from the slush pile. It was *The 13th House* by Adam Zameenzad, which won the

David Higham Award for best first novel in 1987. The following year, 4th Estate was named Best Small Publisher 1988 by the *Sunday Times*. Literary agents began to take notice; would-be writers were getting in touch.

An unlikely success story was a book called *Margaret Thatcher's History of the World*, a droll collection of *Guardian* readers' views. It sold so well that the *Guardian* bought a 50 per cent stake in Barnsley's company. She used the money to set up a dedicated sales team and decided to paperback her own books instead of selling the rights.

Her big bestseller didn't arrive until 1995 – Dava Sobel's *Longitude: The True Story of a Lone Genius Who Solved the Greatest Scientific Problem of His Time*, about the race to measure navigational longitude at sea. Soon after publication, it headed the bestseller list, sold millions of copies and was named Book of the Year.

In 1999 Barnsley decided to open a trading office in New York. She asked the *Guardian* to help with development cash and, when they said no, offered to sell 4th Estate to HarperCollins. The UK's third-largest publisher said yes. Not only did they buy her baby company for £10.2 million, they installed her as chief executive and publisher of HarperCollins's entire UK operations – an astonishing vote of confidence. Overnight, Vicky Barnsley went from having thirty-six people on staff to overseeing more than a thousand underlings.

The other new publishing house was Bloomsbury. When most established publishers were being swallowed up by international conglomerates, four people with impressive pedigrees left their jobs in September 1986, to launch a major new independent, in the heart of literary London.

One was Liz Calder, last seen joining Jonathan Cape in 1981. By 1986, Maschler and his partner Graham C. Greene had grown set in their ways; having once been so avant garde, they were now coasting along. They didn't even have a paperback division. And they refused to give their employees any shares in the company.

Liz had overseen Salman Rushdie's and Anita Brookner's ascension to Booker Prize glory at Cape, but was now dispirited and open to offers.

The brains behind Bloomsbury was Nigel Newton, the tall, slow-talking, California-born son of a Napa Valley winemaker and an American mother. In 1984, aged thirty-one, he was deputy MD of Sidgwick & Jackson and on paternity leave with his first daughter, Catherine, when he thought of starting a new company. A year later, at the London Book Fair, he met David Reynolds (from the Shuckburgh Reynolds imprint, which gave the world *The Illustrated Lark Rise to Candleford*) and with him and a venture capitalist called Mike Mayer, put together a sixty-four-page business-plan-cum-fundraising document, which included one unusual feature: the Bloomsbury Authors Trust, which offered authors shares in the company's equity when it floated on the stock market. In May 1986, they raised £1.75 million from investors while signing up the sales director of Penguin, Alan Wherry, to run their team of reps, and Liz Calder to come in as editorial director, in charge of all fiction. The City's faith in their combined talents raised enough cash to make Bloomsbury the biggest publishing start-up to date. They made other undertakings about the company: they would lavish unusual care on book design and spend a fortune on marketing, employing three publicity directors, the better to manage the public branding of authors.

The new company needed a new logo for branding itself – they had to have a sexy new design style in time for the Frankfurt Book Fair in October. So the directors held a meeting to kick some ideas around. Liz Calder had bought a little statue of Diana the Huntress, and happened to have it in the office. She presented the huntress to a design consultancy called Newell and Sorrell, and gave them four days to find a 'basic kit' of graphic elements around it. They designed a colophon of the goddess as a naked girl drawing back the string of a huge bow, whose outline formed a capital B, which would feature on the spine of every jacket. 'Won't people think,' asked one of the male directors, 'we're a feminist publisher?' Calder pointed out that Diana was also the goddess of creativity and midwifery, both publishing-related virtues. That swung it.

In August 1986 the four directors resigned *en masse* from their current jobs on the same day and, in September, the trade press, the *Times* and the *Guardian* were all briefed about the new venture. Newton had booked a stall at the Frankfurt Book Fair in the name of 'Bloomsbury' three months earlier, so they had to be there. Just before Frankfurt, Liz Calder signed up a novel called *Trust*, by the American author and former Warhol devotee Mary Flanagan, about dark behaviour in the art worlds of London and New York, and they were away. In their first year, Bloomsbury published one hundred and fifty books and had a turnover of £2 million.

The new company's launch party had to be splendiferously stylish, so the directors had to sign up a publicity director worthy of the firm's all-round fabness. They looked at the throng of publicity dames in literary London – and decided: it had to be Caroline Michel or nobody. The only drawback was that she'd only recently been signed up by Weidenfeld & Nicolson. In fact, the day they decided to ask Michel to join Bloomsbury was her first day there. What could they do? Kidnapping seemed the only option. Nigel Newton and Alan Wherry drove to the company's Clapham headquarters, grabbed the publicity diva, said, 'You're coming with us!' and led her to the car. Luckily she agreed to be abducted and spirited away to the new company. But she forfeited her place on Lord Weidenfeld's Christmas card list for ever afterwards.

The party itself was held at Braganza, a restaurant in Frith Street, Soho, where a bulky, distressed-steel construction of a human head poked out of the top-floor like a giant with a migraine. Four hundred of London's finest writers, publishers, agents, editors, liggers and rubberneckers flooded the venue's three floors, drank champagne and agreed that this was undoubtedly the party of the year (until the next one.) Nigel Newton led the speeches and called his glamorous co-director Liz Calder 'the one who puts the "Oo!" in Bloomsbury'. The smouldery-eyed actor Terence Stamp was there, having recently co-starred with Michael Douglas in *Wall Street*.* Eleanor Bron was there, too, fresh from appearing in the film of Russell Hoban's *Turtle Diary*. There was music, and an outbreak of dancing at the end. And the hot gossip was that our hostess, publicity director Caroline Michel, had recently become a hot item with Matthew Evans, chairman of Faber. Several people swore they'd witnessed the moment when he'd said to her, 'I dreamt about you last night, Caroline,' to which she'd replied, 'I dream about you *every* night, Matthew.' Love was in the air, along with success, style, drama and lots and *lots* of money.

In the shops where the new generation of literary fiction-lovers went to buy the genre-bending works by the new authors, things had also been moving. Only three weeks after Tim Waterstone opened his first shop in Old Brompton Road, his eye was drawn to a female customer browsing at the fiction tables. It was the veteran Hollywood glamour-puss, Ava Gardner. Standing beside her was Christina Foyle, owner of the eponymous London mega-bookshop, now a byword in rackety chaos. Foyle introduced herself to Waterstone, complimented him on the excellence of his store and invited him to her flat for a drink – where she offered to give him the building next door to Foyle's 'on an extended lease at a peppercorn rent', Waterstone later wrote, 'simply because she liked what she had seen, had understood that we had virtually no money, and wanted us to have a chance to succeed.' Seizing this quixotically generous offer with both hands,

* Bloomsbury were about to publish Terence Stamp's autobiography, *Stamp Album*. I interviewed him soon after the party. He was the most tactile interviewee I ever met. He'd put his hand on your wrist to make a point; then touch your arm just inside your elbow; then your upper arm; soon he'd be making a beeline for your shoulder. I put it down to nerves, rather than my devastating appeal to the very heterosexual Terence, ex-lover of Julie Christie, Jean Shrimpton and Brigitte Bardot.

Waterstone raised more capital, and the second branch opened in Charing Cross Road on 30 December 1982, four months after the first. For five days, before the recruited staff arrived, Tim Waterstone ran the place single-handed, and watched as £20,000 flooded through the single till.

Four months after that, the Gods of Retailing smiled on him once more: a huge empty warehouse on High Street Kensington was looking for a buyer. How could he raise yet more capital? Fortuitously, an article appeared in the *Evening Standard* by Max Hastings, singing the praises of Waterstone and his small but burgeoning empire. A cabal of small private investors got together to press investment money into the bookseller's hands. They included Sir Laurence Olivier.

The juggernaut rolled on. By the end of 1985, it had ten profitable bookshops. By the end of 1989, they had forty-eight. As the empire expanded – new shops appearing in Bath, Guildford, Cheltenham, Newcastle, Aberdeen, Belfast, Cardiff, Norwich, Canterbury, Birmingham, Manchester – more and more Eng Lit graduates arrived to manage the Art section, the (huge) Poetry section, the Movie-art section, the Mind, Body and Spirit section, the section that featured esoteric books from small companies in America . . . Section heads were responsible for what was ordered; there was no central buying department, no manager to report to, no hierarchy of power. Waterstone encouraged his staff to take new books home and read them, to check out the review pages of the national and regional press for inspiration; to take chances.

John Mitchison, co-founder of the crowd-funded Unbound publishing house and co-founder of the *Backlisted* podcast, enjoyed the conversations in the company staffrooms: 'I've often thought that the emergence of [the Best of Young British Novelists], the adoption of the B-format paperback for the literary backlist, and the arrival of Waterstone's, all at roughly the same time, transformed bookselling from a strange, semi-academic profession into something universal and mainstream . . . And the conversations in

Waterstone's staffrooms – knowledgeable, passionate, unashamedly egg-headed – were an essential part of that culture.'

As the literature-savvy managers changed the way books were sold, another transformation took place. The shops became more than retail outlets. They were now venues where authors could read their new work, meet their public and sign their books. This hadn't happened before in any structured way. In the Charing Cross branch, Martin Amis and Julian Barnes came to visit and read – and soon afterwards, Edward Said, Noam Chomsky, Gore Vidal and Norman Mailer came from America, like the gods descending from Olympus; later, Raymond Carver, Richard Ford, Tobias Woolf and John Irving dropped in to read too. Waterstone's started a series of debates at Stationers' Hall. The first was 'Fiction versus Biography' starring A. S. Byatt and Anthony Burgess, pitted against Michael Holroyd and Philip Ziegler.

Donna Tartt gave her first reading from *The Secret History* in Charing Cross Road. After the fatwa had been issued against him in 1989, Salman Rushdie gave his debut recital in the same place, while nervy punters watched the doors. Senior politicians queued to appear: Roy Jenkins, Edward Heath, Alan Clark, John Major. When Tim Waterstone visited the Manchester branch in 1993, he was amused to discover Irvine Welsh giving a spectacularly foul-mouthed reading from *Trainspotting* on one floor, while a Buddhist monk presided over a packed-out meditation event on the floor below.

Waterstone claimed to have invited one thousand authors to give talks over the years. He tried to persuade Umberto Eco to come and perform, but was told this would never happen. But when he rang Eco's Milan publisher, to ask the fuming semiotician in person, Eco agreed to come – to work in the bookshop for a day, wearing his sinister black hat.

When Ted Hughes came to the basement of the Camden Town Waterstone's, to read his poetry, talk about his career and take questions for an hour, he found hundreds of locals crammed into the store, standing on the staircase and sitting on the floor. He stayed for three hours.

Not everyone was ecstatic, however. While most authors were delighted to have yet more meet-and-greet events to attend on their publicity 'tour', some objected. I received a note from Margaret Forster, the prolific novelist (best known for *Georgy Girl*) and biographer (best known for *Daphne du Maurier: The Secret Life of the Renowned Storyteller*) in December 1988, saying she was thinking of writing a column 'about a row I've just had with Carmen [Callil] which has resulted in a new clause in my next contract. It will insist that "The Publisher's publicity schedule does not include either signing sessions in bookshops or a party of any kind, or long journeys for local interviews." This whole wheeling-out-of-the-author is just getting ridiculous & publishers now act as if the author has a duty to do it. Well, I don't think *I* have.'

CHAPTER 8

———•◆•———

A Street Called Fleet

The noise was fantastic. The cavernous, high-ceilinged editorial floor of the *Evening Standard* clacked and growled and roared and howled as though a million animated football rattles were having a party on board a Boeing 747 as it achieved maximum take-off decibel climax. An undisciplined, hooligan ambience prevailed on the second floor of Beaverbrook House in Fleet Street, and it was a lot to do with the typewriters.

In 1985, the world of computer technology and plasma screens was becoming the norm in newspaper land but, at the *Standard*, things were stubbornly Mesozoic. The dinosaurs sat at rough-hewn desks bashing Remingtons. These were solid, heavy objects, like the ones you'd see in revivals of *The Front Page*; the keys sat pertly upright and you had to peck at them precisely or several would rise up rebelliously to clog the machine; also you had to wind small, fiddly sheets of A5 paper, each with six carbons, onto the typewriter spindle. The pecking, the clacking, the bang-whoops of the carriage return, and the whiny winding of the carbons together conjured a sonic assault that was exhilarating, then deafening, then merely the noise of what happened all day. It was punctuated by human voices shouting over the din, 'Copy down!', at which a Dickensian urchin would gather a hundred typewritten sheets of journalism and transfer them to the Stygian depths of the ancient, hot-metal composing room.

It was wonderful to be there at last. I'd walked down Fleet Street a score of times in my twenties, wondering if I would ever get to work in this hallowed boulevard. I'd lingered outside the Wig and Pen Club in the early afternoon, wondering if I might spot a High Court judge emerge, brushing the ash of his Romeo y Julieta from his tweed lapel, as he finished giving a political journalist the lowdown about an aborted power grab at the top of the Chancery. I'd peered through the glass frontage of El Vino, the ancient wine bar where the nation's finest word-spinners congregated at lunchtime (though women, being notoriously frail and fainting creatures, weren't allowed to stand at the bar).

And there was Beaverbrook House. Several dozen times I'd gazed up in wonder at its spectacular chrome frontage, where the words 'Daily Express' and 'Sunday Express' were emblazoned, and marvelled at the art deco magnificence of the front hall, the model for the offices of the fictional Lord Copper's *Daily Beast* in Evelyn Waugh's novel *Scoop*.

It was 10 July 1985. I'd arrived to join the team on the *Evening Standard*'s gossip column. It felt marvellous. I'd been asked along by a friend from my south London gang, Nigel Reynolds. He was a restless, bald-headed, super-energetic man with a wicked chuckle, to whom I'd steered the odd diary story gleaned from Carol Kennedy at the *Director*. An early adopter of anything fashionable and gossip-worthy, he was the first of our friends to become a member of the Groucho Club, whither he invited me for a drink one evening. 'How busy are you?' he said. 'You don't fancy a few shifts on Londoner's Diary, do you?'

Indeed I did. I was now in the elevated role of a contributing hack, paid by daily shift to supply titbits of tittle-tattle worked up into fancy prose that aimed for the style of the seventeenth-century antiquary John Aubrey and mostly missed. But I was also part of history. I was reminded on my first day that anyone who'd ever been *anyone* in journalistic history had started their career on Londoner's Diary. Its line-up of past editors and contributors included Harold Nicolson, Randolph Churchill, John Betjeman, Malcolm Muggeridge, Nick Tomalin, Mary Kenny, Magnus Linklater and Max Hastings.

There were ten of us in the mid-1980s version of this sainted confederacy. At the head of a long table sat the diary editor Geoffrey Wheatcroft, a handsome man of forty with silvery hair and a grumpy, unwelcoming manner. He was impossible to speak to because he kept headphones on all day, apparently listening to Wagner; if approached, he would look furious and proceed to remove the phones with slow exasperation. I learned that he'd started his career in publishing, switched to journalism with remarkable ease, become literary editor of the *Spectator*, then legged it to South Africa in the early 1980s before returning to edit the premier gossip organ of the British press.

He had a reputation as an enthusiastic race-goer and drinker (he was known to *Private Eye* as 'the rigid man of Cheltenham' after allegedly overdoing things at the famous racetrack) and a notorious skirt-chaser. I was told to read a novel written by an old girlfriend of Geoffrey's, which featured a description of a fictional chap who enjoyed having a woman squeeze his naked frame, from his toes to his nose, as though squeezing a tube of toothpaste. But whether this was a memory or a metaphor I never learned.

Looking around, I couldn't help wondering if the current diary staff would prove an epoch-making, scoop-breaking throng. But they would. Nigel was later to become arts correspondent of the *Daily Telegraph* and *Independent on Sunday*. Victor Sebestyen, a boffin-like figure with wine-bottle spectacles, wrote an excellent biography of Lenin, and Deirdre Fernand was later to relocate to the *Sunday Times*.

Now I watched, with an amateur's fascination, how Nigel wrote a diary story when up against a tight deadline. He'd wind fresh paper onto his Adler, glance at the scribbled words in his reporter's notebook, poke tentatively at the keys for a few minutes – then stop. He'd yank the abandoned story from the machine and hurl it disgustedly into the overflowing bin under his desk. More paper would be wound in, readied, attacked with typewriter keys, found wanting, abandoned, and yanked out again in disgust. At the third attempt, Nigel would start off tentatively . . . begin to nod his head encouragingly as the words appeared before him . . . take a drag of his ever-present cigarette, smouldering in its ashtray . . . start to type faster . . . whack the carriage return as though smacking someone across the face – and BANG! He'd signal that he'd finally cracked it by seizing his tie and flinging the end over his shoulder, as if determined not to allow *any*thing to get between him and the urgent piece he was inscribing for tomorrow's pages.

I loved reading gossip in the newspapers, but I didn't have access to the inner rooms of power and money where the best stories lurked – the kind that started: 'I understand that Pongo, second son of the Marquis of Havergo, is up to his old tricks again . . .' Wheatcroft, with his wide acquaintance in stately homes across the land, was more the chap for that kind of thing. But by 1985 I knew the book world a little, its party circuit and publicity departments. Through my old boss George, I heard lots of stories about businessmen with indiscreet mistresses, and senior churchmen with tales of Vatican impropriety.

My favourite stories to write weren't about people misbehaving, but organisations making mistakes – such as the time a charity, pitched somewhere between the Wildlife Trust and the Nature Conservancy, ordered seventy-five thousand calendars to be sent to every school in the UK. It was to feature twelve photographs of birds and animals snapped in sweet, child-friendly poses – pictures that had been inspected on a lightbox and approved by the charity. Only when the photos came in, now poster-sized, from the printers did the charity spot an unfortunate detail: November's cute little squirrel, sitting with bushy tail and pile of nuts, was sporting an impressive and unignorable erection. Nobody had spotted it at the lightbox stage. Amid jokes about naming the priapic rat 'Squirrel Foreskin', the squillion-quid project had to be postponed while they found a less excitable inhabitant of Woodland.

I grew accustomed to the sight of Valerie Grove, the *Standard*'s thrilling literary editor, approaching the diary editor's chair and – apparently heedless of the iron rule about never speaking to Wheatcroft – engaging in jolly, guess-what gossip while still a few yards away: '. . . At the Folio thing last night I was standing there with Carmen and Melvyn, when who should come striding along but Germaine, shaking her curls in fury, with mad, glaring eyes, advancing on poor Bron, saying, "*You* don't think I'd hit you because I'm a woman, but I could *smash* your *glasses*!"'

Valerie was the most urgent talker I'd ever come across. She punctuated the most innocuous tale with dramatic emphases. She spoke, not in capitals, but in *italics*, her face a picture of indignation, as if every part of her story was not just riveting (and it always was) but morally shocking. Just as you thought of asking why she was so outraged, she would break into a sweet, girlish laugh, as if acknowledging the absurdity of being so indignant.

Valerie had joined the Diary in 1968, the day after graduating with an English degree from the feminist fortress of Girton College, Cambridge. She had shrewd, appraising brown eyes, and thick, dark-brown hair which never seemed to vary in style. She was always in a tearing hurry: off to do the school run (she had four children under ten, and was writing a book about the experience) or taking a taxi to Westminster to grill some political luminary, but seldom missing lunch at El Vino's. I admired her close, matey friendships with the newspaper's stars, especially the humorists Oliver Pritchett (son of V. S.) and Angus McGill, and most of all with the legendary Maureen Cleave, the petite, perceptive, bob-haired doyenne of interviewers, who had elicited from John Lennon the news that The Beatles were 'bigger than Jesus', and was said to be the inspiration behind 'Norwegian Wood'.

I'd been on the Diary a few months when I boldly tapped on the door of the Books Office. 'Hi Valerie,' I said, 'I'm John Walsh. I've been reviewing books and interviewing writers for *Books and Bookmen* for a couple of years now and, erm, I wondered if, at some point, but obviously only if you're, you know, short of someone better, if you'd like me to cast an eye over a novel, say, unless, that is—'

'This is the new Peter Ackroyd,' she said briskly, taking it from the shelf of hardbacks beside her. 'It's called *Hawksmoor.* Can you do me four hundred words by a week today?'

Could I? Would I, in fact, pursue *any other* activity in the repertoire of human behaviour except devouring *Hawksmoor*? I would not. This was my first newspaper commission. I was not going to fuck it up.

I'd read Ackroyd's first novel, *The Great Fire of London*, set in the 1980s, and found the treatment grey, the prose rather flat and the conversations oddly stuck in the 1950s. *Hawksmoor,* set in the eighteenth century, was by contrast bouncingly alive and growling with menace. We hear the voice of Nicholas Dyer, an architect charged in 1712 with building seven churches in London and Westminster under the supervision of Sir Christopher Wren. The book became a fight between the Enlightenment and the Counter-Enlightenment, played out in a London where migrating souls flit from the past to the present.

I admired *Hawksmoor* and ended my review: 'This is a coldly brilliant, immensely satisfying intellectual mystery tale – a metempsychotic masterpiece.' I was pleased to have got the word 'metempsychotic' into the *Evening Standard*, quite possibly for the first time.

And so I began reviewing for Valerie's pages. I loved our conversations, which combined gossip with exchanges of enthusiasm about books and cartoons – her father, Doug Smith, had been a cartoonist on the London *Evening News* and she was a connoisseur and collector of the *bonsai* artworks.

She told me about her early days as literary editor. She'd got the job in 1980, when she was breastfeeding her second daughter, Emma, four months old. The *Standard*'s premises were then on Shoe Lane, and the Books office was a shoebox upstairs from her chums on the newsroom floor. 'It was *filthy*,' she said, 'never tidied since the days of Arnold Bennett.'

One index of the changes brought by the 1980s was her revelation that, in 1980, some reviews would arrive *handwritten*. Her two chief reviewers, *mirabile dictu*, never mastered the typewriter. Valerie would collect Margaret Forster's copy from her house (she lived nearby), and transcribe her (entirely legible) fountain-pen script, then wait for Auberon Waugh's review to arrive by post from Combe Florey, handwritten on lined paper, complete with blottings, crossings-out, smudges and scribblings in the margin. 'Neither of them spent more than an hour on their reviews, nor bothered re-reading their words,' Valerie complained. 'I used to think: for *this* I have an honours degree in Eng Lit – to transcribe and type out the hasty scribblings of these Luddites? Good job I loved them.'

I still kept up my connection with *Books and Bookmen*, writing reviews and interviewing authors. Being the servant of two masters sometimes led to trouble. One day Sally Emerson asked me to write a round-up of first novels. She sent me a pile of six from which to select three. I wrote my seven hundred words and sent them in the post. Two weeks later, by coincidence, Valerie asked me to inspect some debut novels and choose the most appealing three. They included one book I'd reviewed in *Bookmen* – namely *Great Eastern Land* by one D. J. Taylor. I'd enjoyed it, with one or two reservations. Could I review it a second time – using different words, of course? Yeah, I thought. What harm could it do?

So I wrote a second piece about Taylor's debut, noting his elegant use of language, his stylistic nods to both Kingsley and Martin Amis, his depiction of the wily southeast Asian, Mr Mouzoukseem, and concluded both reviews by saying that, although the plot machinery didn't amount to much, if Taylor managed to shed some pretentious follies, he'd be a writer to watch. The *Standard* review appeared three days later; but when the new *Books and Bookmen* arrived, I was startled to discover that my final summation of *the book* had been cut. Instead of ending with a criticism, it ended by saying Taylor was a hot new writer. Too late I learned that *Bookmen*'s policy was to say nothing negative about an author's first book.

So that was embarrassing. But not as embarrassing as the party I attended later, in the Greyhound pub off Kensington Square. I was flooring an indifferent Sauvignon with Tim Satchell when someone tapped me on the shoulder. I turned round. An irritable-looking school-boy stood before me, in a smart Sunday-best suit. A lock of brown hair brushed against his unlined brow. Since he was clearly only about fifteen, I was surprised to see he was holding a pint of Guinness.

'Are you,' he enquired, 'John Walsh?'

'I am.'

'Pleased to meet you.' (He was very polite. Was his mother nearby?) 'My name is D. J. Taylor.'

'Ah,' I said.

'Forgive my asking,' said the schoolboy, 'but I—'

'Good to meet you,' I said. 'Congratulations on your debut.'

'Thank you,' he said neutrally. 'Only I couldn't help wondering—'

'Did you see the *Evening Standard*?' I said. 'I reviewed it.'

'Indeed you did,' he said. 'And also in *Books and Bookmen*. I couldn't help wondering how you came to review it twice, once positively, once negatively.'

'Let me explain,' I said. 'The fact of the matter is—'

'Was it that you couldn't make your mind up?' he asked. 'Or that you read it twice, only in a different mood the second time?'

'It's very simple,' I said. 'You need to know how book reviews work . . .'

I couldn't bring myself to tell him I'd simply forgotten the no-negativity clause.

'Look,' I said, 'why don't I get you a drink and discuss what you might like to review for me if you fancy it?'

'Very well,' he said. ('Very well'? 'Indeed'? Why did this callow youth talk like someone out of Trollope?)*

---

* The callow youth turned out to be twenty-six at the time.

'Does this mean I have to read everything twice? The first time when feeling content, the second when dyspeptic?'

'I'm starting to think,' I said, 'that you're taking the piss.'

'Perhaps,' he said, 'but I may be feeling different next time I see you.'

One evening, shortly after my thirty-third birthday, life abruptly changed. It was the night of the Jonathan Cape party, 9 December 1986. Cape didn't do parties like other publishing houses did. They behaved as if the standard white-wine-with-prawn-canapés-and speeches format was beneath them. The Cape party was an annual thing, held in the company's Bedford Square HQ. Unlike other shindigs, it began at 9 p.m. and went on beyond midnight. Also unlike the competition's idea of what parties were for, it tended not to invite the gentlemen of the press – not the gossip columnists, at any rate, only the literary editors (if they were *very* fortunate). As a result, you'd probably see some Cape authors who'd never otherwise appear in public – Bruce Chatwin, say, or Anita Brookner – in unbuttoned party mode. I found myself there with Sally Emerson and Carolyn Hart. We stood on the sidelines, watching the remarkable spectacle of the Cape chairman, Tom Maschler, doing his stuff.

He was the most intensely tanned Caucasian I'd ever seen. Between unruly wings of flyaway hair, his shiny forehead was as darkly burnished as a conker. His intense brown eyes regarded his guests with an amusement that bordered on disparagement, while his voice soared to girlish shrieks of remonstration. He seemed to be in a permanent state of aggrieved hilarity. Despite his considerable reputation as a ladies' man, he was as camp as a sequinned bivouac. I watched him moving between the big beasts of his publishing stable – Martin Amis, Clive James, Doris Lessing, Madhur Jaffrey, Ian McEwan, Bernard Levin, Claire Tomalin, Anita, Bruce, Salman – like a fond zookeeper doing the rounds, but never pausing for too long between the wildlife.

During the evening, Valerie Grove came up to me to unload a big secret.

'John, I think you should know that I'm leaving the *Standard* in the spring. I'm going to the *Sunday Times* to write interviews for Andrew Neil.'

'Oh no!' I said in dismay. 'Who's going to replace you? Who do I have to suck up to now to get reviewing work?'

'That's just the thing,' she said. 'I think you should do it.'

I gazed at her. 'Are you serious?'

'I'm quite serious. You'd be perfect. You know all the publishers, you go to all the parties, you hang out with other reviewers, you write well, you've got a good ear for bookish gossip . . .'

'Stop, stop!' I said. 'This is really kind but I'm sure there are dozens of others who would kill to fill your shoes.'

'No there aren't actually,' she said. 'I shall recommend you to John Leese.'

I left the party dancing on air, but that night my dreams were full of concern. John Leese was no pushover. A craggy-faced, chain-smoking, Black Country veteran of the *Coventry Morning Telegraph*, the *Standard* editor looked like someone who wouldn't stand for much nonsense on the Books pages. The swishy paragraph, the Wildean paradox, the pretentious value judgement, any *hint* of 'metempsychosis' – none of these would go down well with such a stern overseer. I could well imagine Valerie turning away his wrath with her Oh-come-now, Girtonian insouciance, her thrillingly defusing laugh, but *moi*?

To my delight and alarm, I was summoned for an interview in Leese's lair. I was invited to tell him about my background, my ambitions, my knowledge of literature and my view of the *Standard*'s Books pages. This was tricky. I could hardly criticise Valerie's wonderful choices of books and reviewers, but I had to show initiative.

What, he asked, would I change about them?

'I'd beg the powers-that-be for more space,' I said. 'We're going through a golden period for British publishing right now, especially in fiction, and we should be steering our readers towards the best stuff around.'

'Anything else?' said John Leese.

'We shouldn't be afraid to be both highbrow and lowbrow,' I said. 'Just because we review a biography of Solzhenitsyn or Marx, doesn't mean we should ignore a novel by, er, Jilly Cooper.'

'You're a big fan, are you,' grated the editor, 'of *Riders*?'

Oh God. Ms Cooper's saucy bonkbuster, set in the world of show-jumping, had been a huge bestseller a year before. Now I'd told the editor of the *Evening Standard* that it was, in effect, my favourite kinda novel.

'Not a *huge* fan,' I said hurriedly, 'but I think her readers would love to see a review of her next one. It doesn't mean we're claiming it's literature.'

'I don't think there's *mooch* danger of our readers complaining we're being insufficiently highbrow,' he said, sending a wintry smile through a cloud of nicotine. 'I think we're pretty safe there.'

Three months later, in February 1987, I moved into my kingdom – the Books office on the *Evening Standard* editorial floor. The literary editor needed an office with a lockable door because books that came in for review couldn't be left on desktops, lest some unscrupulous hack might fancy removing them, to parlay them for cash at the second-hand-book dealers in Chancery Lane.

Into the office I brought a stack of new stationery from Ryman's, a Rolodex which I hoped to fill with the names of top-class book reviewers (Could I get Angela Carter to review fiction? And Martin? And maybe Philip Roth, given the right book of course . . . ?) and a small, functional, two-seater sofa from Heal's, where I could entertain visiting authors and reviewers who would obviously start dropping by when I was better known.

The first few weeks were a glorious flurry of organisation – learning to open a hundred Jiffy bags a week without bursting a cloud of choking grey Jiffy-shit into the office air; starting a file of commissioned reviews, a ledger of payments, a folder to house my correspondence with reviewers and publishers, and an in-tray for party invitations. I hummed with satisfaction. To the outside world my bustling form must have resembled a bookish Mrs Tiggywinkle, but I was as happy as a sow in a sauna.

Valerie Grove had bequeathed me a wonderful family of reviewers, and I busied myself with the task of taking them all out for lunch, one by one, and seeing if they'd like to work with me. It's hard to convey the many levels of pleasure I had in making the acquaintance of Rachel Billington (regal and gossipy), Paul Bailey (sleek and outrageous), Lucy Hughes-Hallett (amazingly well-read, gleefully opinionated), Duncan Fallowell (yawningly decadent, tending to over-share about his sexual exploits), Roy Porter (portly, dishevelled, and the most brilliant historian of his generation), Rupert Christiansen (as much at home with grand opera, romanticism and goings-on at *Harper's & Queen*), Penelope Lively (motherly but with a streak of steel) and Brian Masters (equally at home writing about serial killers and duchesses).

Paul Bailey proved to be a whizz at take-no-prisoners abuse: he called A.L. Rowse's study of W.H. Auden 'this preposterous little book... this repellent memoir'. Maureen Cleave, my new colleague at the newspaper, had a lovely way of congratulating publishers in her reviews. When Bloomsbury launched its first list with the debut novel *Trust*, she wrote: 'How clever of Bloomsbury to kick off with Mary Flanagan, whose writing suggests an unfathomable store of riches yet to come.' I enjoyed commissioning famous names to review books supposedly outside their comfort zone: Margaret Drabble on Pol Pot and Cambodia, for instance; Grey Gowrie on new thrillers by the hard-boiled Americans, George V. Higgins and Elmore Leonard.

I busied myself with the look of the pages. I started a little weekly feature called 'Writers Reading', in which 'London's literati' revealed what they were reading for pleasure: Angela Carter was deep in Judith Krantz's raunchy *I'll Take Manhattan*

('The sex scenes are so explicit!' she girlishly cried) while Andrew Motion was soberly buried in Henry James's *Diaries*, I signed up Peter Reading, the Liverpool-born poet – a grumpy, abrasive, caustically funny alchemist of words, who plucked horror stories from the newspapers and turned them into poetry balanced between disgust and regret – to supply a monthly round-up of recent verse. And I arranged to host a slightly down-at-heel 'salon' in the Cheshire Cheese pub every other Friday, to bring together recently published novelists, historians and biographers. I wish I could pretend I was doing some serious managerial work in these endeavours, but really I was just indulging a blissful dream of being the *Evening Standard*'s Book Bloke, some way after (and a long way below) Arnold Bennett's seat at the table in the 1920s.

Morning Conference at 8 a.m. was a revelation. I'd expected it to be a convocation of like-minded intellectuals, discussing vital sociopolitical issues of the day, and fizzing with ideas of how best we might hold the Thatcher government to account (or support it). In reality it was a noisy two hours of raillery, badinage, name-calling and piss-taking, with the occasional moments of serious analysis.

The editor brought two packets of Marlboro Reds to every morning conference in his office, smoked grimly throughout and delivered a considerable toxic fug around us by 9 a.m. Leese, fifty-nine, was by nature a grouchy chap, but I noticed he was judicious and fair in his dealings with the rowdy factions around him.

By his side sat the deputy editor, Genevieve Cooper, a striking presence at forty-five. She was tall and fantastically stylish. The combination of her blonde waves, her long white skirts and high-heeled boots gave her the look of a feminist Bo Peep as she strode around the editorial floor. Born in Nottingham, she'd been a secretary at sixteen and had risen from *Forum* (the high-class smut mag owned by *Penthouse*, with the eye-poppingly confessional letters page) to *Cosmopolitan*, the *Mail on Sunday*'s *You* magazine (where she'd met Leese) and the *Sunday Times*'s colour supplement, before jumping ship to the *Standard*.

Another alumnus of *You* was the managing editor, Craig Orr, possibly the craggiest Scot from the many crags of his native Dumfries and Galloway. He was a quietly spoken but passionate regionalist, who insisted on drinking only the whisky of his Speyside ancestors.

Another notable, and considerably more voluble, Scot was Peter McKay, a beaming mischief-maker who, on my second day in the job, as I stood apprehensively outside the editor's office, appeared behind me, and cooed in my ear, Iago-like, 'You luke pensive, Mr Walsh – and you have much to luke pensive about . . .' He was an unmissable figure: his head was the size of a 1950s television set. His face was broad and pudgy. His merry blue eyes were often lost in crow's feet of amusement. His hair was a curious construction, starting way back on his scalp like the chap in *Eraserhead*, and curling up in dark, oily tendrils.

He tended to express right-wing opinions in tones of twinkling hilarity that sometimes hardened into seriousness. The editor indulged his flights of fury because McKay was held to be the most seasoned newspaperman in Fleet Street, combining an infallible nose for a story with, when the occasion demanded, a thunderous show of moral righteousness he'd learned from his one-time boss, Sir John Junor of the *Sunday Express*. Everyone I met in the Street of Shame had stories to tell about McHackey – about his foreign jaunts, expenses claims, practical jokes, gossip techniques, rows, vendettas and rumoured affairs.

His most spectacular wind-up occurred when he edited the 'Town Talk' page of the *Sunday Express*. His assistant there was Lady Olga Maitland, daughter of the Seventeenth Earl of Lauderdale, and later Conservative MP for Sutton and Cheam. In the office one day, Lady Olga was on the phone, trying to interview Aristotle Onassis, the famous Greek shipping magnate. As the interview stumbled on, McKay silently pushed a note across the table. It read: 'Be sure to ask if he's friends again with Mr Epiglottis after their long feud . . .'

She nodded and went back to listening to Onassis in full flood.
Finally he subsided.

'One last thing,' cooed Lady Olga. 'Have you finally patched up
your long-running and damaging row with Mr Epiglottis?'

The effect was electrifying. 'Whad you talk about?' demanded
Onassis. 'Is CRAP, is never happen. Epi-whatty? I never fucking
'eard of 'im. What are you, the fuckin' police? You ask me about
people I never fucking 'eard of?'

Leese was less indulgent towards Christopher Monckton –
more correctly, the Honourable Christopher Monckton, later to
inherit the title of Viscount Monckton of Brenchley. (He later
became Deputy Leader of UKIP.) Monckton had made journalism
his career since Cambridge, interspersing it with a spell at
Conservative Central Office. He'd edited the Catholic weekly
paper, the *Universe*, had written leaders for the *Standard* from the
early 1980s, and was now its consulting editor. He had a
disconcertingly exophthalmic gaze, affected the garb of a City gent
– grey suit, rolled umbrella, even a bowler hat – and used to occupy
the sofa on the left of the editor's desk, as a kind of upholstered
fiefdom.

He was staggeringly right-wing. Among the leading social issues
of the time was the HIV/Aids crisis. In 1987 the US Department of
Health and Human Services added HIV to their list of
'communicable diseases of public health significance', which
meant refusing to allow immigrants or short-term foreign visitors,
who had tested positive with the virus, from entering the States.
How should the UK treat HIV victims seeking to enter the country?
It was the signal for a lively debate – but I was stunned by
Monckton's take on the problem. He suggested the only way to
deal with Aids was to subject everyone in the UK to a blood test
every month, and to incarcerate every carrier in quarantine *immediately*
and *permanently*. Everyone with HIV, he said, should be locked up
pronto, with no prospect of release, ever.

I remember the uproar Monckton's arguments caused among

my new colleagues. How they shouted and denounced him as a fascist crackpot – and how John Leese, with astonishing calm amidst this fury, raised a hand for quiet. 'This newspaper, Christopher, thrives on argument and confrontation and points of view,' he grated. 'What you are offering here is a point of view. And I am never going to publish it.' I believe Monckton finally published his article in the *American Spectator*; the magazine's assistant managing editor denounced it in the letters page of the same issue.

The editor of Londoner's Diary was now Richard Addis, a charming chap most remarkable for his non-resemblance to any journalist in hack history. He'd spent two years, after Rugby School and before Downing College Cambridge, as a novice Anglican monk. Perhaps as a result, his demeanour was serene to a Zen degree. His long face, that of an El Greco saint, was given character mostly by his black spectacles and severe side-parting. And his contributions during Conference were wonderfully oblique: wherever they started, you never knew where they were going to end up. One morning, he began like this:

'The black beanwood tree, which flowers in North Queensland in eastern Australia, holds a holy significance for Aboriginal people. Its wood was used to make spears. Its seeds have been eaten for two thousand years. The beanwood tree was a cultural gathering point for Aborigines, and the site of religious ceremonies down the generations. The wood is very hard to find outside Australia . . .'

In the editor's office we all waited. We could tell Addis knew what he was doing.

'. . . but one place it *was* used was in creating the Speaker's Chair in the House of Commons in 1926. Which is why, last night, in the Commons chamber, police arrested four men trying to slice bits off the chair, in the hope of returning them to where they rightly belong . . .' As Addis left the Conference room half an hour later, to prepare the Diary for publication, Leese watched him go. 'There,' he said benignly, 'goes one of the great eccentrics of modern journalism.'*

Sometimes, literary issues or authorial misbehaviour would appear in the list of news stories, and I would be expected to write something for the News desk. One bookish kerfuffle seemed likely to upset sensitive Islam thinkers. It concerned a collection of short stories called *Down the Road, Worlds Away* by a young Muslim woman called Rahila Khan, thirty-seven, born in Coventry. Her agent sent the stories to Virago, where Carmen Callil and Lennie Goodings admired them and decided to publish them in the Virago Upstarts series. They asked to meet the author, but the agent explained that this wasn't possible: Ms Khan wanted to keep her writing a secret from her family, she didn't live in London – and to sneak away from her repressive home would be difficult. They went ahead and published the book anyway. Three weeks later, with copies now in the shops, the Viragos got an embarrassed phone call from the agent. She said she'd finally met the lovely Rahila. Unfortunately, she wasn't a woman. Or Muslim. Or indeed a writer, first and foremost. She was a British Anglican vicar called Toby Forward.

Virago's response was remarkably speedy and impressively thorough. They withdrew the book from sale, wrote to all the shops that had taken copies of the bogus tales, asking for them back, pulped the warehouse stock, and issued a press release denouncing the deception. There was an immediate firestorm, from breakfast TV to the tabloids, but the drift of sympathy was not towards the publishers. In vain did Carmen complain about the iniquity of Forward's passing himself off as a black woman; the media said she was being 'sexist' and humourless; the red-tops found it hilarious that a gang of feminist publishers should be defrocking a vicar.

---

* And one of the most successful. After the *Standard*, he became, successively, deputy editor of the *Sunday Telegraph*, features editor of the *Daily Mail*, and editor in chief of both the *Daily* and *Sunday Express*, where he would often ask the papers' regular astrologist to sit in on editorial conferences to provide 'added perspective'.

The Asian community seemed weirdly un-insulted about a British writer fooling a gullible British public by pretending to be a young Islamic woman believer. So I didn't have to defend the publishing world against the rage of Islam.

Much nearer to the front page was the Jeffrey Archer scandal. The story went like this. In 1974, Archer's early political career had hit the buffers. A fraudulent investment scheme had left him £500,000 in debt and he'd resigned as MP for Louth. To pay his debts he began writing fiction, starting with a bestselling thriller called *Not a Penny More, Not a Penny Less*. In 1985, he was back in Westminster, after one of his biggest fans, Mrs Thatcher, made him deputy chairman of the Conservative Party, in the teeth of objections from Norman Tebbit, Edward Heath and William Whitelaw.

Just a year later, he was forced to resign when the *News of the World* splashed a story under the headline 'Tory Boss Archer Pays Vice-Girl'. The paper claimed to have filmed an intermediary of Archer's handing over £2,000 to a prostitute called Monica Coghlan. The exact nature of the transaction for which Archer had allegedly paid up wasn't specified. But after the Sunday paper led the way, the *Daily Star* followed with a story that said Archer had paid for sex with Coghlan; Archer sued the *Star* for damages.

The trial in July 1987 was the court case of the year, partly because of Ms Coghlan's revelation that Archer had an acne-ridden back, and partly because of the judge's apparently love-struck paean of praise for Mary Archer's 'elegance', 'fragrance' and 'radiance'.

In his study of bestselling postwar books, *Reading the Decades*, Professor John Sutherland pointed out the 'eerily prophetic' quality of Archer's fictions. 'His novels,' he writes, 'foretell his imminent disasters with the doom-laden prescience of the soothsayer in *Julius Caesar*.' *First Among Equals*, published in 1984 (and third-bestselling hardback novel of the year following a TV adaptation), featured four British politicians vying to become UK prime minister. One of them learns that the *News of the World* has contacted his estranged wife and offered her £100,000 to spill some no-holds-barred revelations about his private life. In the book, the MP buys her off. It is positively spooky that Archer should have anticipated a real-life sex scandal, involving a senior MP, a pay-off and the *News of the World*, just two years before the same thing happened to him. One might almost conclude that he was tempting Fate.

It was riveting to be, every day, among a roomful of professional journalists – to be right in the, as it were, engine room of Fleet Street. In this heady atmosphere, my books pages couldn't help but seem a little marginal, a bit niche, an adjunct of Showbiz or Lifestyle. I had to fight my corner every Wednesday, when I attended Conference to explain which reviews were to appear next day.

'The lead review,' I once began, 'is a book called *The Embarrassment of Riches* by Simon Schama, the English historian and one of the world's leading academics, currently a professor at Harvard. The book's been praised by heavyweight critics here and abroad, including Robert Hughes and John Gross in the *New York Times*.'

'What's it a history of?' asked John Leese, in his blunt way.

'It's a history of Holland in the, um, seventeenth century.'

'Remind me. What was happening to Holland in the seventeenth century? Were they at war?'

'Not exactly,' I said, struggling a bit to remember. 'It's more about how all the countries of the Netherlands, despite not having the same language or form of government, shared certain things, in a cultural way, and became the Dutch empire.' (Or was it the Dutch Republic? Shit. Or was there a king involved?)

Conference silently digested my exciting news.

'It's reviewed by the brilliant young historian Roy Porter,' I continued, 'and he loves it. He calls it "a watershed in the history of history".'

'What's the title again?' asked Craig Orr, sarcastically. 'I must order it from my local library.'

'It's called *The Embarrassment of Riches: An Interpretation of Dutch Culture in the Golden Age*.'

There were, I'm sorry to say, snorts of derision from the assembled hacks.

'I'm sure *that'll* go down a storm with the housewives of Tower Hamlets,' said Peter McKay. 'I believe they're *avid* for information about Ghent in 1682.'

'OK, OK,' I said, 'obviously it's not for everyone, but it's one of the major historical works of the year, and that's why we're telling readers about it.'

'Have you,' asked Vicky Summerley, the features supremo, a super-efficient woman whose arms seemed permanently akimbo as she ticked off her quaking sub-editors, 'actually *read* this book?'

'No of course not,' I said, 'I can't read every book. That's what reviewers are for. But I dipped into this one. There's a marvellous description of something called a drowning cell, where they used to put especially idle prisoners. It would fill up with water, and the only way you could survive was by pumping the water out as fast as it came in . . .'

By now I had, as they say, 'lost the room'. I got through the remainder of my list without mishap or mockery, but a precedent had been set. I was outed as a pretentious would-be highbrow, who failed to realise he was working on a middle-brow newspaper, with pictures of pretty girls on the news pages, and kids' cartoons at the back. In the weeks that followed, I grew used to McKay's sleek enquiries: 'Nothing this week on Byzantine ceramics, laddie?' or, 'No new works on Mesopotamian hieroglyphics, Mr Walsh?'

There was a predictable reaction when, months later, I announced that the lead review would be of *A Brief History of Time* by Stephen Hawking. The hype that preceded the book had been massive, most of it concerning the eminence and physical disarray of the author, rather than the contents of the pages. There was a manufactured excitement from the publicity department about Hawking's motor-neurone disease. It was, they said, a Race Against

Time: would he be able to crack the Secret of the Universe and the Meaning of Life before His Time Was Up?'*

'It's a work of popular science like no other,' I told Conference, 'because in it the most brilliant British scientist since Isaac Newton explains all the *really* hard stuff – cosmology, quantum mechanics, black holes, relativity, everything – in a way that ordinary people can understand.'

'I stopped being interested in that stuff around the time I failed Physics O-level,' said a voice. 'I think a lot of people feel the same.'

'Nevertheless,' I said, 'it's a vastly important book about the biggest subjects of all. Time and space and gravity and, er, E equals MC squared . . .'

'Does he touch on time travel,' asked the picture editor, 'or alien civilisations?'

'No,' I said coldly. 'I think he sticks to what's actually been discovered.'

'But black holes haven't been *discovered*,' said the sports editor. 'I mean you can't *see* them through a telescope. You don't know they're actually there, or at least you can't prove it, can you?'

'They're just an idea, aren't they?' said the deputy fashion editor. 'Just a possibility. You know? Like unicorns.'

'This discussion would be a lot more sophisticated,' I said sternly, 'if everybody here had read the book.'

'That's settled then,' said John Leese. 'The literary editor will buy us all copies for Christmas.'

An unusual book called *This Small Cloud: A Personal Memoir* came in for review. It was the posthumous confessions of Harry Daley, a London policeman from the 1920s to 1950. Its unique selling proposition was that Sergeant Daley was openly gay, at a time when

---

* Yes, he would. Hawking lived on until 2018, thirty years after the book's publication. It stayed in the *Sunday Times* bestseller list for a record-breaking 237 weeks.

such a thing was unimaginable for a copper; he was cultured and literary and became the lover of E. M. Forster and J. R. Ackerley. He met the Bloomsbury Group, and Duncan Grant painted his portrait (complete with helmet). It seemed a good choice for London's evening paper to review.

Gays and policemen – who might be familiar with both? My mind leapt to James Anderton, the chief constable of Greater Manchester who had, he'd claimed, 'a direct line to God' and had recently said that homosexuals, prostitutes and drug addicts with HIV/Aids were 'swirling in a human cesspit of their own making'. Perhaps he might enjoy reading about—but no. The thought of his response on the phone was enough to freeze the blood.

Then I thought: what about John Stalker? Anderton's deputy was a policeman of high public profile and broad public sympathy. In 1984, he'd headed the Stalker Inquiry, investigating the alleged 'shoot-to-kill' policy used by the RUC against unarmed IRA suspects two years before. In 1986 he'd been removed from the inquiry by Anderton and suspended from duty. Allegations (clearly fictional) were made that some of Stalker's associates were dubious characters; it was all nonsense. He emerged from a farrago of defamation cleared of wrongdoing, smelling of roses and effectively bankrupt.

I asked the News desk for a contact number, rang his farm in Cheshire, talked to his wife ('He's up at the piggery,' she said. 'I'll just go and call him'), and asked if he fancied reviewing the book. Not only did he jump at the chance; he said he'd been considering a writing career for a while. When the review arrived, it was obvious that a natural journalist had always lurked inside his serious blue uniform. The editor signed him up to write serious feature articles about London knife crime, British drug trafficking, UK illegal immigrant legislation, you name it.

It was the start of a new career for Stalker. He published a bestselling autobiography, wrote for broadsheet newspapers, made TV commercials for garage doors and patio awnings, hosted

Crimestalker for six years on Central Television, appeared on *Question Time* and *Have I Got News For You* – even turned up in a sketch on *Harry Enfield and Chums*. It's amazing where a good book review could get you in the 1980s – that and a reputation as a good man in a shabby world.

I interviewed Martin Amis again in April 1987, around the publication of *Einstein's Monsters*. We'd met a few times at parties and chatted to each other at sit-down lunches, but, since our slightly awkward encounter over *Other People: A Mystery Story* in 1981, this was my first proper one-to-one with the literary hero of my early twenties.

We met at the Waldorf, an ornately pillared Victorian hotel near the Royal Opera House. The restaurant seemed the size of Wembley Stadium, the chairs were plush black, the tables round and glass-topped, and the white napery so pristine it dazzled the retina. He'd arrived before me and was sitting, looking entirely at home, reading the *New Statesman*.

I'd brought along a copy of that day's *Standard*, hot off the press, and plonked it on the table, murmuring '. . . a little present for you'. Amis looked at it without enthusiasm. I remembered his father's line in *Lucky Jim* about the guy who presents Jim with 'the smallest drink he'd ever been seriously offered in his life'; the noonday *Standard* was probably the most infinitesimal gift Amis had ever been seriously handed.

He summoned a waiter. 'Tomato juice,' he said, 'heavily spiced,' in a perfect, if perhaps unconscious, echo of Bob Hope in a tough saloon in *The Paleface*, ordering 'Orange juice – in a dirty glass.'

Like the room, the menu was almost aggressively plain, short on adjectives and brusque in manner. 'Take it or leave it' seemed to be the subtext behind 'Mussels in white wine' and 'Boiled beef and parsley dumplings'. Martin ordered the former, I the latter. 'And,' I added, 'can I get a side order of mixed vegetables?'

We talked about the book, and its dual response to the threat of nuclear destruction. First came an essay, 'Thinkability', Amis's passionate non-fiction denunciation of the arms race, slightly hobbled by an oddly American-slang disgust ('I am sick of nuclear weapons . . . they make me want to throw up, they make me feel sick to my stomach . . .'); then five short fictions on themes of time, plague and mortality. Amis explained how he was spurred into action by reading Jonathan Schell's book *The Fate of the Earth*, which offers the blunt prediction that nuclear war will produce 'unthinkable' consequences: the destruction of humanity and the end of life on Earth.

Pre-interview, I'd briefed myself on the state of the arms talks between Presidents Reagan and Gorbachev, and pointed out to Amis that the Reykjavik Summit, six months earlier, had come close to both sides agreeing to eliminate all nuclear weapons within ten years. Did that make his fears in the book redundant?

Amis flashed a smile of killer sarcasm. He'd spent the morning, he said, talking about the arms race with the provincial press. 'They kept asking me if the book and its warnings have been "overtaken by events". I told them, "Yeah it's a real *bitch*, this arms deal of Gorbachev's coming along just as the book is published. I mean, thanks a *lot* . . ."'

John Carey's *Sunday Times* review of *Einstein's Monsters* said that, while Amis had always had a style 'as fast and efficient as a flick-knife', he had only now found himself a serious subject to match his cool prose. And Amis's seriousness showed itself in the (slightly over-rehearsed) gravity of his pronouncements. On President Reagan's 'Star Wars' initiative, he said, 'I hate it because it's another waterfall we can tumble over – the militarisation of space'. On Reagan himself, 'He thinks in free enterprise terms – if you're going to claim material supremacy over the rest of the world, you've got to have the biggest arsenal. He thinks it'll ensure him a place in history – but for that you need a guarantee that there'll be some history.'

I asked about the stories, which (with terrific wit and invention) gave a voice to, among others, an Immortal who's watched human life from the outset and is about to witness its demise. Wasn't it kinda *frivolous* to make undergraduate jokes about the end of the world?

'It's all about perspective,' said Amis. 'Looked at in a hundred-year period, the human race might seem very progressive. From the perspective of eternity, on the other hand, it becomes a farce . . .'

Much of the emotion in the new stories was centred on families, on fathers and children, on the vulnerability of the young and the weak. A master of deduction would be tempted to link this theme to Amis's own fatherhood, of Louis (two) and Jacob (six months). Had they changed him a lot?

'Becoming a father repaired my damaged sense of time,' he said. 'I had ceased to care, in a sense, about the future. I was passive about it. Children represent your attachment to the future and remind you that you're attached to the past as well.'

The food arrived. My guest's *moules marinières* were served on a black plate in the Normandy style, with chopped onions, bay leaves and parsley. One of the world's simplest dishes, they were a startling sight, a score of soft, miniaturised vulvas with tiny teeth round the edges, like something out of *Alien*. My own lunch, by comparison, was a slab of grey, rectangular brisket, surmounted by wet suet lumps; the vegetables were a blokeish *mélange* of carrots, leeks, parsnips and pickled walnuts – the lunch of an eighteenth-century bumpkin outside a Suffolk inn, a kerchief around his neck, a clasp-knife in his meaty paw . . .

I watched Amis devour his plate of mussels while he talked. His eyes were fixed on the orange bivalves, extracting them from their shiny black coffins with speed and precision, like a skilled knitter. I must have seen someone else do that trick of using the empty shell of one mussel to tweezer out the mollusc-meat from the next, but Amis's skill seemed like his writing: selecting the best words from the lexicon, yanking them from his memory with the pincers

of his creative mind, savouring them, dipping some in the marinad-
ing wine . . .

The waiter reappeared beside me, bearing a gigantic silver dish.

'The mixed vegetables you ordered, sir.'

What the *hell*? I'd ordered them because the menu hadn't
mentioned that vegetables came with the beef. Now I had two
helpings, and I looked like a greedy trencherman, an endomorphic
yob. Without asking, the waiter spooned the second sack-load of
leguminous horrors onto my plate. Somewhere in the cascade, I
could identify chunks of turnip, cubes of beetroot, unpeeled
horseradish, boiled mangelwurzels . . .

I looked at Amis coming to the end of his compact, stylish lunch,
delivering the last mussel to his gourmet lips, clacking the last black
shell down on what resembled a pile of Japanese lacquer boxes.
I looked at my plate. It resembled an inverted hubcap crammed
with steaming root vegetables, as though I was in a Crimean War
field kitchen.

Amis showed no sign that he'd noticed my dismay but continued
his fluent dilations on children and Mr Gorbachev's intentions.

Martin is, I thought, a different quality of human being from the
rest of us. He is the 'tiny ironist' with the gift for absolute precision,
for finding the right word, the right image, the stylish response, the
cool remark, for everything. He hovers over my workaday, literary-
hack life like the Mekon in the *Dan Dare* comic strip, the tiny
Treen with the giant brain, hovering above the terrestrial world,
sure of domination. I had, in the past, sometimes found fault with
his work, but now I was right back in total fan mode.

I listened hard, to get back into the conversation.

' . . . and if Reagan wants his legacy as president to be as a great
peacemaker, that should be the strategy he pursues.'

'Hang on, Martin,' I said. 'Ten minutes ago, you said you
thought Reagan wanted to be remembered as the guy who confronted the Soviets and forced them to see reason. He can't be
the gunslinger in the O.K. Corral *and* the peacemaker, can he?'

Amis smiled. 'Did I say that? Maybe I did. I'm a bit of a dolt about politics.'

Even when he contradicts himself, I thought, he makes it seem the right response. Martin Amis – a master of disarmament.

Sometimes, I would be asked to write a column for the *Standard*'s leader page. This was a heavyweight commission because a leader article had to be a) the calm, friendly voice of the newspaper; and b) judicious, seeing both sides of the argument, before reaching a clear conclusion.

Christopher Hudson, my office-mate, was a leader writer of many years' standing, capable of turning his hand, at short notice, to anything from nuclear disarmament to the ordination of women. He kept a box file in his desk, in which the arguments For and Against every imaginable topic, from Abortion to Zionism, were written on file cards. I'd watch Christopher at his desk riffling through the cards, mulling over the Pro and the Anti arguments before tapping out the perfect opening: 'There are two kinds of mercy . . .'

Anyway, in Conference one day, the subject was the IRA, and what should be done about a Republican gunman called Owen Carron. In 1985, the RUC had arrested Carron after he'd been found in his car with a passenger, James Maguire, who was holding an assault weapon. Both men were charged with firearms offences but Carron was granted bail; before he could be tried, however, he legged it across the border to the Republic. Now, in November 1987, the Ulster court issued warrants for his arrest, supported by the Irish police, who expected to send him back to Belfast to stand trial. But Carron had spotted a loophole in the Extradition Act. As a judge ordered his extradition to the UK, Carron brought up a clause which said the High Court could order the release of an accused man if the offence with which he was charged could be 'connected to a political offence'. Which, the High Court conceded, it could. Whereupon the extradition proceedings, barely begun, were aborted.

The editor had a sizeable bee in his bonnet about the IRA, perhaps because of the days when they bombed stores in London and pubs in Birmingham. 'We need a leader on this,' he said. 'How about you, John? You're Irish, and also English. You can tease out the legal stuff and say something colourful about the rights and wrongs, can't you?'

Could I hell. This was no time to reveal my astonishing ignorance about Irish politics. But I couldn't disappoint the editor.

'Sure thing,' I said. 'I'll start right away.'

Four hours later, at 1.15 p.m., I was floundering like a carp on a hot rock. I'd read up on Extradition Acts and inter-government treaties, I'd pillaged the library on UK–USA felon exchanges and prisoner deals with Saudi Arabia. I'd read many sentences like this: 'While on remand in custody, pending his extradition, Keane applied for a writ of *habeas corpus*, claiming that the magistrate's extradition order was contrary to Section 2(2)(b) of the Backing of Warrants Act'. The will to live had slid from my brain down my spine, entered both legs, descended to my feet and was now leaking out of my shoes.

Behind me, from the doorway, I heard a familiar voice:

'All worrrk and no play makes John a dull boy. Come to El Vino's, dear chap.'

'I can't,' I said feebly. 'I've got a leader to write.'

'Ach, no problem,' said McKay. 'Have you got your conclusion?'

'*Nooo!*' I groaned. 'It's incredibly complicated. It's all about how you can't send a potential murderer to another country to face trial if there's any hint of politics about the case. Which of course, with the IRA, there always is.'

'A glass of white Burgundy will make everything clearer.'

Conscious that I was being led astray by the wickedest boy in the playground, I followed him downstairs.

El Vino was packed, fuggy with fag smoke, and noisy as the Babel Tower at chucking-out time. Peter joined two women and a florid-faced man, clearly all daily visitors to the famous watering-hole. One woman was Ann Leslie, the legendary foreign correspondent who'd once punched Muhammad Ali on the chin to get his attention, and been propositioned by a naked David Niven in her hotel room. The other was a *Telegraph* political writer called Helena, groomed and coiffed as if about to appear on a chat show. The florid man, Chris, was an unsmiling news guy from the *Mail*.

'This is John,' said Peter, 'he's writing his first leader, and is feeling a bit stuck. Drinks, anyone?'

Peter took their orders and disappeared to the bar. The veteran trio regarded me without enthusiasm.

'What's your piece about?' asked Helena.

'It's about the extradition of IRA prisoners to British courts. And it's *incredibly* complicated because the courts keep changing the rules about sending people for trial in other countries.'

This was pathetic. Any minute now I'd be wailing: 'It's just not *fair* . . .'

'What's your conclusion?' said Ann Leslie.

'I haven't got one yet,' I said. 'I'm still trying to explain the rulings from 1971.'

Peter reappeared with a tray carrying three glasses of wine, a sherry and a Scotch.

'Well you can't argue that the Irish can claim political immunity for Mr Carron . . .' said Ann.

'Bunch of cunts,' Chris put in, helpfully.

'Do you mind?' I said. '*I'm* Irish. At least my parents are.'

'Bunch of *charming* cunts,' Chris amended.

'. . . And you can't let the Northern Irish courts set precedents for what is or isn't a political offence . . .'

She was brilliant. It felt as if the lady carrying the Scales of Justice on the Old Bailey roof had climbed down from her perch and popped into the wine bar for a snifter.

'So you need to bring London into it. Demand a new law is passed. Demand the Attorney General advises on a new definition of "political" . . .'

'And don't be afraid to say, "This is terrorism",' said Helena, taking a sip of Tio Pepe, as if we'd all briefly returned to the 1950s. 'Say that, for an accused crook to be allowed to claim that carrying an Uzi is some kind of political statement – well, it doesn't help the crackdown on terrorism that we'd all like to see.'

'Wow,' I said. 'That sounds like a final paragraph.'

'Bleeding obvious really,' said the charmer, Chris.

'You've obviously both written about this topic a lot,' I said.

'Not once,' said Helena.

'I wrote something a coupla years ago, about some guy who escaped from the Maze,' said Ann, 'but not since.'

'But how can you be so fluent?' I asked. 'So certain about what to say?'

The three looked at each other.

'We just read the papers,' said Ann. 'And possess a conscience.'

'And decide what the story should be before we start writing,' added McKay.

Four glasses of Sauvignon later, I was back at my desk. It was a quarter to three. The deadline was a quarter past. I was writing my conclusion:

'. . . a travesty of legal language . . . a noisome zoo of weasel words . . . "political offence" used as a Get Out of Jail Free card . . . The Attorney General must act . . .' (I took a swig of Ribena from its cardboard carton. *Christ*, I was thirsty) *and* . . . if the British government . . . should *FLAG or FAIL* in this endeavour . . .'

It was getting a tad Churchillian. Perhaps it needed a second draft. But it had a ring to it. I looked back over the fine phrases, many taken straight from the ladies in El Vino, and took another swig of blackcurrant squash. Really, for a first go at a leader article, it wasn't bad at all.

I found myself on the judging panel of the Catherine Pakenham Memorial Award for aspiring female journalists under thirty.

Since its inception, many winners of the prize had gone on to make their names in the inky trade. Polly Toynbee (doyenne of the *Guardian*'s women's page) had won it, as had Sally Beauman (arts interviewer and now bestselling author of *Destiny*), Bel Mooney (ubiquitous columnist and novelist), Anna Coote (of the *New Statesman*), Tina Brown (ex-editor of *Tatler* and now *Vanity Fair*) and two *Evening Standard* contributors, Lucy Hughes-Hallett and Jaci Stephen.

The seventeenth award was announced in June, and the judges met in September. There were six of us: Lady Rachel Billington, a novelist and one of my reviewers, one of Lord Longford's children and sister of Catherine; Peregrine Worsthorne, editor of the *Sunday Telegraph*; Charlotte Lessing, editor of *Good Housekeeping*; Sebastian Faulks, literary editor of the *Independent*; Valerie Grove and me. We met in an office at the *Standard*, and sifted through one hundred and twenty entries. The prize was only £500 for the winner, while five runners-up would get a princely £100, but it hardly mattered. They'd all get to mingle at the newspaper's exalted premises, presumably trembling with awe that they were in the heart of Fleet Street, surrounded by some of its finest hacks and a few editors. Chances were strong, in those days, that the young women might find themselves being appraised at the party for virtues not entirely connected to their glittering prose, but it was assumed the girls could take care of themselves.

We, the judges, had been directed to look for writing that communicated with the reader, presented facts, descriptions and opinions in a clear and lively (and with any luck, entertaining) manner. 'Polemical writing, academic treatises and indulgently overripe prose', read the rule-book, 'will be viewed with less enthusiasm than clarity, elegance and wit.' All of the last-named were on display in the final shortlist, which was headed by three women: Clare Kavanagh, the daughter of a Belfast JP, later to become a television producer, Ysenda Maxtone Graham, whose biography of her grandmother Jan Struther (pseudonymous author of *Mrs Miniver*) would later be a big hit, as was *Terms and Conditions*, her oral history of girls' boarding schools; and Amanda Craig, born in South Africa, reared in Italy and schooled at Bedales, whose series of social novels on British society since 1990 have been compared to the work of Anthony Trollope.

It was Amanda Craig who finally won the prize, for a scorching piece of reportage about an NHS emergency ward over a single Saturday night. Ms Craig would later be at the centre of a scandal in 1996, when her third novel, *A Vicious Circle*, was due to be published. When proof copies were sent to literary editors, one of them – David Sexton at the *Evening Standard* – decided that a character in the book closely resembled him; he and Craig had been a couple while they were students at Cambridge. He threatened a libel suit. The publishers reacted like spooked horses and withdrew the book from their production schedule. It was, however, picked up by 4th Estate, who brought it out, minus certain Sexton-shaped episodes, three months later. On the party circuit, people discussed the likely identity of a character in the book, Ivo Spunge, a rackety, lecherous literary editor, renowned for perpetrating the 'Spunge Lunge' on innocent women in the book world.

It was wonderful to meet the next generation of women writers, to praise their talent and toast their success. The party was gleeful, the winners delighted, and the feeling of encouraging young talent very satisfying. Later, Valerie and I discussed other prizes. 'I've just been judging a Young Readers' contest,' she said, 'organised by Dillons, the bookshop people, for writing an essay called "Why I Like Books". The winner was only thirteen. She came down from Wolverhampton to collect her prize. And guess what, it was her first trip to London and her *first-ever* train ride. And her writing really is like nobody else's.'

'Gosh,' I said, 'how precocious. What's her name?'

'Well, she calls herself Tatty Moran,' said Valerie. 'But her first name is Caitlin.'

* * *

Meanwhile life in the Books office proceeded on its merry way. I shared the room, and much elevated chat, with Christopher Hudson, and Gilly Filsner, my clever assistant. She and I had met in unusual circumstances. Two weeks before I'd started the job, I'd been at the launch of *Don't Panic: the Official Hitchhiker's Guide to the Galaxy Companion*, written by Neil Gaiman, the talented writer of comic books and graphic novels; the French had started calling them *bandes dessinées*, to give them some respectability. I mentioned my new job to Neil, and promised I'd find space for his cool pictorial excursions. He told me about his newest book – *Black Orchid*, about two elfin sisters and their adventures with Batman and Swamp Thing.

What, I asked Neil, did the sisters look like? Wonderwoman? 'That's easy,' he said. 'They look like this' – and he touched the elbow of a girl standing behind him. 'Gilly? This is John. John, this is Gilly Filsner.' She was the model for Black Orchid.

She turned round. I looked into a face straight from Hollywood – the face of the bad girl from a John Hughes high-school comedy, cool, sharp, taking no shit from anyone.

'Hi,' she said. 'Whadda you do?'

I told her I was shortly to begin an important job at the famous London newspaper, commissioning book reviews and talking to famous writers. Bookish stuff, but at a high level.

'Just starting, huh?' she said, with a condescending smile. 'Got any vacancies?' There was a pause, in which I wouldn't have been surprised if she'd burst a chewing-gum balloon in my face. 'Anything I can help you with?'

The DC Comics super-heroine turned out to be a Rhodes scholar – meaning that she'd won a coveted transatlantic tenure at Oxford University, the first-ever female student from Concordia University, in Montreal, to gain such an honour. She was utterly, one might even say *stupendously* over-qualified to spend her time writing the titles and publication dates of new books in a ledger, and putting little stickers on book spines so that her boss could see which ones might be due for review.

Her other role in the building was to be a magnet for one hundred and fifty pairs of male eyes as she trotted across the office floor in her tiny denim skirt.

Once I returned from lunch to find her holding court to five crime reporters on the News desk: a lairy quintet who, in their leather jackets and jeans, resembled a hardened gang of recidivist jailbirds. God knows how they'd managed to strike up a conversation with Gilly, but they'd got to this stage:

'So, Gilly,' said the criminal called Dennis, 'what d'you make of English men? You think they're a lot of poofs and stuck-up twats?'

'*Twats?*' She raised a perfect eyebrow. 'What are twats?'

'They're, er, annoying people,' said Dennis. 'Not nice or interesting.'

'I've found lots of English guys who are nice and interesting, once they stop talking about *soccer*,' said Gilly. 'And if by poofs you mean gays, I haven't met any of those over here. But it wouldn't bother me, because, back home, gay men are *real* entertaining.'

'So what kind of English guys you fancy then, Gills?' asked a younger one called Bruce.

Her hazel eyes revolved dreamily.

'Oh my *Gahd*,' said Gilly. 'That guy on the TV? The funny guy? What's his name?'

'Les Dawson?' asked Bruce. 'Frankie Howerd?'

'Ben Elton!' said Gilly with a little squeak of delight. She pronounced it Benell-TON. 'He is *soooo* sexy. So fast and so clever. He talks, like, a million miles a minute, and I just look at him and I think, Jeez . . .'

Into a stunned silence, Dennis asked, 'And what would you like to do for him, Gills?'

I thought about suggesting she was needed at the Books office. But she was unstoppable.

'Well, first I'd have to take off that sparkly jacket of his,' she said, smiling sweetly, as if addressing a class of infants, 'only I'd do it *real slow*, so he wouldn't be distracted and stop talking. And then I'd have to take off his glasses. And then I'd have to take off *all* of his clothes . . .'

Her voice had slowed to a soft, rapturous purr.

'. . . and then I'd just *lick him all over.*'

A silence hung like a nuclear cloud over the seated hacks. All the typewriters on the second floor seemed to have fallen silent. Gilly coolly regarded her captive quintet of wide-eyed newsmen.

'Gotta get on,' she said briskly. 'Work to do. Bye guys!'

And she was gone.

Genevieve, herself not unacquainted with male desperation, was suspicious of Gilly.

'This girl you've brought in, John,' she said. 'Is she any good at her job ? Or is her function solely decorative?'

'She's a Rhodes scholar from Canada,' I explained. 'She's actually very clever.'

'Oh I'm sure she's very *smart*,' said Genevieve, 'and could wind *anyone* around her little finger. But can she write? Can she bring any expertise to a journalistic environment?'

'Yes of course she can *write*,' I said crossly. 'She's writing a feature for me about the rise of graphic novels.'

'And she's knowledgeable about that, is she?'

I explained about Neil Gaiman, and Gilly's *alter ego* as Black Orchid, hoping the deputy editor would be impressed. She wasn't.

'Are you telling me you've employed a character from a comic strip to join the staff?' she asked. 'I suppose we must be grateful you didn't hire Wilma Flintstone. Or Minnie Mouse.'

Along with the thoroughbred stable of *Standard* reviewers, I liked to commission pieces from outside the literary world, just to keep things lively. One day, a biography came in of Federico García Lorca, the great poet and playwright who was killed at the start of the Spanish Civil War. It prompted a memory of something

I'd recently read – the news that Nickolas Grace, the British actor, had been signed up to play Lorca in a new Spanish film or TV mini-series. Some Hispanic thespians and filmgoers with nothing else to do had voiced their annoyance that, despite all the home-grown actors who could play the man convincingly, the producers of *Lorca, muerte de un poeta*, had cast a *gringo* in the role.

I'd absolutely loved Grace's performance as Anthony B-B-B-Blanche in the 1981 TV adaptation of *Brideshead Revisited*; I'd loved his saucer-eyed exoticism, his fabulously rhotic delivery – in a bar, he'd ordered four brandy Alexanders for Charles Ryder and himself to drink, two each. Charles arrives but declines any alcohol, because he needs a clear head to write an essay. So Anthony drinks all four cocktails, to the students' astonishment, saying at the end: 'Down the little rrrrred rrroad they go!'

He must have read reams of background material about the great man. Might he fancy rrrreviewing the biography? It wouldn't hurt to ask. I contacted the Arts desk, was given the name of his agent, rang him, explained what I was after and said the fee would be the standard reviewer's fee and was non-negotiable. It was, he replied, entirely up to Nickolas whether he'd do it and he might call me if interested.

I gave him my number. Five minutes later, that sleek, indefinably wicked voice murmured in my ear: 'Mr Walsh . . .'

'Mr Grace.' I explained about the biography. Could he review it?

He said he had indeed immersed himself in Lorca's life, very recently. 'But is it *very* long?' he asked.

'It's not *enormous*,' I said. 'After all, as you know, he died at thirty-eight.'

'Why don't you send it to me, and I'll have a look. If I can't face it, I'll send it straight back to you in a taxi.'

'That's marvellous,' I said. 'Thanks, er, Nickolas.' I wasn't sure how soon one might start first-naming a famous actor.

'Thank you for thinking of me, *John*.' Oh gosh. We were practically pals.

'You've been on my mind lately,' I said, 'because I've just been visiting friends in Boston, and everyone I met was watching *Brideshead* on Public Broadcasting Service.'

'Indeed,' said my new best friend, in a not-terribly-interested voice.

'So these days,' I babbled on, 'the Yanks are mad keen on having British people around, speaking posh English. And they *love* hearing people doing their Anthony Blanche impression.'

There was a silence.

'You mean you did *me?*' asked Nickolas neutrally.

'Er, well, yes I did, actually.'

'Let's hear it, then.'

'No *no!*' I protested. 'I couldn't *possibly*. It wasn't very good, I assure you.'

'I want to hear your Anthony Blanche *right now*, or I won't review this book.'

'What?'

'Impression – book review. No impression – no book review.'

I was, as Nigel Molesworth might have observed, a rat in a trap.

'It was only a couple of lines,' I said, or indeed stammered, only it was a *real* stammer, not an affectation, 'from the time Anthony is thrown in the fountain by the rugby team. It's when he says: 'But then, evvv'ry b-boatman is a G-G-G-Grace D-D-D-Darling to *meeee.*'

There was another silence, a real humdinger.

'Nickolas?'

'Take my advice,' he said. 'Don't rrr*rush* to abandon the day job . . .'

In October 1987, the *Evening Standard* brought out a weekly colour magazine entitled *ES*. It was decided that every issue would carry a big arts interview, and I was asked to do the first one. Clive James was the quarry. I went to meet him at the Groucho Club with our photographer and some mixed feelings. While I'd admired Mr James from the early 1970s for his hilarious TV reviews in the *Observer*, and the cleverness of his rhyming couplets in *Peregrine Prykke's Pilgrimage Through the London Literary World* in 1976, and been amazed by the cool slanginess of his 'middle style' criticism, I couldn't stand his fiction.

Being who he was, the nation's favourite adopted smart-aleck, he couldn't just write a novel; in his debut, *Brilliant Creatures* (1983), he supplied an academic commentary on each chapter, making sure that no allusion was allowed to go over the reader's head. He also thoughtfully added an index, in case you needed to look up some important plot twist or character development. It was probably meant to be a parody of the novelist's self-absorption and conceit, but came across as a *wholly sincere* expression of the artist's self-absorption and conceit.

The 1987 follow-up, *The Remake*, was equally self-regarding. Not only did a character called 'Clive James' appear, halfway through, glimpsed through the window of a Barbican penthouse (where the real Clive James lived in London), jogging through the twilight; but two other characters – the narrator, Joel Court, and the book's media hero Chance Jenolan – bear his initials, straight and reversed. Egomania or what?

He came barrelling through the revolving door of the Groucho Club, looking entirely at home in this media grotto. The burnished confidence of the TV presenter was missing, however: his clothes were nondescript, his arms filled with a capacious holdall and a sheaf of papers; he resembled a flustered removals man. I watched him greeting staff with seigneurial off-handedness, ordering 'the usual' (a glass of Schweppes bitter lemon) and asking the doe-eyed waitress about her forthcoming acting job abroad. 'Ring me before you go,' he told her with the I-may-be-able-to-help expression perfected by 1930s Hollywood casting agents. Despite all this he was, when he finally sat down, charming, fast-talking, confiding and witty.

I brought up the walk-on appearance of 'Clive James', CJ and JC in the book. Wasn't it, I said, a bit much to write about three versions of yourself?

'I'm glad you spotted that,' he said. 'Actually there are five. You're forgetting Jeffrey Chaucer and Jean-Louis Cravache. They represent the five orbits of a star cluster in a complex configuration but with a simple signal at its heart which . . .'

'Yes, jolly interesting,' I said, 'but how can you write *so much* about yourself?'

The great dome creased in puzzlement. 'But it's my only subject,' he said, 'the multiplicity of the self.'

This shouldn't have come as a surprise. By this stage of his career, Clive James inhabited a range of personae diverse enough to bewilder the most devoted schizophrenic. To *Private Eye*, he was Sir Cleveland Jaws, the knighthood-chasing media shark. To the tabloid press, especially the *Daily Star* and *Daily Express*, he'd become 'TV's Mr Sneer'. In certain London drawing rooms, he was known as 'Magwitch' after the bald ex-convict in *Great Expectations* who makes a fortune Down Under. To his mother, back home in Sydney, he was presumably still Vivian, the name with which he was saddled at the font. To *Observer* readers, he was the TV reviewer whose witty judgements people often read out to their partners over breakfast. To TV audiences, he was the impresario of Japanese competitive excess, and the chat-show host who could match Jonathan Miller and Barry Humphries.

To a considerably smaller audience – the audience for literature – he'd become a slight embarrassment. Once a scourge of dilettantes and poseurs, he had appeared wilfully determined to join them. His career seemed an attempt to establish his *bona fides* as a creative artist – poet, lyricist, literary critic, novelist – in order to disprove Kenneth Tynan's dictum that a critic is someone who knows the way but can't drive the car.

His conversation at our meeting was full of compliments about his friends, especially those – Martin, Julian, Craig, Terry, Blake,

Christopher, James – from his *Observer* days with whom he'd shared Friday lunches at Mother Bunch's or Bertorelli's, where he'd played master of the revels. It was also full of Culture Vulture Clive showing off, peppering his conversational stew with allusions to Mahler horn motifs, Pushkinian one-liners and snippets from literary history ('I mean, Proust was a third of the way through *À la Recherche* when he . . .').

I asked him why, when describing a night sky in *The Remake*, he felt impelled to drag in an allusion to James Elroy Flecker. 'Because when I look at the moon and a star, I think of the design of Flecker's books. Literary allusions are just as alive to me as natural phenomena. Maybe it's a failing. Maybe it's because I came to it all quite late.'

Despite the occasional panning by critics, he had learned to trust 'the intelligent British reading public, which is the best anywhere, a dream. They're so amazingly tolerant of obscurity, of difficulty. I love the way they'll stay loyal to an author, and put up with an occasional bad book.'

Though he wouldn't admit to being competitive ('Only against myself. I'm an over-achiever but I don't compete with other novelists and poets') Clive liked to measure himself against his peers: 'I think Martin Amis is astoundingly talented. He gets a tremendous amount of judgement into every paragraph. I'm not as good a writer, although I may just be funnier.' 'The trouble with Ken Tynan was that he put far too much into his table talk. If I thought I was talking away something I should be writing, I'd stop.'

I reminded him that the society portrait painter Dominic Elwes (Nancy Mitford's nephew and Evelyn Waugh's godson) was reputed to be the only man to whom Peter Ustinov would defer in conversation, if both men started speaking at the same time. Who would Clive allow to out-talk him? 'I never draw breath when Ustinov is around,' he said. 'I'm happy to act as his feed-man. But I don't necessarily talk a lot. If it was a relaxed dinner party, and there were some girls I was anxious to impress, I might let rip; but

I'm happy to let others take over. Hitchens is a marvellous talker, even better than Martin. I'm happy just to goad and challenge and help it along. And doing television,' he concluded, perhaps half-seriously, 'spoils you for any audience that's less than three million . . .'

He despaired of ever persuading British commentators to accept the idea that a clever piss-taker about TV shows might *also* be a cultural sage, the dual role he'd nursed into life for fifteen years. 'There are two accusations I always get: that I'm frittering my talent away by writing for a popular audience, and that I'm too allusive and pretentious in the stuff that I do produce. They can't *both* be right. But I think my reputation is in danger. I may fall between the two stools, in which case I may have to choose between serious writing and entertainment. I'll probably go for entertainment, because you've got to pay the rent. But I work hard on my TV programmes. I practise everything as an art form.'

I asked what form of success would give him most pleasure? 'Oh, I think [Eugenio] Montale's notion of "the second life of art" – having a line of your work quoted or a bar of your music whistled in the street. And it doesn't really matter from which source it comes.'

Upon which he had to leave, presumably to take tea with Vivien Guinness, nip down Wardour Street to check the rough-cut of *Clive James: Postcard from Hafnarfjordur* on Channel Four, or head home to finish reading *Eugene Onegin* in the original Russian. It was a treat to meet Mr James, so clever and funny about both TV game shows and Pushkin sonnets. But what an odd phenomenon he represented: a man who's done so much, who's added to the stock of the world's amusement and edification, but who never seemed as pleased with his achievements as he would like to be.

Then the day came – 7 June 1988 – when I got to meet Anthony Burgess. The hum of excitement in the Books office was audible a mile away. My nerves twanged like the bedsprings in Soho at lunchtime. I'd been a fan of the great man since I'd discovered *The Doctor Is Sick* while studying in Dublin in 1977. The titular hero wasn't a doctor of medicine, but a philologist called Spindrift, and his 'sickness' sees him wandering about London after he's been anaesthetised for brain surgery, encountering multiple lowlifes, darts players and friends of his wife, who spends all her time drinking in local pubs. It may not sound a riot, but I loved its sentence-by-sentence zip and precision, its linguistic pedantry and notations of metropolitan grot *circa* 1960. Later I devoured *Inside Mr Enderby*, with its down-and-out poet, who composes his verses while on the lavatory, and is taken up (improbably) by a rich Catholic society woman called Vesta Bainbridge. Its three sequels, *Enderby Outside*, *The Clockwork Testament or Enderby's End* and *Enderby's Dark Lady* (written to placate readers who were furious that their hero had been killed off) were all sprightly combinations of social satire, airy learning and dazzling wordplay.

And there he was in person, seated in the lobby of the Britannia Hotel in Park Lane: exuberantly cravated in green silk, his blue eyes creased in a critical frown, he resembled a gruff, modern-day Doctor Johnson, weathering the rival claims of publicity directors, press photographers, TV show researchers, tea-dispensing waiters and my questions with weary stoicism. When he rose from the sofa, extended a hand and shook mine, it seemed less a gesture towards a stranger than a kind of episcopal blessing.

'My wife Liana,' he said, indicating a short, unsmiling, black-frocked woman on the sofa. Then he pulled out a pack of panatellas, lit one, and waited for a question. It was plain that small talk held no appeal for him.

He was in town from his current home in Lugano (an Italian-speaking region of Switzerland) to talk about his life – or at least that version of it, rich as a Lancastrian fruitcake, presented in *Little Wilson and Big God*, the first volume of his *Confessions*. But, characteristically, any enquiries about his autobiographical art prompted a flood of excoriation about his native land, a few swipes at rival authors and a recital of his multiple current projects.

Burgess had long propagated a myth about his non-acceptance in British book circles. However much critics and word-of-mouth popular acclaim tried to turn him into a Grand Old Man of English Letters, he always refused to buy it. Part of the trouble was his constantly being seen in Britain as something other than a novelist: as the doyen of book reviewers, the workaholic, the bed-becalmed prose factory of essays on the Spanish Inquisition and articles on Italian cuisine, the maverick composer of cantatas and oratorios, the writer of movie scripts about Jesus Christ – and, above all, as a phenomenon of linguistic inventiveness.

He was the man who flung words like 'demotic' and 'adventitious' around in bars. A story was told that, when he met his near-namesake, Jorge Luis Borges (who is reputed, like Burgess himself, to speak a dozen languages fluently) at a reception in the Argentine Embassy in Washington, some American journalists wondered which language the two great linguists might choose to converse in (English? Russian? Icelandic?) and drew near to find out. Seeing what was going on, the story goes, Burgess and Borges chose to speak in Old English. The former recited the opening lines of Caedmon's *Hymn*, and the latter followed with the next line. It must have seemed *amazingly* cool to any fluent speakers of Old English standing nearby.

Now seventy-one (though he looked a bruised and grizzled sixty-three), his legendary energy and invention were far from flagging. In fact they were positively boiling over. He'd just finished his thirtieth novel, *Any Old Iron*, about the discovery of Excalibur in a German bog. Without pausing to draw breath, he was now mining the imaginative potential of half a dozen disparate anniversaries the following year (1989): the French Revolution, the death of Browning in Venice, and of Gerard Manley Hopkins in Dublin, the birth of modern music, when Debussy finally worked out how to turn Mallarmé's poetry into notes . . . But wasn't all this yoking together of such incidental events a wholly arbitrary operation?

'Oh absolutely,' said Burgess happily. 'Almost impossible.'

London was now, he said, 'a foreign city' to him. Its currency baffled him, its inflationary prices (to one who remembers beer and Player's cigarettes in single shillings and sixpences) appalled him. The languages and personalities of its culture brought him emotional heartburn.

'I remember seeing some advertisement that read "Milk has gotta lotta bottle" and could not get over it,' he said with disgust. 'And who are these people on television who are thought so important? This Wogan person, a man with a little Irish charm but nothing else. Who is this "Hattersley"?' Burgess sounded indignant, as though he suspected the shadow foreign secretary of having made up the name in a moment of self-importance. 'These people are simply not interesting. The British only find Mrs Thatcher so because they live here. You wouldn't if you saw her from a European perspective. She has a terribly mediocre mind. When you consider that she claimed to be *re*-reading Freddie Forsyth's *The Fourth Protocol* . . . Even *Lloyd George* would have been found *re*-reading something like *Gibbon*. But then it's a most unliterary time. Can you imagine a really good novel set in the Thatcherite present? I can't.'

He was dismissive about the reputations of some current high-fliers. 'Howard Jacobson? His literary quality isn't up to much. William Trevor? Too bland. As with Fay Weldon, I wish I could read him and I can't. I wish I could like Salman Rushdie or any of the magical realists, but I can't. I think Kingsley is still the best we've got. He's the one writer who will be used in the future to tell new generations how English people used to sound – how they'd say "corm beef" and "vogka".'

Burgess used to live in Monaco, along the Riviera from his fellow Catholic novelist, Graham Greene (though Burgess always liked to claim the superior status of being born a Papist, not converted). Had they been in touch lately?

'Greene has, I'm afraid, become very *difficult* in old age,' said

Burgess sadly. 'I went to Antibes to interview him for a magazine when my left leg was bad, and he – the older man – was clearly delighted by my disability. He was also delighted by the fact that, every night, the husband of the woman with whom he now lives passes by and shouts "*Salaud! Bastard!*" – through the window."*

A cradle Catholic, lapsed from the faith if not the racial identity, Burgess faced the prospect of the afterlife with understandably mixed feelings. He still went to Mass ('Because it makes me feel better'), had occasional chats with priests and could easily conceive of Hell but had no concept of Heaven, 'except in terms of sexual ecstasy or hearing music, neither of which ideas would find favour with theologians.' He was, oxymoronically, a lapsed atheist.

'I'm quite prepared *not* to just fade out when I die,' he said in a businesslike way. 'I'm quite sure there'll be something there.'

Would there be a special Valhalla for writers down the ages? 'Oh yes, I firmly believe *that*,' he said. 'Joyce drinking with Jane Austen and Robert Louis Stevenson ... Their total contemporaneity means they're always alive. Oh yes.' The bright blue eyes in the great tortoise head widened in delight. 'They won't be dead at all.'

To steer the mood away from the subject of death, I asked a very specific question. 'Can you explain,' I said, 'how you came to use the word "onions" three times consecutively in one sentence in *Enderby Outside*?'

He looked startled but not un-pleased, as writers can be, when they find that the supposedly pitiless interrogator before them stands revealed as just a fan with a typewriter.

'Why? Because I *could* in those days. I suppose I thought it was clever.' He paused. 'How did the sentence go? "Rawcliffe strode across the restaurant to where Enderby was sitting and"—'

---

* This piece of information caused a rift between the two men. Someone sent Greene a cutting of my *Standard* piece, and Greene hit the roof. He wrote to Burgess on 13 June 1988 to say: 'I have now received [a] cutting in which you claim I told you of an aggrieved husband shouting through my window (difficult as I live on the fourth floor). You are either a liar or you are unbalanced and should see a doctor. I prefer to think that.'

'No no *no*,' I cried. 'It's "Rawcliffe lurched across the restaurant and breathed upon Enderby, bafflingly (the restaurant refused to serve, because of the known redolence of onions, onions) onions."'

'My God,' said Signora Burgess from the sofa. 'You must be Cattolico to have a memory like that.'

'Well I was brought up a Catholic,' I said. 'But what does that have to do with memory?'

'Ees simple,' she said. 'The Catechism. When boys and girls have to learn the whole Catechism by heart at young age, they develop a fine memory.'

'Tell me, signora,' I said. 'Do you read all your husband's books?'

'*Now*,' she said, 'I do not. But I read all the reviews in the newspapers. When they are rude, I say to him, "Antonio, don't read *theese* one!"'

Burgess beamed. Liana gave a sweet laugh. Despite Burgess's pedantic and professorial schtick, I felt oddly warmed by their company. They were a loving, and lovely, couple.

As I was to learn, as well as showing off his skill with languages, Burgess liked to throw around Ancient Greek quotations, dilate on abstruse religious dogmas and explain complex philosophical concepts in a breezily matter-of-fact way. I soon realised his most natural mode was *magisterial*, literally being a teacher, expatiating on any subject in his emphatic northern-schoolmaster voice, his eyes crinkling in the cigar smoke. He was also, it must be said, a terrific ham. He liked showing off his massive knowledge in public, even on television. In February 1982, he'd appeared on the TV show *Friday Night, Saturday Morning*. The actress Siân Phillips (then appearing in the TV adaptation of *Smiley's People*) was also a guest. Their host, Frank Delaney, asked her about the TV show, then introduced Burgess, who sat on the sofa beside her.

'Now Anthony,' said Delaney, 'you're a well-known wordsmith, and you know every word in the dictionary. But can even you produce a word sufficient to describe the great beauty of Miss Siân Phillips?'

Burgess regarded the veteran actress though narrowed eyes. 'Oh, I dare say I could,' he said, rather ungallantly. '*Orchidaceous. Poly-pulchritudinous* . . .'

The audience gave him a round of applause. It was as if Burgess had been brought on to do a routine, a music-hall *turn*.

I became just slightly obsessed with Anthony B. He was like nobody I'd ever met, a throwback to a literary past, when Johnson was writing the first dictionary and couldn't understand why people weren't as passionate about the meaning of words as he was.

Frank Delaney and I were introduced by Sue Bradbury of the Folio Society. We discovered that we shared a birthday (24 October) and became firm friends. He had worked for a time in Dublin at the Bank of Ireland, then as an RTE announcer, before heading to London, and he was immensely charming. He was a big man with a huge square head, twinkling eyes and a very fruity delivery, his Tipperary accent ideal for reciting poetry on the radio, as we shall see. He wrote a history of the Celts, a guide to the Dublin of *Ulysses* called *James Joyce's Odyssey* (which traces the route taken around the Irish capital by Leopold Bloom, and discovers that it's, basically, a giant question mark) and later a sequence of novels, based on Irish folklore.

Women fell for him like pheasants at a Windsor shoot. He was married four times and had stacks of girlfriends. During lunch one day at a restaurant called Smollensky's Balloon, he told me about his most notable conquest.

At a party at Broadcasting House, he met Princess Margaret, who told him about her love of Irish poetry. 'And of course, Mr Delaney,' she said, 'you run that radio programme on Saturdays, *Poetry Please*, don't you?'

'I do indeed, ma'am,' he said, smiling. 'Are you a fan?'

'I never miss it. Tell me, do you know the work of James Clarence Mangan?'

'Yes indeed.'

'Are you familiar with his poem "My Dark Rosaleen"?'

'Why wouldn't I be, ma'am? I learned it at school in Tipperary.'

'Jolly good,' said the princess. 'Do you think you might be able to recite it for me on your radio show?'

'Well, I suppose I could find some pretext that might . . .' said Frank, dubiously.

'I mean as a *special favour* to me,' said Princess Margaret firmly.

'I would be honoured, ma'am. Consider it done.'

I'm not sure how Frank managed to make it obvious to his readers why he was reading the work of an obscure Irish poet, a Coleridgean/ De Quinceyan figure – depressive, alcoholic, addicted to opium – who, after the Irish famine, wrote seditious (or at least patriotic) verses published in the anti-Unionist magazine *The Nation*. Or why it should be particularly topical that day or that week (or year). But he managed it.

After the broadcast of *Poetry Please* on Sunday afternoon, he was in his flat in west London, wondering if he might receive some kind of royal acknowledgement (a note? A telegram? A *phone call*?) But nothing. *Pas d'un oiseau de Dicky*. He was a little downhearted, but what, seriously, could he have expected?

The next Saturday evening he was, by chance, alone again. He listened to the repeat of the show, listened to his own voice caressing the fabulous climactic words:

> *O, the Erne shall run red,*
> *With redundance of blood,*
> *The earth shall rock beneath our tread,*
> *And flames wrap hill and wood,*
> *And gun-peal and slogan-cry*
> *Wake many a glen serene,*
> *Ere you shall fade, ere you shall die,*
> *My Dark Rosaleen . . .*

And just as the signature tune played out at the end, the phone rang.

Frank lifted the receiver and heard a voice say, 'Mr Delaney?' With great presence of mind, he said, 'Your Royal Highness.'

'She said, "I listened to your programme. Thank you *very* much for including 'My Dark Rosaleen'. I thought you read it *beautifully*." All Frank could think of to say was, 'It was my pleasure, ma'am.'

The princess was all businesslike. 'I think we should meet,' she said. 'Will you come to me or shall I come to you?' Frank replied, 'It might be better if you were to come here.' He gave her the address, which she wrote down to give to her chauffeur. And forty-five minutes later, she walked through the door of Delaney Towers in Hammersmith.

'She stayed until Monday morning,' he said in a dazed voice. 'John! I saw her *eatin' corn flakes*!'

'Did you actually fancy her, though,' I asked, as though this were a perfectly normal conversation. 'After all, she is about ten years older than you.' (Twelve, to be exact.)

'Oh *God* yeah,' he said. 'Her skin was so *soft*.'

'Just out of interest,' I said, 'did it turn you on, being an Irishman, reading a nationalist poem about Irish rebellion to the sister of the Queen of England, and then having her come round to have sex with you?'

'That didn't cross my mind,' he said. 'I was just amazed at what was happening.'

'What about her?' I enquired relentlessly. 'If you don't mind my asking, did she . . . display . . . enthusiasm?'

He creased his noble brow. 'She was pretty matter-of-fact about it. When things had gone a certain way, she said to me: "Don't worry about me. Just – *get on* with it."'

I never established if the story was true. The princess was certainly known to have a thing about Irishmen. And Delaney was a torrential charmer of middle-aged women. But he never mentioned giving the princess his phone number. And I can't find 'Rosaleen' in the Index to poems recited on *Poetry Please*.

But the story was so detailed, his report of the princess's fascination for the poem so plausible, I can't help hoping it might have been so.

In the summer of 1988, the editor asked if I'd consider becoming features editor of the *Evening Standard*. This was not in itself an arduous task – the *Standard*'s only features were the big daily political essay alongside the paper's thunderous editorial, and five features a week, usually interviews with the kind of people you might see in the Groucho after midnight, or else light pieces on London Style or Modern Etiquette by writers who thought they were Peter York – but I felt it wasn't really up my *strasse*. Noticing my reluctance, John Leese said: 'It would mean more money, more responsibility on the paper, and . . .' (a meaningful pause) '. . . and you would enjoy my full support.'

Nobody could resist such an approach from the boss. But I told him I had come to the newspaper as literary editor and didn't want to lose that connection – nor those writers, that army of reviewers, that immersion in the literary world. So I wound up doing two jobs. I signed up my old friend Pat Miller from the *Books and Bookmen* days to be my deputy and run the office (the lynx-eyed Black Orchid had long departed to drive men crazy in the world of business media). So here I was at the end of the Features desk, exchanging early morning chitchat with Jak the cartoonist; dictating letters to my secretary, Doreen, a lady who would have been thrown out of the cast of *EastEnders* for excessive vulgarity; fencing with David the commissioning editor (Politics) who felt he should be sitting in my chair and mostly pooh-poohed my ideas; and generally feeling miles outside my comfort zone.

There were some good things. I signed up a chap called John Preston as a feature writer. He was personable, funny, arty and industrious – many of his evenings, he confessed, were spent writing a book about a trip he'd made with a friend to the Mountains of the Moon in Uganda. He became arts editor of the *Standard*, then of the *Telegraph*, published four novels, and hit the jackpot when *A Very English Scandal: Sex, Lies and a Murder Plot at the Heart of the Establishment*, his retelling of the Jeremy Thorpe/Norman Scott debacle, was televised in 2018.

I was also impressed when a clever and sweet-faced woman called Annalena McAfee answered an ad in the *Standard* looking for a reviewer of London fringe theatre and, on being asked by the editor for her opinion of the current London fringe, replied 'I think 99 per cent of it is absolute crap.' Leese had beamed. 'That,' he said, 'is a *very* good start.' She joined the paper, wrote some lovely features (one about being the girl in the corn-flakes advertisements *circa* 1960), later became editor of the *Guardian Review* and left journalism to write an excellent novel about Fleet Street called *The Spoiler*. She also married Ian McEwan, whom she met when she interviewed him for the *Financial Times*.

As summer headed into autumn, it was clear that John Leese was far from well. Unscheduled single days off gradually became several days' absence at a time, and Genevieve Cooper had to take the editor's chair at Conference. She was unflappable in the face of the argumentative alpha males – judicious, decisive and charming, but I missed the craggy irascibility of John Leese, the way he kept you on your toes. I started to wonder if I might be happier elsewhere. But where?

An answer soon suggested itself. A word on the grapevine suggested that the *Sunday Times* might be looking for a new lit ed. Formal interviews were not being conducted, I was told, but conversations were being had. Soundings were certainly being taken. Straws were decidedly in the wind. The circumlocutory fog was like something out of *Yes Minister*.

I conjured up the image of Fate – a stumbling, mumbling old windbag, shuffling about the Universe, telling people they're stuck with whatever future has been assigned to them – and said: 'Hang on. What is going on? This is what I set my heart on, seven years ago. You cannot dangle my ambition in front of me now, like it's some kind of *game* . . .'

Five days later, it happened. A voice on the phone asked if I might be available to have lunch with Simon Jenkins, former editor of the *Standard* and now Andrew Neil's *consigliere* at the *Sunday Times*.

I asked what kind of lunch.

Oh, just an exploratory chat, said the voice.

Yeah, I said guardedly, I might be available. Where would it take place?

I mentally ran through the ideal venue for such a high-powered encounter. The River Room at the Savoy? Rules in Maiden Lane? Le Gavroche?

'The Wapping canteen,' said the voice, rather briskly. 'Mr Jenkins will see you in Reception.'

CHAPTER 9

Launches, Lunches and Lechery

The launch parties we attended in the 1980s were, or seemed in hindsight, golden and Gatsby-like extravaganzas. From the Faber garden in Queen Square to the Orangery in Holland Park, from the guest room at the Garrick to the long room at the Reform, from Kettner's, the upmarket Soho pizza joint, to the Steinway-and-cheese-plant Palm Court at the Ritz, from the ballroom of the Arts Club to the Raphael Room at the V&A, from L'Etoile to L'Escargot, from Bedford Square to Berkeley Square, men and women of a literary persuasion flickered and swooned, glass in one hand, cigarette in the other, up marble staircases, along verdant parterres, down Soho basement steps and across threadbare carpets, greeting and flirting, kissing and squeezing, talking and joking about pretty well everything *but* books.

About Princess Diana's first baby, the Falklands War and the government's I-speak-your-weight-machine briefing expert, about Greenham Common, about Mrs Thatcher being described by President Mitterrand as possessing 'the eyes of Caligula and the mouth of Marilyn Monroe', about Live Aid on TV and the clothes of the music tribes, from New Romantics in their Cossack-style trousers and brocade headbands, to the leathery fans of Frankie Goes to Hollywood; about Prince Andrew's hoydenish bride Sarah Ferguson; about the pronouncements of Edwina Currie, the junior health minister who claimed that 'good Christian people don't get Aids', that people from the north of England die of 'ignorance and chips' and, notoriously, that 'most of the egg production in this country is now affected with salmonella.' About Lockerbie, the massacres in Hungerford and Loughgall, Arthur Scargill and the painfully protracted miners' strike, President Reagan addressing Parliament, the proposed ordination of women, the archbishop of Canterbury's advice that the church should see homosexuality as 'a handicap, not a sin', and the spectacle of the House of Commons on live TV. Partygoers who had visited the new 'American-style' chain of Waterstone's mega-bookshops remarked on how *very cool* they'd found their matt-black box-shelves. Controversialists brought up the iniquitous prosecution, by Mary Whitehouse, of Howard Brenton's *The Romans in Britain* at the National Theatre.

The parties were held on Tuesdays and Thursdays; no other days seemed to count. In the early 1980s, the *Books and Bookmen* gang sometimes took in three parties in one evening, like an upmarket pub-crawl. 'Oh, *there* you are, Sally,' a famously cross Irish publicity director once greeted our leader. 'I see you've brought yer *onn-too-rahhhje*.' Later in the decade, when I was a literary editor, I should have grown out of books parties. But they kept getting bigger and more flashy. And the flesh was weak.

The launches were no longer evidence of publishers making a special fuss of some star author; now they seemed to make a fuss about *everyone*. This cannot have been true – not with fifty thousand new books being published in the UK each year – but it seemed that way. It was a far cry from the 1970s, when the attitude of publishers to publicity was to send proof copies of a new book in the first-class post to the literary editors of the *Sunday Times*, the *Observer*, *The Times*, *Guardian* and *Telegraph*, perhaps also to the *Listener*, *Spectator* and *New Statesman*, with a covering letter that read, in its entirety, 'Dear Mr Jones, I have pleasure in sending you the new novel by Septimus Penge, and look forward to your review.' That was the lot. As for trying for coverage on TV and radio, you could forget it. Occasionally they might risk a tiny advertisement in *The Times*. Of launch parties, or author dinners, there were few signs.

In the garden of Faber & Faber we toasted the launch of *An Artist of the Floating World*, the follow-up to *A Pale View of Hills*, written by a short, weedily moustachioed, rather diffident young Japanese-born guy called Kazuo Ishiguro; everyone was soon referring to him as 'Ish', as though they'd known him for years. At the launch of *An Ice-Cream War*, we marvelled at the industry of its author, William Boyd, who just a year earlier had brought out *A Good Man in Africa* (which won the Somerset Maugham) and a collection of stories called *On the Yankee Station*.

Whether it was the new atmosphere of splashy, aristo-chic party-going engendered by Tina Brown's *Tatler* since 1979, or the after-effects of the 1981 royal wedding, or the rise of the Yuppies, and Sony Walkmans that made the difference, the more commercial publishers put on ever more ridiculous displays of money and style.

Pavilion celebrated their book about David and Elizabeth Emanuel, designers of Princess Diana's bridal gown, by launching it in a candy-striped pavilion at the Chelsea Flower Show. Webb & Bower, who in 1977 had one of the biggest bestsellers in history with Edith Holden's *The Country Diary of an Edwardian Lady*, brought out a follow-up, *Nature Notes of an Edwardian Lady* ten years later. Their launch wheeze was to smuggle guests in among the royals enjoying the opening party for the Burleigh Horse trials – a shocking cheek, but it worked. More modest in numbers but vastly more expensive was the day *Reader's Digest* helicoptered a gaggle of privileged hacks to a thatched inn in Kent for lunch to celebrate the launch of their *Living Countryside* series; as a cute extra, each guest discovered beneath their chair a pair of green gumboots in their size, in anticipation of a bracing post-prandial walk – as if that were something Fleet Street's finest would ever think of doing.

When Pan Books decided to celebrate the paperback incarnation of *The Life and Times of Little Richard*, they hired the London

Hippodrome for a suitably huge party, of which the climax, they fondly hoped, would be a performance by the author. The great man appeared on stage amid flashing strobe lights, lasers and volumes of dry ice – only to explain that his new-found religious beliefs forbade him from doing anything as wicked as singing.

A less glamorous stage event was the publisher Headline's launch of a book by a male stripper. To guarantee the right mood, they drove sixty guests by charabanc to glamorous Ilford, Essex. In the music venue, the crowd drank cocktails with suggestive names, ate rudely titled canapés and watched the author going through his routine. He was 'Fabulous Frankie – Agent 007 And A Half Inches', probably *not* his name at the baptismal font.

The most reliably spectacular launch parties were those given by Lord Weidenfeld at his luxurious apartment on Chelsea Embankment. It was generally agreed that, should His Lordship ever stoop to getting a Filofax, its bulk would rival the National Theatre. He knew everybody. He was the biggest networker in Europe. Unless they were already wildly famous, first-time guests at his SW3 oak-panelled drawing room, with its capacious sofas and Thames-side balcony view of Buddha in his Peace Pagoda across the river, might feel a little intimidated by their fellow guests. I know I did. A Weidenfeld party characteristically featured a royal, a couple of transatlantic film stars, some international statesmen, a handful of notoriously reclusive and party-hating authors, some bookish parliamentary backbenchers, a handful of gregarious peers of the realm – and a scattering of nervous journalists.

In my first couple of visits, I found myself chatting to the serving staff, rather than daring to initiate a conversation with (on my left) Edward Heath or (on my right) Lord Snowdon. Once, stranded in the middle of the room, I told myself, 'Don't worry. The fourth Test Match is on at Lord's. Take a deep breath, turn around and, whoever is behind you, say, "Have you been following the cricket?"' I took a deep breath. I turned around. I found myself standing in front of Harold Pinter and Simon Gray, both fanatical cricket-lovers. 'Have you been—' I began. The former turned a face of thunderous hatred in my direction. I kept on turning, like a sheepish revolving door. Several Weidenfeld parties later, I became more adept at mingling and hung out in some interesting company. During the Iran-Contra affair in Reagan's second administration, I experienced a weird conversation between Martin Amis and Shirley MacLaine as they discussed whether Lieutenant-Colonel Oliver North could defeat General Manuel Noriega of Nicaragua in a fist fight.

Who were the guests at the weekly parties? A hardcore of journalists, of course. The literary editors, who decided which books got reviewed, had to be invited, and thanked for their 'loyalty'. The reviewers themselves (mostly freelancers engaged in writing their own books) were welcome if they tended to admire the party-giving publisher's stable of talents. The *quidnuncs*, the young gossip hacks from the newspaper diary columns, were vitally important for giving an air of urgent topicality to the new book, whatever its subject. Louis Baum from the *Bookseller*, and Auberon Waugh from the *Literary Review* were ubiquitous. TV faces such as Melvyn Bragg, John Birt, Ned Sherrin and Alan Yentob carried about them the air of seraphic conceit that is the mark of the instantly recognisable Telly Bloke. Lady Antonia Fraser was always to be found at Lord George's, wearing her beatific, though non-directional smile. A throng of ageing hacks, who might not be terribly useful in getting the book talked about, were nonetheless welcome because of their seen-it-all celebrity – people like Robert Kee, Bernard Levin and Keith Waterhouse. The last named – playwright, author of *Billy Liar* and long-standing *Daily Mail* columnist – was easily spotted by the lanky wisps of grey hair that hung like curtains around his whisky-reddened face.

I always enjoyed meeting Keith, because he radiated wisdom about journalism and told good stories. He would dilate, for instance, upon the difficulty of keeping a twice-weekly column fresh. 'Couple o' years ago,' he once told me, 'I went oop to Coventry to give a talk to the Rotary Club, and afterwards, because

I'd 'ad a few drinks, I decided to walk back to me 'otel to clear me 'ead. Outside a pub, some youths started making remarks and askin' for the time, like they were plannin' to take me watch off me. I swear to God, *even as I were runnin' away*, I was composin' t'first two paragraphs of me Friday column in me 'ead.'

Many writers would tell you that the Jonathan Cape Christmas party – the only one given by Cape all year – was the most exciting event in the party calendar. Others would bang on about the international cast of Lord Weidenfeld's glittery thrashes. But a small and privileged group swore that nothing outshone the parties held by the boss of Picador, Sonny Mehta. Those privileged to enter would find the drawing room at his flat in Chesham Place pullulating with writerly talent – Ian McEwan, Graham Swift, Hermione Lee, Julian Barnes, Edmund White, Clive James, Salman Rushdie, Angela Carter – but, sadly, no journalists were allowed. When Mehta left England for New York in 1987, to become the boss of Knopf, there was much weeping in Authorland.

The hostesses at these glittering occasions were the publicity directors – a score of young professional women who presided over the revels with a delicate cocktail of glad-handing welcome and diplomatic firmness. They were *not* at the parties just to amuse men. Their function was to greet with smiles, welcome with an arm-squeeze, reassure with a name-drop ('Your friend Sir Nigel is over there . . .'), hijack the passing drinks tray for you, usher you towards other new arrivals, and ask the question that never got a keen affirmative reply: 'Would you like to meet the author?' The PDs had nonetheless to keep nervous authors happy by steering them into conversational groupings where admirers might be found, ensuring they had their speech prepared for the toast, and reminding them of the fabulously exciting publicity trip to the northern cities, university campuses or coastal bookshops that was coming their way.

The publicity director at Heinemann, Susan Boyd, to whom all her husband William's books were dedicated, always threw brilliant parties. Her launch for Graham Swift's *Waterland*, a novel set in the flat, eely Fenlands, was a humdinger: among the guests was a gigantic real-life eel, being handled by guests like a pet tarantula at a kids' party. Others in the top rank of thrash-flingers were Helen Ellis at Hamish Hamilton, Serena Davies at Secker, Jacqueline Graham at Pan, Angela Martin at Macmillan, Rosie Glaisher at Viking, Morven Knowles at Collins, Sarah Hodgson at Penguin, Susan Lamb at Century Hutchinson; also the independent publicists Belinda Harley (whose attractive associates were called the Harlettes) and Dotti Irving, who started Colman Getty in 1987 and saw it later take on the Booker Prize as a client.

The queen bee among publicity directors, though, was Caroline Michel, a thrillingly sophisticated, brown-eyed, auburn-haired, Chanel-scented, heftily maquillaged ('I just *eat* lipstick,' she used to say) and designer-clothed woman with a laugh in her voice and a core of tungsten steel in her dealings with men. The daughter of a German commodities dealer (although it was commonly believed that 'arms dealer' was more accurate), she studied Sanskrit at Edinburgh and started life on *Agenda*, a poetry magazine which turned down her own (anonymously offered) poems. Her first publicity job was at Chatto, where she might have lasted only a few hours (she couldn't type, though she'd claimed she could at interview) if her knowledge of John Henry Newman hadn't meant she was able to promote a new biography of the great Papist thinker that was part of the Chatto list.

At twenty-five, she was fun to meet, a shameless flatterer who seemed to tremble with the pleasure of knowing, or hearing, secrets. At lunch she encouraged the literary editor sitting across from her to chat away, but if he went on too long, she'd signal her ennui by gradually leaning to the right as if planning to fall over sideways – then she'd put her right hand behind her head and, while regaining the vertical, would gather her mane of hair upwards and *whompf* it up and over her head (channelling, incidentally, the first appearance of Rita Hayworth in the film *Gilda*) so that it crashed down on her left cheek – making her interlocutor abruptly lose his thread. She was a terrific flirt and a dazzling *salonnière*, in the tradition of Ottoline Morrell and Sonia Melchett.*

Invitations to her flat in Eaton Terrace were guarantees of interesting company. One evening, I found myself at dinner beside Inge Feltrinelli, the German-born queen of Italian publishing, who started out as a photographer (her most famous snap was a selfie taken with a very pissed Ernest Hemingway and a thirty-foot marlin) and took over her husband's publishing company after his death, guiding the careers of Nadine Gordimer, Isabel Allende and Amos Oz.

A favourite of mine was Joanna Mackle at Faber & Faber. Born in Belfast and educated by Catholic nuns in Wimbledon, she was for years the guiding star of the company's Premier League writers: Seamus Heaney, P. D. James, Ted Hughes, Kazuo Ishiguro, Paul Muldoon. She spoke with an irresistible breathy urgency and affected large and striking hats – not the wide-brimmed Gertrude-Shilling-at-Ascot kind, more the brimless sort that made her look like a sexy matador or a kindly-but-determined female bishop. Joanna laughed a lot, and her authors doted on her. When she got married, Seamus Heaney came to the wedding.

If you were a literary editor, or a regular reviewer of books for the national press, your phone would ring importantly twice a year, and you'd be invited to lunch with the publicity directors, one by one. They were, as I've tried to emphasise, serious-minded, intelligent and well-read people, but it would be disingenuous not to mention that they were almost all women, invariably blessed with good looks and considerable charm, indisputably classy, well-dressed and *soignée*. The point of the lunches was to persuade literary editors (mostly male) to make a special fuss of their company's books and authors in that spring, or autumn, publishing season, and to do so as a Special Favour to Helen, or Angela or Susan or whoever. The

---

* When her husband Matthew Evans, chairman of Faber, became a life peer in 2000, Caroline became Lady Evans.

1980s was not an enlightened, asexual decade, and a lot of flirting went on. I'd be lying if I said I never got a kiss from a publicity director as we parted, post-lunch, but it was never part of a sordid transaction, oh no. Publishing ladies, by and large, did not misbehave.

Which is *not* to say that journalists, editors, writers and male publishers didn't. On the contrary. From what I gathered, sexual propositions pretty much rained down on men and women scribes all through the 1980s. Umpteen lunches were concluded with a frank invitation to stray from the path of virtue at the early convenience.

Sometimes the invitations were quickly withdrawn, as if they'd been made in jest. A woman colleague was startled to find, at the start of lunch, her guest Magnus Magnusson, inquisitor of *Mastermind*, laying a hand upon hers and saying 'I think you should know I've booked a room where we can go and make love.' (He was, he said, only kidding.)

My friend Naomi was asked to lunch by Tom Rosenthal, the hugely distinguished, bearded and bow-tied chairman of Secker & Warburg and later Andre Deutsch, after they'd met at a talk he gave on art publishing. After they'd eaten, he said, apropos of nothing, 'I want to make a suggestion. For years I've been lucky enough to keep a mistress. Recently a vacancy for the job has become available, and I wondered if you would like to take it on. I admire you very much and I think you would enjoy it.'

Naomi blinked. 'Don't get me wrong,' Rosenthal continued. 'I won't take up much of your life. I'm happily married. But I've always needed a mistress as well. Will you think about it?' She said she'd never heard such a bizarre proposal in all her days. And she said, emphatically, no. Rosenthal looked crestfallen. Then he took a paper napkin, extracted a pen from his inside pocket, and proceeded to draw what looked like a long and substantially proportioned banana, after which he pushed the napkin across the tablecloth to his lunch guest. She left shortly afterwards. Heaven knows if he was serious. Perhaps he just enjoyed winding up the extremely serious (and rather proper) Naomi.

'Don't defy me!': *Sunday Times* editor Andrew Neil at work.

(Steve Pyke/Getty Images)

(above) The Books Department *en vacances*, 1989. L to R: the author, Cheryl, Penny, Harry, Nicolette, Austin. Our glamorous stenographer Joanna took the picture. *(Author's collection)*

(above) Mistress of foxhounds: Jilly Cooper, inventor of the Bonkbuster novel. *(Nikki English/ANL/Shutterstock)*

(left) Brat Pack bombshell: Tama Janowitz launches *A Cannibal in Manhattan* at London's Montcalm Hotel, 1989. *(Nils Joorgensen/Shutterstock)*

Galactic giant: Douglas Adams, who made hitch-hiking both cosmic and hilarious. *(ANL/Shutterstock)*

(above) Ghosts of Nagasaki: a brooding publicity shot of Kazuo Ishiguro in 1982, on the publication of his spooky first novel, *A Pale View of Hills*. *(Sueddeutsche Zeitung Photo/Alamy Stock Photo)*

One of the brilliant caricatures by Richard Willson (1939–2011) published each week in the *Sunday Times* Books section. This one accompanied a review of *The Invisible Woman: the Story of Nelly Ternan and Charles Dickens* by Claire Tomalin (1990). *(Author's collection)*

Elder statesman: three decades after his publishing career began with *Lucky Jim*, Kingsley Amis wins the 1986 Booker Prize with *The Old Devils*. *(PA Images/Alamy Stock Photo)*

Wizard of Oz: the pan-cultural coruscator Clive James.
(Paul Popper/Popperfoto/Getty images)

The extended judging panel for the 1991 Whitbread Book of the Year. Along with two of the previous year's winners, Nicholas Mosley and Ann Thwaite, the judges (Hilary Spurling, Liz Lochhead, Barbara Trapido and the author) are joined by celebrity culture vultures Michael Howard, Sir Roy Strong, Timberlake Wertenbaker, Michael Cole and Donald Trelford. *(Author's collection)*

John Carey. 'He brought the book review to the zenith of sound judgement and readability.' *(Colin McPherson/Getty images)*

Peter Kemp. 'One finished his reviews amazed by the machine-tooled precision of his sentences.' *(The Royal Society of Literature)*

Diamond miner: Sally Beauman was woken by her agent at midnight to be told she'd snagged the world's biggest-ever advance for a first novel. *(Stuart Clarke/ANL/ Shutterstock)*

Sue Townsend: the creator of Adrian Mole was the biggest-selling author of the 1980s. *(Mirrorpix/Getty Images)*

Anthony Burgess with the author, soon revealed as 'a fan with a typewriter', August 1988. *(Author's collection)*

Ramshackle chic: visitors to Hay-on-Wye Literary Festival browsing for bargains.
(Philip Dunn/Shutterstock)

Master of ceremonies:
Hay Festival co-founder
Peter Florence.
*(© Kathy De Witt/Bridgeman
Images)*

Twin Crags: Ted Hughes, Poet Laureate from 1984 to his death in 1998, with Seamus Heaney, future Nobel Prizewinner for Literature, 1995. *(Mark Douet/ArenaPal)*

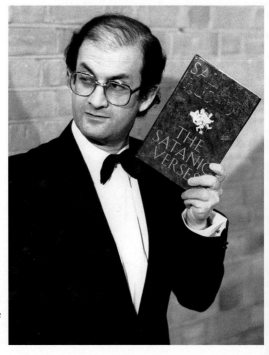

Salman Rushdie launches *The Satanic Verses* in October 1988. Four months later, he was under a death sentence, after Ayatollah Khomeini of Iran introduced the world to a new word: *fatwa*.
(© Guardian News & Media Ltd 2022)

A senior editor I knew well on a Sunday paper kept a room at the Strand Palace Hotel booked on constant standby every Friday afternoon, in case his lunch appointment that day, across the road in Simpson's restaurant, developed into something more promising. Mick Brown, the handsome rock-and-spirituality correspondent of the *Daily Telegraph*, once asked me, 'John, tell me, how do *you* deal with it when a woman propositions you at the end of lunch?' to which my only answer was, 'I should be so lucky.'

Did the publicity ladies ever fall for their authors? Jacqui Graham, the glamorous Pan publicity director, fell into a well-documented and loving relationship with Douglas Adams when the first volume of the five-volume *Hitchhiker's Guide* trilogy was published. They were both single at the time, and nobody turned a hair. And Polly Samson, publicity director of Cape when it published *Whale Nation* in 1988, went so far as to have a baby with its author, Heathcote Williams. She took him on his one and only book-signing tour, which was, he said, 'enough to cripple a rock star'.

Polly was a serial bewitcher of men. With her dark glossy hair and Sino-Caucasian good looks (her father was an English journalist, her mother was of Chinese extraction and was once a major in Chairman Mao's Red Army) she turned a lot of male heads, and made wives jealous. Some friends and I were leaving a party one evening and watched as Julian Barnes was upbraided by his wife Pat Kavanagh for lingering too long in the vestibule, saying goodbye to Ms Samson. No matter how much he protested his innocence – 'I was just leaving look I have my coat here in my hand I was just saying goodbye' – Pat's sharp eyes were unamused and suspicious. 'Look at that,' said Sebastian Faulks beside me. 'Flaubert's Polly . . .'

When she and I met for drinks about publicity matters, she would occasionally bring an admirer along. I don't mean a boyfriend – just one of her court. Once she brought Peter Hillmore, the Sunday columnist, with her. 'You don't mind if Peter sits here, do you?' she asked me, 'He won't be any trouble.' He was installed, with a drink, on a chair just behind her. As Polly and I talked about future publications, she would occasionally break off ('Just a sec . . .') and root around in her handbag until she found something therein to amuse the silent beau behind her. It could have been one of Ralph Steadman's *Paranoids* (Polaroid photos grotesquely manipulated) that Cape was about to publish, or an amusing invitation to a party to which Peter wasn't invited. She'd hand it over silently, then turn her attention back to me ('Where were we?') while Peter digested the titbit. The procedure was repeated four or five times in an hour. It reminded me of a moorhen gliding across a pond, occasionally remembering she has a baby moorhen behind her and turning to bung it some grub.

I got the impression that Polly had three or four such admirers – all male journalists – who would be allowed to squire her around and be amusing company, without any suggestion, let alone guarantee, that they might ever be allowed to part the Anglo-Chinese dreamboat from her foundation garments.

While we're discussing such sordid matters, did authors ever try it on with their publicity directors – perhaps forgetting, in the midst of a long book tour, that the women were highly valued colleagues in the publishing enterprise, and not freelance *horizontales*? A group of PDs who'd formed a mutual-support club called the Publishers Publicity Circle, used to award an ironic prize every year for the author who'd failed to conduct himself (or herself) in an appropriate manner during a publicity tour. Sometimes the behaviour that won the award was on the crude side; sometimes it was no more than a spot of gallant waist-encircling, of which John Julius Norwich, the diplomat and historian, was said to be El Maestro Absoluto.

Joanna Mackle had a spot of bother with the father of rock 'n' roll, Chuck Berry, in 1989, when Faber bought the rights to his *Autobiography*. She was in New York when the news came, and decided to fly to St Louis to see the grizzled hellraiser at his home, modestly named Berry Park. 'It was frankly surreal,' she told me, 'to find myself sitting on a sofa in Chuck Berry's house beside Chuck Berry's wife and being offered Kool-Aid to drink, which was *disgusting.* I said, "D'you want to come over to England for an author tour?" and he seemed very amenable. When I left, he accompanied me to the airport, right up to the departure gate. As he walked away, a stewardess came up to me and said, "So – are you the new Chuck Berry *eye-dem*?"'

It's possible that Berry may have got the wrong end of the stick about Ms Mackle's function in the publicity machine. He had, after all, spent half a lifetime being pleasured by groupies of all shapes and sizes, and might have assumed all women were available for his delight. Fearing that Joanna might encounter some trouble, her boss Matthew Evans, the Faber chairman, came to the hotel where Joanna was meeting Chuck, and asked her afterwards, with fatherly concern, how it had gone. She was hazy about what exactly happened, but it involved Berry urging her thus:

'Relax, honey . . . Would you like to lie down on this bed . . .? Would you like to take off your shoes . . .? Would you like to take off your *hat*?'

To all of which Joanna replied, 'No, Chuck! *The Times* of London is waiting outside to speak to you!'

'He didn't rape me or anything like that,' she said, 'but it was not a situation anybody would like to be in. He was a pretty nasty man.'

When Alan Franks, *The Times* journalist, wrote about the Chuck encounter in the newspaper next day, Joanna didn't seem to mind; her only objection was Franks referring to her as 'a publicity girl'. And despite her down-playing what went on, a rumour flew around literary London that Berry had exposed himself in the hotel room. Fanciful but wholly fictitious descriptions of the sight and dimensions of the offending body part were exchanged by the gossiping classes. The phrase 'game biltong' gained a certain traction.

The downstairs loos at the Groucho became, for a limited period, resorts of opportunity for the lustful and the drug-crazed. High-speed sexual encounters were shockingly common. A woman friend, said to be adept at oral sex, told me that when she moved to New York, she met an Englishman who claimed to have bought her several drinks at the club a year earlier. When she said she had no recollection of their encounter, he replied in exasperation, 'But you *must* remember! The evening ended up with you giving me a blow job downstairs in the Ladies.' 'I'm sorry,' said my friend, 'that doesn't really narrow it down . . .'

The club forbade any drug-taking on the premises, and signs in the downstairs lavatories carried dire warnings that indulgers in the devil's dandruff would be handed over to the police. It didn't stop members making bad-taste jokes about the level of consumption that went on. When one of the WC cubicles was closed for repairs, a sign on the door read: 'Out of Order. Ceiling Collapsing.' Soon, an unknown hand had crossed out 'Ceiling' and substituted 'Nose'.

It didn't have to be cocaine, of course. Some people, sharing the spirit in which Ozzy Osbourne once knelt down and snorted a line of soldier ants to impress the guys from Guns N' Roses, would snort anything. I was having a late drink at the Groucho one evening with some friends that included a New York novelist and his wife. It had been a long day. We were all rather sloshed and dead tired. I remember the novelist laying his head on the table and going straight to sleep, an innocent smile on his weary face. The late-night chat rumbled on. A few minutes later, he opened his eyes. His face still lay on the table, but his fingers now took a little walk across the surface and ve-ry slow-ly up-ended a miniature glass tray of black pepper. Nobody noticed him, but I watched in fascination as his index finger combed the teeny pile of black grains into a line, his finger dabbed the line and he ran it under his left nostril with the enthusiastic sniff of a drugs connoisseur. It must have taken all of four seconds before the first crashing, bone-shaking, deranged first *blast* of the mother of all sneezing fits rocked the Groucho dining room like an earthquake.

CHAPTER 10

———— ·•· ————

A Home on the Highway

The lack of noise was fantastic. As I walked through the newspaper complex at Wapping on my first day at the *Sunday Times*, what struck me most was the ghostly quiet. Not silence, exactly, just a discreet hum of 'white noise' – a vaguely companionable susurration, designed to make the resident drones feel they weren't working in a morgue. As I passed through the News section into the allegedly more frivolous territory of the Arts, Books, Style, Travel and Design sections (known as 'the Shallow End'), I was also struck by its resemblance to both a high-tech warehouse and a low-ceilinged, strip-lit cathedral. Not only was it as cloistered and monastic as the *Standard* offices had been raucous and rambunctious, but everyone worked on computers, not typewriters. The journalists and sub-editors sat bolt upright, as though directed by their mothers not to slouch, making hardly more sound with their busy fingers than a dormouse skittering across a plastic tray.

My guide was Simon Jenkins, the Fleet Street columnist and commentator, former editor of the *Evening Standard* and soon to edit *The Times*: a god-like presence, journalistically speaking, shrewd, wise and all-knowing about politics, London history, English churches, the English countryside, food, literature and the habits of American actresses (his wife was the glamorous and *haut ton* Gayle Hunnicutt). What he was doing introducing me to my new staff was a mystery.

'Here we are,' he said, 'the Books department . . .'

In a glass box the size of a British Rail waiting room, four women sat at their desks. As Simon introduced me, they kept their eyes fixed on him, as if reluctant to grant their new boss any unearned show of respect. Then, one by one, they emerged from their desks, to shake hands and say Hi to their new boss.

Penny Perrick was the outgoing lit ed, a stately woman like the hostess in a Henry James novel, with huge, humorous eyes and an abstracted manner. She had a way of holding her hands before her as though trying to evoke some shapely Venetian pot. I discovered that her mother had been fashion editor of the *Sun*, and she herself had worked as a fashion editor at *Vogue*. Cheryl Younson, the production editor, was an elegant, rather combative presence, her eyes appraising and watchful under a dark-auburn fringe. The secretary was called Margot, thin, bird-like and fifty-something, her hair in a grey bob like Anna Massey's.

The last of the quartet was Nigella Lawson.

I'd heard of the chancellor's beautiful daughter, of course. Everyone in Fleet Street knew of her. She'd been working in publishing at Quartet Books, owned by the Arabian entrepreneur Naim Attallah, and was the leading light of his aristocratic female workforce, rudely known as 'Naim's Harem'.* The parties in which they'd featured at Quartet's Goodge Street headquarters had been legendary. More discussed than her sub-editorial skills were her Gina Lollobrigida looks, her intelligence and humour. Nigella had bewitched and bewildered dozens of would-be boyfriends – writers, poets, lawyers – all over London. Just turned twenty-nine, she now regarded her new superior (ha!) with cool amusement and a faint hint of welcome in her fathomless brown eyes.

My first day was spent learning the ropes: the location of the lavatories, the post room and the downstairs composing room; the whereabouts of the Arts section, the Design and Layout staff (I

---

* They included Emma Soames, Lady Cosima Fry, Virginia Bonham-Carter and Evelyn Waugh's granddaughter Sophia Watson, among many others.

was expecting bow-ties and floppy black curls, and I was right), the photography library, the canteen and, of course, the proximity of good pubs just off The Highway, which would surely soon become my spiritual home in Wapping.

In the canteen, I met an old *Evening Standard* pal, Mark Law, who shook his head sadly at my enquiry. 'The days of the pub lunch in Fleet Street have gone, I'm afraid,' he said. 'The most levity you can expect around here is someone saying: "Have a break from that article – come with me to the canteen for a *cuppa* . . ."' He snorted. 'Have you ever heard anything more *dismal*?'

I explained to my staff how I liked things done – how long before publication we should commission reviews, where books for-review should be marked with date-stickers on their spines, how I liked separate folders for letters of complaint and fan mail . . . I could tell they were impressed by my streamlined managerial skill.

One area in which I needed instruction was in computer skills. When I'd left the *Standard*, typewriters were still being used, but for my home operations I'd bought an Amstrad PC, one of Alan Sugar's television-sized computers with a rickety plastic keyboard. At the *Sunday Times*, everyone had gleamingly cool, state-of-the-art screens that used Atex software, which I'd never seen before.

I jabbed at the keys, checked the manual and jabbed some more, but the keyboard sulkily refused to give up its secrets.

Nigella came and stood beside me as I poked and prodded.

'Like this?' I asked.

'No,' said Nigella. 'Go to the tab, click and wait for the drop-down menu.'

I fiddled and faffed some more, without success.

'This key here?' I said, 'the one which says F6. Do I . . .?'

'*No!*' she said. 'You have to click on *this*' – she poked a key – to get the drop-down . . .'

'Nigella,' I said firmly, 'I'm rather at sea about electronics, OK? Could you just *show* me how it's done and I'll try and copy you.'

Without a word, she straightened up, put one hand on the arm
of my chair, the other hand on my shoulder and rolled the whole
ensemble, on its castors, back from the desk. Then, without so
much as a how-d'ye-do, she turned round and sat on my lap.

It's hard to describe my exact feelings at that moment. Thirty
seconds before, I'd been cursing myself for being a technological
birdbrain, who should have acquired some rudimentary knowledge
of Optrex or Andrex or whatever the bloody system was called.
Now, all thoughts of software had fled from my brain, as it struggled
to process the fact that, like some exotic nesting bird, one of the
great beauties of the twentieth century had just settled herself
upon my seated person.

'Can you see all right?' she asked, shifting to the left so I could
follow her hand movements on the keyboard. 'It's really simple.'

'Mmm-hmm,' I said into a face-full of luxuriant chestnut hair
and a heady whiff of Diorissima. 'What you're doing is very helpful
indeed.'

'You press this *here*, wait for the menu to appear, then click on
that, and Bob's your uncle.' Nigella shifted her weight to the right,
to look over her shoulder at where my face was emerging, slightly
dazed, from the mass of hair. 'Have you got it now?'

'Absolutely,' I said. 'Fully briefed.'

In the first few weeks of my, ahem, reign, Simon Jenkins appeared
on my behalf at the Tuesday Conference, in which the paper's
departments revealed their plans for the forthcoming Sunday
paper, and were approved or shot down in flames by the editor.
It was just as well I had some breathing space in these early days,
so that I could commission some weeks' worth of exciting pieces.

Redmond O'Hanlon, the world's most genial naturalist, had a
new book coming out. A sequel of sorts to *Into the Heart of Borneo*,
which had told scary/hilarious tales of head-hunters and waterfalls
and the candiru fish that can swim up a chap's todger, requiring the

victim to have it amputated *pronto*, the new work was called *In Trouble Again: A Journey Between the Orinoco and the Amazon*.

I felt we should make a big fuss of this sublime teller of tall tales. So I signed up Jonathan Meades, something of a connoisseur of the grotesque, to go to Redmond's house in Oxford and interview him. What larks, I thought, to have two such vivid characters (and fine writers) locked in conversational battle. Soon afterwards, I talked to Nigella about her love for the work of the novelist Margaret Atwood. I asked her to interview the Canadian *grande dame* about her new book and she readily agreed.

Two fine interviews! What a brilliant start that would be!

The day after the Redmond meeting, the phone rang. It was Meades. He sounded a little distrait, a touch woebegone. 'Look, I'm sorry . . .' he said without preamble, 'but there's been a bit of a problem. The interview didn't really work out.'

His explanation was long and barely coherent. He'd gone to the house in Oxford. O'Hanlon had been in terrific form. He'd given Meades a welcome drink . . . After that, things had become fuzzy. Life had unwoven. The fabric of reality had yielded to the logic of dream. Caipirinhas had been involved, and rough Amazon tequila. No other details were forthcoming, except that nothing of actual substance had found its way onto tape.

'Can't you do it from memory?' I wailed. 'Surely you must remember *some* things he said?'

'Absolutely not,' said Meades. 'Hardly a word. So I propose . . .'

'What?'

'I thought I'd go back to Oxford tomorrow and have another go.'

The conversation ended soon after that. I couldn't bear waiting to see if my commission got drowned a second time in an Orinoco of sugar-cane-based liquor.

Thank God I had Nigella's encounter with Atwood to look forward to. The novel was called *Cat's Eye*, and told the story of a painter, Elaine Risley, whose life and relationships are blighted by her friendship with three girls who befriend, then bully her, from schooldays into adolescence and maturity.* The book was about feminism, resilience and the growth of identity. Just up Nigella's street, surely?

Amazingly, this one crashed and burned as well. Nigella returned from the meeting physically shivering from the frostiness she'd encountered in Ms Atwood's company. I'd heard about the author's reluctance to answer questions about her personal circumstances *vis-à-vis* those of her characters, and about her habit, on hearing any question beginning with the words, 'In your books you often . . .' by asking exactly *how many* books the interviewer had read. Nigella had, unfortunately, strayed into both these bear-traps. She typed up the piece, but we agreed that the Atwood responses were so blood-curdlingly hostile as to make the interview unusable.

Well, that was marvellous, wasn't it? Two hot commissions, one thwarted by drink, the other by writerly deep-freeze. This was no way to stamp my authority on the new-look Books section. This was like being given a fabulous item of stately furniture, a Sheraton bookcase, say, or a Chippendale sofa, to look after for years, before giving it back unblemished – only to break the glass door of the former or rip the silk lining of the latter shortly after it arrived.

The section was, I should point out, a fantastic thing – the only serious stand-alone literary supplement that came with a British newspaper. As serious, in its reviews and analyses, as the eighty-six-year-old *TLS*, but more readable, and with more well-known names writing the reviews.†

---

* *Cat's Eye* was shortlisted for the prestigious Canadian Governor-General's Award and the Booker Prize. She didn't win the Booker in 1988, but did so with *The Blind Assassin* in 2000 and, jointly, with *The Testaments* in 2019.

† The idea for the pull-out had been Andrew Neil's. He had flown to New York in 1987 to impress on Rupert Murdoch the need for a stand-alone tabloid Books section, and came home with the go-ahead. Neil anticipated generating no revenue from the Books pages, however, because, as he wrote in his memoir, *Full Disclosure*, 'unlike their American counterparts, Britain's publishers are an uncommercial bunch who do not think they need to advertise'. This was a criticism he repeated many times in the next few years, sometimes directing it straight at the publishers themselves when they attended our literary-prize dinners at Grosvenor House.

The first separate Books section, a sixteen-page tabloid, had come out earlier that year. Neil and Simon Jenkins had together decided the roster of big-name reviewers that launched the section. John Carey led the team, as he'd done for years, along with George Steiner, Frederic Raphael, John Mortimer, Victoria Glendinning, Melvyn Bragg, Rabbi Julia Neuberger, Miranda Seymour, Deborah Moggach, Norman Stone and Conor Cruise O'Brien. An astonishing Premier League team, and a daunting prospect for the new manager, who'd come straight from the *Evening Standard* XI . . .

The business of commissioning reviews from well-known philosophers, academics and politicians wasn't, as it turned out, terribly hard. Compared to breaking rocks in an Alcatraz chain gang, it was a breeze. Asking my A-team of reviewers to write about a meaty biography or revisionist imperial history for a large sum of cash seldom resulted in an outraged silence. The conversations went like this:

'Hi, John Mortimer. John Walsh here from the *Sunday Times*. Look, next month there's a reassessment of the Profumo scandal coming out and I wond—'

'I'd love to.'

'Hello Miranda. John here from the *Sunday Times*. I know you're an expert on Bertrand Russell, but how much do you know about Bertie's brother Frank and his disastrous first marriage to—'

'Mabel Scott? Who spent years getting a legal separation from him on grounds of sodomy, and ended up having to make a living by singing in variety shows? I know a little.'

'Er, yeah, exactly. Well, there's this new book out which exam—'

'I'd love to.'

'Good afternoon, Enoch Powell. I hope you're well. I thought you might like to look at a new book on the politician Roger Casement, his travels among the Putumayo Indians and their enslavement by the Peruvian Amazon Company. It looks very int—'

'Please send it over as soon as is convenient. Goodbye.'

See what I mean? I was dealing, week by week, with exceptionally clever, well-read and well-informed people, who devoured new books with relish and served up a thousand words of well-balanced, richly anecdotal and unarguably *right* analysis. Along with the aforementioned talents, we regularly signed up Anthony Quinton the philosopher, A. S. Byatt the future Booker winner, Sheridan Morley the showbiz expert (and Noël Coward's godson), Asa Briggs the historian . . . We had politicians galore: Barbara Castle, Roy Jenkins, even a sighting of Tony Blair, then shadow home secretary, who wrote about a study of Keir Hardie ('. . . the inspirational founder of the Labour party, his name a source of reverence and pride') several years before he led the party to win the 1997 election.

Our go-to reviewer for anything about music – folk, jazz, rock, blues – was Robert Sandall, tall, seraphic, ridiculously good-looking. I was delighted to renew our acquaintance. I'd known him at university, where we'd both performed, with contrasting degrees of skill, in rock bands; I was the singer in Flying Wedge, he the lead guitarist of Frothy Green Stools.*

In the first dizzy rapture of commissioning stuff from the God-like figures on the Murdoch payroll, I did little reviewing myself. But Penny asked me to evaluate some interesting new novelists. One was Nicholson Baker, the matchless American describer of things traditionally considered beneath literary notice, the laureate of paper-towel dispensers, milk-carton wing-flap spouts, staple guns and drinking straws. His debut novel *The Mezzanine* took place during one man's lunch hour in a Manhattan office and minutely described everything he does, sees and thinks in this tiny timeframe. It was a kind of Joycean stream-of-consciousness inside the head of a modern, obsessively enquiring, tech-savvy inhabitant of Planet Earth.

---

* Tony Blair, our exact contemporary at Oxford, sang with the band Ugly Rumours. It's a shame the three of us never collaborated, to form The Ugly Green Wedge.

I especially praised Baker's use of footnotes, some of which extended over a page. There was even a two-page footnote *on the subject of footnotes*, which incidentally brought the interesting factoids that the philosopher Wittgenstein loved to watch cowboy movies, and the poet Milton preferred to wear laces, rather than buckles, on his shoes.

The day after the review appeared, to my amazement, Nicholson Baker rang me from New York to convey his thanks. This had never happened before, to me or possibly any literary editor in history. 'I was very pleased that you compared me to Flann O'Brien,' he said. 'I'm a great admirer of the guy.'

'I didn't think any writer could use more footnotes than he did,' I said, 'but you managed it. And by a weird coincidence, there's a new collected edition of his newspaper columns coming out soon. Shall we say nine hundred words?'

He agreed to review O'Brien's droll ephemera, and turned in an excellent piece. I rang him to express my pleasure in having him on the payroll. 'What would you like to do next?' I asked. 'There's a biography of Jack London out soon, that's a bit conventional but you might care to—'

'No no,' he cut through my commissioning patter. 'I can't do any more book reviews.'

'Whyever not?' I asked. 'You're *really good* at them. We can give you regular work. And maybe pay you a little more if you . . .'

'I'm sorry, John,' he said. 'I appreciate the offer, but I wanna write books. I can't afford to be distracted by journalism, whatever the money. I have to think of the future.'

'Nicholson,' I said, 'I admire your dedication to being a serious writer. But maybe you could do, say, half a dozen pieces for us between now and summer, while your stock is so high, and make some money reading things you'd probably be reading anyway . . .'

I suddenly realised, to my shame, that I sounded exactly like the appalling Mr Vampire in Cyril Connolly's *Enemies of Promise*, the literary editor who seduces the innocent young Walter Savage

Shelleyblake into a lifetime of writing lucrative book reviews and getting nothing creatively worthwhile done at all. Baker and I said goodbye – me regretfully, he firmly, having tussled with the siren call of the newspaper byline, and won. It left me wondering if I should have had his willpower when I was starting out; if I should have turned down the reviews and interviews that filled my late twenties and early thirties, and concentrated on getting a decent novel out. But I cheered myself by thinking a) that literary criticism was itself a creatively legitimate thing to do and b) just how long would it have taken me to try writing intensely about milk cartons and drinking straws?

Sometimes my conversations with literary titans went awry. When a fat collection of Craig Raine's literary essays, entitled *Haydn and the Valve Trumpet*, came into the office, I decided to make a big fuss of them, and thought of Al Alvarez. He was the grizzled, all-action cultural commissar of the 1970s – poet, essayist, critic, novelist, mountain-climber, poker-player and possibly the last lover of Sylvia Plath. Also long-serving poetry critic of the *Observer*, and editor of the anthology *The New Poetry* which suggested that, quite frankly, British poets were a mewling chorus of genteel bedwetters compared to their tough-minded American counterparts.

Our conversation went like this:

'Hi Mr Alvarez. John Walsh here from the *Sunday Times*. I'm ringing to ask if you'd be interested in reviewing Craig Raine's collected essays, which are out in three weeks. Obviously you'll know Craig's poetry over the years, but I thought his essays might amuse you.'

'Mr Walsh, I'm not sure this is a wise commission,' he said, craggily. 'Craig and I haven't got on well over the years. There have been . . . strong words between us. I don't think we see eye to eye about many things.'

'I'm not expecting you to agree with his views, Mr Alvarez, only to appreciate his attacking style, which, if I may say so, is not dissimilar to your own. We need one thousand words. Do say yes.'

'Tell you what, Mr Walsh. I'll do as you ask – for a grand.'

'A *thousand quid*? I'm afraid that's impossible, Mr Alvarez. We never go higher than £600. But I'll gladly pay you that if you'll review it.'

'Nine hundred.'

'Did you hear me? I said we never go above six— oh for God's sake, *700 quid* then. And that's my final offer.'

'I'm happy with that, Mr Walsh. It's a deal. Sling it over, and I'll do my best. Do you have my address? I'm in *Who's Who*.'

'Fantastic. It'll be in the post tomorrow. And thank you *very much*, Mr Alvarez, for being—'

'Look, John,' he said, with a sudden warmth, or less gruffness, 'there's no need to be so formal. We've had a conversation, we've struck a bargain . . .'

'And . . .?'

'I'm just saying that, henceforth . . . You can call me Al.'

'In that case,' I said, my voice trembling with hilarity, 'you can call me Betty.'

There was a silence that could freeze champagne.

'I'm sorry?' said Al Alvarez.

'It's a song,' I blurted out. '*You* know. By Paul Simon, "You Can Call Me Al". It came out a couple of years ago.'

'What on earth . . .?'

'In 1987, I think. It's a famous song lyric,' I babbled. 'So when you said, "You can call"—'

There was a click and a burring noise as the hard man of British poetry rang off.

Christ, I thought, what now? Will he ring his friends and say: 'Do you know the new books chap at the *Sunday Times*? He's *most* odd. Encourages people to call him Elizabeth on a *very* brief acquaintance . . .'*

* * *

---

* Although he turned in an excellent, and (given what he'd said) surprisingly appreciative review.

Not every reviewer was 100 per cent scrupulous about what they wrote or how they wrote it. I had a slight problem with Norman Stone, the famous historian, a professor at both Cambridge and Oxford. He had a reputation as a ferocious drinker, smoker, Soho poker-player and serial groper of his students (of both sexes – he seduced a famous thriller writer and his famous sister, though obviously in different tutorials).

In the late 1980s, he'd become a speech-writer for Margaret Thatcher, in front of whom he'd once collapsed from drink, but she forgave him; he was given a column in the *Sunday Times* by Rupert Murdoch. To amortise his substantial contract, he was expected to write a certain number of reviews each year. I grew to dread them. Mostly they would arrive on time and make sense; but, every so often, a chaotic typescript would appear, in which, after six hundred words of perfect sense, the review would dissipate into random phrases inexpertly linked by ellipses, like this:

'Scheidemann resignation . . . Baeur telegram . . . plebiscite on B. sovereignty . . . letter to Empress Eugenie . . . Danzig and Vistula delta . . . mandates of Togoland and Cameroon . . .'

Along with this unhelpful burst of historical shards (reminiscent of Mr Jingle's speech patterns in *The Pickwick Papers*) would come the handwritten instruction: 'Get one of your history graduates to fill in the gaps. NS.' One can imagine Professor Stone's mood at 3 a.m., perhaps befuddled by Glenmorangie, when his interest in pursuing consecutive thoughts and writing a coherent argument was eclipsed by an overwhelming desire to go to sleep.

One morning, Nigella dropped a small bombshell. She'd had enough of the Books department and wanted a weekly column on the paper, a job that involved fewer interactions with annoying male bosses and zero encounters with beady-eyed Canadian prima donnas.

I was asked to choose a new deputy. Where could I start? A small
ad in the *TLS*, the *LRB*, the *Guardian*, *Time Out*? I thought of the
multitude of literary wannabes out there in the cultural metropolis,
bursting with excitement for books and all the palaver that now
attended their publication. I wondered if, rather than having to
choose from a gang of strangers, there might be someone I'd
already met . . .

I thought of my reviewers at the *Evening Standard*, but couldn't
picture any of them (especially the women) relishing the idea of
having me as their boss in an office environment. Then, over a
solitary lunch in the canteen, a name, a face and a book appeared
in my head.

I remembered the launch of *Success Stories*, about the literary
scene in the 1950s, in particular the Angry Young Men phenomenon.
It had been adapted from an Oxford DPhil thesis and reviewed in
every newspaper and magazine in the world except *Flat Earth
Monthly*. The poet John Wain, who used to be bracketed with the
Angries, had reviewed it excitedly for the *Sunday Times*.

I recalled the jolly launch party at Faber – and I certainly
remembered the author. Harry Ritchie was thirty, Scottish, tall,
handsome, curly-haired, talkative, ironical, mad keen on football
(especially Raith Rovers, the local team from his home town,
Kirkcaldy in Fife) and terrific company. He was part of the
Charming Young Men phenomenon, of which there wasn't a huge
membership in 1988.

He must, I thought sadly, be tied up in academe now, doubtless
persuaded by a massive research grant from Stanford, California, to
do a PhD on the Black Mountain poets of 1950s Carolina. Was
there any point in asking him?

I rang Joanna Mackle, his publicity director at Faber, and asked
what she knew. She confirmed that Harry was still in the UK,
employed as a sub-editor on *Harper's & Queen*. She didn't think he
was earning a fortune but he liked the easy working conditions.
In particular he liked sharing an office with 297 women, many of

whom were about twenty-five, well-connected and uncommonly attractive.

I rang the magazine and suggested we have lunch at the Groucho.

'I'll come straight to the point,' I said, as we took our seats. 'I've been made literary editor of the *Sunday Times*, and I'm looking for a deputy.'

'Oh aye?' said Harry.

'Nigella Lawson was the deputy when I arrived a few weeks ago, but she's leaving to be a writer.'

'That's a shame,' said Harry neutrally.

'So tell me,' I enquired. 'How are you enjoying life at *Harper's*?'

'It's lovely,' said Harry. 'Very laid-back and relaxed. The deadlines are always about three months away, so everyone swans around having a really *agreeable* time and joking with the Art department.'

It sounded like he was perfectly content, goddammit.

'Do you get on with the editor?'

'Nicholas Coleridge? He's lovely. He's young and preposterously posh but very approachable. He has these catchphrases. You can hear him on the phone to some advertiser, saying, "Oh hurrah *hurrah*!" It's that kind of place.'

'Are you used to working on a computer all day?'

'I've never worked on a computer in m'life. At *Harper's*, it's still mostly quill pens.'

By the time the grilled octopus arrived, I felt it was pointless to continue.

'Well,' I said, 'you sound very happy in your job . . .'

'No, wait,' he said. 'I'm saying it's oh-*kayyy* where I am. But it's not exactly fulfilling, spending my days writing headlines for articles about the correct headgear for shooting parties or choosing a kid's blanket in the nursery.'

'What headline did you come up with for that?'

'"They Tuck You Up, Your Mum and Dad".'

'That's brilliant!' I said. 'And how many of the staff recognised the Larkin allusion?'

'About three.'

'Harry,' I said, 'would you like to get back to literature, work beside me and some attractive colleagues, commission book reviews, interview authors, write pieces about modern poetry and go to hundreds of parties?'

'What – you're *offering* me *the job*?' His soft Kirkcaldy voice rose to a squeak.

'What did you think we were discussing?'

'I thought you were going to ask me to suggest someone suitable.'

'I don't want a *suggestion*,' I said with perhaps excessive passion. 'I want *you*!'

Harry beamed. 'Being Scottish, though, I have to know,' he said, 'is there a fee attached?'

'What are you earning at present?'

He told me. It was a pittance.

'I'm sorry to break it to you, Harry, but you'll have to start seeing yourself in a completely different income bracket.'

There was a meaningful silence between us, as we considered how this lunch – indeed, this conversation – would change our lives for years.

Harry beamed. 'In that case, John, I would love to work with you at the *Sunday Times* Books section.'

'Great!' I said.

'Hurrah!' said Harry.

In the following weeks I got to know my Books office colleagues better. I discovered that Penny, whom I knew only as an excellent reviewer of novels, owed her position to an unusual circumstance: the Wapping dispute, that ran for fifty-four weeks from January 1986, after Rupert Murdoch moved production of the *Sunday Times* and other newspapers from Gray's Inn Road to the Wapping plant, where journalists could input their articles directly, without having to use the ancient hot-metal printing method. The typesetters and printers saw their jobs hanging by a thread. Six thousand union members came out on strike and were served with dismissal notices, their places taken by workers from a non-print union. Demonstrators arrived daily to surround the Wapping plant. There were ugly scenes, cries of 'Scab!' greeted arriving journalists and outbreaks of violence ensued: four hundred policemen, van drivers and members of the public were injured, and twelve hundred arrests made.

Claire Tomalin, the literary editor at the time, described in her memoir, *A Life of My Own*, the shock of the move. 'Murdoch sprang the closing of the Gray's Inn offices and the move to Wapping on us skilfully, acting with all the brutality he had found necessary to defeat the print unions. Their own intolerable behaviour had brought this on them, and cost them the support of the journalists. The journalists were summoned to a meeting, offered rises of £2,000 a year and membership of a private health insurance scheme if they turned up the next day at Wapping. Otherwise they would be sacked. A majority went, many reluctantly.'

Tomalin and her deputy Sean French were surprised when, on going back to their office, they found that the proofs of the following Sunday's books pages had gone missing. Their whereabouts soon became known. Penny had come from her desk at the *Sun* and smuggled them to Wapping. Tomalin was asked to go there and be filmed walking into the new building alongside Sean French, perhaps offering a cheery thumbs-up to the cameras. Instead, she resigned. French was told that Penny was now literary editor, and that he was being replaced by Nigella Lawson.

I discovered what the Books section's more recent problem had been. While Penny had been put in charge as a reward for her loyalty, and though she adored literature, she had no experience of commissioning reviews, and suffered torments of indecision. Faced with a shelf of soon-to-be-published novels and biographies, she'd panic about which deserved to be sent for review. Then she hit on a solution: a speed-reading course. 'It works very well with fiction,' she said, 'because you can pick up the story easily, and if there's some especially fine writing, you can re-read it later. It's harder with non-fiction because there are so many facts to digest. And,' she concluded with a smile, 'it's absolutely *hopeless* with poetry.'

The only flaw in this plan was that it meant Penny spent every week whizzing through forty or fifty books, effectively reviewing them all in her head, rather than choosing a dozen interesting-looking ones and getting other people to do the analytical stuff.

Harry Ritchie duly arrived and was, as I'd anticipated, a big hit with the staff. The atmospheric levels of oestrogen and testosterone were substantially rebalanced, and an atmosphere of contentment prevailed. Harry was taken in hand and shown the ropes by Nigella, an arrangement he accepted without argument. He was, however, rather baffled by her choice of clothes. She invariably wore loose black frocks that, he said, reminded him of bin liners. 'The thing is,' said Harry, 'Nigella is really, actually, a genuine 1940s Hollywood movie star. She should be swanning around in a red dress with red lipstick and her hair up . . .'

Harry learned from Nigella the black arts of commissioning reviews. One day, weighed down with work, I asked them to find someone to review a study of moral philosophy that was due out in a month. Harry checked his contacts book but no obvious name jumped out. He asked Nigella's advice.

'Hmm,' she said, 'I suppose I *could* ask my stepfather.'

Harry was dubious. 'Shouldn't we set our sights a bit higher than asking members of our immediate families?' he said. 'I was thinking of getting a university professor of philosophy or something.'

'Well,' Nigella conceded, 'my stepfather *is* A. J. Ayer . . .'

At the time I joined the *Sunday Times*, in September 1988, Salman Rushdie was pretty much king of the British literary world. In terms of book sales, important prizes, laudatory reviews and height of international profile, nobody could hold a candle to him. Winner of the Booker Prize in 1981, and a runner-up in 1983, he'd launched his fourth novel *The Satanic Verses* on 26 September and the Booker judges had voted it onto the shortlist.

The reviews in Britain were enthusiastic – Victoria Glendinning in *The Times* began by saying 'This book is better than *Midnight's Children* . . . because it is more contained – but only in the sense that the Niagara Falls is contained', while Bill Buford, in the *Sunday Times*, called the book 'a masterpiece of a novel that is more ambitious than any other fiction being written today.' Rushdie must also have been pleased, and possibly relieved, to read an encomium in the *Bombay Times*, where Nisha Puri said it 'sweeps everything before it in an imaginative avalanche which is both wondrous and uplifting' and praised, with stupendous irony, its portrayal of the tensions between East and West. He called it 'an intensely sad look at the brutal incomprehension with which man and his inflicted and chosen worlds face each other.'

Trouble, however, was coming. On 2 October, two Muslim politicians, Syed Shahabuddin and Kurshid Ayad Khan, leading lights in the Janata party, which represented most of India's 150 million Muslims, called the novel 'suggestively derogatory' and demanded it be banned. Neither MP had read it nor, they said, had any need to do so ('I do not have to wade through a filthy drain to know what filth is' said Shahabuddin). They were effectively telling the prime minister, Rajiv Gandhi, that he'd be wise to heed their demands. Three days later, Mr Gandhi ordered the book to be placed on a list of proscribed texts and the Indian Ministry of Finance, no less, announced that *The Satanic Verses* was now banned under Section 11 of the Indian Customs Act.

Events began to ramify, both East and West, in a pandemic of condemnation. In England the UK Action Committee on Islamic Affairs was formed for the sole purpose of banning *The Satanic Verses*. Although the book won the Whitbread Best Novel Prize in

November, the Islamic Defence Council held a protest march in London, followed by rallies in Bradford, Bolton and other northern cities with large Muslim populations. A photograph showing a furious Muslim nailing a copy of the book to a wooden stake before burning it, went around the world.

In December, *Kayhan Forangi*, the top literary journal of the Islamic Republic of Iran, claimed the book offered 'false interpretations about Islam and wrong portrayals of the Koran and the Prophet Muhammad. It also draws a caricature-like and distorted image of Islamic principles which lacks even the slightest artistic credentials.' By early February, the book had been banned in India, Pakistan, Iran, Bangladesh, Sudan, Sri Lanka, Egypt and Saudi Arabia. Worse was to follow. Public protests in Bombay and Dhaka led to rioting in Islamabad where, on 12 February, six people were killed and over one hundred injured. Next day a riot in Kashmir left one more person dead.

Then the balloon went up. On 14 February, Ayatollah Khomeini of Iran went on Radio Tehran to tell his co-religionists: 'I inform the proud Muslim people of the world that the author of *The Satanic Verses* book, which is against Islam, the Prophet and the Koran, and all involved in its publication who were aware of its contents, are sentenced to death.'

The day of the announcement was, of course, St Valentine's Day. It was also the day of Bruce Chatwin's memorial service in San Sophia Cathedral, the Greek Orthodox church off Bayswater.

At the church, Rushdie sat in a pew beside Martin Amis and endured the humorous joshing of Paul Theroux across the aisle. ('Next week, Salman, we'll all be back here for you!') Later, policemen came to his home and told him and his wife, the American writer Marianne Wiggins, that men from Special Branch would be visiting them the following day. They would be entering a new life in hiding, under police protection, indefinitely.

The day after the fatwa, Salman Ghaffari, Iran's ambassador to the Vatican, was asked if he would personally shoot Rushdie, should he walk through the door. 'Yes, certainly I would,' he replied. 'The law of God is clear ... But why do you find this behaviour strange?'

Among the responses to this incitement to murder was the very British suggestion that, if Rushdie were to grovel, to promise to remove the offending passages, even to suppress the book and lock it away in a vault, everyone might calm the hell down. Rushdie issued an apology of sorts on 18 February. It read: 'As author of *The Satanic Verses*, I recognise that Muslims in many parts of the world are genuinely distressed by the publication of my novel. I profoundly regret the distress that publication has occasioned to sincere followers of Islam. Living as we do in a world of many faiths, this experience has served to remind us that we must all be conscious of the sensibilities of others.'

The ayatollah wasn't impressed by this sanctimonious flannel. Next day he declared that Rushdie's statement fell far short of a proper act of repentance and repeated the sentence of death, adding, 'Send him to hell.'

It was the most significant, and scary, literary event in centuries. Of course, it wasn't actually a 'literary' event, but a religio-political-cultural-diplomatic row with, at its centre – amazingly – a really terrible book review. In the fundamentalist implacability of the ayatollah and his associates, and in the way the dispute ignored the old diplomatic safeguards of national boundaries, it felt as if we'd been time-travelled back to the Crusades.

The response of the British literary establishment was almost wholly supportive of Rushdie; nobody would question his right to say whatever he liked on any subject. British newspapers, however, raised objections. Some questioned his enjoyment of setting a match to the tails of large, international tigers, as he'd done in previous books with General Zia and Indira Gandhi. Some asked: 'Did he know that this was likely to happen?' – a question expecting an affirmative response and the follow-up, 'Well, it serves him right then.' The *Sun*, remarkably, took Rushdie's side, insisting that 'Freedom of speech is a precious British tradition.' In an interview, Rushdie told Valerie Grove he worried about unwittingly inspiring a wave of 'Paki-bashing' if *Sun* readers were told, in effect: 'Let's teach these savages how to behave in our civilised society!' A leadenly jocose leader in the *Daily Telegraph* said that, if Muslims wanted to shell out £12.95 to burn the book in the privacy of their homes, then 'many Christians who have struggled with Mr Rushdie's impenetrable novels will warm their hands at the fireside.'

The archbishop of Canterbury and the foreign secretary, Sir Geoffrey Howe, agreed that the book was offensive both to Islam and (in its portrayal of 'Mrs Torture' the British PM) to Britain. The far right argued that, since Rushdie had been a fierce critic of both the police and British society in general, he should face the danger he'd brought on himself without the benefit of police protection. Rushdie's old English master at Rugby, Geoffrey Halliwell, was asked for his memories of the schoolboy Salman. 'He had a way with words,' said Halliwell. 'But I would never have thought that such a quiet boy would have ended up in such trouble.'

Quiet? Bryan Appleyard considered the role of the author's ego in precipitating a crisis: 'Rushdie was never quiet. Revelling in the fame and controversy he could inspire, he constructed ambitious doctrines of the power of literature and his duty in the world. The beliefs horribly and unjustly backfired. But his own character, in its touchiness, its pride and its egotism, endowed the affair with its final uneasy ambiguity: that perhaps all we had here was a smart salon lefty who had simply gone too far.'

There was, inevitably, a flood of hate mail and death threats to the offices of his publisher, Viking Penguin. In the press, Rushdie said he hoped that other religious leaders – bishops and rabbis, for instance – might try to defuse the situation; but there seemed to be an unbridgeable gap between the mild, inoffensive leaders of the Church of England and the unsmiling, non-negotiable imams of Muslim fundamentalism.

At the *Sunday Times*, it was deemed a good idea for the Literary department to explain just what had enraged the Ayatollah, and the wider Muslim world, so much. It fell to me to have a stab, so to speak, at an exegesis.

In my piece, I explained that Rushdie's main narrative thrust was to reimagine, through the dreams of a film star, the beginnings of Islamic culture. Through Gibreel Farishta's human eyes, the prophet's original visions of heaven and earth are set down in the dissolving sands of an Unreal City. The trouble lay in Rushdie's giving the fictional not-quite-Muhammad a non-divine nature.

I explained at length that at no point does Rushdie refer to the Prophet Muhammad by name, nor the city of Mecca, nor to sharia law, nor to anything directly concerned with Islamic faith. All the fundamentalists' objections concerned the symbolic representation of religious figures and events – as one might condemn George Orwell's fictional Ministry of Love in *Nineteen Eighty-Four* for satirising the Ministry of Defence. The book's status as a novel, however, cut no ice with Muslim critics. The Grand Sheikh of Cairo's Al-Azhar, the thousand-year-old seat of Islamic theology, called on all the nations in the Islamic Conference Organisation to suppress the book, saying it contained 'lies and figments of the imagination' about Islam which were 'passed off' as facts, and that the Jahilia sequences were insulting distortions of Islamic history. The fact that Rushdie had always presented his material as fictional 'figments of the imagination' – nothing factual about them – was not considered an excuse.

I felt I needed a flesh-and-blood Muslim voice to explain how belief in a divine being could translate into murderous revenge for the supposed representation of the divine being in a novel. So I rang up a Mr Faruqi, the editor of *Impact International*, the guy who'd written at length about Rushdie's chronic 'sadomasochism' and itemised the blasphemies he'd committed. I told Mr Faruqi that *The Satanic Verses* was a work of fiction, and that all UK readers would know that everything in it is an imaginative creation, invented to raise questions or illustrate truths about the human condition, about behaviour or morality or society. Did he appreciate that it was a fiction, not a presentation of factual reality?

'What we are talking about here is an insult,' he said. 'There is no problem about it being fiction or not. It doesn't matter if it's a fiction, a serious book, a dream – the point is that the language should be decent. And the problem is the abusive and insulting way the Prophet is described, in the most filthy language. That is what cannot be forgiven.'

'In Western culture,' I said, perhaps a little pompously, 'followers of Christianity have been speaking lightly of Jesus Christ and his life, have questioned his teachings and made fun of the Trinity and the saints and the Bible for two thousand years without the Church fathers condemning anyone to death. We tend to believe that scepticism is a sign of a healthy society, and shouldn't affect anyone's belief. Why do Muslims become so enraged about a made-up figure in a made-up book?'

'Mr Walsh, let me put this very simply for you. If someone insults your father, would you not retaliate?'

'Well,' I said, 'I expect I might send them a rather stern letter.'

He continued. 'If someone insults your mother, would you not retaliate?'

'Well I suppose so, yes.'

'If someone insults your child, would—'

'Absolutely. Yes of course I would.'

'And so, Mr Walsh,' his voice slowed down dramatically, 'if someone insults your *God*, who is more important to you than *any* of these, and who is *within you*, would you not retaliate all the more?'

It was useless to try and explain that, to British Christians, God is an external deity that one believes to exist in some numinous form, with some power or agency in the world and in the fate of one's life, especially the whereabouts of one's soul after death. But it's at best a distant relationship, like that between a peasant and a king in a far-off country. Mr Faruqi and I had to leave it there, in mutual metaphysical bafflement.

In February 1989, I went to interview William Golding, the nation's most eminent writer (Booker Prize 1980, Nobel Prize 1983, knighthood 1988). I'd read *Lord of the Flies* as a teenager, and been haunted, not just by the story of pre-teen schoolboys turning feral with sharpened sticks and homicidal intentions, but by an elemental dread that hung over the chapters and revealed itself when the revellers at the feast tore Simon apart with their bare hands. A grammar-schoolboy, I hadn't run into anyone who sounded like Jack Merridew, the posh leader of the public-school choir, or Piggy, the fat, specky, picked-on loser who *didn't 'alf talk funny*. I didn't know that a damning indictment of the British education and class system was being played out in its pages. I just knew the book had snuck its way inside me. So, in meeting the author, I felt I was meeting someone from pre-history.

My first sighting helped disperse this impression. Standing at Truro Station, Sir William cut a rather comfortable figure. With a beanie hat clamped over his white hair, his portly frame clad in oatmeal jumper and overalls, he put one in mind of slippers, toast and spaniels. His greeting was warily distant – he said he had a streaming cold, so don't come near – but he flung his Jaguar around the Cornish lanes like a boy racer. His ragged King Lear beard showed some storm damage, but age (seventy-eight that year) hadn't withered Britain's most renowned literary knight.

After half a lifetime in Salisbury, Golding and his wife Ann had moved to their elegant Cornish mansion five years before. Golding was born in Cornwall, and his mother was a local. So had the move been nostalgic? No, he said, he'd gone there to escape the press. 'Salisbury was a place to which London media types could nip down in an hour and, as it were, have lunch on my back,' he said feelingly. 'People were crawling over the hedge. I'd become a tourist object. We simply *had* to get further away.'

The reason for our meeting was the publication of *Fire Down Below*, the last of the trilogy of novels collectively called *To the Ends of the Earth*. When the first book, *Rites of Passage*, came out in 1980 and won the Booker Prize, critics had marvelled at the new Golding it revealed: his astonishing vigour, his vivid characterisation and, especially, his bounding good humour. There were definite notes of Jane Austen about the on-board social comedy. The second and third books continued the transformation and brought the story to a triumphantly ambiguous rest.

Golding taught naval cadets for five years, picking up all the nautical arcana – stuns'l, tricing, careen, binnacle, larboard, tompion, orlop – that studded the *Sea Trilogy*, and his memories of childhood pungently entwined the sea and his boyish imagination. He grew up in Marlborough in a fourteenth-century mansion of which he was afraid. 'I disliked the house intensely. I used to be terrified because I didn't see visions, and felt, in a house that old, that one should ... There was a graveyard in the garden, where my father once dug up some human bones; I already knew, intuitively, that they were there.'

His father, a Quaker's son turned super-rational polymath, taught science at Marlborough Grammar School. His mother, by contrast, was full of superstition: the sinking of the *Titanic* in 1912 profoundly affected her; afterwards, the whole world had become, for her, a risky place to be. Golding heard chilling ghost stories from her lips: 'In St Columb's parish, where I was born, a terrible cry can be heard at certain times, first by sea, then sweeping up the valley – it means someone is going to be drowned. It's called The Crake, and across the side of the headland, round by Newquay, a phantom ship could sometimes be seen, disappearing through the cliffs and coming right into the land.'

He grew up in the sunny Wellsian optimism of the 1930s, to have it blown apart by the war, which taught him about the horrors of which men were capable.

'I was at Portsmouth Barracks when it was bombed to pieces. The only place to go was a slit-trench with a thin concrete roof and a wooden seat to one side. I was there alone throughout the raid, listening to a machine gun outside. Afterwards, the machine-gun nest was all right. But twenty yards away, a petty officer had been trying to calm a couple of unruly seamen who'd joined up that day. To show them they shouldn't worry, he'd stood up, said, "Look, you can even stand up in an air raid . . ." and instantly had been blown in two. That night, we went to sleep in hammocks with a five-hundred-pound, delayed-action bomb under the floor a few yards away.'

Asked about his religious convictions, he said: 'Religion as a subject always ends in boredom because it's impossible to find an answer . . . The arguments about the Big Bang and the First Cause are valuable and proper intellectual arguments; but the only real apprehension of God is a feeling, a knowledge that he exists. All you know is that there's a light there – a stumbling, fumbling, torch-like perception of God.'

Did he worry about death? Did he fancy the idea of an afterlife? 'I'd sooner there wasn't an afterlife,' he said. 'I'd much rather not be *me* for thousands more years. Me? *Hah!* I don't mind extinction. The important thing is that God exists, not that man exists.'

Later he played a Schubert 'Impromptu' on the Bechstein grand piano in the drawing room (it was once his ambition to play at concert level), encouraged with silken sarcasm by his cherubic wife Lady Ann. As he played she leaned across the sofa to me. 'He really does play,' she confided, '*very loudly*.' Sir William was definitely not a fan of modern music. 'I loathe it. Not just pop music, but show tunes – all that mock emotion.'

Puritan and aesthete, sage and man of action, drawing-room charmer and Nobel-decorated visionary, Golding seemed a bluffly English version of a Renaissance Man. As we said goodbye, I wondered what he might have become if he'd been born two centuries earlier, and was the same age as his young hero, Edmund Talbot. A sailor? A teacher?

'*Not* a sailor,' he said with a shudder. 'The ordinary seaman had a hell of a time two hundred years ago. Probably a writer, although it was so much more difficult in those days. But far more likely, I think I would have been a *highwayman*. A rather *timorous* highwayman ...'

How much did I know about my new editor, Andrew Neil? I knew he was thirty-nine, four years older than me, and that he was Scottish, from the town of Paisley, which is washed by a tributary of the River Clyde, and gave the world both the Paisley shawl and that strange embryo design that turns up on fabrics from Tootal ties to Liberty-print squares. He'd read Politics and Economics at Glasgow University and rocketed into a job at *The Economist* two years after getting his MA. Ten years of covering the waterfront of UK and American news later, he'd arrived at the *Sunday Times* in 1983.

At my interview for the job, Andrew had been affable and charming, but behind his cooing and reassuring Renfrewshire delivery, I could hear a hum of scepticism. He beamed at the news that I was born to middle-class Irish parents, that I'd had a grammar-school education and taken an English degree at Oxford, despite having no connection with *Burke's Peera*ge or public school. His beam wavered when he saw the mess that my books pages on the *Standard* had become in that day's paper – the result of a wildcat strike in the Production department that had left the reviews almost entirely unillustrated. But it returned when I showed him some recent interviews I'd written for the magazine.

We shook hands, I went home, Andrew rang some newspaper friends to ask if I might be any good at the job, and, on hearing positive replies, offered it to me.

I said yes. I was just approaching my thirty-fifth birthday. It took me a few hours to register that I'd achieved my life's ambition (OK, not the *actual Times*, but the Sunday version, which was bigger, had a larger circulation, and used to be the literary home of my hero Cyril Connolly) with exactly *twelve days to spare*. Hurrah!

I'd heard that Andrew Neil remained fixated on politics and finance, but was less in tune with cultural matters. My friend Mick Brown, rock music scribe and connoisseur of all things spiritual,* told me that, a year before I arrived, he'd been staying late at the newspaper, writing at his desk. Neil had walked past, turned, come back and said:

'You're here very late, Mick. What are you working on?'

'I'm writing a big colour piece for the Features section,' Mick told him, 'on the Summer of '67.' To which Neil had replied: 'The summer of 1967? The summer Harold Wilson applied for membership of the EEC?'

I'd also heard that, in his early days in the editor's chair, Andrew's interests had been dominated by two things that weren't politics and economics, namely women and new technology. His passion for both had been expressed by a staff member's summation: 'If he can't fuck it, and he can't plug it into the mains, he doesn't want to know.' I'd assumed he must have been enraged by this vulgar one-liner; later I learned that he'd been so pleased by it, he'd had the line printed and framed for his office wall.

I also knew that he had an alarming side. I'd heard him described as 'menacing', and there was something about his big-browed face and hunched, round-shouldered truculence that rang alarm bells. By all accounts, rage was an emotion to which he was no stranger. People told me how alarming he could be if thwarted or disobeyed. Someone who'd worked on the News desk near the editor's office said the most bloodcurdling sound he'd ever heard was of Andrew bawling out a hack from the Insight section. It was a sustained verbal assault that climaxed with the words:

'DON'T *DEFFFYYYYYYYY ME!!*'

---

* It's an unusual hybrid of interests, rock and religion, but it gave Mick Brown certain advantages. Mick was known to be the only rock critic liked by Van Morrison, because they could converse at exactly the same level of sonorous mystical bollocks.

The editorial Conference, held every Tuesday, was quite different from the bear-pit of raillery and badinage I'd enjoyed at the *Evening Standard*. For one thing, it was much quieter. Twenty people, mostly men, ranged themselves in Neil's office on sofas and chairs around Neil's emperor-sized desk; some sat behind his sightline, as if hoping Neil might not realise they were there. Michael Williams, the puckish and humorous head of News and Features, took up a counter-strategy, sitting actually *at Neil's desk*, directly opposite him, in what seemed almost suicidally close proximity – were the editor to lose his temper, surely Williams might get a punch in the face? A roving eye, such as mine in my first Wapping Conference, might have noticed the basketball hoop perched above Neil's waste-paper bin – a rare sighting of levity – and the photograph of Neil interviewing Ronald Reagan at the White House, a trophy displayed with pride.

Neil sipped coffee from a mug and glanced through the story-lists brought by the section heads: the news stories, the list of possible features, the lists of arts reviews, the list of sports reports, and so on. Andrew knew, of course, what was coming in news, but greeted the other revelations mostly with a neutral silence. This is *OK*, the silence implied, but it ain't *earth-shaking*. Where, it asked, were the *must-read* stories?

One week, he asked the seated conferencers what ideas they had for a big feature – or investigation – the following Sunday. You're all talented journalists, he told them, you read the papers, you have many contacts – so what big question should we be asking? The assembled hacks regarded him in silence. (You what?) Neil looked around with an expression close to contempt.

'In that case,' he said, 'I say we postpone this Conference until 2 p.m. when we all come back with inspired suggestions about what should go in our paper.' We trooped out like schoolkids with smacked bottoms, most of us thinking, 'Bugger! Bang goes lunch!'

Most weeks, he would tick off a section head for offering a story that had been already covered by another paper; the City section head, Roger, a nervous, bespectacled man with the air of an anxious-to-please provincial accountant, was regularly chastised or mocked for some business news that was ancient history to Andrew. Sometimes a section editor might counter the editor's rebuke and an argument would follow, in which Neil's voice would grow softer and more dangerous. The combative spirit of Paisley Grammar School Debating Society clearly had never left his soul.

I thought myself mostly out of the danger zone because Andrew didn't take the Books section seriously; as far as he was concerned, it was a place for intellectual dilettantism and thousand-word essays on Thackeray or the Plantagenets. But sometimes, the Neil gaze turned on me. When I announced that the fiction lead would be *The Innocent* by Ian McEwan, he enquired, looking straight in front of him, 'I recall that McEwan's last novel, *The Child in Time*, represented quite a departure from the grisly and macabre material that made his name. Now comes *The Innocent*. Is that a work along the same lines?'

'You're, er, quite right about his last book,' I said. 'But I couldn't say for sure about the new one. I haven't had a chance to read it yet.'

'Let me understand this,' said Neil evenly. 'You are the literary editor of the *Sunday Times*, home of the finest Books section in the land, and you have *no opinion* about the latest work from an author popularly thought to be one of the finest British novelists since the war ...'

'I've had a lot to read lately ...' I countered feebly, like a squadron leader explaining that a broken shoelace has rendered him incapable of leading a bombing raid over Dresden.

Neil shook his head sadly and moved on to Sport.

'Never again,' I silently promised myself, 'will I be caught without a firm opinion of *every fucking book* published in this country.'

CHAPTER 11

———•·•———

Christopher Marlowe and the Sheep

By the summer of 1989, the Books section staff, had turned into a nest of singing birds. Harry, Cheryl, Penny, my super-smart secretary Joanna Duckworth, Austin McCurtain the paperbacks editor (a former Catholic priest), the children's editor Nicolette Jones and I had become a jolly septet in our polished glass home, operating in an atmosphere of mutual amusement, constant raillery and, I blush to recall, borderline sexist jokes. Harry and I once spent half an hour trying to establish exactly which kind of ocean-going vessel Cheryl most resembled in her stately progress down to the composing room. 'A galleon' didn't really convey the full-sailed magnificence of her transit. We finally settled on 'a flotilla of quinqueremes'.

Harry and I worked late on Thursday evenings, putting the Books section to bed, reading the proofs, checking corrections and dreaming up clever headlines. Harry was exceptionally good (and fast) at headlines. Once he was returning from the canteen when he found the Arts department standing around their desks at 9 o'clock in the evening, racking their brains. They'd been trying to think up a headline for an article about a forthcoming made-for-TV film about the Princess of Wales, and the news that she'd be played by Catherine Oxenberg, the daughter of Princess Elizabeth of Yugoslavia. 'It's driving us mad,' they said. 'Can you help?'

'The Di Is Cast,' said Harry, hardly breaking his stride back to his desk.

His annoying good looks, and the fact that he was single, had not gone unnoticed on the party circuit. Girls of aristocratic or academic pedigree were always hovering near him: Jane Wellesley, Julia Hobsbawm, Sabrina Guinness. He even showed up in *City Limits* magazine, in a feature about the 'Ten Most Eligible Bachelors in London Media'. It began, gallingly: 'Taller, younger and, to be brutally honest, easier on the eye than his boss, John Walsh, Harry Ritchie is . . .'

Every month, we'd ask a chap from Thomas J. Gaston, the second-hand book dealer, to come and take away the books that hadn't been sent out for review. His shop paid a percentage of the cover price of every one, meaning that, after six months, we had a bulging sack of fivers to spend. Technically, I guess, the money belonged to the *Sunday Times*, but we were the people who went to the trouble of converting books into cash, so we regarded it as a legitimate departmental perk. In early summer we decided to spend the windfall on a holiday – a bit of *esprit de corps* in action. I booked the seven of us a weekend trip to Amsterdam in mid-May, and felt mighty pleased. Then a blow struck.

I'd been asked to write a book called *Growing up Catholic* for Macmillan Publishers – an English take on a similar book published in the US. It was supposed to be a work of humorous intent, but I'd injected some personal wrath and venom into the stuff about Catholic sex education and the lurking proximity of Hell to every-thing you did*. Now it had been taken up by the Irish media. I'd been asked to appear on *The Late Late Show*, Ireland's number one TV chat show. The date was Friday 12 May, the day we were due to fly to Amsterdam.

---

* It's not a book I'm terribly proud of, but it brought me the great fortune of meeting Kate Jones, my editor at Macmillan. She was brilliant, passionate and well-read, a hyper-articulate feminist and *bonne vivante* who went on to become editorial director of Viking and Penguin General, looking after authors of the calibre of Barry Unsworth, Sara Paretsky and Esther Freud; she died of cancer at the tragically early age of 46.

What could I do? I could hardly miss the TV appearance, despite the fact that I might mortify my mother, who lived in Galway and was staunchly Catholic. But I didn't want to let down my staff on our Works Outing. In the end, unable to choose, I did both.

I was met at Dublin Airport by a genial chap called Brendan. He explained we had three hours before live transmission. He was, he said, 'the man who looks after the Talent' and suggested we went to the pub. I wondered if this was a terrific idea. The few times I'd appeared on BBC TV, a drop of gin in the Green Room beforehand had been relaxing. But going to Durty Nelly's bar for a couple of hours before appearing on Ireland's most popular gabfest (and *live* to boot) promised disaster. My sister, Madelyn, who also lived in Ireland, told me in 1983 how shocked she'd been to see R. D. Laing, the great Scottish psychiatrist, appear on *The Late Late Show* one Friday, clearly the worse for wear, slurring his words and lapsing into silences.

'Professor Laing,' the host, Gay Byrne, eventually said crossly, 'may I ask why you have chosen to appear on my show in a state of intoxication?' Laing replied that he thought their encounter would be more a warm little fireside chat than an interrogation, and had enjoyed a few snifters accordingly. Some of the studio audience called out, 'You're a disgrace!' Others noisily demanded, 'Why shouldn't a fella have a few jars on a Friday night for the love o' Jaysus?' and things broke up in disarray.

The car pulled up in Donnybrook, home of the nation's TV network. I met the other guests – a politician and a very polite folk band called The Rocking Chairs – and we went to a bar somewhere in the complex, where Brendan gave a fine impression of a carefree Dublin jackeen on a night out with the lads, rather than a well-paid RTE executive tasked with keeping six nervous TV guests calm and relatively sober. But he went too far by saying: 'Now! Two hours to go! Anyone for a lovely curry?' Six laughing guests abruptly remembered where they were, and how much they did *not* fancy a bout of diarrhoea while appearing on live TV.

I didn't realise that, when it was your turn, the studio guys wouldn't spend any time reassuring you about your imminent ordeal. They stand with you beside the big green curtain through which you reach the stage – and when the host ends his introduction by announcing your name, they do *not* squeeze your hand and mutter, 'You'll be fine'. A hand on the small of your back gives you a hard shove, like a parachute sergeant, and projects you into the dazzling lights, the applause of one hundred and fifty people in the studio audience – and the howlingly insincere smile of Gay Byrne, Ireland's favourite broadcaster.

My slot was twenty minutes long. Byrne began by asking about my schooldays, the nuns and Jesuit priests I'd encountered, and what a good education I must have enjoyed, to have got where I was. I said I hoped my brain might have flourished just as well in a Protestant public school, where I wouldn't have had to suffer the torture of being a Catholic sinner, forever forced to examine my conscience and be wary of Occasions of Sin (such as being on a beach with a girl) or Sins of Omission (failing to rescue someone from being assaulted by shiv-bearing thugs).

Byrne adopted his most headmasterly expression. 'Is this not,' he boomed, theatrically, 'just intellectual arrogance, Mr Walsh?'

I was familiar with that phrase, and had a reply. 'There's nothing remotely intellectual about wishing people would stop telling you you're wrong all the time,' I said. 'But I know that phrase very well. My father used to say that. It's obviously a phrase Catholic fathers are taught to say to their children if they show signs of backsliding in their faith.'

Things became more fun when we got onto sex. I mentioned how much I'd enjoyed reading the Irish *Sunday Press* (my parents subscribed), whose famous agony aunt Angela McNamara would give advice about sex to young men and women. Asked whether French kissing led to pregnancy, she'd say, No, but it was still 'sinful outside marriage' or outside a phenomenally long betrothal. We were rollicking along, with much audience laughter, until I complained, with sudden vehemence, about 'the Catholic Church's creepy fascination with what boys and girls do together', and asked why grown-up people should have their sexual behaviour dictated by 'a cabal of geriatric virgins'.

That was a step too far. I realised too late that everyone in the audience had priests and nuns as friends, neighbours and relatives, and they weren't going to hear them being insulted. The questions became heated, then hostile and shouty. I was relieved when Byrne turned his gaze to the Irish minister of Turf and his trenchant views on the economy.

Next day, over breakfast, Brendan told me he'd drop me in O'Connell Street where the capital's biggest bookshop might ask me to sign copies of *Growing Up Catholic*. 'They're expecting you around noon.'

I thought of the angry faces in last night's audience. I imagined myself sitting on a chair, imprisoned in Eason's bookshop shortly after noon, under a heavy fire of eyes. And insults. And, shortly after that, eggs . . .

'Sorry, Brendan,' I said, 'I hate to disappoint but I can't do that. Got to be at the airport at noon. I'm catching a plane to Amsterdam to see some dear friends . . .'

Every week, to hear John Carey's lead review inching its way through the office fax machine was to experience a thrill of anticipation. His pieces were single-space-typed, as if any kind of interlinear editing from me was obviously out of the question; they were always exactly 1,200 words and shout-out-loud brilliant.

We had an understanding that I would ring him within the hour to acknowledge receipt and offer comments. Seldom did my comments amount to more than praise and the singling out of an especially good line. Carey had been at this game since 1975, and had brought the book review to the zenith of sound judgement and readability.

He was fearless in his assessments of literary superstars, silkenly expressed. Reviewing Michael Holroyd's biography (Volume 1) of George Bernard Shaw, he mocked the playwright's prolixity by drawing attention to the author's photograph on the back cover: 'Glum and costive, [Holroyd] looks like a man whose otherwise desirable residence is sited directly beneath the main flight path of an international airport. For years now his life has been disrupted by a shattering and virtually incessant din, which banishes reflection and repose . . .' He meant, of course, the voice of Shaw – 'optimistic, argumentative, maddeningly genial' – that 'has harangued him daily.'

Reviewing a biography of Yeats, Carey wrote: 'Was he really all that intelligent? Some bits of evidence suggest the contrary. He was substandard at school. He never learned to spell: even as a grown man, simple monosyllables foxed him . . . His gullibility was, seemingly, fathomless. Mysticism and magic, to which he was introduced by the half-batty George Russell, occupied much of his waking and sleeping life. He believed he conversed with the old Celtic gods and a copious ragbag of other supernaturals . . . In his relations with Maud Gonne, too, he comes across as a credulous simpleton . . .'

A child of south London middle-class parents (his father was an accountant, his mother a secretary), and a passionate defender of grammar schools, Carey detested snobbery, privilege and contempt for popular culture, as he made clear in *The Intellectuals and the Masses: Pride and Prejudice among the Literary Intelligentsia 1880–1939.*[*]

Many of his reviews inspected the private lives of celebrated writers and held them up for critical inspection. But he never lost sight of genuine achievement, no matter how squalid or hypocritical

---

[*] The book argued that the chief exponents of modernist literature (Lawrence, Forster, Woolf, Pound, Shaw, Wells, Huxley, Yeats) were repulsed by the culture of 'the masses', and came to regard them as vermin, ants, creatures worthy of extinction; an attitude which, elsewhere in the 1920s and 1930s, led to the concentration camps.

the life of its achiever. When the *Selected Letters of Philip Larkin 1940–1985* was published in 1992, and the literary world collectively clutched its pearls with horror at their casual racism and Larkin's fondness for watching pre-pubertal girls gyrating on TV, Carey detected 'the howling inner emptiness, the shrunken mental horizons, the boredom, lassitude and hypochondria' that lay behind them. He concluded his review, 'This is the most enjoyable, as well as the most enlightening, collection of letters I have ever read by any writer.'

One of my favourite Carey reviews, showing his mastery of tone when dealing with shocking subjects, was of Fiona McCarthy's biography of Eric Gill, the sculptor. It began:

'Fiona McCarthy's life of Eric Gill uncovers a lot that has not been made public before. It appears from Gill's diaries that he enjoyed incestuous relationships over a long period with two of his sisters and with his two elder daughters. He also had sexual congress with a dog. For a lay brother of the order of Saint Dominic, who wore the girdle of chastity of the Confraternity of Angelic Warfare, this is obviously not a good record.'

Note how Carey does not condemn the incest, let alone the bestiality (I love the fastidious shift from 'incestuous relationships' to 'sexual congress' with the dog, as if to stress that the latter didn't count as a 'relationship'); he wants to condemn the hypocrisy involved in the high-minded Gill's misbehaviour. (And don't you love that 'obviously'?)

Carey makes his disapproval clear, but qualifies it by giving it context. Here he is remarking on the fact that the artist required a bare white cell to work in, but also needed regular sex every day: 'Gill was a great artist . . . and the contradiction between rigour and voluptuousness, which made him look a fraud to outsiders, was vital for his work. In his nude studies, the tension between clean hard lines and luscious female roundness is the key to the eroticism.' This shrewd combination of art appreciation and human understanding is very Carey. But when he wants to show his disgust at his subject's behaviour, he does by emphasising Gill's amoral

322   CIRCUS OF DREAMS

practicality in a way that gives the reader a chill: 'He did not think females worth educating so his daughters never went to school. Their ignorance and isolation must have made it easier for their father to abuse them.'

Carey was an expert handler of the pungent detail. Here, describing life on Gill's farm commune, he puts the reader uncomfortably in the centre of the action:

'After dinner would come Compline in the Chapel, and then Gill might show you his drawings of his own private parts in various states of arousal – exact in every detail, he would explain, the measurements having been taken with a footrule by his secretary.' That word 'footrule' gives Carey's picture-painting extra pungency, and the reader a fastidious shudder. And that poor secretary of Gill's. Did they tell her, when she attended typing school, that her future duties might include measuring her boss's cock every afternoon?

The only modern critic who could hold a candle to Carey was our own chief fiction reviewer, Peter Kemp. I'd admired his stuff for ages. His review of *The Bonfire of the Vanities*, published shortly before I arrived at the newspaper, was stuffed like a Thanksgiving turkey with pungent verbal details. He seemed able to match Wolfe himself in evoking several shades of dread in a single paragraph:

'Wolfe sends his couple skidding with accelerating alarm round blocks razed to the ground, down pot-holed streets, through nerve-wrenching blasts of noise from crumbled buildings and past glimpses of ugly fights. Lost in what seems a giant junkyard over which darkness is falling, they cower – she in her smartly shoulder-padded Avenue Foch *couture*, he in his Huntsman jacket and Jermyn Street shoes – as what seem to be faces from another species peer and leer through the electronically locked windows of the *de luxe* car halted at a red traffic light . . .'

Peter had published books on Muriel Spark and H. G. Wells. He was the editor of the 499-page *Oxford Dictionary of Literary*

Quotations, a bulging anthology of things that two hundred and thirty writers had said, over three thousand years, about Creativity, Drink, Money, Sex and (especially amusing) Other Writers. Although he always wore a flat cap and collier's woolly scarf when visiting the Books office, and proudly claimed never to have missed an episode of *Coronation Street*, there was nothing provincial or Little-England-ish about Peter's tastes in literature. He was one of the first reviewers to champion the rise of the post-colonial novel and the work of Salman Rushdie, Timothy Mo, Rohinton Mistry and a score of others.

About British writers he could be crushing. Peter Ackroyd's *English Music*, one of a sequence of novels about English culture, featured a character called Timothy Harcombe. In the book he works as the security guard in an art gallery where he has several vivid reveries about English literature, music and painting. Kemp mercilessly undermined the novel's visionary core by wondering why the gallery should employ a chronic narcoleptic to oversee its surveillance facilities.

Reviewing Douglas Adams's *The Long Dark Teatime of the Soul* in October 1988, he laid on a verbal feast of scientific and aeronautical imagery: 'In *The Hitch-Hiker's Guide to the Galaxy* and *The Restaurant at the End of the Universe*, Adams soared hilariously away from the portentous atmosphere enveloping much contemporary science fiction . . . Then a law of physics, like those with which Adams so entertainingly played, began to take its toll. Entropy – loss of energy, running down, falling apart – showed itself. Later books failed to make the lift-off into buoyant burlesque and nose-dived into soggy facetiousness.'

Kemp's conclusion was regretful but still appreciative of the author's wild imagination: 'At one point in *The Hitch-Hiker's Guide*, a character was strapped to a battery of electronic equipment, "imagery intensifiers, rhythm modulators, alliterative residulators", designed to boost his literary powers. Something similar now seems urgently called for to re-activate Adams's comic flair and rescue his talents from their plummeting trajectory.' Here, as so often with Kemp, one finished the review convinced of the rightness of his judgement, but also amazed by the machine-tooled precision of his sentences.

I enjoyed having lunch with John Carey. We'd meet twice a year at the Savoy on a Friday at 1 p.m., consume a Dover sole each, drink a bottle of Chablis and chat. Sometimes we'd talk about recent reviews in the Books section, sometimes about things we shared (we were both south Londoners – he from Barnes, I from Battersea – and both grammar-school boys) and sometimes people we both knew: my friend Philip Kerr's wife, Jane Thynne, for instance, was Carey's beloved niece.*

We compared notes about writers we admired (Martin Amis, Craig Raine, Seamus Heaney, Stevie Smith), and mocked the idiocy of the new literary-critical orthodoxies of structuralism, postmodernism and similar atrocities. John smartly remarked that the title of David Lodge's explanatory book *Working with Structuralism* sounded to him as alluring as *Living with Sciatica*.

Once I told Carey about my habit (inspired by Clive James) of reading the odd work of bestselling popular fiction – a thriller by Tom Clancy, say, or historical romance by Philippa Gregory – to see if it could tell us something about how great fiction works. 'If Maeve Binchy,' I suggested, 'can make the reader care for two whole chapters about whether Mrs O'Flynn gets herself new curtains in time for the visit from her son and his horrible new wife, then surely one can admire . . .' Carey came over all John Ruskin. 'You cannot seriously suggest,' he said gravely, 'that this has *anything at all* to do with literature . . .' After which I'd move on to, say, D. H. Lawrence, about whose work he always talked with passion.

John Mortimer liked being lunched at The Ivy, which had recently reopened in Covent Garden, and featured its new co-owner,

---

* Jane was to become a prolific and successful novelist in her own right after 1997.

Jeremy King, as a greeter. I'd never come across the concept of a greeter before. It meant having a handsome but unknown alpha male looming before your table, asking if you were enjoying your meal and encouraging you to gossip about which eminent people you'd seen lately. Whoever they were, Jeremy would always know them – The Ivy was *the* London place-to-be in the late 1980s, if you weren't a Groucho member.

The Inns of Court's most famous champagne socialist, Mortimer always kicked off with a glass of Dom Pérignon, and followed it with a proletarian plate of liver and bacon, to balance things in his political system. He told lots of legal jokes, often about Lord Mackay of Clashfern, recently appointed the UK's lord chancellor. Mackay was a man of frugal tastes. I loved the story of the small party he threw for the Faculty of Advocates, at which he offered tea, toast and a minuscule pot of honey. One of the guests regarded the honeypot and said, 'I see your lordship keeps a bee . . .' Mortimer also liked talking about his many children, especially Emily, who'd done work experience for me at the *Standard*, and was soon to make a reputation for herself as an actress.

I greeted with slightly less delight the prospect of lunch with George Steiner. He'd been reviewing for the *Sunday Times* since the mid-1970s, and was considered quite a clever chap. No, let me try that again. He was regarded as an absolute intellectual giant, the polymath's polymath, a colossus in a dozen disciplines, some of which he'd invented. He'd held key academic positions at Oxford, Cambridge, Princeton, Harvard and Geneva. He was a one-man bulkhead against the forces of philistinism and the democratisation of high culture, but also (like Carey) against the bogus sophistication of modern literary theory.

I'd read about his parents, who brought him up to speak three languages: his father made him read Homer's *Iliad* in the ancient Greek when he was six; and although he was born with a withered arm, his mother brought him up to use it like a normal one.

I'd heard about his row with Cambridge academe: when the English faculty refused to grant him a full lectureship, relations between Steiner and the university turned to permafrost. The dons thought him a bit of a charlatan, while he thought them borderline antisemitic. Normal relations were resumed only when he was elected to an 'extraordinary fellowship' at Churchill College, which he'd co-founded in 1961, as a consolation prize. Academic people spoke of Steiner with respect for his genius, but a suspicion that he was a fake. 'It wouldn't surprise me,' one said, 'to find he has a perfectly serviceable right arm behind his back.'

So you can understand my apprehensiveness about spending two hours at the Savoy Grill with this alarmingly brilliant man. I'd read his novel, *The Portage to San Cristobal of A.H.*, in which Adolf Hitler is found in the Amazon jungle, put on trial and allowed to defend his outrages, but I was reluctant to chat, over lunch, about such a fizzing bomb of a book.

Was it too late to read *After Babel*, his study of translation and hermeneutics, published fourteen years earlier? How about his first book, *Tolstoy or Dostoevsky: An Essay in Contrast?* Perhaps I could skim-read *The Brothers Karamazov* and *Anna Karenina* in the week I had available . . .

You can imagine what happened. The week was stuffed with appointments – two book launches, dinner with an agent, fatherly duties at home, reading *Each Peach Pear Plum* to my sweet daughter Sophie, rather than Steiner's *On Difficulty and Other Essays*.

Suddenly, out of the blue, Friday morning arrived. Lunch was planned for 1 p.m. I had reviews to commission, phone calls to make. Could I ask the cuttings library to find me some recent articles by George? Noon drew alarmingly near. As I tried to keep a lid on the rising panic in my breast, I became aware of a commotion in the Arts department outside. There was laughter, and knowing remarks. I saw people leaving their desks to look over the shoulders of colleagues.

Cheryl came in, clocked my enquiring look and said, 'It's the

Daily Mail. Everyone's terribly excited. Day Five of the Pamella story, as told to Lynda Lee-Potter.'

One of the year's big revelations had been about Andrew Neil's girlfriend Pamella Bordes, a staggeringly beautiful former Miss India, whom he'd dated the previous summer. In spring 1989, the *News of the World* revealed that she'd been a prostitute and had been given a House of Commons security pass by a Tory MP.

'What,' I asked coldly, 'is so exciting about Day Five?'

'It's about the editor,' said Cheryl. 'Pamella's spilled the beans about going out with Andrew. Where he took her, how he behaved, and what they got up to at weekends. She says she did his laundry and washed the stains on his pillowslips – which she says were caused by a hair-restoring tonic.'

'Cheryl,' I said disapprovingly, 'I'm just going to lunch with the world's most brilliant man for a lengthy discussion about hermeneutics. I cannot sit here listening to tittle-tattle.'

I looked at my watch. It was 12.46. Holy shit! I was going to be late. I leapt from the desk, rushed to the entrance of the Wapping complex. Thank God, a taxi was idling at the traffic lights on the Highway.

'The Savoy,' I yelled, 'and step on it!'

It took seventeen minutes. I was three minutes late! My heart was pounding. A dozen fascinating questions jostled in my head, like paratroopers waiting to jump. Should I ask about how different translators handled Dostoevsky's religious beliefs? About Tolstoy's attitude to the serf? About, er, the weather in Geneva . . .?

In the entrance to the Grill Room stood a short, dapper-looking figure, clad in a grey business suit, smiling a thin smile behind professorial specs. I stammered my apologies. He waved them away with his left hand. We sat down. I ordered champagne, and he bowed graciously.

'I think the main problem I have with Tolstoy . . .' I began airily.

He put his hand on my arm. 'Before we have our serious discussion,' he said, 'you must tell me. This thing in the *Daily Mail*?

About your editor and the beautiful girlfriend and the hair tonic?
Do you think it's *true*?'

I had an interesting encounter with Rupert Murdoch. It was August
1989, and the world was exploding with news: Tiananmen Square,
the collapse of Communism, the Princess Diana revelations. Before
morning Conference that Tuesday, we were told that the meeting
would take place, not in the editor's office as usual, but in the
boardroom, in an unfamiliar part of the Wapping complex.

We'd no idea why the venue had been changed but when we
got there it was clear that something (or someone) important was
afoot. In the boardroom, tubular-steel chairs lined the perimeter of
a long table festooned with water bottles, glasses and notepads.
A multi-coloured summer buffet groaned on a cream-clothed
sideboard: yellow slices of melon with Parma ham, platters of pink
roast beef and pale orange salmon, white Alps of potato salad and
swathes of healthy greenery – beans, asparagus, lettuce. Bowls of
strawberries, tubs of ice cream and sorbet waited for those who
made it to the end.

I was the last to arrive and, by the time I did, most of the chairs
had been bagged, except for two. One was on the editor's immediate
right, a little too close to Andrew Neil, in the boss chair, for comfort.
The other empty chair was placed slightly behind the editor's at a
slight angle to it – at first slip, so to speak.

Conference began. We discussed the appalling tragedy of the
Marchioness pleasure steamer that had sunk in the Thames, with
the loss of fifty-one lives, after it was hit and crushed by a dredger
called the *Bowbelle*. It had happened at the weekend, too late for
the Sunday papers, so we would have plenty of time to investigate
the cause and talk to survivors 'and,' said Neil, 'we will insist on a
stringent review of safety measures on the Thames in general.'

The news list went on: developments in Eastern Europe,
scandal at the BBC, misbehaviour at the Vatican ... Then, ten

minutes into the meeting, the door opened and a bespectacled, bald head appeared.

'Rupert! Come in! Come in!' called Andrew Neil, as the Grand Panjandrum of the Popular Press walked in.

He cut, to my surprise, an unprepossessing figure for a global media Titan. His face was always moving: making little grimaces, awkward little smiles, little moues of concern, eye-narrowings, eyebrow-raisings – he resembled one of those Popperfoto contacts sheets, depicting the complete range of expressions available to mortal beings.

The editor ushered him to the first-slip chair, where he sat, uncomfortably close to me. I had never been so close to a billionaire before. I felt self-conscious before his gaze. Among my colleagues on the paper, I was a chap with a pretty wide knowledge of literature and the world of criticism, and possessed a serviceable if mildly pretentious prose style. To Mr Murdoch, I knew, I was just another fucking journo.

Conference restarted. The sports editor went back to his predictions about the sale of a famous football club, but hardly had he begun to speak when Murdoch interrupted him.

'If ya don't moind me sayin' so,' he said, 'shouldn't we be discussing the levels of safety on the Tims? Afta that accidint? That seems to be most *voidal* topic of the moment.'

Around the table, the *Sunday Times* section heads voiced their agreement with noisy delight. Despite the fact that they'd been chewing the topic pretty thoroughly only ten minutes earlier, they greeted Murdoch's suggestion as pure genius. 'Absolutely!' they said, and, 'Of course!' They (perhaps I should say 'we') stopped just short of smiting our brows and shouting, 'Why didn't *we* think of that?' So, river-based London safety initiatives came under discussion for the second time that afternoon.

We continued with the Foreign News agenda, then Sport, then Arts, and then it was (gulp) my turn. But hardly had I embarked on my list of commissioned book reviews when Murdoch cut across me.

'I was readin' this noo book on the pline over,' he said. 'About that appeasement business before the war? Bloody interestin' about Churchill goin' off to see Hitler and talk peace!'

'Chamberlain surely?' I said, before I could stop myself. I sounded like a murmurous pedant at High Table in All Souls.

'What?' barked Murdoch.

'I think,' I said, 'it was Neville Chamberlain who visited Hitler in Munich. Not Churchill, although of course he . . .'

'Churchill, Chamberlain, whatever,' said Murdoch, as if anyone whose name began with 'Ch' would have done in 1938 political circles. 'Ah we reviewin' it?'

'Ah – not at the moment,' I said, random thoughts reeling around my brain. I had no idea which book he was talking about.

'WHOY NOT?' Murdoch demanded. There was a horrible silence. My job – indeed my newspaper career – suddenly hung by a gossamer thread.

'Oh, I remember now,' I lied. 'The book is called, er, *Chamberlain and the, er, Quest for Peace*' (it was a wild guess but a pretty good one – it turned out to be *Chamberlain and the Lost Peace* by John Charmley). 'We're, um, reviewing it next month along with some other books about the run-up to the war.'

Murdoch nodded. The meeting continued. I could breathe again.

At 1 p.m. we adjourned for lunch. At the buffet I helped myself to roast beef and potatoes, plus fruit salad and peach sorbet, and bore them back to the table. I ate the first course with relish, glad to have survived a sticky confrontation, and chatted to the woman on my right.

'You were really on the spot there,' she commented. 'Good job you knew what he was talking about.'

Abruptly the meeting restarted, and I turned back towards the editor's (and the proprietor's) chairs. Murdoch had ignored the pudding course and now sat in a more relaxed pose, his left ankle perched on his right knee. He seemed very close to my chair. As the editor called us to order, I reached forward for a spoonful of fruit salad and sorbet. But I couldn't reach it. Something was stopping me.

I looked down. Murdoch's foot was resting against the tubular arm of my chair, his shoe parked immovably against my jacket. I reached forward again, spoon aloft, hoping to shame him into letting go his shoe's restraining pressure. But he seemed to be oblivious, talking animatedly to the room about the likelihood of his buying Manchester United. He was also making damn sure I wasn't going to have my peach sorbet.

Was it just carelessness? Or was it a petty revenge for being contradicted, in front of his Pommy section editors, by an annoying git from the Books cupboard? It took a couple of practice pulls and a final admonitory tug to release my garment. I thought of flicking a spoonful of sorbet at his crotch but decided, on the whole, better not.

One thing you couldn't fault Murdoch for was spending money on book-related initiatives. He invested heavily in a stand-alone Books section in his beloved *Sunday Times*, even though it was, technically, a rival to his *Times Literary Supplement*. He spent what sometimes seemed a fortune on serialisation deals with non-fiction books, and took part in expensive serial auctions. For while it seemed there was no former Cabinet minister with a memoir in the pipeline to whom he would not offer a vast sum (£75,000, £100,000?) for the serial rights.

Sometimes, however, you could find Murdoch using his oceanic financial resources to back something small-scale and worthwhile – something that might not produce a massive return on the investment, but simply bring to life an event that would please many people. One such was the Hay-on-Wye Festival of Literature and Arts.

The idea of the festival was dreamed up in 1987 around the kitchen table of the Florence family of Hay-on-Wye (pop. 1,500). They comprised Norman and Rhoda Florence and their son, Peter. Norman was an actor who'd been in films (he was in *The Singer Not*

the Song, in 1961, with Dirk Bogarde and John Mills) and had run
Sam Wanamaker's Globe Playhouse Trust in the late 1970s. Peter,
twenty-three, a Cambridge graduate, was starting out in the same
ballpark, performing a travelling one-man show using the words
and poetry of Wilfred Owen. At the kitchen table, the Florences
discussed setting up a literary festival with the £100 they'd won in
a card game, or so the family mythology goes.

Hay-on-Wye had no literary reputation before the 1960s. In
1922, the year that saw the publication of *Ulysses* and *The Waste
Land*, the town's only famous event was the hanging of a local
solicitor called Herbert Rowse Armstrong who had murdered his
wife. In 1961, however, a guy called Richard Booth opened his first
second-hand book shop in the town's fire station. Four years later,
he opened a second in the disused cinema. Over the next fifteen
years, Booth was joined by more aspirant booksellers, apparently
heedless of the danger of competition. By 1977, Hay-on-Wye was
'the world's first book town' with thirty second-hand shops. That
year, the monomaniacal Booth declared it an independent kingdom,
of which he was ruler: he even produced his own currency. The
nation's press began to take notice. Martin Amis travelled to Wales
for the *Observer* and glumly pronounced the contents of Booth's
flagship emporium almost entirely worthless.

A decade later, twelve months after the kitchen-table conversation, the first Hay festival got under way in 1987. Details of
performers and audience are hazy, but three important things
happened. 1) Norman Florence died, and his widow and son
resolved to continue the festival in his honour. 2) Peter Florence's
capacious address book, and his fearlessness in approaching
important writers, paid off when he found himself speaking to
Arthur Miller, the American playwright. Asked if he would like
to attend a literary festival in the town, Miller replied: 'Hay-on-
Wye? What is that, some kinda sandwich?' And 3) Once Miller was
involved, word of the festival reached the ears of Murdoch. He
offered to sponsor it for the next few years, putting the resources of

the *Sunday Times* Books section to work on it. This meant having a chap from the Books section there in the thick of it. Which is why I found myself barrelling down the M4 on 26 May 1989, turning off at Swindon and heading north to Ross-on-Wye and the dark majesty of the Brecon Beacons.

I hadn't known what to expect, but I loved Hay-on-Wye from the outset. The long main street full of wholesome, home-made, honest-to-God produce, the butchers, the bakers, the jam emporium, the exotic-spices bazaar, the four or five bric-a-brac shops selling Victorian fire-dogs or lengths of parachute silk – and on either side of each one, it seemed, yet another pair of bookshops. Dog-eared Penguin Classics ran the length of the windowsills in the ruined castle. Garish hardback thrillers brought a dash of drama to the medium-density fibreboard shelves in the old cinema.

In these early days, the festival action was confined to the Kilverts Hotel, a grand, Grade-II-listed Victorian house overlooking the Wye valley. Round the back, you emerged into a bosky garden where a candy-striped marquee welcomed the festival's visitors. Hay bales lay around the canvas floor, for rustic effect, but, thank God, proper seats were available for the literary stars.

Who were they? A mix of highbrow and middle-brow literature could be seen in the presence of Peter Levi, former Jesuit priest, poet, traveller and outgoing professor of Poetry at Oxford; Ben Zephaniah, the dreadlocked Brummie dub poet whom Levi had beaten to the professorship in 1984; and P. D. James, the Queen of Crime, whom Levi was to introduce at her own event. Her most recent book, *A Taste for Death*, had been submitted by her publishers, Faber, for the Booker Prize, a pleasing elevation of the crime genre. Despite being a crime writer, Dame Phyllis was nobody's idea of a middle-brow; she was a fellow of Downing College, Cambridge.

Fiction was represented by Ian McEwan, Mary Wesley, Beryl Bainbridge, Shena Mackay, David Lodge and Lucy Ellmann. Among the poets was Peter Reading, whose collection *Stet* had won the Whitbread poetry prize. Fiona Pitt-Kethley, who'd been described by Laurie Lee as 'the most beautiful English poet since Rupert Brooke', would read with Liz Lochhead – and, a little surprisingly, with Norman Willis, the burly general secretary of the TUC. Willis told the audience that, when he was in Russia, people were much more impressed that he was a poet than that he was a trades' union boss. And Heathcote Williams, the poet and visionary, who had triumphed with *Whale Nation* and *Falling for a Dolphin*, was at Hay to launch his new project, *Sacred Elephant*. You could see him outside the candy-striped marquee, teaching Polly Samson, the mother of his son Charlie, how to juggle.

I'd been signed up for two events. One was to chair a discussion of Coleridge's 'Kubla Khan', 192 years after its composition in 1797, between Richard Holmes (whose wonderful biography of the *Ancient Mariner* poet would be published in 1998) and A. S. Byatt, whose novel *Possession*, about the secret love affair between two Victorian poets, would win the Booker Prize in 1990. I remember it being an elevated conversation about two questions that had been asked for almost two centuries – first, was it any good as an actual poem, as opposed to a fragment of mysticism as fake as a séance?, and second, was the 'mighty fountain' that 'momently was forced' midway through the poem, supposed to be an orgasm? The main thing that sticks in my memory, however, is the sight of Ms Byatt being attacked by tiny spiders, abseiling from the canvas roof and landing in her hair.

The other event was a discussion about fiction and fact, starring Julian Barnes with *A History of the World in 10 1/2 Chapter*s, Marina Warner with her novel *The Lost Father*, shortlisted for the previous year's Booker Prize, and a twenty-five-year-old ex-public schoolboy called Paul Watkins, whose novel *Calm at Sunset, Calm at Dawn* was set among the Rhode Island fishing community. I was there to tease out the borders of that which is experienced and that which is imagined.

Julian Barnes's book offered a series of essays, told in dry, sometimes argumentative prose, about historical (or biblical, or even metaphysical) events reimagined through a filter of art or fantasy: here's an insider's report on life inside Noah's Ark; here's the ghastly true-life survival strategies behind Géricault's *Raft of the Medusa*, and here's a report of the daily grind in Paradise. Marina's novel was concerned with a woman imagining her Italian mother's family's life as they emigrate to New York; and how it chimed with her belief that her grandfather had died fighting a duel. Lastly Paul Watkins's book turned his experiences among the crew of a scallop trawler into a coming-of-age novel about a youth rejecting his grand family to embrace real life at its harshest.

The discussion was lively but superficial.

Julian Barnes wondered if Watkins (Eton and Yale) had encountered many other Old Etonians in the fishing fleets, all seeking gritty *realismo* as research for their books. Someone in the audience wondered how hard it had been for Watkins to find he had the same name as one of Charles Manson's homicidal 'Family' who had also written a book. A wag asked Marina Warner if she was proud of being the titular scribe in the Dire Straits song, 'Lady Writer on the TV'.

That strain of mild misbehaviour could often be found at Hay-on-Wye. Like the invariably muddy opening weekends and the Shepherds ice cream, it became part of the Hay experience. Something about being so far from London society brought out a wayward element. When Arthur Miller arrived in the town, as the star of the 1989 festival (and believe me, it was disconcerting to walk across Hay Bridge in the sunshine and notice the Great American Playwright, the bald eagle of twentieth-century US drama, striding towards you), they had to cancel plans to film his talk live for Sky Arts TV. Why? Because the organisers were told that too many local geezers had promised their mates in the pub that they planned to join the ensuing Q&A session, just so they could ask Miller: 'So Arthur, tell us – what was it like to fuck Marilyn Monroe?'

After the excitement of my first experience of Hay, I couldn't wait to return for more larks in the sunshine and pints in the

Kilverts Hotel (and the Swan and the Blue Boar and the Black
Lion). I'd quickly grown to love the setting, the golden light on the
fields in May, the *al fresco* lunches in the ruined church, and the
strangely un-Arcadian experience of listening to Charles Nicholl
reading, from his book *The Reckoning*, the shocking details of the
fatal stabbing of Christopher Marlowe in a London tavern while,
through the tent flap, you could see the sheep placidly cropping
grass on the mild Welsh hillside.

We Hay fans soon discovered that this end of the Brecon Beacons
wasn't a recent discovery by bookish Londoners. Several literary
figures had country retreats up there. One was Brenda Maddox, the
Massachusetts-born, London-based biographer of D. H. Lawrence
and Nora Joyce. She'd bought a cottage near Brecon with her husband,
Sir John Maddox, long-time editor of the rarefied scientific journal,
Nature. Together they threw parties at the cottage for luminaries in
both the literary and scientific worlds. Once I turned from chatting to
Richard Holmes about Shelley and found myself in a frankly weird
conversation with James Watson, co-author with Francis Crick of the
paper that proposed the double-helix structure of DNA and won the
Nobel Prize for Medicine in 1953. Prof Watson didn't want to talk
about that, though; having clocked that I was a journalist, he wanted
to air his view that racial stereotypes about black people or Jews have
their foundation in genetics. After fifteen minutes of hearing that
black skin means its owner has a bigger libido than a white skin,
I looked around wildly for my hostess to bail me out.

Another local dweller was Arnold Wesker, the prolific playwright,
who was introduced to Hay by Tom Maschler, who helped him buy
a beautiful but semi-ruined cottage from a Welsh hill farmer for
£2,500. The Cape chairman had bought his own cottage, Carney,
when he was only twenty-four; he'd been enchanted by its remote-
ness, with sheep and wild ponies scattered around the hillside.
He also liked its literary connections: Eric Gill, the sculptor, had a
studio at nearby Capel-y-ffin, and Francis Kilvert, the diary-writing
clergyman, came from Clyro. Maschler himself added to the

bookish reputation of Carney, by having his author Bruce Chatwin stay in the cottage while writing *On the Black Hill.*

One summer Tom asked me to join him and his wife Regina for dinner at the cottage, and I was delighted to find that among the guests was Redmond O'Hanlon, whom I knew well, and Ian McEwan, whom I knew only by repute and by my having read everything he'd written, including his TV plays and opera libretto. Dinner was fine, the food chilled salmon and strawberry fool from Hay's finest delicatessen, the conversation gossipy and hilarious. I was struck by McEwan's hesitant, rather feline manner in company. He was courteous of other people's desire to hold the floor with anecdotes, while restricting himself to quiet comments and questions that would keep things going.

Night fell, the moon rose, stars appeared through the window and, by ten-thirty, the company was flagging. Tom and Regina saw their other guests off the premises, looked at Ian, Redmond and me, and said: 'There's a bottle of claret here which I haven't opened. Why don't you three take it with you to your hotel? We're off to bed. We'll see you all tomorrow.'

This was a generous offer. I was, in fact, prosaically billeted back in town at the Swan; but, having a car and being marginally less pissed than the others, I was elected to drive them home … which was the Abbey Hotel, next door to the ruins of Llanthony Priory, a fabulous Norman Gothic extravagance dating back to 1100. Its south-west tower was part of the Abbey Hotel. Redmond, the intrepid traveller, had typically chosen the room right at the top. He suggested we climb up there, open the wine in his room and finish off the evening in manly carousing.

Brandishing the claret, he led the way. It was a bugger of a climb – about a hundred winding steps, narrow and perilous, with minimal lighting on the stone wall. Finally we reached the top. Redmond let us into his room, where he proceeded to open the single window and let a gust of cold air, a hundred feet above the ground, slice our flushed faces.

Ian and I sat on the bed while Redmond fussed about, looking for a corkscrew. Naturally there was none, so he forced the cork with a Yale key.

'The only problem now,' he said, 'is finding some glasses. You can hardly drink a Saint-Émilion straight from the neck.' He tried the bathroom cupboard and the chest of drawers without success, then got down on his knees to check under the bed.

'Ah-ha!' he cried. 'Just the thing!' And from under the ancient divan, he extracted a large – really large; *full-bottomed*, so to speak – flowery china chamber pot.

Ian and I peered inside. We saw dust. No stains, nor evidence of sordid night-time voidance, only dust. But it clearly hadn't been washed in weeks. Months. Possibly a century. Even an historic era.

'This'll do,' said Redmond, sploshing gouts of the expensive liquid into the bowl.

'Chin chin!' he said, raising the chamber pot to his lips.

'Redmond!' yelled Ian McEwan. '*Don't!*'

'Mmmmm?' said Redmond, tilting the noisome receptacle with both hands.

'*Do not drink from that thing!*' Ian shouted. '*It's disgusting! It's full of germs!*'

Ian wasn't just being a bit fastidious. He sounded aghast, spooked, appalled. He put his hand on the chinaware and removed it from his friend's grasp.

I watched with fascination as the master of the macabre, the connoisseur of grotesquerie, the doyen of human depravity and bodily revulsion, responded with abject disgust to the sight of someone applying their gob to a dusty chamber pot in a hotel bedroom.

Five minutes later it was all over. Ian had chucked the pot's contents down the sink. We took it in turns to swig the remaining wine from the bottle, talked about this and that and bade each other good night. I saw Ian downstairs to his room and drove away in my car, rather pleased to have witnessed the great writer confronting the final frontier of the unacceptable.

* * *

Back in the metropolis, the highlight of the autumn was Lord Weidenfeld's seventieth birthday thrash at the National Portrait Gallery, off Trafalgar Square. Everyone was there. Well not everyone in the *world*, or in the Groucho Club, but every literary or political or media grandee over the age of fifty was working the room: Cabinet ministers, prize-winning authors, captains of industry, society beauties, peers of the realm. Harold and Antonia Pinter, Ann Getty, Edward Heath, George Melly, Sonia Melchett, Lord Gowrie . . . Perhaps a handful of other people could have invited *some* of these names, but only George could have got them all to come.

Past a tense-making greeting of tuxedoed bouncers, I rode up in the world's slowest lift with a member of Her Majesty's upper house. 'What George is marvellous at,' he said, 'is judging to perfection the right mix of types, old and young, eminent and, ahm . . .' – he glanced at my shoes – 'less so.'

Inside, past the looming portrait of Dr Johnson, the first-drink corridor was crammed with literary agents. This furtive and shadowy breed were at their most unbuttoned: instead of talking money, they were talking the imminent Frankfurt Book Fair, the forthcoming Booker Prize (would it be Rose Tremain this year, for *Restoration*? Or John Banville, for *The Book of Evidence*? It couldn't be Kazuo Ishiguro for *The Remains of the Day*, could it?) and the latest royal family scandal: the Duchess of York had appeared on Sue Lawley's TV show to discuss her two *Budgie the Little Helicopter* children's books and told her hostess all the proceeds would go to charity; later it turned out that only one-tenth would do so. At the party, Giles Gordon, publishing agent for most of the royal family, tonight sporting one of his amusing collection of 1967 neckties, repeatedly declined to comment on the brouhaha.

A shoal of public intellectuals could be found noisily exchanging views beside the devils-on-horseback display: Bernard Levin in a cream suit, clearly on his way to the Proms, Roger Scruton and Paul Johnson standing together like some upmarket Red-Headed

League of Irascible Thinkers. Distinguished media faces – Melvyn Bragg, Alan Whicker, Sir Robin Day, Robert Kee – beamed at each other as though they'd just met outside the BBC. The room seemed full of noble lords: Longford, Quinton, Briggs, Gowrie, Grafton, Sieff. By some way the most striking was Lord Longford, who tonight was sporting a spectacular cranial Band-Aid the size and texture of a rubber bathing cap. He explained that it was the result of an unfortunate collision with a cupboard, but had to endure joshing enquiries about his wife and the ancestral rolling pin.

He was not the only casualty. Lord Snowdon was on a crutch. Lady Longford, a meltingly sweet-faced octogenarian, affected an adjustable cane. Kathleen Tynan, whose biography of her husband Kenneth was published by Weidenfeld, arched her spectacular, leopard-skin-clad shoulders and claimed that an ill-advised ride through the Colorado desert might have tweaked her spine. Beside her, several gentlemen admirers sighed audibly.

It was very hot. Beads of sweat appeared on the nose of a young diarist from the *Evening Standard*, after he'd ill-advisedly approached Harold Pinter for an amusing quote about Weidenfeld and was bluntly directed to perform an erotic act with himself.

Suddenly there were speeches. Christopher Falkus, the company's managing director, silenced the cawing multitude and introduced the raffish, seventy-two-year-old Nigel Nicolson, co-founder of the publishing company forty years before in 1949. Nicolson, a charmer of the old school, let the room in on Jonathan Cape's classic Rules of Publishing, as told to the two young partners many years earlier. 'Rule 1: Books on South America never sell. Rule 2: Books on Mary Queen of Scots always sell. Rule 3: that's it.' He introduced a pinkly spectacular Antonia Fraser, whose Mary biography had made the firm a fortune.

She recalled lunching with someone who had said 'the only trouble with George is that he thinks all his geese are swans.' The room was silent as several guests wondered if they were ever considered geese. Mrs Pinter ringingly concluded her speech by saying there was nothing grey about George at seventy. 'His only colour is evergreen.'

Moved to reply, Weidenfeld winningly hoped to continue his espousal of good writing up to whatever terrestrial rest might claim him – and beyond: 'Even in the grave,' he said, 'I expect to find a fax machine.' Prolonged applause followed.

The last hour found things beginning to unweave. Edward Heath put an arm around a choleric Sir Robin Day and muttered, 'Sir Roy, how nice to – I mean, Sir *Robin*.' Rupert Murdoch chatted to David Owen, who was one month away from renaming his new party the Liberal Democrats. A ravishing blonde novelist in black silk gazed at his rugged features and told me: 'I sat beside David Owen at dinner last month. He looked in my eyes and said: "Tell me, do you believe in proportional representation?" I was *so* disappointed.'

The less discreet paparazzi were loosing off flashbulbs at gatherings of three or more. Nigel Dempster arrived, complaining volubly about the press treatment of his biography of Christina Onassis. Alistair Horne drifted amiably past, murmuring about his hippie-style trip to Morocco. And, as though drawn by an unseen signal, wave upon wave of ladies *d'un certain âge*, arms emblazoned with pancake-sized freckles, prodigious bosoms shimmeringly swathed in designer chiffon and organza, descended on His Lordship to convey their final birthday wishes. George moved happily, steadily and (sorry, girls) valedictorily through their Balenciaga-clouded mist.

My last encounter was with a puzzled Felicity Bryan, the tiny literary agent. She told me: 'I said goodbye and thanks to Lord Weidenfeld. He put an arm around me and whispered, "My dear . . . so many *happy memories*." I wonder who he thought I was.'

I went home more than slightly intoxicated, made a jug of strong coffee, fired up the Amstrad and wrote up the evening as best I could. Next morning, I brought it in to the Style people and said, 'This might make a Style front. Lots of names . . .' To my delight it was splashed over the front with lots of terrific photographs. Lord Weidenfeld saw it, called me up and asked me to pop round to his flat. He told me how much he'd enjoyed the piece, praised my writing and said, 'Maybe you'd like to write a book for me.'

It took a few seconds for this to penetrate.

'Sorry,' I said. 'What did you just say?'

'I would like you to write a book for me,' said Lord Weidenfeld. 'I like books of social history, particularly ones that take a single decade as their subject. Go away and think about it and choose your decade. Then let me know.'

I'd never encountered this kind of high-speed commissioning before. I went home and, in the days that followed, weighed up his suggestion. I didn't want to write up a decade before the twentieth century, being no historian. I thought I'd love to write something like Ronald Blythe's sparkling *The Age of Illusion*, a great favourite of mine. But Blythe had covered the years 1918 to 1939, so I could hardly till the same field. The 1940s would necessitate some research into the war, a subject far too unwieldy and grim for airy treatment. The 1950s were all about retrenchment, the Festival of Britain, Suez, skiffle and Angry Young Men, maddeningly over-familiar. The sixties were equal parts Carnaby-Street-kipper-tie-Beatles-pop and druggy-psychedelia-burnout-Manson-family. The 1970s was all unions and strikes, Bowie and punks, three-day weeks and terrible haircuts.

I rang His Lordship and had a brief conversation with him.

'I've considered your proposal about the decades,' I said. 'And the only one I want to write about is the one that's just ending: the eighties.'

'You're too late,' said His Lordship. 'We've got someone already doing it.'

'In that case,' I said, 'I'll start next year on *The Nineties*. We'll talk again in ten years' time.'

'Goodbye, Mr Walsh,' said Lord Weidenfeld.

CHAPTER 12

Side-Splitters and Bonkbusters

Not everything notable in the 1980s book world was about success, innovation and the challenging of taboos. In a remarkably British way, books that celebrated failure, hopelessness, embarrassment, social climbing and celebrity worship made an absolute fortune while making the nation laugh at the same time. 'The 1980s were, above all, a golden time for British comic writing,' wrote John Sutherland in *Reading the Decades: Fifty Years of the Nation's Bestselling Books*. 'Books designed to amuse display the same vitality and buoyant national genius as that evident in, say, Ealing comedies of the 1950s or stage dramas of the Restoration period.'

Things kicked off, as did so many things in this elongated decade, in 1978, with *The Book of Heroic Failures* by Stephen Pile, a collection of newspaper tales of howling ineptitude. You could read about the Least Successful Lying in State (in March 1896, the late Bishop of Lesbos lay in state in a Greek Orthodox church, clad in episcopal garb, for two days. On the third day, he sat up, glared at the mourners and demanded, 'What are you staring at?') or the Least Successful Spy (he was a guy who, working for Russia, broke into the NATO naval base near Naples, removed top secret documents – and left behind his overnight bag containing a file, a Bible, a copy of *Playboy* and full details about himself, including his address). My favourite, though, was the Worst Burglar. This was Mr Philip McCutcheon, who was arrested twenty times in his career. When he appeared at York Crown Court in 1971, the judge spelt out why he was perhaps in the wrong job. 'I think you should give burglary up. You have a withered hand, an artificial leg and only one eye. You have been caught in Otley, Leeds, Harrogate, Norwich, Beverley, Hull and York. You are a rotten burglar.' No matter how ludicrous the subjects, the entries were written in a calm, sympathetic, non-judgemental way that tickled an audience of millions.

The same year saw *The Dieters' Guide to Weight Loss During Sex* by Richard Smith, a book of fathomless silliness which combined, in a shockingly unserious way, two bestselling books of the previous ten years, Dr Alex Comfort's *The Joy of Sex* and Irwin Stillman's *The Doctor's Quick Weight-Loss Guide*. The *DGTWLDS* explained exactly how many calories you could burn in a sexual context depending on what you were doing. The section on Locations for Sex disclosed that you could burn 20 calories by Doing It on a bar stool, but 38 calories if you were on the boot of a Honda Civic. I liked the surrealism of Achieving Orgasm Under Unusual Circumstances, which included 'While donating blood' (45 calories) and 'While negotiating for a bank loan' (100 calories).

The next year introduced British, then transatlantic, then world readers to a comic masterpiece. *The Hitchhiker's Guide to the Galaxy* (see Chapter 3) emerged in book form in October 1979, a year and seven months after its aural incarnation knocked BBC Radio 4 listeners for six. I'd found Douglas Adams's fascination for – and delight in – cosmic sound effects sometimes got in the way of his peerless verbal invention; now, on the page, minus the whooshing and bleeping, readers could luxuriate in the fabulous mash-up of history textbook, surrealism and satire. Take the *Guide*'s description of Golgafrincham, a planet 'rich in legend, red, and occasionally green, with the blood of those who sought in days gone by to conquer her.' I yelped with laughter at 'and occasionally green'. The book was an instant hit: in three months it sold seven hundred and fifty thousand copies.

Just as the *Book of Heroic Failures* proved, ironically, to be a resounding success, *Hitchhiker* managed to conquer the book world – it spawned four sequels, became a TV series, a talking book, a Christmas Book for Comic Relief, a computer book at Infocom (which sold millions in the US), and eventually a feature film – while the engine of its comedy was mostly self-belittlement and bathos. It begins with Planet Earth being obliterated to make way for a hyperspace bypass. Later we learn that the entry for 'Earth' in the actual *Hitchhiker's Guide* reads (in its entirety) 'Mostly harmless'. *Hitchhiker* showed how an improbability generator could be created 'when a Brambleweeny57 sub-meson brain is linked to an atomic vector plotter suspended in a nice hot cup of tea'. It argued that the most crucial piece of knowledge an interplanetary traveller can possess is 'knowing where your towel is'. Towels, tea and harmlessness – could anything be more British?

The main demographic for *Hitchhiker* readers was students and teenagers. The readership of *The Secret Diary of Adrian Mole aged 13¾*, first published in 1982, which narrowly beat Adams's achievement in total sales over the decade, was a puzzle. It's a book that started off being bought by parents and ended up being bought by teens to show their friends in school playgrounds. At first read, I thought it too thin and childish to interest adults, while its references to wank magazines, feminism, left-wing politics and sensible dieting seemed a bit grown-up for young readers.

It follows the fortunes of the titular schoolboy, growing up in Ashby-de-le-Zouch, an only child with problem parents: his father drinks too much and his mother is conducting a furtive affair with Mr Lucas next door. At school, Adrian swoons unrequitedly over his dream girl, Pandora Braithwaite. He has to pay protection money to the class bully, Barry Kent. Then, as the year opens, Adrian's parents split up, the family home is plunged in darkness because of unpaid electricity bills, and our hero discovers that he's been living in poverty for years. But things improve. Adrian's grandma confronts the bullying Barry and retrieves Adrian's money, and Adrian's firm stand over not wearing school socks wins the heart of Pandora.

The burgeoning of Adrian's sexual feelings was fun, and rather shocking, to read. After scrutinising a copy of *Big and Bouncy* magazine, Adrian measures his 'thing' and reports that it's 11 centimetres. That's a nice detail for a thirteen-year-old boy: '11 centimetres' sounds so much better than 'four and a bit inches'. And I liked the unconscious eroticism of Adrian's poem to Pandora's horse, Blossom:

> *Little Brown Horse*
> *Eating apples in a field,*
> *Perhaps one day*
> *My heart will be healed.*
> *I stroke the places Pandora has sat*
> *Wearing her jodhpurs and riding hat . . .*

But I was still amazed by Ms Townsend's runaway popularity. In March 1984, sales of the paperback *Diary* were six hundred thousand copies. In August the sequel, *The Growing Pains of Adrian Mole*, came out. By September it had sold two hundred and fifty thousand copies in hardback, and Sue Townsend had nabbed the number 1 slot in both hardback and paperback. At the Frankfurt Book Fair that month, *Mole*'s publishers sold translation rights to every country in Western Europe. And all for a book which represented, according to the entry in *British Council Contemporary Writers*, 'a particularly British story; that of continued, almost heroic, failure.'

Another bestselling piece of creative anarchy was *The Henry Root Letters*. They were presented as the work of a former wet fish tycoon who likes to correspond with famous people – politicians, newspaper editors, TV personalities, members of the royal household, foreign tyrants – to discuss important issues of the day. To help his correspondents ignore the fact that he sounds like a smug, prejudiced, right-wing, racist buffoon, and to encourage them to reply, he encloses a £1 note with each letter.

This brilliant wind-up was the invention of William Donaldson, novelist, theatre producer, philanthropist (he bankrolled the early careers of his Cambridge contemporaries Ted Hughes and Sylvia Plath) and crack-smoking brothel-keeper. It was a bestseller for months, securing for him, according to *The Times* obituary, 'a place as a cult figure amongst twentieth-century satirists.' The missives drew an astonishing number of replies from people who took them seriously. The wonderfully named Major General Wyldbore-Smith, at the Conservative Board of Finance, replies to Root's enquiry about the 'going price' for a life peerage by making it clear that 'there is no question of buying honours from the Conservative Party'. Willie Whitelaw writes to reassure him that the Party has no plans to legalise cannabis. Mrs Mary Whitehouse at the National Viewers' and Listeners' Association thanks him for his concern about a (fictional) *Penthouse* columnist's promise to pull Mrs W's knickers down next time they meet. When Root writes to General Zia of Pakistan praising him for 'the smack of firm government', and calling for the return of capital punishment in the UK, the general replies by sending a signed photograph and commending his 'very pertinent views'.

The arrival of 'Sloane Rangers' on the London social scene announced, like a butler at Highgrove, the arrival of a whole new area of comedy: posh people laughing at posh people. The phrase, meaning a young, upper-crust inhabitant of the Chelsea or Kensington districts of London, usually a young woman of good schooling, with a fondness for Hermès scarves and shopping in Peter Jones, had been around for years before it became a defining cliché of early 1980s England. It was coined by Tina Margetts, a sub-editor on *Harper's & Queen* magazine. Ms Margetts had found herself part of the Chel/Ken milieu while doing a course on Fine Art at the V&A Museum. In 1975 her witty definition was taken up by the style writer Peter York, and the features editor of *Harper's*, Ann Barr. Margetts, York and Barr developed the concept further, nailing down the quiddity of the typical Sloane: her (or his) parentage, education, living quarters, clothes, haunts, drinks, friends, music and sexual choices. Their findings were immortalised in hard covers when York's collection of journalism, *Style Wars*, was published in 1980.

Then a game-changing phenomenon appeared. Diana Spencer became engaged to Prince Charles in February 1981. Style watchers everywhere registered the fact that the most perfect living embodiment of the Sloane Ranger was joining the British royal family. After the royal wedding in July 1981, Diana's popularity with the public led to a tidal wave of royal books. *An Invitation to the Royal Wedding* sold one hundred and fifty thousand copies in weeks. *Debrett's Book of the Royal Wedding*, published two months before the occasion, sold one hundred and sixty thousand copies. But hardly a year later, a book arrived to eclipse all the monarchical folderol. *The Official Sloane Ranger Handbook: The First Guide to What Really Matters in Life* became one of the great successes of the decade. 'Suddenly, a Sloane – as we saw her – was the most interesting and publicized person in the world,' York said later. 'It did click with me that, if we could expand the taxonomy of the breed and make it funny but with illustrations, we would clean up.'

The book was presented as a piece of cod anthropology, noting the markings, habitats, social rites, modes of transport, grooming habits and mating rituals of the upper-middle-class dwellers of London W2 and SW3. Identifying how 'Caroline' (the archetypal Sloane) furnished her drawing room or laid her dining-room table became vitally important. Passing on the news that one was expected to cry at a carols service but not at a funeral was the most crucial advice since the days of Gloria Vanderbilt. Sloane men were christened Hooray Henrys, and characterised as working in the City (if clever) and property (if not – because the job requires no training, and pays so badly it needs a private income to bolster the tiny salary). Off duty, 'Henry' can be found in corduroy trousers, Burberry sheepskin jacket and Hunter wellingtons.

The book's success was attributable to three things: it showed how the British social élite could be identified by clothing and trappings; it showed the upwardly mobile how an affectation of élitism could be adopted; and, because it was done with affection, it amused the Sloanes, who enjoyed reading about themselves.

The same year saw something never seen before: the convenient marriage of anarchic TV show and respectable highbrow publishing house. *NOT 1982* was the work of the team behind *Not the Nine O'Clock News*, the BBC satire show which had run through four series since 1979. Having delivered a spoof Charles 'n' Di tribute, *Not the Royal Wedding*, the producer John Lloyd put together a brick-sized, 365-page calendar for 1982 with a gag on every tear-off page. He enlisted a crew of writers (which included Douglas Adams) to supply the laughs, and looked for a publisher to produce and distribute it.

Robert McCrum at Faber made an offer. 'I am strongly in favour of this,' he wrote to the firm's elderly editorial director Charles Monteith, 'as not only is it likely to be extremely profitable but I think it will enhance our reputation in the marketplace as a publisher prepared to do new, good and interesting things.' Indeed it did. But McCrum received a memo from an anonymous 'staff member', more than likely Monteith himself, who was far from happy: 'I have all along found the idea of this enterprise distinctly unappealing ... I think everyone here wants to see [our books] edited, produced and sold to the best of all our abilities. *NOT 1982* is something else, and energies which could have been employed on worthwhile projects have been dissipated. I am disappointed to have been associated with it.'

Despite its regrettable lack of worthwhileness, *NOT 1982* was a bestseller, and earned Faber £250,000 in gross profit. They were at it again four years later when Faber published the spin-off *Spitting Image* book in early 1986. This time they made £214,000 profit. Nobody complained.

The year 1987 saw another collaboration between Faber & Faber and the High Command of TV comedy. The book was *Who's Had Who*. Despite the grammatical solecism in the title, it was a funny and eye-opening guide to historical sexual daisy-chains. It explained, for instance, how Marlene Dietrich is distantly related (sexually speaking) to Des O'Connor, because Ms Dietrich once had it off with Douglas Fairbanks Junior, who rogered Joan Crawford, who forgot herself with Clark Gable, who buried the baldy-feller in Ava Gardner, who succumbed to the silver tongue of Howard Hughes, who shagged Hedy Lamarr, who climbed aboard Stewart Granger, who danced the blanket hornpipe with the 'actress and ballet dancer' Gillian Vaughan, who married the popular TV entertainer Des in 1960. See how it works? Astonishing historico-politico-cultural connections could be made via the bedroom, the sack and the royal couch: Ronald Reagan is connected to the top 1960s DJ Tony Blackburn in eight 'rogers', while it takes as many as fourteen to get from Elvis Presley to Prince Charles (via Jayne Mansfield, Marilyn Monroe, both Kennedy brothers, Mick Jagger and Jackie Onassis among others). Astonishingly well designed, awash with footnotes, fizzing with unexpected items of historical gossip and written with boundless verve and wit, this was my favourite funny book of the 1980s. The authors were Simon Bell, a prolific London journalist and film critic, and two others whose names have almost entirely faded into obscurity: Helen Fielding and Richard Curtis.

Another favourite was the best literary spoof of the decade, *The Wordsmiths of Gorsemere*. It was the work of Sue Limb, a Cambridge graduate who specialised in Elizabethan lyric poetry and staged a production of Sheridan's *The Rivals* starring Douglas Adams as Sir Lucius O'Trigger. I'd reviewed her first novel, *Up the Garden Path*, in *Time Out* and admired her footloose heroine Izzy's adventures in finding love. One particular phrase stayed in my head: after enduring the ferocious pounding of less sensitive boyfriends, Izzy entered a new world of 'fat, voluptuous ticking' courtesy of a boisterous Welshman.

The Wordsmiths, subtitled 'An everyday story of towering genius', began life in February 1985, and dealt with events in March 1799, when William and Dorothy Wordsmith have just moved into 'Vole Cottage' in Cumberland under the majestic peaks of Flabbergoat Fell. This take on the Lake Poets didn't just lampoon the pretensions of their poetry (full of noble leech-gatherers and rhapsodies upon a *Withered Turnip*); it was also a silken feminist satire in which Dorothy did all the vital housework – carrying beds and cupboards upstairs, scrubbing the floors, digging the cottage garden and sowing Shaggy Persiflage in the orchard – while the menfolk, who include Samuel Tailor Cholericke and Percy Jelley, are too busy composing verses, or trying to kill themselves, to be of any use. I laughed at Ms Limb's way with writers' names (Thomas de Quinine, William Bloke, John Sheets) and the *double entendres* in her dialogue, as when the rascally seducer Lord Biro tries it on with his hostess:

Dorothy: 'Pray, unhand me, Lord Biro. I must go and toss the salad.'

Lord Biro: 'Oh fortunate lettuce!'

A book version in 1987 presented the whole two radio series in diary form, with spidery handwritten entries and marginal notes which move between sketches of Norfolk Nobbler butterflies to doodles of startlingly vaginal Wild Arum lilies soon after Lord Biro has come a-calling.

The milking of Cynthia Payne, if that's not too gross a phrase, was an episode that typified one side of 1980s British publishing: whatever's done well, try it again and again (and again).

Ms Payne was the brothel queen whose house in Ambleside Avenue, south London, was raided by police in December 1978. Officers discovered fifty-three men, many of advanced years, standing in the hallway waiting to have their go with one of the thirteen prostitutes operating (if that's the word) in the four bedrooms. To general hilarity, the men were found to be clutching luncheon vouchers as proof of payment – the down-at-heel passport to sexual paradise in Streatham, SW18.

In 1980 Ms Payne was in court for keeping a 'disorderly house'. The nation was entertained all over again by details of her sex parties, especially her clients' delight in being whipped, humiliated and enslaved; they included a bank manager who was turned on by having mud flung at him while he stood naked against a wall. Ms Payne hinted that members of the judiciary, a peer, several vicars and an MP had attended the high jinks *chez elle*, and that 'the posher they were, the kinkier they were'.

Payne was found guilty, fined £4,000 and sentenced to eighteen months in jail. Inevitably, a book was commissioned. Ms Payne's memories were extracted by the novelist and gay scandalmonger Paul Bailey in *An English Madam: The Life and Work of Cynthia Payne*, published in 1983. It sold extremely well. Four years later, it was republished as a paperback tie-in with *Personal Services*, a film 'inspired by' *An English Madam*, directed by Terry Jones and starring Julie Walters.

A further suck at the sauce bottle in 1987 was offered by Gloria Walker and Lynn Daly, who returned to the 1980s court hearings and published the proceedings as *Sexplicitly Yours: The Trial of Cynthia Payne* in Penguin. Remarkably, the famous paperback house looked for a further draught of the ketchup and approached Terence Blacker with the suggestion that he write *Cynthia's Book of Entertainment*. 'Penguin pitched it to me as a joke,' Blacker told me, 'because Harrods published a *Harrods Book of Entertainment* and this would be something similar, only with luncheon vouchers. I was offered £10,000 to ghost it. So I went to her garden in Streatham and explained what was required. She said, "Terry, I just don't get it. *Cynthia's Book of Entertainment* – what's that even mean?" I explained about the Harrods book but she was still blank. The problem was, she could only talk about sex, and she'd already told all the stories about the bank manager, etc., once for the book and once for the film.'

The as-yet-unwritten book was then selected by Boots as part of their Christmas Selection. Penguin explained that there couldn't be too much about sex in it, because it was for the Christmas market; it had to be family-friendly. 'To sum up,' said Blacker, 'this was a book whose author didn't understand the point of it; the only thing she could talk about was sex, and I wasn't allowed to write about that. But I managed to cobble something together.' *Cynthia Payne: Entertaining at Home. 101 Party Hints from Britain's Most Popular Hostess* came out in October 1987. Blacker regards its publication as 'one of my finest professional achievements'.

The late 1980s were full of evidence that publishers had gone mad for a bestseller – *any* kind of bestseller – from any source. They didn't want to rely on the traditional method of cultivating authors through half a dozen books, over several years of modest sales, until they had a successful seller and could guarantee chart success with each new book – who had time for *that*? Instead, the modern publisher looked for something new – the Instant Bestseller. His or her gaze turned upon men and women who'd already acquired celebrity in some field – who had 'a media profile'– and he wondered: just how hard would it be to persuade them to produce a book?

Everybody would win. The celebrities would feel proud to have a previously undreamt-of connection to literature; the publisher would feel glamorous by association; the author would get free promotion on the media circuit; the booksellers would put the books (with instantly recognisable cover photos) in their windows; and readers would expect some of the authors in glamorous occupations to dish the dirt about the businesses in which they worked.

In early 1990, Nicholas Shakespeare, literary editor of the *Sunday Telegraph*, summed up the phenomenon: 'The result of this trend is a full-scale invasion of literature by other media, embracing authors from the worlds of film, television, newspapers and, most noticeably, women's magazines – all of whom have come to books from media which, in Marshall McLuhan terms, are "hotter".

Put another way, where once someone might have parlayed into perfumes or designer tights, they now parlay into a book.'

So that's where we'd come to – fiction as a fashion item, the book as the creative effusion of a C-list actor, starlet, comedian, model, TV presenter, athlete or musician. The recent works of Jackie Collins (*Hollywood Wives*, *Hollywood Husbands*) and Jilly Cooper (*Riders*, *Rivals*) had pushed the boat of sexual explicitness right out to sea, so (logic dictated), with the right ghost writer to help, the new breed of celebrity author could let their hair down.

On to the fiction shelves came *Dance with the Devil* by Kirk Douglas, *The Scarlet Thread* by Mandy Rice-Davies (a wartime saga, since you ask, set against the backdrop of the Ottoman Empire), *Fantasies* by Vidal Sassoon's wife Beverly and *Prime Time* by Joan Collins.

A rumour circulated that a famous catwalk model, let us call her Scheherazade, was signed up to put her name to a novel called *Swan*; she would supply the characters' names and a plot outline, and Caroline Upcher, editorial director of Century fiction and the doyenne of designer novels, would do the actual writing. The story goes that Upcher visited Scheherazade in Paris, backstage at a fashion shoot. She told the supermodel: 'Your novel *Swan* is finished. I have it here for you to take home.' Scheherazade was pleased until Upcher reached into a capacious tote bag, extracted the three-hundred-page manuscript and plonked it on a table. 'I can't *possibly* carry *that*,' said the model. 'It's *far* too heavy. I'll wait for the paperback.'

Some fine comedians took to fiction with success: Ben Elton with *Stark* and *Gridlock*, Stephen Fry with *The Liar* and *The Hippopotamus*. Female journalists became a category of their own for writing polysexual blockbusters with one-word titles: *Lace* by Shirley Conran, *Pearls* by Celia Brayfield, *Ambition* by Julie Burchill.

Special mention should be made of Sally Beauman, the convent-educated daughter of a RAF officer. She was a Cambridge graduate, a journalist on *New York* magazine and the historian of the Royal

Shakespeare Company. Possibly bored by her immaculate pedigree, she started writing romance novels for Harlequin, the American version of Mills & Boon. Then, seized by an impulse to try something raunchier, she began a story about an aristocratic jewellery tycoon, his Alabama-bred wife and his stable of prostitutes. She called it *Destiny*. In 1985, several publishers fought over the US rights. Her agent, Pat Kavanagh, banged on her door at midnight, woke her up and told her the rights had gone to Bantam for $1 million – the biggest advance ever paid for a first novel. A week before publication, *Destiny* appeared at number 6 on the *New York Times* bestseller list.

In a moment of jaw-dropping cheek, Bantam's marketing department approached Tiffany's, the Fifth Avenue jewellers and asked if they'd be interested in a promotional tie-in. Why? Because one of the prostitutes in *Destiny* wears a Tiffany diamond in her *labia majora*. Tiffany said no thanks. Their customers preferred earrings.

CHAPTER 13

———— •◆• ————

The End of the Beginnings

In March 1990, the indefatigable, access-all-areas books impresario, Martyn Goff, asked me to help him suggest to HM the Queen which books she might read over the summer. Obviously, this came as no surprise to me – hardly a month went by without a phone call from some European or transatlantic head of state, asking me to recommend a good beach read or murder mystery. 'Not now, Helmut,' I usually replied, or 'I'm sorry, Mr President, I'm kinda busy . . .' but sometimes I was happy to help.

Goff's request came in a letter on the creamy vellum paper and curlicued signature of Sotheran's of Sackville Street, the venerable antiquarian booksellers (founded in York in 1761, est. London 1815) where he was chairman for years. His letter began:

'Dear John, I think you know that for some years now, Book Trust makes an annual gift of a small library to the Queen. This usually gets quite a lot of publicity for books. Would you like to be one of this year's selectors?'

You bet I would. Pat Miller from *Books and Bookmen* was also signed up to do the selecting, along with a bookseller called George. We were to choose books not just for Her Majesty but for her guests at Balmoral to enjoy on those afternoons when they weren't shooting pheasants or dismembering a stag.

We trotted along to Martyn's cool house, on the north side of

Clapham Common, which he shared with Rubio Lindroos, a Finnish poet of a cherubic and lecherous disposition, whom he met after Rubio wrote him a fan letter praising Martyn's gay novel, *The Youngest Director.**

George, Pat and I had brought our own suggestions of novels, biographies, works of history, art books, travel books and nature notes. Suggestions for poetry collections were swiftly vetoed. Several books pretty well selected themselves: *English Country House Interiors*, *Scottish Colourists*, Mark Girouard's *The English Town* and Robert Gray's *The King's Wife: Five Queen Consorts* might already be on the Balmoral shelves but we sent them anyway. In fiction we chose Rose Tremain's lushly descriptive and earthily physical *Restoration*, Mary Wesley's *A Sensible Life*, John Mortimer's *Titmuss Regained* (the sequel to *Paradise Postponed* about the ghastly, rapacious Tory MP and city developer Leslie Titmuss), *The Light Years* by Elizabeth Jane Howard, *Devices and Desires* by P. D. James, *Family Sins* by William Trevor and *Lies of Silence* by Brian Moore.

This last was a controversial choice because the plot concerned the Provisional IRA forcing a hotel manager to drive a truck laden with explosives to blow up his own hotel and kill several members of the Orange Order who are attending a function. Did the royals need a reminder of the Troubles (and the blowing up of Lord Mountbatten ten years earlier)? But once you started asking if this or that book might give offence, there was no stopping. No sooner had we chosen *The Mambo Kings Play Songs of Love*, Oscar Hijuelos's hot and sexy evocation of New York City's Cuban neighbourhood and the mambo dance craze in the late 1940s, than we worried – was it too raunchy, too erotomaniacal, too Cuban backstreets, to beguile the British royals? 'We don't need to worry,' said Patricia

---

* *The Times* obituary of Martyn Goff mentioned how a fan letter *from* Martyn changed literary history. While he was in the RAF, as part of his national service, he had written to Siegfried Sassoon, praising his war poetry. He was amazed to receive a reply – and even more amazed to learn, from Sassoon's biographer, that the poet had written to John Maynard Keynes saying: 'I haven't written a word for two years. Now here's an aerogram from an unknown airman somewhere in the western desert, praising my work, and I've started writing again.'

(who came from Kansas). 'It's won the Pulitzer Prize. It's ring-fenced with respectability.'

Some of the non-fiction choices gave us, as they say, pause. Tim Jeal's life of Lord Baden-Powell, of *Scouting for Boys* fame, was a shoo-in, as was *A Sparrow's Flight*, the memoirs of the lord chancellor, Lord Hailsham, A. N. Wilson's respectful life of C. S. Lewis, and Lucy Hughes-Hallett's rave-reviewed *Cleopatra: Histories, Dreams and Distortions*. But would, say, Prince Philip relish the details (of relentless gay pursuit, of cottaging in public lavatories, of double-agent spying) in Francis Wheen's *The Soul of Indiscretion: Tom Driberg, poet, philanderer, legislator and outlaw*? 'Sod it,' I said. 'It'll make a nice change after *The Oxford Book of Humorous Prose* edited by Frank Muir.'

The list ended on a note of cuteness. Shrewdly noting that the Prince and Princess of Wales's summer holiday would involve two children, William (eight in June) and Harry (six in September), we added Kathleen Hale's *Orlando the Marmalade Cat Goes on Holiday*.

After we'd chosen our thirty-two titles, and Martyn opened another bottle of Chardonnay, I asked if his yearly selections ever got any feedback from Balmoral. 'Nothing from the Queen herself,' he said, 'but we get a formal thank-you from her staff. And an occasional request that we send more picture books or art books or horse books next year.'

'So we never know,' I said, 'if the Queen has read any book, or if she enjoyed it?'

'As a matter of fact,' said Martyn, 'there's one book we *definitely* know she's read because I heard about it, in confidence, from one of her private secretaries.'

'My God,' I squawked. 'What? Which?'

'It wasn't at Balmoral,' said Martyn. 'It was on a royal visit to Singapore last October. The chap who told me said that, the evening the Queen and Duke of Edinburgh arrived, the Queen said to him after dinner: "It's very annoying but I've left my book on the plane. Do you have anything I could read when I retire?"

The secretary replied, "Why yes, ma'am, I have a novel you might like. It's just won the Booker Prize for the best novel of the year. It's called *The Remains of the Day*. Would you like to try it?" She said, "Yes all right," so he handed it over.

'A few days went by without any word from the Queen about the book. After a week, the private secretary could stand it no longer. "I hope you don't mind my asking, ma'am," he said, "but I hope that the book I recommended hasn't given any . . . offence." The Queen looked at him. "Not at all," she said. "I'm enjoying it. But there's one thing I want to ask you. Is it *really like that* – below stairs, I mean," said the Queen. "Is that *really* how they talk?"'

I love this story. I love to think the Queen might take Kazuo Ishiguro's studiedly neutral prose style – pitched somewhere between English politeness and Japanese formality – as the natural mode of discourse downstairs, where valets are, naturally, discussing back-collar studs and exchanging rumours about allegedly 'flashy' new ways of cleaning teaspoons.

The Rushdie Affair rumbled on. A year after the fatwa, there was no sign of its being lifted. Rushdie, displaying considerable amounts of courage, or perhaps driven mad by being cooped up with police minders in a dozen safe houses, had made some appearances in public. A friend at the *Guardian* told me he'd attended a dinner party in Greenwich and was surprised to find Rushdie sitting at the table with other guests, as if life was perfectly normal. The stilted conversation went as follows:

Friend: Hi everyone. Hi Robert. Hi Lucy. Hi Blake.
            Oh hi Salman. Er – how're things?
Rushdie: Oh, you know. Can't complain . . .

The author was still under sentence of death, with a cash bounty of a million dollars on his head that could be claimed by any one of forty million Muslim bounty hunters, should they be inclined to make a move. To mark the occasion he was interviewed by Sebastian Faulks, now at the *Independent on Sunday*. The interview was set up by Gillon Aitken, the agent of both Rushdie and Faulks; it cost the *Sindie* a cool £100,000. But at least it contained one colossal scoop.

'Rushdie said that he'd discovered Islam,' Sebastian told me later. 'He said that he'd found "an Islam-shaped hole" in his heart and his life. I felt so sorry for him and so utterly outraged by the fatwa that, instead of quizzing him about his conversion, I wrote a front-page leader about the traditions of Islam and how respected it was by other world religions, for its mercy and loving kindness. I felt passionately that this was the most outrageous rupture of international relations, diplomatic behaviour and human decency since the Crusades – and aimed at one of our own.'

At the *Sunday Times* we published a fascinating perspective on the fatwa – the view of a Westernised Islamic insider.

I'd barely registered the name of the Egyptian writer, Naguib Mahfouz, when he won the Nobel Prize for Literature in 1988. Now, in March 1990, the US firm of Doubleday, recently established in the UK, bought the rights to his novels, and were giving the world Mahfouz's *Cairo Trilogy* in translation for the first time, starting with *Palace Walk*, 'an intricate evocation of family life in Cairo around the First World War.'

Mahfouz was the first Arab ever to win the world's top writing prize. This was a hot occasion. How could we mark it? I spoke to the publicity department at Doubleday. No, I learned, Mr Mahfouz would *not* be flying into London, staying at Claridge's and expecting a rip-roaring thrash at the Groucho; he was seventy-nine years old, rather frail, half-blind, deaf and diabetic. Right, I said, can we send someone to Cairo to interview him? Does he speak English? They weren't sure. No UK newspaper had hitherto expressed an interest. OK, I thought, we can be cultural pathfinders here. But whom should I get to interview the great man?

A name suddenly popped into my head. It was D. J. Taylor, my friend, frequent contributor and, more to the point, literary polymath.

I rang him straight away. 'David,' I said, 'have you heard of Naguib Mahfouz?'

Of *course* he had. Not only had D. J. heard of every single writer published anywhere in the world since the death of Queen Victoria; he could recall the thinly disguised caricature of Lloyd George in their first book, the plot-twist in their second, and could recite by heart the shocking final paragraph of their third. Of *course* he knew of Mahfouz; he knew how political a writer he was, and looked forward to reading the *Trilogy in translation*.

'Do you have,' I asked, 'an up-to date passport?'

I had to ask. I'd never heard him mention going anywhere outside London or Norfolk.

'Yes of course. Why?'

'I'd like you to fly to Cairo, book into the Giza Hilton for two nights, make contact with whomever speaks English at the publicity office, interview Mr Mahfouz at Cairo's equivalent of *The Times* for an hour, and try not to get mugged in the backstreets while looking for local action afterwards. Can you do that?'

'I can't do it today,' he said. 'I'm writing a column for the *TLS* about the use of the future conditional tense in early Huxley. Is tomorrow OK?'

It was.

They met at the offices of *Al-Ahram* in downtown Cairo. Mahfouz had a 'visiting day' once a week, and D. J., accompanied by a Reuters snapper and a Japanese camera crew, found himself in a hall crowded with security guards, Egyptian functionaries and a rumoured ambassador. Fifteen months since the Nobel, the tide of international visitors was still baying. His face and works were everywhere – hotel bookshops and kiosks in Tahrir Square displayed copies of his most famous work, *Midaq Alley*.

After studying at Cairo University in the 1930s, Mahfouz had joined the civil service and most of his thirty-odd novels were populated with civil servants, nationalist students and denizens of the bazaar. The curious thing about his work, however, was the Rushdie-ish echo that sounded when his novel *Children of Gebelawi* (also known as *Children of the Alley*, first published in Arabic in 1959) came out in England in 1988. It was only months before the announcement of his Nobel Prize – and of course the launch of *The Satanic Verses* in October 1988. *Children* was a religious allegory in which Muhammad, Jesus and Moses wander through the Cairo rubbish heaps. Its portrait of the Prophet as a worldly womaniser made Muslims furious; even now, a complete version of the book has never appeared in Egypt.

In the wake of the Rushdie affair, in 1989, fundamentalist leaders tried to apply retrospective blame to Mahfouz. Sheikh Omar Abdel-Rahman, leader of Islamic Jihad, demanded Mahfouz's death on the slightly weird grounds that, had a fatwa been pronounced on him thirty years earlier, it would have scared Rushdie off publishing *The Satanic Verses*. The fact that nobody saw any reason for a fatwa in 1959 didn't seem relevant. But the death threat was still out there – his home and family were still under guard.

Mahfouz told Taylor that a bilingual friend had guided him through *The Satanic Verses*. So what did he think of it?

'It was insolent, very insolent,' he said. 'Not a book of thought.' It was the 'immoderation' of Rushdie's work which disturbed him more than its message. Rational criticism of Islam, he said, was one thing – 'we accept that and we discuss it. But if you insult . . .' here Mahfouz snapped his fingers expressively. At the same time he defended Rushdie against the fatwa, which he said was 'against law, against Islam'. It was sentiments like these, rather than the stale controversy of *Children of Gebelawi*, which inflamed the wild-eyed sheikhs, along with his description of Khomeini as a 'terrorist'. Hardline Islam also disapproved of his matter-of-fact portrayals in his books of physical relationships, and his accounts of women striving for greater equality. He was well known as a moral libertarian in a land where the imams routinely called for belly-dancers to be flogged.

The first book of *The Cairo Trilogy* was about to hit British shelves. Did he, Taylor asked, acknowledge Western influences in his fiction? Indeed yes – Tolstoy, Thomas Mann and, er, John Galsworthy. '*The Forsyte Saga*!' cried Mahfouz in rapture.

Did he feel the weight of nineteenth-century Western classics on his shoulders?

'It is natural,' he said. 'We know Western literature here. In fact, we love it *too much*.'

I was delighted that we'd been given this perspective on Islamic attitudes, glad to find that the imams' attitudes weren't shared by all, pleased to discover that, although the fatwa was a sanction upheld by the ultra-hard-line 1980s Muslim fraternity, it wouldn't have held much sway in the 1950s. I felt we'd learned something of the gap between fundamentalist rage and the stirrings of enlightened Muslim tolerance.

I never knew what books Andrew Neil was reading. He was such a political animal, such a connoisseur of business matters, had such airy acquaintance with the government's economic strategy, it seemed unlikely he'd spend much time reading books for enjoyment. I don't remember him ever telling me that he was enjoying/ hating any recently published book, though he once waved a title under my nose and said, 'The new million-seller!'. It was *Dirty Weekend*, Helen Zahavi's fantastically violent piece of feminist revenge porn, which went on to be filmed by Michael Winner, to universal howls of dislike. Andrew was given a sit-in role in the movie, as a newsreader. I found out later that he and Winner were part of a celebrity friendship group (they included John Cleese) who occasionally holidayed together in the Caribbean, and he was doing Winner a favour.

Now and again, though, Andrew would query my choice of a book, and we'd have a little confrontation.

One day in Conference, I read my list for the following Sunday.

JW: The lead review this week is the thousand-page biography of Charles Dickens by Peter Ackroyd, whose previous lives of T. S. Eliot and Ezra Pound were very well received. It's reviewed by John Carey who—

AN: I notice that further down your list is a biography of Arnold Schwarzenegger. Do you not think more readers would be interested in the life of a modern movie star than a dead Victorian novelist that even their parents found boring?

JW: Actually no, I don't think so. The Arnie book contains no revelations beyond the news that his dad joined the Nazi party in 1938, but I think we knew that. And Dickens is still British readers' favourite novelist, and of course his stuff is TV-dramatised and filmed all the time for new generations. So all in all—

AN: I don't agree. I think we should put the Schwarzenegger on the front, and the Dickens can go on page three.

JW: Andrew, look. (*Takes out wallet and extracts some money*). This is twenty quid. I bet you twenty quid that, in two weeks' time, the Dickens book will be in the top three of the bestseller list, and the Schwarzenegger book will be nowhere to be seen.

AN (*considers for a moment*): Well *if* that's what happens, it will only be because you, and people *like* you, have arranged it that way.

JW: I assure you, it doesn't work like that.

AN: In the meantime, please let me see proofs of both reviews, and I will decide which to lead with.

I never could persuade the editor that the world of book-review journalism was not run by a shadowy cabal of literary editors, sitting in the Groucho Club smoking Cohibas, drinking hock and seltzers and deciding how we should promote certain modern biographies, novels and historical works. But Andrew was always fair about good writing. The morning after I delivered the proofs of both reviews to his office, he rang me at home (always an occasion to chill the blood, when you're still in pyjamas) and said: 'Hi John, you were right. The Dickens review is much the better. So go with that.'

Despite Andrew's dim view of my world, I had to admire his stewardship of the newspaper during these crazy political times. The dissolution of the Warsaw Pact. The democratisation of Eastern Europe satellite states, starting in Poland and Hungary. The scarcely believable dismantling of the Berlin Wall. The break-up of the USSR. The million-strong demonstrations in Tiananmen Square. The Iran–Contra affair. They all presented the Foreign pages with a nightmare of dizzyingly complex reportage, as did the Lockerbie bombing over Scotland. The events that led to the fall of Margaret Thatcher were momentous in British politics and needed scrupulous and comprehensive (and fair-minded) treatment. It was a heady time to be alive, to be witnessing twentieth-century history at a major turning point – and to be on a major newspaper that watched incredulously as it all came down, and faced the task of making sense of it all to half a million readers each week.

In March 1990, the editor and I had a heated encounter. A year earlier, the Thatcher government had promised to replace local-council rates with a tax called the community charge. Instead of raising revenues by taxing the estimated rental value of a home, this imposed a fixed-rate tax, set by the local authority on every adult living there. It meant that a large poor family in a small house would find their rates increased a lot, while a rich family in a big house would pay proportionately less. It was the infamous 'poll tax' and it went down like a rat sandwich with the population at large. It first appeared in Scotland in 1989, and was to roll out across England and Wales from 1 April 1990.

The day before, 31 March, a huge demonstration, coordinated by unionists and Militant Tendency and (according to police computation) two-hundred-thousand-strong, started in Trafalgar Square, spilled down Whitehall and came to a halt at Downing Street. At one point, mounted police charged down the street and knocked a woman under clattering hooves. Some demonstrators headed north and shops were vandalised in Oxford Street and Covent Garden. Windows were broken, cars overturned, Stringfellow's nightclub was at-

tacked and wine bars set ablaze. Running battles with police continued into the evening. Over three hundred people were arrested.

The following Monday, Hanif Kureishi was on Radio 4's *Start
the Week*, to discuss his first novel, *The Buddha of Surburbia*. In a
preliminary discussion, Melvyn Bragg asked his guests for their
reaction to the riots on Saturday. 'Terrific!' said Kureishi at once.
He may have been simply voicing his pleasure at seeing a full-
scale, real-time, protestors-versus- police riot that closely resembled
the street riot that featured in his second film (as scriptwriter),
Sammy and Rosie Get Laid (1987). For Andrew Neil, though, it was
an outrageous endorsement of anarchy.

He called me into his office, and asked about the book discussed
on the show. Was I, he asked, planning to review it?

I told him it was Faber's lead fiction debut for 1990, and Paul
Bailey, the double-Booker-shortlisted novelist, was reviewing it.

'Take it out, John,' said Andrew shortly.

'Come again?'

'Take it out of the Books section. I'm not having that man's
name appearing in the paper.' He explained about Kureishi's blithe
endorsement of the riots, the missiles, the broken glass, the looted
shops and torched offices, the anti-police mayhem and Militant-
Tendency-organised chaos.

'You really can't do that, Andrew,' I said. 'People will call it
censorship.'

'I don't care what they call it,' he said. 'It's a matter of principle.
Take it out of your pages.'

I'd seldom seen him so fired up – and about a single word,
'Terrific'. Three days passed. I called on Andrew a few times to
make the point that his principle (withholding publicity from a
vocal supporter of anarchy) might seem to outsiders an attack on
free speech. He stayed firm.

'I know what the literary world will think,' I said. 'And I wish
you'd be guided by me about this.'

'Yes, John,' he said. 'I know you do.'

At the last minute, Andrew told me to go ahead and publish Bailey's review of Kureishi's debut. I wish I could take the credit for changing his mind, but I can't. What changed it were the magic words: 'People will not understand *the subtlety of your motives* in cancelling the review.' At least three people claimed to have said them. For myself, I was pleased that the editor had shown he could listen to reason, once his fury had abated.

I had, over the years, met Seamus Heaney several times. Our paths first crossed in 1977 when I was studying for a degree at University College, Dublin, and he was visiting one of my tutors, his friend Seamus Deane.*

I have an embarrassing memory of muttering, in the English Department common room, something about his being a god of the modern lyric. He waved it away, and steered me towards a face-saving conversation about Patrick Kavanagh.

A decade later, I met him at a Faber party just after *The Haw Lantern* was published. I told him how much I admired the sonnet sequence called 'Clearances', about the death of his mother. He wrote about the moment of her death in the penultimate poem; the final sonnet, though, was about the chestnut tree in the family's garden, now cut down and ghostly:

> *I heard the hatchet's differentiated*
> *Accurate cut, the crack, the sigh*
> *And collapse of what luxuriated*
> *Through the shocked tips and wreckage of it all . . .*
> *Its heft and hush become a bright nowhere,*
> *A soul ramifying and forever*
> *Silent, beyond silence listened for.*

---

* The ubiquity of their first name prompted a witty couplet from Clive James in *Peregrine Prykke's Pilgrimage through the London Literary World*: 'There sat the Belfast poets – all called Seamus/Of whom the best-known one was Seamus Feamus.'

How on earth, I asked him, did you come on the word 'ramifying' (meaning, of course, 'branching out', 'creating offshoots') which so perfectly expressed the tree's, and his mother's, absence? Heaney smiled. He pointed heavenwards and replied, 'I just said, "*Thank you very much*!"'

It had been a long time since poets spoke about having 'divine inspiration' or indeed any inspiration at all, but he genuinely believed in it. He also believed (and told Sue Lawley on *Desert Island Discs*) that between the mouth, the ear and the brain there's a direct poetic correlation and sympathy in everybody.

I interviewed him again when I joined the *Standard*, but I have no record of the occasion except for his letter in reply, which called my write-up 'hearteningly well-disposed', a wonderfully Dickensian formulation.

In October 1990, I was pitched into the heart of Heaney Country, when I found myself in the Guildhall in Derry, a stone's throw from the walled citadel of the Bogside. Heaney was born in the county, in the town of Tamniaran, and was meeting his people after the premiere of his first and only play, *The Cure at Troy*. The cream of Derry society was there: both bishops of Derry, Catholic and Protestant, local dignitaries, buddies like Stephen Rea, Brian Friel and Tom Paulin from the Field Day Theatre Company (created in 1980 to rethink Irish drama as a way of helping to unify a divided community), and thrillingly coiffed Ulsterwomen who darted about the draughty cloister like loose racehorses.

The great man sat at a table, drinking whiskey with Harp chasers. Now fifty-one, he listened to the praise from joshing fans, professorial specs perched on his nose. His huge head always put me in mind of a medieval castle through whose narrow windows – the wary slits of his eyes – shafts of murderous intelligence could rain down on the incautious. Encased for the occasion in a grey suit, he resembled a social-climbing Visigoth.

In 1990, Heaney was routinely held to be the most important poet writing in English. His Nobel Prize for Literature was still five years off. Favourable comparisons with Yeats, uttered since the publication of his third collection, *Wintering Out*, had become the critical orthodoxy. His early lush evocations of the rhythms of working the land – thatching, dowsing, ploughing, threshing, milk-churning – gave way to reflections on tribal violence in Ulster, her cultural identity ('O land of password, handgrip, wink and nod/Of open minds as open as a trap') and the role – indeed the point – of being a poet in a society that demanded the taking of sides.

The Cure at Troy was a version of Sophocles's *Philoctetes*, set during the Trojan War. The action sees Homer's Odysseus, King of Ithaca, and Neoptolemus, son of Achilles, visiting an island where Philoctetes, the great Greek archer, has been left stranded and solitary; a bite from a snake has given him an ulcerated wound on his leg that stinks beyond endurance. The visitors have come to get the stricken hero because, without his famous bow, they cannot win the Trojan War. The play's main concern was to portray friendship and loyalty as morally superior to duty or service to a cause; its relevance, as a plea for understanding and charity in the teeth of sectarian ideology, was obviously relevant to modern-day Ulster, if unlikely to convulse audiences hoping for a good night out.

I listened in, at midnight, as playgoers asked Heaney about his references in the play to 'the hunger-striker's father' and 'the police widow in veils' as examples of tortured humanity. Did it mean he was now a political writer, speaking directly to modern events? Heaney wasn't having it: 'That's not politics,' he said, 'it's sentiment. People misunderstand the idea of a play, any play, if they think it's a cure for life. There's a sealed border between the house and the stage. The Berlin Wall may come down, but the wall between make-believe and the real world will never come down.'

He also denied there was no link between classical theatre and modern Irish emotion. 'I use a rural Catholic idiom in the play because in so many usages – saying things are "meant to be", talking about "going to the altar" – the two have a lot in common.

I think the folk-church element in Catholicism is close to the communal Greek sense of Fate.'

Next day, as reviewers criticised the Field Day dramaturges for bringing classical dramas to audiences who'd probably prefer a modern comedy (local wits thought the play might usefully be retitled 'Pus in Boot' or 'Ulcer Says No!'), I drove by the banks of the Foyle to visit Heaney at the home of his friend, the great playwright Brian Friel, on the northernmost tip of Ireland. Across the bleak, gull-tormented strand I could make out the grey pillbox of an internment camp.

Heaney was recuperating from his first-night revels. He was hungover, but game to talk. We sat in a bright conservatory, hung with hessian rugs, and drank tea. I asked him about his Catholic education and how much of it had stayed with him. He said no, he didn't go to Mass. And no, he didn't believe in sin, 'But I believe in offence, to yourself and others. The first thing a Catholic does in the outside world is secularise his religion; people with any gumption respond to the world around them, away from their education – but it remains inside you like a subterranean command. There's a terrible temptation to go back to it because as a system it's perfect. But generally the self-satisfaction of Catholicism is reprehensible and' – he narrowed his eyes to slits – 'gives offence'.

He talked about the impulse writers felt to express themselves. 'Take Wilde and Synge,' he said. 'They had a need to be heard. Synge chose to take the language of pre-literature and make it literature. Wilde took the language of literature and took it up a notch. They were employing different methods, going for different effects, but were replying to a similar impulse . . .' He took a deep breath, 'Synge going under the cuticle, Wilde gliding along the nail, like varnish.' I was impressed that a chap with such a monster hangover could pull off such a brilliant double-image.

I asked how he saw himself now, back in his old tribe in Derry, in the bosom of his people. He considered for a minute. 'The most admirable writer we've known in our time is Samuel Beckett,' he said, presumably not using 'we' in the royal sense. 'Beckett was purely The Writer, but he was also purely himself. He did not behave as he thought The Writer should. My own sense of The Writer's function is of an impersonal stand-off. But I myself, a creature living in my own temperament and times, I can't do it.'

Oh come on, I said, you've become the modern spokesman of an ancient culture, the universalised Ulsterman, someone who manages to bind history, language and feeling into a single grand sensorium and strides the torn streets of Derry like a god.

'That's a lot of blarney,' said Seamus Heaney. 'Complete blarney.' It was not.

When it was over, Heaney asked if I could give him a lift to Derry Station in my hire car. I said 'Of course' coolly enough, but my heart was pounding as I unlocked the passenger door. It was like having T. S. Eliot, or Walt Whitman or Alfred Lord Tennyson settling themselves into the seat beside me and making small talk about the grim Bogside weather – except that they probably wouldn't have presented such a charming, crinkly-smiling face to the outside world as Heaney did, the morning after his successful First Night.

I can't recall what pleasantries we exchanged on the way, but I remember him asking, out of the blue, 'Tell me honestly, John, what'd you think of the play?'

I blathered the sort of stuff you blather to a playwright about their new creation – more about the acting and production than the words – but I did have one tiny problem with *The Cure at Troy*. I thought I'd risk it.

'At the end,' I said, 'when they've finished arguing about whether Philoctetes should go to Troy and join the war, there's a big speech from the Chorus, and lots of thunder-and-lightning special effects . . .'

'I remember,' said Heaney, a bit sarcastically.

'And Philoctetes says he's just seen Hercules in the sky. And someone in the Chorus speaks in Hercules's voice.'

'Uh-huh,' said Heaney. 'And?'

'There's nothing *wrong* with it,' I said. 'But it's a classic *deus ex machina*, a god descending from the sky to bang the characters' heads together ...'

'Indeed it is ...' said Heaney.

'Well, I just wondered, why didn't you *dramatise* the most dramatic moment in the play, and have Hercules, played by someone not previously seen, come down to earth in, you know, awesome splendour amidst the thunder and lightning, and make the big speech and tell everyone what to do? Wouldn't it make for a better climax?'

Ahead of us, Derry Station appeared in its bleak glory.

'Thanks for the lift,' said Seamus Heaney, manoeuvring his great Celtic bulk through the car door. 'And for the advice.' His big face came back inside. With a charming, crinkly smile, he said: 'I'll have another look at the script, and see if anything can be *salvaged* ...'

I sat in the car for five minutes after he'd gone, thinking: Did I just give a lift to one of the Titans of modern literature and, while doing so, give him a 'note' about his newest creative work? What was I *thinking*?

I checked the text of the play a couple of years later. There was no sign in the later editions of an actual guest appearance by Hercules, as I'd suggested. Perhaps I should have suggested fireworks.

Later in the year, Salman Rushdie published his first work since *Satanic Verses*. It was a children's book called *Haroun and the Sea of Stories*, and was dedicated to Rushdie's son Zafar, from whom he'd been separated by the fatwa. The book followed the eponymous Haroun and his father Rashid, a professional storyteller, through several plonkingly allegorical regions, including the Sea of Stories, whose existence is under threat. Rashid's neighbour is Mr Sengupta, who despises stories and the imagination; he later appears as the villainous Khattam-Shud, the 'Prince of Silence and Foe of Speech', who wants to plug the Source of Stories at the bottom of the sea.

The book's major themes were utterance, censorship and silence.

I wondered whom we might sign up to review such an important book. I told myself: Be bold. Think outside the box. This review should be An Event.

I went to my address book, rang a transatlantic number and spoke to someone in the Scott Meredith Literary Agency. I explained who I was and whom I wanted to write the piece. I offered £1,000, possibly even £1,500. They got back to me in an hour. 'Our client,' they said, 'is not interested.'

'Perhaps,' I said, with the air of a pushy diner at the Ritz stuffing a ten-pound note into the *maître d*'s breast pocket, 'if I offered a larger emolument, your client might think again.'

'I don't think so, sir,' said the voice, rather shortly.

'Let me put it this way,' I said, 'we're very keen for this to happen. You might tell your client he can name his price . . .'

The agent came back again an hour later with the price. I went straight to Andrew Neil.

'The hot news, Andrew,' I said, 'is that I've signed up Norman Mailer to review Salman Rushdie's new book, *Haroun and the Sea of Stories*.'

'You have?' said the editor neutrally. 'What's it going to cost us?'

'That's the thing,' I said. 'His agent says they'll want ten thousand dollars.'

'Ten grand,' said the editor, faintly, 'for a children's book review.'

'It's certainly a lot,' I said. 'But it is obviously a big event so—'

'A big *non*-event,' said the editor, 'because the answer is No.'

I was going to upbraid Andrew for stifling a valuable contribution to the Rushdie debate when I suddenly remembered I had an urgent lunch appointment in the canteen.

In January 1991, I became one of the judges of the Whitbread Fiction Prize. The Whitbreads had been going since 1971 in competition with the Booker Prize, but differed in having five categories: Novel, First Novel, Children's Book, Biography and Poetry Collection. From 1985, they brought in a special prize, the Whitbread Book of the Year, which was chosen from the five category winners, and greeted by much razzmatazz, despite the absurdity of judging a children's book against a poetry collection, or a biography against a first novel. It was like judging a prize aubergine against a prize egg.

It was my second go as a judge. In 1989, I'd judged the First Novel Award and with my judicial companions had given the prize to James Hamilton-Paterson for *Gerontius*, his exquisite imagining of the composer Edward Elgar's 1923 cruise up the Amazon to Brazil, musing on the waning of his powers and the ruin of postwar Europe. That year, the Book of the Year Award went to Richard Holmes's biography of Coleridge, which was fine with me because it was wonderfully researched and sublimely written.

I think by then the Whitbread organisers had begun their policy of calling in a couple of external judges to give the climactic chinwag some extra significance. There were now so many book prizes around (the *Writers' and Artists' Handbook* listed over a hundred, including a prize for a second novel, another for a debut novel by someone over fifty – and a novel that, in the judges' view, did most to further public interest in Oriental carpets) that any extra touch of celebrity heft was considered vital. So when my colleagues and I sat in judgement on the Best Novel Award, and gave it to Jane Gardam's touching, funny and mischievous epistolary novel *The Queen of the Tambourine*, I wasn't surprised to hear that the final judging panel had now expanded to ten outsiders.

What a line-up, though. Michael Howard, Secretary of State for Employment; Sir Roy Strong, former director of the V&A Museum, Donald Trelford, editor of the *Observer*, John Cole, the BBC's political editor, Timberlake Wertenbaker, the political playwright, Nicholas Mosley (son of Oswald), who'd won the previous year's Best Novel prize, Ann Thwaite, who'd ditto the Best Biography prize – plus some of this year's category judges:

Liz Lochhead (poetry), Hilary Spurling (biography), Barbara Trapido (first novel) *et moi*.

From the start it was obvious which book would win. Standing out from the others like a sequoia in the New Forest was the first volume of John Richardson's *A Life of Picasso*. The author was the world's number one Pablo expert (he'd known Picasso, Braque and Cocteau when living in the south of France for twelve years after the war) and this book had already been praised beyond idolatry ('The finest biography of an artist I have read' – Waldemar Januszczak in the *Guardian*). It meant that the poetry of Michael Longley, the first novel by Gordon Burn and the children's book by Diana Hendry weren't going to be in with much of a shout.

The eleven-strong, round-table discussion of which book should win the big award took about ten minutes, before deciding that Picasso was the only horse in this race. I tried to interest the Secretary of State for Employment, seated on my right, in my trenchant views on the proposed closure of the Ravenscraig steel plant in Scotland, but he could tell I was only pretending to be a political animal and escaped to talk to Cole and Trelford. As book-prize judging panels go, it was all a bit nonsensical. They could all have phoned it in. But the presence of the arty-journo-politico celebrities just showed how dizzyingly high the status of the book world, and the evaluation of its best works, had now become.

In February 1991, I interviewed Kingsley Amis about his *Memoirs*. I'd met him a few times in the past, at the Garrick Club and in the Haycrafts' garden, of which he would have had no recollection, but this was a serious face-to-face.

I was startled to find that the pop-eyed, misogynistic crypto-fascist of legend turned out to be a charming and beguiling chap, from his warm handshake to the repertoire of grimaces and vocal grotesqueries for which he was famous. He treated me to some of his famous vocal impressions (President Eisenhower, Lord David

Cecil) then threw in a new one: himself. He did an impression of the irascible old bastard he was rumoured to become when being interviewed: '"So, Mr Amis, how do you think your career has gone?" "Oh, not bad," he *yelled*. "Do you enjoy writing?" "Yes I quite like it," he *bellowed apoplectically*. "Thank you very much for dropping by," he *snarled, his mouth twisted with fury*.'

Within four minutes of meeting him, I was laughing like a fool.

His new book took the form of a trip through a rogues' gallery of horrible people: in forty-eight chapters, Kingsley had nailed, skewered, humiliated and (surely) embarrassed a few dozen eminent and respectable figures, including some long-standing friends. It was quite a performance from the sixty-nine-year-old. Names were named. Rebuffed homosexual propositions were recalled. Moments of ghastly indiscretion or yelping conceit, perpetrated by ex-chums twenty-five years before, were held up to a new, embarrassing light.

The poet John Wain, once a great friend, was portrayed as a condescending, vainglorious lout. Bruce Montgomery, better known as the crime writer Edmund Crispin, came across as a talentless drunkard. Roald Dahl was shown advising Amis to try writing for children because, no matter what nonsense he came out with, 'the little bastards'd swallow it.' Sometimes I felt as if I was reading a moral tract in which figures from the literary, political and media worlds were being brought on stage as embodiments of sins: laziness (Malcolm Muggeridge), pedantry (Enoch Powell), gaucheness (John Braine), hypocrisy (Dahl), naivety (Philip Toynbee) and above all, meanness. 'If there's a recurrent vice I mention, it's that,' said Amis. 'I think, in the last couple of decades, meanness has become the vice that people dislike the most, and across all classes.'

When I asked why the *Memoirs* didn't feature many warm or positive judgements about his old pals, he was blunt. 'I've had several marvellous friends in my life, of whom there's nothing to be said except I've enjoyed many amusing hours in their company, getting drunk, learning things – but you can't make an interesting chapter out of that. And I can't stand *virtue* as a writer,' (here his voice took on a *faux*-sanctimonious purr: 'It was about *this* time that I fell under the influence of what I can *only* call one of nature's *good men*, Parson Blah . . .'), 'and I loathe piety. That's why I can't read autobiographies now.'

I said there was a distinct whiff of grudges being borne and scores being settled down the years. Was the book about getting his own back? 'It's a question of whether they made me *cross*,' he said, emphasising the nursery word. John Wain, for instance – 'his allegations about my first wife' (Wain apparently told a friend that the reason he turned down invitations to visit the Amises at home was his conviction that Hilly would 'break down the bedroom door' to seduce him) 'made me very cross and still does. He deserves what I said about him. A lot of the other stuff isn't very serious; the spirit in which I'm writing is to say: "Oh pull yourself together, what absurd behaviour."'

There was one story of bad behaviour in the book that rather shocked me. It concerned a visit made in the 1940s by Philip Larkin to Shrewsbury, to visit Bruce Montgomery, a schoolmaster, and to attend a meeting of the school literary society. Bruce was a ferocious drinker and, before the meeting, took Larkin for 'a prolonged session' in the local pub. Larkin found himself seated as far from the door as possible, with hundreds of boys, many sitting on the floor, between him and the exit. He felt his bladder sending panicky urges to his brain and, reluctant to disrupt the event by walking out, reasoned (ill-advisedly) that, because he was wearing a heavy overcoat of super-absorbent qualities, it would probably be OK if he let fly. Unfortunately, he miscalculated, and a shame-making pool of urine appeared under his chair and began to spread across the linoleum.

'Round about here,' Amis wrote, 'rather late on, I thought, Philip broke off telling me this story and said he wished he had never started on it. He went on to extract from me some sort of promise not to go round repeating it, which I interpreted as a ban on any sort of publication. But now I consider myself released from that undertaking . . ."*

I told Amis that I was shocked by the story, but also a bit surprised that he should have reneged on his promise to Larkin to keep *schtum* about it. Didn't he feel he'd – what was the word – betrayed his trust?

'I don't see why you should say that,' Amis said crossly. 'Nobody who knew Philip at all would have thought any the less of him after hearing that story.'

'I'm not talking about the people who *knew* him,' I pressed on. 'I think he didn't want people *in general* to know he'd done such a thing. You know – the outside world.'

'Well, how very – *high-minded* of you,' he said, possibly muttering '. . . *you little shit*' under his breath.

He was genuinely annoyed to be accused of betraying a friendship. It took several closing questions about his army career – especially his hatred for officers who abused their power to win arguments against lesser ranks – to allow us to part company with gruff good humour.

Hatchet-job reviews are, of course, regrettable in a civilised environment such as a Book section, but sometimes they led to actual physical trouble. In October 1991, John Carey reviewed a rather gushing biography (by Rosemary Sullivan) of Elizabeth Smart, the Canadian author of *By Grand Central Station I Sat Down and Wept*, the famous prose-poem about being stuck in a *ménage à trois*.

Headed 'Rebel Without a Clue', Carey's review pointed out that Ms Smart, though anxious to live a life of cultural distinction, was strikingly ungifted. 'She studied piano but soon gave it up, and tried to prepare for Oxford entrance but lacked the scholarly

---

* The essay published in *Memoirs* was mostly a reprint of the piece Amis wrote for the book *Larkin at Sixty* (edited by Anthony Thwaite) in 1982. That piece didn't mention the peeing episode.

temperament. A spell at drama school established that she had no theatrical talent. She longed to be a poet but found writing difficult.' Carey's real target in the review, however, wasn't Smart but George Barker, whom he described as 'a minor English poet who enjoyed some vogue in the 1930s' and with whose poetry and person Smart became infatuated.

The story of Smart's life becomes a saga of Barker's neglect: 'According to Smart, he would take money from her to go to the pub when she was struggling to feed the children. She lived in a series of wretched cottages, without electricity or plumbing, and felt at times that she was going mad.' George Barker, having fathered six children by three women, leaves Smart to go to the south of France with a younger woman and, when she leaves him, returns to Smart for comfort. A fight ensues in which she bites right through his lower lip and he is rushed to hospital for stitches. 'You feel,' says Carey, 'like cheering.' Though clearly unimpressed by Barker, he plays fair by him, saying that he might have had a different story to tell about the stormy relationship.

At one point Carey had written, 'Barker is, one gathers, still alive ...' By a cruel twist of Fate, by the time the review was published, what Carey 'gathered' was no longer the case. Amazingly, George Barker died on 27 October, the day the review came out. Next day, a gossip columnist, noting the coincidence, floated the possibility that Barker might have been reading Carey's review that very morning, and that it had effectively killed him. Ridiculous. of course, but on the morning of 31 October, I looked at the invitation to the evening's launch party of *By Heart: Elizabeth Smart, a Life* and thought, 'Should I give this one a miss?'

Discretion, I thought, would be better than having to explain to Elspeth Barker, the great man's widow (whom I'd met a few times and liked) why I'd given the book to the nation's most fabulously forensic critic to kick. I told Harry Ritchie I'd skip it, go to the Groucho instead, and looked forward to hearing about the party afterwards, at Kettner's.

I was indeed joined there – but not by Harry. Around 8.45 p.m., just as my Capricciosa pizza was arriving, I was aware of a kerfuffle in the restaurant. Three adolescents were heading my way with the unmistakable figure of Elspeth Barker. Had they come to attack me with one of those circular-bladed pizza knives? No, it turned out. She was sad about the review, she said, but many people had been rude about George Barker's behaviour over the years. What bothered her was the timing – having her husband traduced in print *on the day he died.* I pointed out, reasonably, that this was hardly Carey's fault, and that George would've agreed with Carey that he could have told a different story about Elizabeth Smart from his own perspective. This seemed to mollify her, but the matter wasn't over. When Elspeth left me to my pizza and gathered her children to leave, one of them (the others called him 'Bruddy') came over to me, his young face twisted with fury, bunched his right fist and shouted: *'Are you John Carey?'*

What a moment! 'No,' I said sadly, 'only in my dreams.'

The family finally caught up with John at the 1991 *Sunday Times* Books Christmas party, held a month after the book launch and the ruckus in Kettner's. Carey was in mid-party conversation when he saw 'a winged fury' bearing down on him. It was one of Barker's fifteen children, followed by their mother. The professor made haste to escape but found himself barred by a large table in his way. Elspeth came up to him and hissed: *'Be wary, Carey!'* like a Maenad, before vanishing.

I was delighted to find the episode described, with a fine sense of drama, in a 2002 biography, *The Chameleon Poet: A Life of George Barker* by Robert Fraser. Anyone who thinks the world of book reviewing is all slim volumes, murmured appreciation and glasses of Madeira in gentlemen's clubs just doesn't know the half of it.

Things at the *Sunday Times* became rather jollier when Tim Willis arrived in 1991 to edit the Style section. Originally from the

Yorkshire Dales, by way of Stonyhurst and Edinburgh University, he came to London full of journalistic ambition and industrial supplies of cheek. He wangled a job as a sub-editor on *World of Interiors* when it launched in November 1981, despite having never subbed anything in his life. He worked through several magazines and, by twenty-nine, was triumphantly named by *Tatler* as sixty-ninth 'Pushiest Person in Britain'.

When he arrived at the *Sunday Times*, he reunited with Geordie Greig, with whom he'd worked on the launch of Eddy Shah's *Today* newspaper, which had opened the door to new printing technology and led to the demise of the print unions. Both Willis and Greig were champion networkers and party animals, and the former decided to bring Andrew Neil into the milieu of metropolitan 'style' and the recreations that accompanied it.

'I could see Andrew needed some new friends, and took it very much to heart,' he told me. 'I spent years carousing with him. Every night, the Style team were invited to magazine parties, restaurant openings, fashion thrashes, perfume launches, so I said to Andrew, "Come along with us" – and he did. At the end of the 1988 Andrew/Pamella Bordes libel trial brought by Peregrine Worsthorne, a group of reporters outside the High Court asked Andrew, "What did it all mean?" and he answered, "It's a victory for the New Britain." He later said it was an off-the-cuff remark, but it stuck – he was now the Prophet of the New Britain, and welcome at parties in consequence.'

Neil was introduced to a crowd of London scenesters he'd not met before. Willis once took him to a bohemian party off Eaton Square, where one guest, who'd seen Neil on television, stroked his hair and said, breathily, 'Your hair – it's like a *badger's bum*.' It wasn't the kind of compliment he was used to receiving in his usual circuit of Whitehall wine bars or Treasury restaurants.

As time went on, the Style section signed up some glamorous writers. One was Helen Fielding, a former BBC researcher and documentary-maker who'd done serious broadcasts from the

Southern Sudan rebel war. There was not, however, the faintest trace of female warco about her. She was dazzlingly pretty, had an irresistibly uncertain what-shall-I-do? way of speaking and a voice in which her West Yorkshire background wrestled with Oxford-graduate polish. She used to say *pants* instead of *knickers*. I seethed with envy when Harry became her boyfriend for a time. Another new recruit was Polly Samson, formerly of Cape publishing, last seen at the Groucho Club, feeding gossip titbits to one of her courtiers.

I didn't realise how things were moving along until my former *Standard* Diary colleague Deirdre Fernand dropped into the office to deliver an article for the Style section. She told me she'd been told by Andrew Neil's secretary to make her way to the Wapping Car Pound at 7.30 p.m. A little unsure about what she'd find, she asked me to accompany her down there. We went and found three other women waiting to be taken somewhere for the evening by the editor. They were Polly, Helen Fielding, and Tim Willis's then-wife, Joanna Rahim, a mixed-race Glaswegian.

Tim, Andrew and the four girls all piled into the back of the motor – I remember it being a fair-sized limousine – which was clearly bound for an evening at Tramp or Annabel's. Andrew smiled at me through the open window and said, either, 'Look, John – the trappings of power . . .' or 'Look, John – the rewards of success . . .' or even, 'Look, John – the wages of sin . . .' before the great car purred away. I didn't begrudge Andrew his fun. I knew that he, like me, had grown up with an image in his head that, one day, he'd be riding to a fancy club in a huge car, surrounded by a harem of beautiful dames like James Bond in the adverts for *Thunderball* or James Coburn in *Our Man Flint*. Though I doubt that he'd have included Tim Willis in the fantasy.

A year later, one of the harem had to leave. Not long after the publication, in May 1992, of Andrew Morton's explosive book, *Diana: Her True Story*, the Princess and her ex-lover James Gilbey were caught on tape, in a conversation from three years before. He called her 'Squidgy' or 'Darling' fifty-three times, and at one point

Diana said to him, 'Bloody hell, after all I've done for this fucking family.' These revelations, along with a transcript of the tape, were published in the *Sun* in August 1992.

Andrew was in New York at the time. As far as he was concerned, Squidgygate was rocking the monarchy. It was an important story and the *Sunday Times* had to feature something on it, in the Style section. Helen Fielding was commissioned to write the piece. She, however, refused to take it seriously, and wrote a funny *jeu d'esprit* instead, making light of it all. On the Saturday afternoon, Neil returned to his Manhattan hotel, saw a fax of the story, rang the paper and told the overseeing editor, Kate Carr, 'This piece is *not* going in the paper. The story is a big scandal, and must be written as such.' The section rang Helen and told her the editor's reaction, but she refused to rewrite it. She was directed to do as she was told, or risk losing her job. She said fine, and duly parted company with us.

Which begs the question: without Squidgygate, and Ms Fielding's northern stubbornness, would *Bridget Jones's Diary* ('one of the ten novels that best defined the twentieth century' – *Guardian*) ever have been born?

In early 1992, I noticed that Anthony Burgess was approaching his seventy-fifth birthday – on 25 February – and rang the publicity department at Penguin to ask if they were planning a celebration. Actually no, they replied, but perhaps they should. Would I like to interview him? As luck would have it, I'd been asked by an arts college in west London to conduct a series of face-to-face events in the run-up to Easter, so I signed up Anthony there and then.

It was always a relief to find *any* audience prepared to come out on a late February night to listen to bookish chat, but the audiences at the talks were a curious bunch. You could tell by the things they asked the authors.

When Ruth Rendell was on stage, the first six questions were, predictably, about her rivalry with P. D. James and her need to invent ever-more-*outré* murder implements. Then, from the darkness at the back of the audience came the strangulated voice of an eighteen-carat weirdo, his lower lip mangling his Rs.

'Miss Wendell,' he said, 'can you confirm for me what I've often suspected mature ladies might suffer fwom . . .'

The audience let out a murmur. Oh God, I thought. Where's this going?

'. . . given the essentially sedentwee posture in which they wight . . .'

Oh God, I thought again.

'Sir,' I said, 'I'm not sure this is the appropriate occasion on which—'

But he was unstoppable.

'My question is, Do you tend to suffer fwom . . . gout?'

The audience laughed, mostly in relief.

Ruth Rendell's face was a picture. Shading her eyes from the lights, she looked to find the voice's owner.

'I can't see where the gentleman is sitting,' she said. 'But may I congratulate you, sir, on asking the first original question I've heard in *over twenty years*.'

The audience cheered. I imagined Gout Man sitting in Row W, surrounded by guffawing neighbours and – like the old guy in Hitchcock's *The 39 Steps* who keeps asking the music hall star Mr Memory, 'What's the cause of pip in poultry?' – feeling a little put out that his question remained unanswered.

Burgess at seventy-five was, I thought, a little shrunken physically, but was still terrific value. He talked feelingly about the 'Jackie Wilson' he used to be,* and about where his early fascination with music came from (hearing Debussy's *Prelude to the Afternoon of a Faun* on the family wireless, apparently). He talked about his unlikely friendship with the comedian Benny Hill, who had recently died. But when it came to questions, the way he handled them had a deep effect on me.

---

* He was born John Anthony Burgess Wilson, in Harpurhey, near Manchester.

The first was: 'Mr Burgess, I've tried to read *Finnegans Wake* a few times, but I've always had to give up. What exactly is *Finnegans Wake* about?'

Burgess had lit a cigar, ignoring the No Smoking signs in the wings.

'Well now,' he began, in his oracular schoolteacher style, 'while *Ulysses* traces its characters through the actions of a single *dayyyy*, *Finnegans Wake* follows the Earwicker family through the actions of a single *nighhhht . . .*' And off he went – five minutes of fluent brilliance, exemplary unfolding and miraculously clear exegesis of the most opaque novel ever published.*

The next question was: 'Mr Burgess, I'm aware that *À la Recherche du Temps Perdu* is considered a great twentieth-century novel, and I'm determined to finish it before the end of the century. But can you tell me: is there an actual *story* somewhere in the middle of it?'

Burgess took a pull on his cigar. 'At the risk of giving away the ending . . .' he began (this got a big laugh), 'I would say one cannot speak of *plot* in the traditional sense when it comes to Proust, more a series of *perspectives . . .*' and again he was off, for six or seven minutes of masterly, indeed headmasterly, explanation of the three-thousand-page book.

The third question was a touch anti-climactic.

'Mr Burgess, I understand you're an accomplished cook. Can you tell us: what is the secret of making a successful tortilla?'

We all laughed at such a bathetic enquiry, after all the literary fireworks before it. Burgess didn't laugh. He furrowed his brow, nodded his head, considered his response.

'The tortilla is nothing more than a *potato omelette*,' he said, 'and I would say the secret is, when frying the cubes of potato, not to allow them to become too crisp at the edge before drenching them in the *ovoid mixture*.'

---

* Of course it helped that he'd brought out *A Shorter Finnegans Wake* twenty-six years earlier in 1966.

It was wonderful, the high seriousness with which he took the question, the judicious advice he gave about a hot snack, delivered in the same way he might explain the Albigensian Heresy or the Diet of Worms. I marvelled at his commitment to Being Right, to intellectual clarity and factual accuracy; I loved his determination to pass on learning and truth, no matter whom he was talking to, as if he had a moral imperative to do so. He was – though the image might dismay him – like a fantastic juke box of knowledge, into which you shyly tendered your 50p, expecting a three-minute single to emerge, and receiving instead a twenty-minute oratorio.

He died a year later, in November 1993. Anthony's widow Liana invited me to read a passage from his last novel, *A Good Man in Deptford*, at the funeral. It was a lovely event in St Paul's Church, Covent Garden, designed by Inigo Jones and known for generations as 'the actor's church'. William Boyd delivered a warm and funny eulogy. The closing music was a burst of Burgess's own composition, *Blooms of Dublin*, a bewilderingly atonal operetta. Alert participants might have registered that among the church's memorial plaques were tributes to Charlie Chaplin, Noël Coward, Gracie Fields, Stanley Holloway, Boris Karloff and Vivien Leigh. I thought how much Anthony, the intellectual showman, would have appreciated being in such ripely theatrical, indeed hammy company. There was also a plaque to one Bransby Williams, a star of early twentieth-century music hall – so it seemed appropriate that, when the back doors of the chapel were opened to disgorge the congregation, the raucous strains of an old barrel organ blared across Covent Garden's piazza.

Everybody laughed and said, 'That's Anthony's spirit, telling us all to cheer up.'

I couldn't shake off a nagging sense that lots of things were coming to an end. With Burgess fading and Angela Carter gone (she died, ridiculously young at 51, in February 1992), my literary heroes were dropping like flies. I had last seen Angela Carter on Booker night, in 1991, speaking wryly about her failure to reach the shortlist with *Wise Children*, published in June to great acclaim; it won the *Sunday Express* Book of the Year Award. She noted with regret that all the Booker-shortlisted novels were by men: *Time's Arrow* by Martin Amis, *The Van* by Roddy Doyle, *Such a Long Journey* by Rohinton Mistry, *The Redundancy of Courage* by Timothy Mo, *The Famished Road* by Ben Okri and *Reading Turgenev* by William Trevor. 'So this is the modern English novel, is it?' she said. 'One black, one brown, one yellow, two green and one . . . written backwards!' This faintly shocking summation was sometimes reported as 'So this is the modern novel, is it? One African, one Canadian-Indian, one East Timorese, two Irish, and one . . . written backwards!' But Timothy Mo later confirmed to me the exasperated words I remembered.

Martin Amis, after the triumph of *Money*, was very much alive, but seemed to have gone off the boil. His *London Fields* in 1989 featured some fabulous paragraphs and some knockabout fun with the working classes in the character of Keith Talent, the darts-playing professional cheat. But the plot made zero sense (American visitor in London, led into a scabby Portobello boozer by his taxi driver (Keith) meets Nicola Six and Guy Clinch and somehow intuits that one of them will murder her and the other will take the rap . . . Hello? Was he psychic?) and the narrative became a repetitive carousel of special effects (feral baby Marmaduke, Keith's toxic racism, Guy's posh fecklessness, Nicola's terminal lassitude) to brighten the entropic gloom. I was a little astonished to find myself, for the first time, closing a Martin Amis novel before I'd reached the end.

I'd heard from Philip Kerr that he'd persuaded the *Granta* editors to continue the success of 1983 by having a poll of Best of Young British Novelists 1993 (in which he himself featured). But by 1992, it was clear that, whoever showed up on the list, there was a distinct new generation of rising young novelists that were quite *unlike* the Amis-Barnes-McEwan generation.

Harry Ritchie was the master-theorist about the key newcomers. Like him, they were born between 1957 and 1962 and began to be published in 1987–92: Nick Hornby with *Fever Pitch*, Robert Harris with *Fatherland*, Helen Fielding with *Cause Celeb*, Irvine Welsh with *Trainspotting*, Roddy Doyle with *The Commitments* ... 'It's a generational shift,' Harry would say. 'By the early 1990s, the glamorous lot – Barnes, Amis, McEwan – had become the establishment, the middle-class English mainstream, prize-winning, utterly pleased with themselves. I think many people born post-1958 wanted nothing to do with that lot. The new writers were lower class – even if they went to Oxbridge, they were outsiders – and unlike Amis, they were unshowy in style, modest in the structure of their books, and they dealt with ordinary life – not with ad men going crazy in New York, not with the heat death of the universe, not even with Frenchified men of letters from London's fashionable Dartmouth Park, having agreeable little adventures in Paris.'*

The concept of Endings was in the air in 1992. The fall of the Berlin Wall and the end of the Cold War had prompted a book called *The End of History and the Last Man* by Francis Fukuyama. It didn't suggest that things would cease to happen, but that, post-Communism, only variants of liberal democracy would flourish.

Fukuyama's startling essay prompted discussion of the part books had recently played in ending things. Hadn't *Diana: Her True Story* brought about the end of the royal marriage? Hadn't it rocked the whole *idea* of the monarchy? And hadn't the almighty ruckus about *Spycatcher: The Candid Autobiography of a Senior Intelligence Officer*, almost brought down the government?†

---

* I think Harry was alluding here to, respectively, *Money* and *London Fields* by Martin Amis, and *Metroland* by Julian Barnes.

† The author of *Spycatcher*, Peter Wright, a former assistant director of MI5, claimed he and his associates had 'bugged and burgled our way across London at the State's behest' in the 1960s, and suggested that Roger Hollis, the former director-general of the Security Service, was a Soviet mole. MI5 denied it all and the book was banned from publication in the UK. It was published in Australia, though. When the British government tried to ban it there, a judge refused to allow them – and the European Court of Human Rights ruled that the British government had broken European law. The embarrassment didn't, in fact, bring down Mrs Thatcher, but it shook the political establishment to its bedrock.

And hadn't a book – or at least its author – helped to bring about the end of Communism? John Sutherland passed on this ingenious theory in *Reading the Decades*. The author was Tom Clancy, author of *The Hunt for Red October*, in which an anti-Communist Russian submarine commander tries to deliver his state-of-the-art sub to the US Navy with the help of Jack Ryan, Clancy's hero in several thrillers. It was a huge bestseller and came to the attention of President Reagan, then in the midst of his *glasnost* negotiations with Mikhail Gorbachev. According to Sutherland, Clancy was invited to the White House where he reportedly 'enthused Reagan with the idea of [having a] "six-hundred-warship" navy ... It is plausible that the expense of matching the USA, ship for ship, was what finally persuaded Gorbachev to throw in his hand.'

The whole nature of publishing and bookselling was changing. In 1987, Tom Maschler, the UK's most imaginative and innovative postwar publisher, let himself be persuaded by the boss of Random House, the huge US publishing group, to sell the conglomerate of Cape, Chatto and Bodley Head for £20 million. Maschler talked his business partner of twenty years, Graham C. Greene, into agreeing. They made £5 million each – but Greene was effectively kicked out in a few weeks and Maschler never got over it. He became depressed, had a breakdown, and split from his wife, Fay. It was pretty much the end of the line for a book-world genius. And since then, a score of independent publishing companies, some of whom had been around for a century, were acquired by the paperback houses Penguin and Pan, and were being swallowed up in turn by the mega-corporations of Random House, Hachette and Bertelsmann.

I remembered the fanfare that had announced the first Waterstone's bookshop in 1982. Now, a decade later, in October 1992, an article in the *Independent* considered the owner's achievement: 'It would be difficult to overstate Mr Waterstone's effect on the book trade, and publishers tumble over each other in tribute: he has changed the rules, moved the goalposts, revolutionised the industry. He has made book buying a pleasurable experience, not an obstacle course. He has made high culture stylish. His shops have proved a godsend to publishers specialising in literary fiction – the Fabers, the Seckers, the Picadors. He staffed them with postgrads who had read a volume or two and were more than likely to be writers themselves. He set in motion an eighties publishing revolution that inspired many other stores to revamp – Dillons, Hatchards, Books Etc – and with the boom in authors' advances and the emergence of the writer as talk-show star, he somehow made the whole business rather rock'n'roll.' In 1990, however, WH Smith acquired a strong minority stake in the chain, and bought Waterstone's outright in 1993. Their bold, independent spirit was compromised and dimmed by the books-and-stationery chain they'd so brilliantly eclipsed in the early 1980s, and – four years later – WH Smith sold Waterstone's on.

The Net Book Agreement, established in 1900, had never been a terribly sexy subject (except, of course, when Pamella Bordes – working for David Shaw, Tory MP for Dover – was researching it in the House of Commons), but it was an important one. The agreement forbade price competition between bookshops. Large booksellers (like WH Smith) weren't allowed to discount their books so they couldn't undercut independent bookshops, who relied on full-price bestsellers for their bread and butter. But in 1991 the Dillons bookshop chain began to discount selected titles. Waterstone's followed suit; other chain stores joined in, then supermarkets. In 1997, the NBA was declared illegal, and there followed a discounting war that led, eventually, to the monopoly called Amazon Books; but it also sharpened the resilience and tenacity of independent bookshops – the ones that hadn't been put out of business – over the next two decades.

When I'd been given the *Sunday Times* job, and achieved my ambition, in 1988, someone had asked what I might do 'afterwards'. My response had been, 'Whaddya mean *afterwards*? This is a job for *life*.' But human nature dictates that such questions stay in your head and demand an answer. So I told myself that, since journalism seemed to be my career, my next ambition might be to edit something with a nationwide audience. Not necessarily bookish. Something committed to stylish writing and, perhaps, the reportage and travel pieces that Bill Buford had become so good at publishing in *Granta*. So when I was approached by the editors of the *Independent*, and asked to edit their magazine from early in 1993, it was tremendously exciting.

Of course I would miss the book world, which had become so colourful, so brash and circus-like, so sexy and friendly and rich in the last fourteen years. I'd miss the dizzy-making succession of new fictions from this crazily talented generation; and the great thousand-page biographies, employing all manner of quasi-fictional tricks in the telling, of literary figures from Chaucer to Shaw by way of the Brontës; and the new genre of science books, post-Hawking, explaining the hardest byways of science with new levels of clarity; and the poetry collections – by James Fenton, Craig Raine, Seamus Heaney, Andrew Motion, Peter Reading, Carol Ann Duffy, Kit Wright – that flung the English language across the wrestling ring of the page in thrilling new ways.

I'd loved being there at the *beginning* of so much – the new magazines, the new bookshops, the new prizes, the ever-more-glitzy launches, the Best of British promotions, the Hay Festival – and would happily greet their later iterations as they fell, year after year. But I'd been there when they were getting started – so perhaps it was time to move on, and do something new.

And I must, I told myself sternly, stop going to parties. Now that Carolyn and I had had a second child (Max Henry Thomas, aged sixteen months), I really should stay home more, and cook supper and introduce him and his big sister Sophie to a world of books. But just before I began doing so, Christmas was imminent, and I had to push the boat out one more time.

Through my old friend Sue Bradbury, a long-term member, I booked the two adjacent drawing rooms at the Reform Club in Pall Mall and invited everyone to a Christmas beano on 17 December 1992: all the publishers, all the publicity divas, all the reviewers, all the authors I'd met over recent years, the literary staff on rival broadsheets, the agents . . . It was a riot, though my memories were inevitably befogged. I wish I'd kept a list of all the glowing, luminous faces whom I spoke to or brushed past on the Reform's mile-long-seeming, double-room carpet – a plush and handy metaphor for the carpet of years down which I'd walked, a soul in bliss, in London's literary world, watching it evolve from the grey, defeated husk of the 1970s into the prancing, coruscating, bejewelled, million-headed, billions-spinning spectacle it had become in front of my dazzled, enchanted (and slightly bleary) eyes.

Afterwords

Were the 1980s a golden age for British literature? Was it true? It was unquestionably a great period for bookselling, for promotional wheezes, for fancy cash advances, for prizes and festivals and meet-the-people stunts and parties and associated razzmatazz. But can the decade be described as a culturally adventurous, artistically coherent, excitingly innovative and inspiring time for UK writers and readers?

In *The Ordeal of Gilbert Pinfold*, published in 1957, Evelyn Waugh wondered how much the novelists of his time might be valued by future generations. His judgement on his contemporaries was lordly and damning: 'The originators, the exuberant men, are extinct and in their place subsists and modestly flourishes a generation notable for elegance and variety of contrivance.' To my fellow readers and me, in our twenties and thirties, it seemed that in the 1980s a new generation of exuberant writers *was* in town – that the English novel had found a new confidence and was noisily asserting itself on the international stage.

We watched as wave upon wave of new talents arrived, their work by turns violent, tender, vulgar, cerebral, argumentative, seductive, hilarious and obscene. The authors were mostly young and brash and keen to shock – and publishers, by and large, were more than happy to let them. Realism, indeed *extreme* realism, was everywhere, as was the breaking of taboos about the human body, sexual relations, racial supremacy, religious fervour, Gothic nastiness, even the presence of gods and monsters in human life.

Older novelists with established reputations (who included Kingsley Amis, John Wain, Doris Lessing, Graham Greene and Beryl Bainbridge) went on offering their readers new work, though some of it carried a distinct whiff of mothballs. Iris Murdoch won the 1978 Booker Prize for *The Sea, The Sea*, but her prose audibly groaned from the weight of the redundant adjectives she now applied to every other noun. Samuel Beckett, born in 1906 and the last surviving dinosaur of modernism, still published – *Company* (1982) was, at eighty pages, a blockbuster by his standards – but his minimalist drone ('You now on your back in the dark shall not rise again to clasp your legs in your arms and bow down your head till it can bow down no further . . .') was all but drowned by the new flood of eloquence.

In the fiction of the 1980s, the English language was cleansed of indolence, fog and banality; in their place came hyperactivity, attack, clarity, surging narrative. Readers could marvel at the twirling swordsmanship of Martin Amis, the forensic creepiness of Ian McEwan, the headlong storytelling verve of William Boyd, the supple luxuriance of Rose Tremain, the vivid ventriloquising of Peter Ackroyd, David Lodge's evocations of sex and rivalry on the academic circuit, the textured historicism of Graham Swift, Angela Carter's Venus-flytrap feminism, A. S. Byatt's skilful mash-up of scholarly romance and Victorian pastiche, the exquisite *bijouterie* of Bruce Chatwin, the suave elisions of fact and invention in Julian Barnes's *belles lettres*, the precocious mythologising of Jeanette Winterson, the gleeful cruelty of Iain Banks, Salman Rushdie's linguistic salmagundi, Ben Okri's dispatches from emergent nationhood, Caryl Phillips's powerful investigations of slavery and self-determination, Timothy Mo's comic topography of Hong-Kong-immigrant Soho . . .

Most of these writers made their debuts in the 1980s; but it wasn't just a period of precocious start-ups. Most went on to make writing their sole career, and develop their art into areas of greater complexity. Amis Junior branched out from the in-your-face solipsism of his early works to take on transatlantic capitalism, global entropy and the Nazi mindset. William Boyd graduated from the fish-out-of-water comedy of Englishmen in Africa and the USA to trace the effects of history on character across the twentieth century. Kazuo Ishiguro moved from dramatising Japanese postwar mortification to inhabit the voice of hapless British compromise. Across the new literary landscape, readers saw a gradual turning away from the provincial or self-centred voice to take on broader themes of historical or political resonance.

The career of Penelope Fitzgerald was paradigmatic. A very late starter in the art of fiction, she was sixty-one when her first novel *The Golden Child* appeared in 1977 – a genre piece about murder in a museum, inspired by the Tutankhamun exhibition. Her next novels were grounded in her own experience: *The Bookshop* (she worked in such a shop in Southwold), the Booker-winning *Offshore* (she lived on a houseboat on Battersea Reach; it sank), *Human Voices* (about wartime life at the BBC, where she worked in the early 1940s) and *At Freddie's* (a thinly disguised portrait of her life at the Italia Conti drama school in the 1960s). Each was characterised by brisk character-drawing, brittle dialogue and revelations of postwar British snobbery and class warfare.

In the 1980s, though, Fitzgerald developed into a different kind of artist. She began to investigate moments of historical change and revolutionary politics. *The Beginning of Spring* (1988) was set in pre-1916 Moscow and followed a British family's involvement with revolutionary forces, political and spiritual. *The Gate of Angels* (1990), set in 1912 Cambridge, offers what seems like a simple love story but quivers with elements of quantum mechanics, religious belief and feminism. Her final novel, *The Blue Flower* (1997), which dealt with the passion felt by Fritz von Hardenberg (later to become the poet Novalis) for a twelve-year-old girl, and with the first stirrings of the Romantic movement, was later commended as 'one of the twelve best historical novels' ever published.

A popular creative activity of the decade was Mixing Things Up: several writers enjoyed playing games with genre and identity. Science fiction flirted with literary fiction in the works of Iain Banks and Christopher Priest. Julian Barnes took time off from writing not-quite-novels to produce (under the *nom de plume* 'Dan Kavanagh') gumshoe thrillers starring a bisexual shamus called Duffy. Novelists and poets tried their hand at libretti (Ian McEwan's *Or Shall We Die?*, Craig Raine's *The Electrification of the Soviet Union*). Bruce Chatwin's *The Songlines* was presented by its publishers as 'a form common enough in the eighteenth century, rare in ours: the novel of ideas.' It turned out to be a non-fiction study of Aboriginal culture, nomadism and 'sacred land', bulked out with anecdotes from Chatwin's notebooks: they included the occasion he and the Sheikh of Omdurman tried to conjure a djinn at sunset by sprinkling a charcoal brazier with Elizabeth Arden *eau de parfum*.

In the 1980s, biography also had a funny turn, as some of its key practitioners embraced the heretical possibility that 'life-writing' might have some connection with fiction. In 1985, two books took a fresh look at the subject. In *The Craft of Literary Biography*, Jeffrey Meyers said he was 'sceptical of much of the fine writing, balanced appraisal and psychological insight that is the hallmark of the English tradition of biography', and suggested that it take a more dramatic form, a 'patterning process' that would be imposed on lives whose motivations were of more interest than their actions.

In *Biography: Fiction, Fact and Form*, Ira Bruce Nadel cited examples of biographical writing, from the days of Xenophon and Plutarch, right up to Lytton Strachey's subversive *Eminent Victorians*, to show that honourable precedents existed for experimentation in 'life writing' – things like 'thematic patterning', 'plausible invention' and other quasi-fictional techniques. The publication of both books sparked responses from practitioners of the craft.

Victoria Glendinning, biographer of Elizabeth Bowen, Edith Sitwell and Vita Sackville-West told me she'd recently spotted some suggestions 'that it's perfectly all right to make up images, myths or whatever you like about somebody, depending on your own creative needs. You can leave out bits that don't suit, you needn't check or verify spurious anecdotes, you can do pretty well anything . . .' She thought this approach worked with fiction or drama, but not biography. She believed, however, that biographies are more than accumulations of facts and memories. 'You have to make an end somewhere and say, "It's *my* book", however much other biographers may feel detached about the whole relationship. I'm not aware of having *fictional* impulses when I write – only what I'd call *formal* ones: like being aware of the boring bits of someone's life and wondering what to do about them.'

Peter Ackroyd's massive, and massively odd, thousand-plus-page *Dickens* raised eyebrows for featuring six imaginary 'meetings' between Mr Micawber, Dickens, Little Nell, Oscar Wilde, T. S. Eliot and Ackroyd himself. He told me that life-writing inevitably required creative skill.

'When Beckett told his biographer [Deirdre Bair] that [the work she planned to write about him] was *her* book, that he wouldn't dream of interfering in its shape or direction, he was reacting from the standpoint of a literary artist and assuming that a biography required creative skills equal to those of any other creative artist. Just as a writer wouldn't dream of meddling in somebody else's novel.' When researching his Dickens book, Ackroyd said, 'I [did] the same with him as I do in my novels – accumulate a body of information in a certain pattern, look at what's there and try to discern an inner momentum. And from that comes the rhythm and tone of the biography.'

For modern readers who were around in the 1980s, these words from Glendinning and Ackroyd would have put them in mind of

Flaubert's Parrot, in which successive chapters played tricks with the reader. In one, Barnes's protagonist, Geoffrey Braithwaite, offered twin chronologies of Flaubert's life to show that it was a) a wild success and b) a wretched failure. In another, he meets an American academic who tells him he's been gifted a treasure trove of letters written by Flaubert to his niece's English governess, Juliet Herbert, about whose relationship with Flaubert scholars have long speculated. Braithwaite dreams of the acclaim that will greet his revelation of their correspondence – but the American reveals he has burnt the letters. All this is fiction, of course, but such is the plausibility of Barnes's telling, some readers (including me) felt shocked by the academic's casual vandalism, as though he'd really existed.

Readers in the 2020s will easily identify the mid-1980s search for new forms of life-writing as leading directly to Craig Brown's bestselling work, *Ma'am Darling: 99 Glimpses of Princess Margaret*, and the equally popular *One Two Three Four: The Beatles in Time*. For both books, Brown trawled through the vast ocean of biographical material available on each subject, identified certain themes and recurrent patterns (and the liveliest anecdotes), edited them and threw in some 'plausible inventions', to produce what reviewers called 'biography with the boring bits left out'.

The usually quiescent and rarefied British poetry world was shaken in the 1980s by alarming rumblings from the Underground. After the arrival on the late-1970s punk music scene of John Cooper Clarke (the 'Bard of Salford' and the first poet capable of holding captive onstage an obstreperous audience waiting for the lethal decibels of The Buzzcocks and The Sex Pistols), a group of acidulous performer poets appeared, strong on street credibility and post-punk aggression. They included Benjamin Zephaniah, Julie ('Joolz') Denby, Attila the Stockbroker, Seething Wells, and a Bradford albino known as Little Brother. Collectively known as the 'Ranters', they performed in pubs, clubs and rock venues, spitting fury about Mrs Thatcher's social and fiscal policies, the supposed Cold War threat ('Russians in the DHSS') and sundry establishment figures.

I saw Attila in 1982 performing his poem 'Contributory Negligence', about a high court judge who let a rapist off with a fine because his woman victim was hitching at night wearing a short skirt and was therefore 'asking for it'. In the poem, the judge picks up a hitchhiking Attila in his flash car and is bashed up for the same flawed reason. He could be found performing the same poem five years later.

In interviews, the Ranters expressed frustration at the poetry establishment: Demanding intelligibility as a basic poetic quality (an attitude that hadn't been voiced since the 1920s), they insisted that poetry should have 'relevance' to the modern world of unemployment, political unrest and urban deprivation. They also disparaged the work of mainstream poets (i.e. the ones published by Faber) such as Christopher Reid and John Hartley Williams, dismissing anything they couldn't understand as 'trivial', 'obscure' or 'bullshit'. The individual members flourished – Zephaniah published several collections to acclaim and aspired to the Oxford Professorship of Poetry, Attila became a skilled musician and an expert on post-English Civil War radical movements – and their influence could be seen in the rise of transatlantic poetry 'slams' in the 1990s.

The poetry mainstream took another hit after the publication, in 1982, of *The Penguin Book of Contemporary British Poetry*. Edited by Andrew Motion and Blake Morrison, it wasn't exactly an arms-wide-open celebration of British bards: in fact, it was rigorously selective. Only twenty poets were given houseroom in its pages, and of those, six were Northern Irish poets reflecting on the Troubles (spearheaded, of course, by Seamus Heaney), five represented a new northern English self-awareness of the poet's distance from metropolitan culture; and Craig Raine and Christopher Reid, the celebrated exponents of the new 'Martian' strain of verse took up two more places. It seemed as though the anthology was mainly interested in only two things: politics, northern-ness and similes.

There were cries of outrage from a ragged band of older poets loosely connected to *New Departures*, a magazine of avant-garde writing that had existed intermittently since 1959. It was edited from day one by Michael Horovitz, a thin, bespectacled, wispily bearded visionary who spoke in a weirdly slow, adenoidal drawl, punctuated by wild laughter. He had been a convenor of the spectacularly successful International Poetry Incarnation at the Royal Albert Hall on 11 June 1965. Literally hundreds of poets, unknown, famous or forgotten, weird or conventional, British, Jamaican, Russian or without-fixed-abode, had passed through the magazine's pages in the intervening twenty-three years – pages that featured contributions by Samuel Beckett, William Burroughs, Stevie Smith, Allen Ginsberg, Yevgeny Yevtushenko and Paul Weller of The Jam.

As part of a series I wrote in the early 1980s for *Books and Bookmen* on literary cliques, I found that Horovitz was part of a starry, mutually supportive group that included the avant-garde playwright Heathcote Williams, who would soon publish the all-conquering hymn to sea mammals, *Whale Nation*; Roger McGough (whose 1967 joint venture with Adrian Henri and Brian Patten, *The Mersey Sound*, sold half a million copies); Fran Landesman, the New York torch singer/songwriter, and R. D. Laing, the brilliant, maverick psychiatrist, director of the unorthodox, humanistic sanatorium The Langham Clinic, and author of *The Divided Self*, a classic (and bestselling) study of madness and alienation. His later works, *Knots* and *Do You Love Me?* laid out the intricacies of human relationships as a litany of syllogisms, marching down the page to resemble poems. He was also an accomplished blues pianist, who joined in jam sessions at Ronnie Scott's Soho jazz club.

To find such a multi-talented, poetry-and-song-and-hip-psychiatry avant garde in the heart of mid-1980s Islington was confirmation for me that we were living through a literary golden age, not just of mad achievement, but of astounding *variety*; where writing could range from the rarefied, Henry-Jamesian sophistication of Alan Hollinghurst to the street-level rodomontade of the Ranter poets, and find an eager audience for both.

Writers in the 1980s never seemed content to do one thing well and do it over and over: they crossed boundaries and ventured into un-broached lands; they took on new subjects, new challenges, even new identities, to see if they could coerce the words on a page to do something different and exciting – to hose down the paths and byways of the imagination, to wipe a squeegee blade across the shop window of the world, to make everything look new, more brightly lit, more real.

The Amis Generation are now mostly in their sixties and seventies and it's only natural to compare their impact on the 1980s with the impact that younger writers are having on the twenty-first century. It's hard, to be brutally frank, to feel many seismic tremors of excitement and awe. Those of us who cut our teeth on Ian McEwan and Angela Carter may be impressed by the bold humour and stylish attack of, say, Zadie Smith, but may feel only puzzlement about the lionisation of, say, Sally Rooney, whose *Normal People* is a blandly written, linguistically unadventurous, Young Adult novel of schoolgirl romance but with more sex than is common in the genre. It seemed to me not a patch on *Exciting Times* by Rooney's Irish contemporary, Naoise Dolan, a novel of wicked wit and breezy questioning of modern-day behaviour in the relationship jungle.

Devotees of old novelistic virtues – such as the gradual revelation of plot and character against a vividly evoked setting – may wonder why so many modern novels read like sincere but unmediated autobiographical testimonies of their authors' problematic libidos, traumas on the dating scene, or real-life experiences of discrimination over their race, gender or sexuality.

In 2020 Martin Amis suggested that the Booker shortlist now had less to do with literature and more to do with socio-politics. He had a point. Modern novels need to have 'relevance', 'relatability', even basic 'acceptability' to succeed. Many come with 'current thinking' and the drive for 'awareness' stamped all over them. You can imagine a class of students being asked, about a novel on the English syllabus: 'How does the character Henry identify the institutional prejudices of UK society that have precipitated his current struggle with mental health?' The modern 'culture wars' precipitated by social media have led some authors to beware of giving offence, or inciting riot, by portraying characters some distance removed from their own 'lived experience' or their own ethnic (or social) background.

Some established authors have started to wonder if the authors who appear on Booker Prize shortlists are being praised for literary strengths, such as believable characterisation, coherent plotting, vivid sense of place and narrative drive, or for their choice of serious world-issue subject matter. Penelope Lively said that, over the last five years, she's regretted the loss of individual wit and exuberance in award-winning fictions. Others have looked askance at politically engaged works of ethical hand-wringing, set in the future and featuring flooded or otherwise damaged places on earth, where characters explain issues such as the perils of climate change to each other. Sometimes it seems as if modern authors are writing to an algorithm of zeitgeisty concern rather than to a personal imaginative pulse.

For a piece in the *Spectator*, Philip Hensher read all six shortlisted books under consideration for the 2021 Booker Prize and concluded: 'Overall I would say that the novels the Booker judges consider worthy of our admiration share a few qualities: serious, real-world issues are preferred, particularly if they involve injustice to women and racial minorities; humour is entirely dispensable, and the art of drawing a vivid character seems quite optional. There is a lack of investment in forward movement – many episodes across these novels end without any incident having intruded or consequence arising.'

There is also a problem with modern *author* acceptability. In the 1980s, female authors seemed to have a harder time getting published than men; the first appearance of the Best of Young British Novelists promotion counted only six women in the twenty writers. Today, new male writers struggle to be signed up. A search of the *Bookseller*'s news archive for 2020 revealed that, of the seventy-seven debut novels that featured in the news pages, only *seven* were by men.

It is, of course, a good thing that the gender imbalance should be redressed; but when in the 2020s, male writers are told that nobody wants to hear their stories, and commissioning editors in modern publishers are advised not to take on books that won't sell until they're part of an acceptable demographic, the literary landscape seems a very bleak place. The question of acceptability also haunts modern publishing houses. At boardroom level, the decision to publish a book is no longer taken by commissioning editors urging the virtues of their authors, or the qualities of their books. Today, the go-ahead for publication seems, more and more, to be given by the sales, marketing and publicity departments. The days of gifted enthusiasts, well-read connoisseurs of literature, or shrewd and commercially minded men and women of letters, are over. If an 'inspired' or 'swashbuckling' figure such as Tom Maschler, a 'passionate' and 'visionary' dealer in 'edgy' or 'genre-busting' fiction such as Liz Calder or Carmen Callil came along today, they would, I suspect, get no further than their first interview. In British publishing, the originators, the exuberant men and women, seem to have, for the moment, well and truly gone.

Appendix

And have the works of the 1980s generation of writers lasted? Have their reputations survived three decades? Here's a brief update of a dozen leading lights of the School of 1978–1992 and their current standing.

Martin Amis's novels suffered a few dips in fortune since the 1990s – *Yellow Dog* was diffuse, uncertain in its humour and roundly abused by critics; *House of Meetings*, set in a Soviet gulag, seemed an offcut from his book on Stalin, *Koba the Dread*. *The Pregnant Widow*, set around the 'sexual revolution' of 1970, took on the feminist movement to little effect; *Lionel Asbo: State of England* addressed Yob Culture in Britain from the vantage point of Brooklyn (where Amis had moved with his family) and was considered by home-grown critics to be ten years out of date. At times, Amis seemed more energised by autobiography (*Experience*) and non-fiction polemic, especially against Islamism (*The Second Plane*). But with the publication, in 2017, of *The Rub of Time: Bellow, Nabokov, Hitchens, Travolta, Trump. Essays and Reportage 1986–2016*, and of *Inside Story* (2020) his melange of autobiography, politics, thoughts on death and sections on How to Write, all misleadingly entitled 'a Novel', Amis's real achievement became clear. It's his commitment to style rather than story, to making war on clichéd words and flabby thinking. He goes so far as to say that 'Style ... is morality.' His whole project has been to find a voice uniquely fitted for expressing, and challenging by wild satire, the preoccupations and grotesque obsessions of the twentieth and twenty-first centuries, whether he's dealing with political false-hood, moral dyslexia or global wrong-headedness. That voice, that style, may be too cool, too machine-tooled, for some; but it seems the voice of the utmost sanity.

Pat Barker followed up her 1980s novels of grainy northern working-class life with the awesomely accomplished *Regeneration* trilogy, a multi-angled examination of psychologists and poets in the First World War. The third book, *The Ghost Road*, won the Booker in 1995. Her later novels explored intense relationships in history, notably her study of the Slade School generation of artists in *Life Class* and *Toby's Room*, and her feminist retellings of *The Iliad* in *The Silence of the Girls* and *The Women of Troy*.

Told at ten by his mother that he had 'too much imagination', **Julian Barnes** has skilfully juggled art and cultural history with fictional dictators, true-life crime and the history of ballooning to create extraordinary patchworks about the complexity and fragility of human life. His reputation shines brightly in the twenty-first century – he won the 2011 Booker with *The Sense of an Ending*, while his 2019 non-fiction study of a 'virtuoso gynaecologist' in *belle époque* France, *The Man in the Red Coat*, was in the bestseller charts for months.

A one-man narrative machine, **William Boyd** has published fourteen novels since his debut *A Good Man in Africa*, many driven by inspections of twentieth-century history and the concept of history itself. All have been bestsellers. He's picked up a sizeable raft of awards, here and in France and the USA for *Brazzaville Beach*, *The Blue Afternoon*, *Any Human Heart* and *Restless*. For a period he wrote in the thriller format, which he pulled off with the same polish and aplomb as his more ambitious chronicles of history and culture.

Kazuo Ishiguro's third novel *The Remains of the Day* won the Booker Prize in 1989, was filmed by Merchant Ivory Productions starring Anthony Hopkins and Emma Thompson, and is the only modern novel known to have been read by HM the Queen (see chapter 13). He was made an OBE, and for a time his portrait hung in Number 10 Downing Street. His *Never Let Me Go* was voted one of the 100 best English-language novels published between 1923 and 2005 and was filmed with Keira Knightley. He was knighted and won the Nobel Prize in 2017. His most recent novel, *Klara and the Sun*, was a bestseller in 2020.

The tirelessly productive **Ian McEwan** has had perhaps the most consistently buoyant career of the 1980s generation. Almost every novel he's published in the last two decades has been regarded as An Event, because of his embrace of modern subjects, such as the threat of climate change (*Solar*), Artificial Intelligence (*Machines Like Me*) and family law (*The Children Act*). He's been nominated for the Booker Prize six times, won it once, holds a CBE and has a long shelf of Distinguished Author and Literary Achievement awards.

When **Hilary Mantel** began publishing in the 1980s (with *Every Day Is Mother's Day, Vacant Possession* and *Eight Months on Ghazzah Street*), she probably couldn't foresee that, by 2020, she would be, uniquely, the holder of two Booker Prizes, and a nomination for a third, for three successive novels – the *Wolf Hall* trilogy. The vividness with which she conjured life (and the constant nearness of betrayal and death) in the Tudor court was compounded by the technical skill she showed in embedding the thought processes of Thomas Cromwell in the minds of modern readers. The *Observer* went so far as to say: 'Her Cromwell novels are, for my money, the greatest novels of the century.'

Mercurial, unpindownable, **Adam Mars-Jones** is the most *intermittent* writer of the 1980s generation. He followed up his 1981 debut *Lantern Lecture* with an Aids-themed story collection, *Monopolies of Loss*, a decade later in 1992, and had the distinction of appearing on the list of Best of Young British Novelists in 1983 and 1993 without actually producing a novel. This was remedied soon after with *The Waters of Thirst* – and fifteen years later, *Pilcrow*, the first part of an immense four-book mega-novel appeared. A second instalment, *Cedilla*, emerged in 2011. In 2020 and 2021, he published two slim comic novels about humiliation, *Box Hill* and *Batlava Lake*. Mars-Jones has also written a family memoir, *Kid Gloves*, and a lot of superior film criticism.

Sir **Salman Rushdie** became by far the world's most famous writer with *The Satanic Verses*, although 99 per cent of those who knew his name and reputation never read the book, or were even equipped to do so. Since then he's produced a stream of dazzling fictions, mostly set in India, often deriving from figures of myth (Orpheus), history (Akbar the Great) and other fictions (*Don Quixote*). His hectically readable third-person memoir of life under the threat of the fatwa, *Joseph Anton*, was an international bestseller in 2012. He was shortlisted for the Booker Prize five times and won it for *Midnight's Children* in 1981. He was made Commandeur de l'Ordre des Arts et des Lettres, France's highest literary honour, in 1999, and knighted by the Queen for 'services to literature', not without controversy, in 2007.

Graham Swift, the most English of novelists, despite his flirtations with the magic-realist tradition of Márquez and Borges, was nominated for the Booker Prize for *Waterland* and *The Light of Day*, and won it for *Last Orders*. He has also published three collections of stories. A keen angler, he used to fish for trout on the River Torridge in Devon with his friend Ted Hughes. His eleventh novel, *Here We Are*, came out in 2020. Four of his works have been filmed, most recently the novella *Mothering Sunday* in 2021.

Rose Tremain, after dazzling readers with fictions set in historical regal courts (*Restoration*, *Music and Silence*) went on to explore more complex themes: the search for a new home, a new country, a new identity (and a new gender in *Sacred Country*, an early consideration of transsexuality), even a new relationship with the past. Her vivid imaginings and lusty prose won her the Orange Prize, the Whitbread Award and the National Jewish Book Award among others, and showered her with honours including a CBE and a damehood.

After startling readers with her Sapphic-missionary debut, **Jeanette Winterson** wrote novels that anticipated crucial matters of social and political concern. She tackled gender fluidity in *Written on the Body*, cyber-identity, social media and fake news in *The Powerbook*, anti-capitalist protests *à la* Extinction Rebellion in *Sexing the Cherry*, the threat of climate change in *The Stone Gods* and AI in *Frankisstein*. She also produced a sparkling 'retelling' of *The Winter's Tale* in *The Gap of Time*. Winner of the Whitbread Prize, the John Llewellyn Rhys Prize and the E. M. Forster Award, she was made an OBE in 2006 and a CBE in 2018, both for services to literature.

John Carey's first published collection (*Original Copy: Selected Reviews and Journalism*) came out in 1987. Its earliest pieces dated back to his 1969 TV reviews in the *Listener*, while the most recent were from the mid-1980s – a sixteen-year spree of intellectual fireworks, lethal snipings at complacent and philistine grandees, and celebrations of real, if uncomfortable, life. Reviewing one TV programme on foetus surgery, Carey inspected the horrific footage and remarked, 'It's impossible to feel detached in these circumstances, and the involvement is humanizing.' The very last review of the collection found him praising Craig Raine's poetry collection, *Rich*, and drawing attention to Raine's poem 'Arsehole', which had spurred controversy in the *Observer*. 'In fact it is a graceful – almost flowery – attempt' Carey wrote, 'to create beauty where ugliness is normally seen.'

Seeing the world afresh, laughing at the pretentious or the over-praised, celebrating writing that's available to 'ordinary intelligent people' rather than elites – these have been his obsession in a reviewing career that's lasted from 1969 to the present day. He's published several books alongside, notably his Faber anthologies on science, utopias and, best of all, reportage ('Dinner With Attila the Hun, c. AD 450' was an early highlight); he's published polemic (*What Good Are the Arts?*) and ferocious literary criticism (*The Intellectuals and the Masses*). It is a thing of wonder that John Carey, now in his late eighties, goes on, week after week, setting a standard of vivid, coruscating, non-academic reviewing, of books about literature and the natural world, that has never flagged, and never been eclipsed, in over fifty years. He is, as you may have gathered, the hero of this book.

The 1980s: 25 Essential Novels

Hawksmoor by Peter Ackroyd
Money by Martin Amis
Regeneration by Pat Barker
The New Confessions by William Boyd
Earthly Powers by Anthony Burgess
Possession by A. S. Byatt
The Bloody Chamber by Angela Carter
The Beginning of Spring by Penelope Fitzgerald
The Swimming-Pool Library by Alan Hollinghurst
The Remains of the Day by Kazuo Ishiguro
The Buddha of Suburbia by Hanif Kureishi
The Child in Time by Ian McEwan
Eight Months on Ghazzah Street by Hilary Mantel
Such a Long Journey by Rohinton Mistry
Sour Sweet by Timothy Mo
The Famished Road by Ben Okri
Cambridge by Caryl Phillips
Daughters of the House by Michele Roberts
Midnight's Children by Salman Rushdie

Loitering with Intent by Muriel Spark

Keepers of the House by Lisa St Aubin de Teran

Waterland by Graham Swift

Restoration by Rose Tremain

Puffball by Fay Weldon

Oranges Are Not the Only Fruit by Jeanette Winterson

Acknowledgements

Many people helped in the gestation of this book, but one stands out. The whole project faced disaster in spring 2020 when the British Library – a primary resource if there ever was one – closed its doors, due to Covid-19 restrictions. Where could I turn for crucially important magazine and newspaper articles from 1978–92? And that was when Valerie Grove introduced me to the stupendous archive she has kept since the 1960s, and said, 'Take what you need (and make sure you give it back).' So, massive thanks to her – and to the following who kindly shared their memories and impressions in interviews: Louis Baum, Terence Blacker, Liz Calder, Nick Clee, Richard Cohen, Sally Emerson, Sebastian Faulks, Jacquie Graham, Ian Jack, Howard Jacobson, Nicolette Jones, Robert McCrum, Joanna Mackle, Tom Maschler, Jon Riley, Harry Ritchie, Patrick Janson Smith and Peter Straus.

Enormous thanks, also, to my first readers: to Sarah Spankie, for her enthusiasm and wise counsel from start to finish; to Valerie Grove (again) for her perfect recall of life at the *Evening Standard* and its personnel, and her eloquent tut-tutting at my cavalier way with famous names ('There is no second "h" in Harold Nicolson, John . . . '); to Jon Canter, scriptwriter, novelist and my friend for nearly half a century, for his beady-eyed editing and ruthless verbiage-slashing; to Sally Emerson, for her warm responses and phenomenal memory of the Olden Days; to Robert McCrum, for his fluently insightful analysis of the period and his cheerful encouragement as I approached The End.

I'm grateful to Andreas Campomar, my publisher – the plan for this book got started with our two-hour conversation beside a swimming pool in 2019; to Matthew Hamilton, my agent, a master of Zoom-call diplomacy; to Steve Baker at the *Sunday Times* archive, who kindly supplied me with an all-important *entrée*; to my friend and neighbour Jules Ansell for reminding me of the alternative comedy of the 1980s; and to Emily Bootle from the *New Statesman* archive for tracking down a notably waspish Martin Amis review from 1975.

My most heartfelt thank you, however, goes to my darling wife, Angie, who has uncomplainingly endured my long spells of creative self-imprisonment, revived my flagging spirits when lockdown ennui settled on us like moss on a gravestone, laughed at my garment-rending fury in failing to track down a vital citation, and provided levels of spousal encouragement not seen since the heyday of Mrs Tolstoy and the second Mrs Dostoevsky.

Sources

Amis, Kingsley, *The Letters of Kingsley Amis*,
  Zachary Leader (ed) (HarperCollins, 2000)

Amis, Martin, *Experience* (Cape, 2000)

Amis, Martin, *The War Against Cliché: Essays and Reviews 1971–2000*
  (Cape, 2001)

Amis, Martin, *The Rub of Time: Bellow, Nabokov, Hitchens, Travolta,
  Trump. Essays and Reportage, 1986–2016* (Cape, 2017)

Amis, Martin, *Inside Story: a Novel* (Cape, 2020)

Bell, Simon, Curtis, Richard and Fielding, Helen, *Who's Had Who
  In Association with Berk's Rogerage* (Faber, 1987)

Biswell, Andrew, *The Real Life of Anthony Burgess* (Picador, 2005)

Brown, Tina, *Life as a Party* (Deutsch, 1983)

Callil, Carmen and Toibin, Colm, *The Modern Library, The 200 Best
  Books in English since 1950* (Picador, 1999)

The Cambridge Companion to British Fiction: 1980–2018,
  Peter Boxall (ed) (Cambridge University Press, 2019)

Carey, John, *The Violent Effigy: A Study of Dickens's Imagination* (Faber, 1973)

Carey, John, *Original Copy: Selected Reviews and Journalism 1969–1986* (1987)

Carey, John, *William Golding: The Man Who Wrote* Lord of the Flies (Faber, 2009)

Carey, John, *The Unexpected Professor: An Oxford Life in Books* (Faber, 2014)

Connolly, Cyril, *Enemies of Promise* (Routledge & Kegan Paul, 1938)

Faber, Toby, *Faber & Faber: The Untold Story* (Faber, 2019)

Frayn, Michael, *The Tin Men* (Collins, 1965)

Gordon, Edward, *The Invention of Angela Carter* (Chatto, 2016)

Gordon, Giles, *Aren't We Due a Royalty Statement?: A Stern Account of Literary, Publishing and Theatrical Folk* (Chatto, 1993)

James, Clive, *May Week Was in June* (Cape, 1990)

Lewis, Jeremy, *Grub Street Irregular: Scenes from Literary Life* (Harper Press, 2008)

Lewis, Roger, *Anthony Burgess* (Faber, 2002)

Limb, Sue, *The Wordsmiths at Gorsemere* (Bantam Press, 1987)

Lodge, David, *Writer's Luck: A Memoir 1976–1991* (Harvill Secker, 2018)

Maschler, Tom, *Publisher* (Picador, 2005)

Neil, Andrew, *Full Disclosure* (Macmillan, 1996)

Rushdie, Salman, *Joseph Anton: A Memoir* (Random House, 2012)

Sutherland, John, *Reading the Decades: Fifty Years of the Nation's Bestselling Books* (BBC, 2002)

Taylor, D. J., *The Prose Factory: Literary Life in England since 1918* (Chatto, 2016)

Untermeyer, Louis (ed), *The Golden Treasury of Poetry* (Collins/ Golden Press Inc, NY, 1959)

Webb, Nick, *Wish You Were Here: The Official Biography of Douglas Adams* (Headline, 2003)

Index